ETHNICITY AND INTRA-STATE CONFLICT

Ethnicity and Intra-State Conflict

Edited by
HÅKAN WIBERG
CHRISTIAN P. SCHERRER

Routledge
Taylor & Francis Group

LONDON AND NEW YORK

First published 1999 by Ashgate Publishing

Reissued 2018 by Routledge
2 Park Square, Milton Park, Abingdon, Oxon, OX14 4RN
711 Third Avenue, New York, NY I 0017, USA

Routledge is an imprint of the Taylor & Francis Group, an informa business

Publisher's Note
The publisher has gone to great lengths to ensure the quality of this reprint but points out that some imperfections in the original copies may be apparent.

Disclaimer
The publisher has made every effort to trace copyright holders and welcomes correspondence from those they have been unable to contact.

A Library of Congress record exists under LC control number: 99072603

ISBN 13: 978-1-138-31259-3 (hbk)
ISBN 13: 978-1-138-31260-9 (pbk)
ISBN 13: 978-0-429-45812-5 (ebk)

Contents

About the Authors and Editors

Tamara Dragadze had her doctorate in political anthropology from Oxford University in 1987; her main research areas are nationalism and regionalism. She is director of the Centre for Caucasian and Central Asian Studies in London and a collaborator at the Institute of Social Research, Surrey University. She is series editor of *Ethnicity and Identity* (Berg) and associate editor of *Central Asian Survey*, and serves as advisor to Parliament, parties and NGOs.

Tuomas Forsberg holds Finnish degrees in political science and international relations and received his Ph.D. in International Relations from the University of Wales at Aberystwyth in 1997. He is a Research Fellow and Acting Director at the Finnish Institute of International Affairs.

Wenche Hauge holds a degree in political science from the University of Oslo and currently has a doctoral scholarship from the Research Council of Norway for work at the International Peace Research Institute Oslo (PRIO) on the project 'Causes and Dynamics of Conflict Escalation: The Role of Environmental Change and Economic Development'.

Anton Ivanov, Ph.D. in anthropology, was a research fellow at the Institute for Ethnology and Anthropology at the Russian Academy of Sciences and became Principal Researcher at the Forum for Early Warning and Early Response (FEWER), London, in 1998. He was coordinator in Russia for UNHCR and guest researcher at the Berghof Research Centre for Conflict Management in Berlin.

Dietrich Jung, Ph.D. in political science (University of Hamburg, 1995) on his thesis *Tradition – Modernity – War. A Methodology for Analysing Belligerous Processes in the Context of Globalisation*, published works in comparative war studies and Middle Eastern affairs. He was Assistant Professor in International Relations at Bilkent University, Ankara, before becoming Research Fellow at the Copenhagen Peace Research Institute (COPRI) in 1998.

Janie Leatherman has her Ph.D. in international studies from the University of Denver (1991). Visiting Fellow and Visiting Assistant Professor at Notre Dame University before joining the faculty of Illinois State University in 1997. Consultant on conflict prevention and resolution to i.a. the United Nations University and the United States Institute of Peace. Lead author of *Pursuing Peace in the Shadow of War: Conflict Prevention in Intrastate Crises* (1999).

Marta Martinelli received her MA in International Politics and Security Studies from the University of Bradford in 1997 for a dissertation on Track II Diplomacy, has been admitted as a Ph.D. candidate at the Conflict Resolution Centre there and a guest scholar at COPRI by virtue of the cooperation agreement between the two institutes.

Bjørn Møller has a Ph.D. in International Relations (University of Copenhagen, where he is now external lecturer). Since 1985, he was (Senior) Research Fellow and later Programme Director at COPRI. He is project director of the Global Non-Offensive Defence Network; editor of *NOD and Conversion*; and Secretary General of the International Peace Research Association (IPRA). He has written and edited several books on (non-offensive, alternative, conventional) defence issues.

Félix Nkundabagenzi holds degrees in law and international relations (University of Louvain, 1986, 1991). Authored several studies and articles on political and social evolution in sub-Saharan Africa and a book on the Rwandan genocide. He worked with the Conflict Prevention Network of the European Commission, is an expert-consultant for the EU and research fellow at GRIP. Founder of COMSOC, a Belgian think tank on Euro-African political relations.

Ralf Rönnquist received his Ph.D. in history from Lund University in 1991 on his thesis in Swedish, *History and Nationality: Scottish Ethno-Territoriality in a Historical Perspective*. He has published several other works on nationalism in the British Isles and has had research and teaching positions at Swedish universities, at present as Senior Lecturer at the University of Halmstad.

Christian P. Scherrer, Ph.D. (University of Berne, 1985) on a thesis on social and cultural impacts of Tourism in the Third World. After Swiss teaching and research positions, he founded the Ethnic Conflict Research Project (ECOR) based in the Netherlands, whose Director he still is. Senior Research Fellow at COPRI in 1997 (CONF programme). Several books and reports on ethnicity, genocide and ethno-nationalism, covering most major regions of the world.

Klaus Schlichte received his Ph.D. in political science from Hamburg University in 1996. He was chercheur invité at the Maison des Sciences de l'Homme in Paris (1996) and visiting scholar/lecturer at the Henry Jackson School for International Stuides, University of Washington, Seattle (1997/98). He is currently a research associate at the Department of Political Science at Hamburg University, working on statehood in 'Third World' countries.

Helena Lindholm Schulz received her Ph.D. in Peace and Development Research from the University of Gothenburg in 1996 on her thesis, *Between Revolution and Statehood: Reconstruction of Palestinian Nationalisms*. She is researcher and teacher at the Department of Peace and Development Research, Gothenburg University (PADRIGU).

Tarja Väyrynen received her Ph.D. in International Conflict Analysis from the University of Kent at Canterbury in 1995 and became *Docent* in 1998. She is now Research Fellow at Tampere Peace Research Institute (TAPRI). She was guest researcher at the George Mason University in 1997.

Håkan Wiberg has his Ph.D. in sociology from Lund University and was professor of sociology there in 1980-88, being in periods guest professor in Seoul, Amsterdam and Oslo. Since 1988 he is Director of COPRI and Programme Director of its CONF project. He was President of the European Peace Research Association in 1989 through 1993. Author and editor of many books on various issues related to peace and war and regional conflicts.

Introduction

HÅKAN WIBERG

By any count the number of cases, number of victims, amount of time and with quite few exceptions, today's wars are intra-state wars, taking place within the boundaries of a single state (in a minority of cases, however, there is also military intervention from other states or by mercenary firms). This fact led the Copenhagen Peace Research Institute (COPRI) to set up a new research programme, *Intra-State Conflict: Causes and Peace Strategies* (CONF), which started to take shape in 1996/97.[1] As part of the preparations for its further development, a number of specialists in various fields relevant to the programme were invited to an authors' symposium in May 1997. From the presentations at this symposium, several were then selected for publication and subsequently revised by the authors. Some lacunae were then identified in relation to the ambitions behind the book, and a few additional scholars were invited to make contributions to this volume.

The logic of the book is related to the crucial terms in the name of the programme: 'conflict', 'intra-state, 'cause' and 'peace'.

The term 'conflict' is traditionally ambiguous.[2] Sometimes it refers primarily to certain kinds of (negative) *behaviour* between parties in general, or military violence in particular, this being seen as the most deadly form of behaviour; an assumption that is not always justified: some economic blockades, such as the Sudanese government against its rebel areas or the United Nations against Iraq, having harvested more lives than most wars.

At other times, the term refers primarily to *contradictions* or incompatibilities between the goals, needs or ambitions of two or more parties, and the analysis deals with the character of these contradictions and various ways of overcoming them.

Part I of the book deals with war and other forms of mass violence as behavioural phenomena. Since the classic war studies half a century ago,[3] there have been several dozen collations of wars in different slices of time and space; and even where these slices overlap in space and time, we rarely find complete agreement and sometimes considerable differences in regard to the cases included.[4] These differences may to some extent depend on varying degrees of completeness in the data collection;[5] many or most of them, however, depend more on different authors or teams using different *empirical* criteria and thresholds: in terms of the number of casualties,[6] the character of the parties[7] and the duration and continuity of the violence.[8] There is also some conceptual variation as to what to count as an *intra-state* war. Even if a war is fought entirely within the boundaries of a single state, armed forces from another state may cross the boundaries or be transported in from far away – to back up some local forces or pursue aims of their own. Apart from sending in troops of their own, third parties may permit 'volunteers' to join the conflict; they may send arms and other military materiel (as gifts, on credit or for cash payment); and they may back up local parties, or try to hit them, by economic, political or diplomatic means.[9] Between the clear and undisputed cases of inter-state and intra-state wars, respectively, we find what different authors call 'mixed cases', 'intra-state war with military intervention' etc.

We find several different typologies, of 'war' as well as of 'internal war', in the literature trying to answer the general questions on intra-state wars, such as:

1. What different kinds of such wars are there?
2. What typologies are made on what basis?
3. What kinds of questions are they intended to answer? (The purposes of classification differ among, for instance, social scientists, lawyers, journalists and politicians; different questions tend to be asked by each group and, not surprisingly, different answers are delivered).

To some extent, though limited, we also find empirical studies that use these typologies, place them in a theoretical framework and relate them to other variables.

Chapter 1 deals, *inter alia*, with behaviour and, specifically, *war*. This term is shown to refer to kinds of collective behaviour that differ considerably in terms of actors, actions, technology, aims and strategies, forms of regulation and victims; they are broadly categorized into *premodern, modern* and two kinds of *postmodern* warfare: the kind of intra-state war that mainly resembles premodern warfare and the use of state-of-the-art military technology by multi-state actors (UN, NATO etc.) when intervening in already existing armed conflicts.

Chapter 2 tries to summarize the 196 wars between 1945 and 1996 it counts with, concluding *inter alia*:

1. their frequency is tendentially increasing;[10]
2. the great majority are intra-state wars and this majority becomes more overwhelming in every decade;
3. 90 per cent are fought in the 'Third World';
4. intra-state wars last longer than inter-state wars; and
5. about one-third of all wars are ended by third-party mediation.

Chapter 3 assembles a more heterogeneous set of violent conflicts, using wider criteria than Chapter 2, *inter alia* by including mass violence where only one party is armed and organized (for instance, genocide). It therefore includes a higher number of cases: 102 in the period 1985–94 and (with much overlap) 80 cases in 1995–96. It deals with seven types of such violence, in order of relative frequency: ethno-national, anti-regime, inter-ethnic, inter-state, decolonization, gang wars and genocide. The order would be different if it were governed by the amount of victims.

The first three chapters already refer to conflict in the sense of *contradictions*. One of the discriminating characteristics used in Chapter 1 is what the war is *about*; Chapter 2 relates wars to the global transformation based on the diffusion and deepening of global capitalism and the conditions they define for the internal and external relations of states; and Chapter 3 notes that some two-thirds of all its cases have as a dominant or at least important feature to be *ethnicized* by the definition it uses.

This book is primarily about such intra-state armed conflicts that at least have significant ethnonational components, however defined; in principle it leaves aside, for instance, left-right conflicts about central power and centre-periphery conflicts that do not present themselves as ethnonational. Pure types, however, are rare – we may often find an interplay (synchronic and diachronic) between class, region etc. and ethnicity. Furthermore, what definitions to use are quite a controversial subject, and the proportion of all wars that are somehow 'ethnic' depends very much on what closer conceptualization has been made. Other studies report about half of all wars to be of this type, sometimes much less.

One of the problems is that wars can be characterized as 'ethnic', 'ethnonational', etc. on very different bases: the ethnonational composition of the parties; the conflict issues appearing in the propaganda of the parties;

whether conflict objects are specifically about ethnic markers; or by the results of causal analyses, etc. By a very inclusive definition, more than two-thirds of all wars are 'ethnic'; by a very strict definition, rather fewer wars fall squarely into this category (see Chapter 13). There are also strong indications that, for example, theoretical frameworks, ideological backgrounds and – especially in the 1990s – 'political correctness' play a role in what definitions are chosen.[11]

Another problem – at least for some of the classifications – has to do with all the problems surrounding the notion of *causality*. Disagreements on how to conceptualize causality and the legitimate methods for identifying causes are just as frequent in peace research as in other areas of social science. Stated in their strongest forms, one view (*Verstehen* in the classical German debate) is that each conflict is unique and that causal understanding means and requires that one has understood the purposes and beliefs of actors, so as to be able to reconstruct their actions rationally.[12] The opposite view, that the only way of establishing the validity of a hypothesized causal relationship is to collect systematic data on the involved variables, and then show that there is a significant statistical correlation between them, that this is not spurious and that the causal direction is as hypothesized.[13] These positions, however, are the versions for epistemological purists; in reality – in the social science workshop, that is – there are many positions in between and combinations of both approaches, the legitimacy of which can often only be challenged precisely by these purists.

There are dozens of statistical investigations on wars in general and on inter-state war in particular, most of which have tested some causal hypotheses by statistical methods. The interesting thing is that solidly established conclusions on the correlates of inter-state wars are so meagre at all levels. At the lowest level, where we relate properties of *individual states* to their being involved in war, the findings that are solid (in the sense of being replicated in several studies) are few enough to be enumerated:

1. great powers tend to be much more engaged in war than other states;
2. if a state has many boundaries, it tends to fight more wars than other states; and
3. a state whose armament level is clearly above the average for states of that size is also more prone to participate in wars.

Very many other properties of states have been run against war participation, with the normal result: close to zero correlation; some such properties of states have indeed been found in single studies to correlate with war participation, but the correlations, even if sometimes statistically significant, are normally quite weak.[14]

The paucity of solid findings may of course be due to the question being asked at the wrong level; after all, it takes two to tango. Let us therefore look at the *dyadic* level, trying to relate relations between two states to their tendency to go to war *with each other*. The robust results at this level include:

1. that great powers are the only states to fight other states apart from their neighbours;[15]
2. when a great power fights a minor power, it is almost always a state that lies in the economic sphere of interest of the great power (and which is usually, although not always, itself an economic satellite of the great power);
3. the risk that a military confrontation between two states escalates into a war increases with their being armed above the average for their sizes, and increases even more strongly if an arms race has preceded the confrontation. If these findings are related to, and further elaborate, findings at the single-state level, this is not true for the so-called 'Double Democracy Hypothesis';
4. whereas single democracies are neither more peaceful, nor more warlike than other states, two democracies do not fight *each other* (there is, however, no agreement as to *why* this is so).[16]

At the *systemic* level, finally, results are also ambiguous and weak, whether we look at cultural factors or such structural factors as (degree of) polarity or balance of power; it appears, furthermore, that their rates of change have more effect than the absolute values of these variables themselves.[17]

With this summary we leave the problematique of wars *between* states. This book is primarily about wars *within* states, bringing in inter-state wars in so far as they are directly relevant for understanding intra-state wars, and the lesson from studies of inter-state wars is that we should also have quite modest expectations when it comes to clearly demonstrated causal factors behind intra-state wars. This is not a clear-cut dichotomy, however; for instance, the very classification of a given war in this respect may often call for cutting through some of the propaganda war surrounding it, e.g. when some kind of military intervention is taking place.[18] In general, the meagre solid knowledge we have about inter-state wars appears to give limited guidance for the analysis of intra-state wars, e.g. because causal relations between them seem to be weak, for which reason generalized causal patterns must be sought inside each category, rather than across them.[19]

That 'cause' is an ambiguous concept has already been noted; in one of its senses, it comes close to equating the notion of 'issue'; and even if they are not equated, the relations between them tends to be interesting. Part II of the book focuses on some conflict *issues*, sometimes also being conceptualized as *causes*.

Territoriality is often used in descriptions of conflict issues or even causal explanations of violent conflict.[20] Chapter 4 deals with non-metaphysical aspects of territoriality as a conflict issue, investigating its content and discussing under what circumstances we may expect a linkage between territoriality and violent conflict. The former is neither a sufficient nor necessary condition for the latter: the likelihood for violent conflict is particularly high when territorial issues are ethnonationally loaded and mythologized, and where the issue has furthermore become one of secession and sovereignty.

Chapter 5 uses *economic development* and *environmental change and scarcity* as guiding concepts to elaborate the observation in Chapter 2 that some 90 per cent of all wars take place in the Third World. It is argued that the weak and even disputed relations between war and indicators of level of development or distribution (land, income etc.) are due to too narrow approaches: such indicators should be seen in relation to the overall economic structure, including environmental change and scarcity. Structural factors usually do not work by themselves in engendering, for example, social mobilization, but are mediated through cultural and perceptual factors, for instance those emphasized in modernization theory. Finally, there tends to be an interplay of forces that are internal and external (e.g. IMF).

Chapter 6 uses *identity* as a guiding concept to investigate one major – or even predominant – group of intra-state conflicts: those where ethnicity has become politicized, with the effect that conflict issues are seen, that is, as issues about identity. It goes through the rapidly expanding literature on the social construction of ethnic identities, and moves on to relate identity formation to modern macro phenomena: the territorial state and the deterritorialization created by modern technology and by the division of labour defined by global capitalism. The results are then used to discuss possible models for conflict resolution by 'dialogical community'.

Chapter 7 looks into a particular aspect of ethnic identity: *ethnonational mobilization*, i.e. investigating the effects on intra-state conflict of the relations between ethnicity and territory (e.g. the institutionalization of regions). One of the constitutive factors of an ethnonation is its *collective memory*, whether or not it agrees with the results of professional historians. This memory may well change over time, e.g. in the course of ethnonational mobilization, where identity is politicized, conflict objects and demands are articulated, mobilization is attempted and conflict methods chosen, so as to obtain desired resolutions. This normally involves challenging an already existing legitimate authority that has predominant power: the pattern of mobilization and choice of conflict methods depends, i.a. on whether this authority leaves any room in the political arena or not. The chapter stresses the multidimensionality and reversibility of these processes, using Northern Ireland as a concrete example.

Part III moves on from the descriptions and causal analyses in the two first parts to the study of *possibilities for peace* and *strategies* to attain them: what kinds of conflicts can be treated in what ways and under what circumstances? When are conflicts best left to the parties themselves and when does an external party appear by invitation from the parties or itself? How do relations between the original parties, or features of the external party (status, impartiality, intrusiveness), decide what processes are most likely to be fruitful?

To the extent that such studies are empirical, they call for tenable generalizations on what types of approaches are fruitful in bringing about de-escalation, ceasefires, political compromises, peaceful division or peaceful integration, reconciliation etc. Some of them go beyond that level to combining empirical knowledge, theoretical analysis and normative concerns into proposals as to who should do what.

Chapter 8 deals with the process of escalation and the timing of conflict management. It present a number of proposals on *conflict prevention* (how to avoid that conflicts take destructive forms) and *conflict management*. One overarching idea is to have states and the international system organized in such ways that no (political, regional, ethnic) group sees its interests as gravely threatened without access to redress by peaceful means.

A dozen different kinds of conflict prevention are suggested, as are half a dozen approaches to conflict management and peace-building. For many of these, historical (if imperfect) examples can be learnt from, whereas others are theoretically derived. What is possible to do for different categories of actors depends on how far a conflict has progressed beyond its dormant phase: from emergence to escalation, full intensity, de-escalation and finally a post-conflict situation.

Chapter 9 deals with *democratization*. There is no 'Double democracy hypothesis' at the intra-state level, violence being rare in economically developed democracies, but more frequent in less developed ones; transition to democracy increases the risks of violence. The waves of new electoral democracies saw many democracies stabilize – and many collapses and political reversals. The 'conflict settlement' approach (about power political issues) has serious shortcomings, as has 'conflict resolution' (about human needs). The transformative agenda should go for consensual, rather than adversarial, democracy to avoid that interest based conflicts get overloaded with identity conflicts. External intervention should strengthen resources for regional problem-solving; threats of or actual negative sanctions are often counterproductive in this respect, even if officially presented as successful. New ways are needed to overcome the political barriers between early warning and early action – and may be easiest to find in post-conflict situations.

Chapter 10 focuses on *third-party intervention*, presenting a typology based on the roles a potential third party may aim at or actually fill. It discusses what conditions a potential third party has to fulfil, e.g. in terms of status, (perceived) impartiality and self-restraint in actions, in order to be accepted as such by the original parties and to be effective by some criterion among the competing ones. This depends, among other things, on who the third party is (individual, NGO, state, international institution), at what phase in the conflict the third party tries to intervene and how intrusive a role it intends to play and actually plays. The final part of Chapter 10 discusses in what situations and under what circumstances traditional state diplomacy and Track II diplomacy have the best chances of playing a constructive role.

Part IV, finally, moves from the generalizing descriptions, analyses and proposals in the first three parts to presenting several analyses of specific concrete cases, illustrating central aspects of these generalizations, but also that they are often too limited to do justice to a complex and variable reality.

Chapter 11 takes up one of the particularly long-standing conflicts, that between *Palestinians and Israelis*, focusing on the element of identity conflict and in particular how this was treated in the Oslo Agreement. Identity is not a static phenomenon, but tends to be problematic, fragmented and changing. This is so because the identity of Self is constituted in relation to Other: nationalism – as a claimed unity of people, territory and state – creates the nation, rather than the other way around, and the homogenizing feature of nationalism, often referred to as 'nation-building', actually often calls for the destruction of previous nations. When the Oslo Agreement contained a mutual recognition between two parties who had long denied each other's legitimate – or even actual – existence, this demanded of both the Israelis and Palestinians a complex reevaluation of Other images and thereby also of their mirror-images: Self images as victims-cum-heroes.

Chapter 12 deals with various aspects of the roots of *Russian nationalism*, with problems that turn out to be quite different from those in Chapter 11. Its genealogy includes an inclusive tradition, Eurasianism, where what is constitutively Russian is seen as belonging to an even wider sphere; an exclusive tradition, sometimes referred to as Slavophile but really more centred on Orthodox Christianity and the idea of Moscow as a 'Third Rome'; and an ideology of *derzhavnost* (state-ness) which has Russians as its focus but which is not in itself limited to them. The chapter then describes the varieties of Russian nationalism that have emerged from these traditions' being combined in different ways.

Chapter 13 treats a set of conflicts in the *Causasian region* and presents brief analyses of them, but has an analytical ambition beyond that in studying how these conflicts have been treated in different discourses. On the one hand, and using quite restrictive criteria, the author argues that none of these conflicts are primarily – or at all – *ethnic conflicts*. On the other hand she points out that most or all of these conflicts were presented as ethnic conflicts. She then discusses the political functions of these conflicts being thus presented. One of them is that when the conflicts are presented as largely irrational, this tends to give the Russian Federation – as an 'old Causacus hand' – predominant roles in dealing with them, thereby excluding or diluting whatever role other actors in the international community may be able to play.

Chapter 14 surveys *sub-Saharan Africa*. As a heritage from the Berlin Congress – and in spite of the OAU ambitions to the opposite effect – the dozen or more recent or present inter-state conflicts are about borders and aspects of these: natural resources, political strategies or socio-political dynamics. Intra-state conflict, on the other hand, is about succession (who is to be in power on what conditions) or secession. Violent intra-state conflicts have cost several million lives and produced an even greater number of refugees and internally displaced persons; severely damaged economic infrastructures; and contributed to the breakdown of several states. There is a vicious circle here: the more the state shrinks economically, whether due to internal war damage or IMF conditions, the more competition is there for what the ruling elite can give their clients or their own groups, and the more likely is a breakdown of the state, with more violence resulting from that very process or from the state being unable to control local conflicts. The chapter reviews the possibilities and achievements of various actors: the OAU and such regional organizations as ECOWAS and SADC as well as various parts of civil society, and finally discusses EU policies.

The process of producing a volume like the present one unavoidably generates debts of gratitude. The Board of COPRI made the authors' symposium financially possible. Christian P. Scherrer assisted in finding the final structure of the plan for the book and provided contacts to some of the authors invited to fill the lacunae defined by the chosen structure. The authors usually had several previous commitments, but nevertheless found the time and mental energy necessary to contribute their chapters at relatively short notice. Martin Noble (Internet: www.martinob.demon.co.uk Email: martin@martinob.demon.co.uk) took good linguistic care of the chapters whose authors are not native speakers of English and which had not been language edited before reaching COPRI. Sidsel Westi Kragh and Tor Nonnegaard-Pedersen went far beyond the call of duty in producing the camera ready copy under circumstances that eventually became more arduous than they had been given to believe.

Notes

1   COPRI has its research organized in major programmes, the three older ones being 'European Security' (EUR), 'Military Restructuring' (MIL) and 'Nordic

Security' (NORD). The Strategy Plan of COPRI as well as the present Medium Term Research Plans for its programmes are presented in *COPRI Working Paper 14/1998*.

2   For a thorough discussion of its conceptualization, see Johan Galtung: *PEACE BY PEACEFUL MEANS: Peace and Conflict, Development and Civilization*, London, Thousand Oaks and New Delhi: Sage, 1996.

3   Pitirim A. Sorokin, *Social and Cultural Dynamics*, Vol. 3, New York: American Book Co., 1937; Quincy Wright, *A Study of War*, Chicago: Chicago University Press, 1942; Lewis Fry Richardson, *Statistics of Deadly Quarrels*, Chicago: Boxwood & Quadrangle, 1960 (posthumous).

4   See Milton Leitenberg, *A Survey of Studies of Post WW II Wars, Conflicts and Military Coups*, Cornell University, 1977.

5   It is true already for the three classics that they show little differences concerning the inclusion of highly lethal conflicts, but considerably more where the magnitude of the conflicts is a few thousand casualties or less.

6   The threshold of 1,000 casualties per year as threshold for 'war' is used in the Correlates of War project (J. David Singer and Melvin Small: *Resort to Arms: International and Civil Wars, 1816–1980*, Beverly Hills: Sage, 1981 – and many later publications). The statistics in SIPRI Yearbook in recent years uses the same criterion for war, but also has a category of 'intermediate conflict' (more than 1,000 altogether, but not in the single year under consideration, and a category 'minor conflict' with 25 victims as its lower threshold. Richardson (1960) has about 300 as the actual threshold for 'deadly quarrels'; some authors indicate no lower threshold at all, whether on principle or by omission.

7   The most rigorous criterion is that all actors are states; others demand that one actor is a state and the other at least a quasi-state in the sense of having a central political leadership and organized armed forces; others yet again are satisfied with two or more quasi-states, or with at least one actor being a state or quasi-state; and some demand none of these.

8   The most important question tends to be under what circumstances we should count as one or more wars a situation where periods of high violence are interspersed by periods of little or no violence.

9   For the conceptual problems (and an empirical study) of military intervention, see Bertil Dunér, *Military Intervention in Civil Wars: The 1970s*, Aldershot: Gower, 1985.

10 The average year in the 1940s contained about a dozen wars; the figure then quadruples until the early 1990s and a peak in 1992, with a subsequent decline. It is still too early to state with any confidence whether that decline marks a clear change of trend or is just another of the variations we have earlier seen around the rising trend. Whereas there is no upward trend in inter-state wars, that in intra-state wars is roughly proportional to the rising number of states in the world.

11 It is illustrative that the statistics which the Department of Peace and Conflict Research at Uppsala University produced for *SIPRI Yearbook* over several years (and which are also used in an annual article in the *Journal of Peace Research* during the last few years) have eliminated references to ethnicity, now merely classifying armed conflicts by the conflict objects as 'Government' or 'Territory'.

12 One major problem with that approach is *embarras du richesse*: the same action can normally be reconstructed by *many* different and *prima facie* credible combinations of beliefs and goals ascribed to the actors, for which reason conclusive proof calls for eliminating all the competitors to the rational reconstruction chosen by the author; its internal coherence and compatibility with known facts are not enough.

13 The problem with this, on the other hand, is that a rigorous adherence to it in the case of such a meagre universe as that of armed conflict makes it *a priori* unlikely that we will ever find many solid results.

14 Vasquez, John A., 'Statistical Findings in International Politics: A Data-Based Assessment', *International Studies Quarterly*, vol. 20, no. 2, June 1976, pp. 171-218.

15 The few exceptions derive from great powers having dragged their own clients into wars, such as Bulgaria's joining the USSR in its invasion of Czechoslovakia in 1968, or the United States for a while dragging Australia and New Zealand into the Vietnam War.

16 Gleditsch, Nils Petter and Håvard Hegre, 'Peace and Democracy: Three Levels of Analysis', *Journal of Conflict Resolution*, vol. 41, no. 2, April 1997, pp. 283-310.

17 For an overview of all levels and the relationships between them, see the chapter by Dina A. Zinnes, 'Why War? Evidence on the Outbreak of International Conflict', in Ted Robert Gurr (ed.), *Handbook of Political Conflict: Theory and Research*, New York: Free Press, 1980.

18 See, again, Dunér (1985).

19 One indication of this is a statistical non-finding that has been repeated since studies published a generation ago: the bivariate correlations between indicators of a state being engaged in external conflict and indicators of internal conflict in it lie quite close to zero; and trivariate elaborations, while sometimes finding stronger correlations, generally fail to present many meaningful patterns about them.

20 In this case, territoriality is seen as an instinct or something like that. Much of the literature is fairly fanciful and undocumented, but there are also solid and sober overviews, such as Torsten Malmberg: *Human Territoriality: Survey of Behavioural Territories in Man with Preliminary Analysis and Discussion of Meaning*, The Hague, Paris and New York: Mouton, 1980.

PART I

WAR AS A PHENOMENON

1   The Faces of War

BJØRN MØLLER

Preface

War has ceased to conform to the Clausewitzian paradigm, for it is no longer predominantly a means wielded by the State for its political ends. Now that the State is, at most, one among several war-waging actors, and that war now occurs more within than between states, there is a need for a new conceptualization of the phenomenon of war which should pay special attention to the causation, motivation, modalities and consequences of what might, for want of a better term, be termed 'ethnic' or 'ethnopolitical' war.

For this purpose, some of the approaches and findings of so-called 'postmodernist theory' appear to be relevant. The value of this rather amorphous agglomeration of trendy new approaches (also known as 'critical theory', 'post-structuralism', '(de)constructivism', etc.) has rightly been questioned: Its claim to constitute a theory is disputed (to say the least), its connotations are unclear, and its explanatory value remains to be proven, to put it mildly. Nevertheless, the postmodernists appear to have posed some pertinent questions overlooked by mainstream International Relations (IR) theory and Strategic Studies as well as to have discovered some truths about (post)modern society, both nationally and globally.[1] This nucleus of truth may be well worth salvaging from postmodernism's cauldron of epistemological obscurity, terminological opacity and theoretical fuzziness. To make an attempt at this is one of the main purposes of this chapter.

It looks first at the question of what postmodern theory might have to say about 'postmodern warfare' and other violent intrastate conflicts. Here, postmodernist theory is also far more successful in explaining the roots of conflicts than mainstream theory, which has long entailed a 'closure' (in postmodern newspeak) against themes such as 'identity', be it national, ethnic or religious.[2] Postmodernism also provides some clues to understanding the actual waging of such 'wars' (if so they are) in contrast to IR Realism which has absolutely no comprehension of such 'irregular warfare'.

Secondly, it attempts a preliminary analysis of the phenomenon of war through a comparison of three types of war, one of which is 'modern', the other distinctly postmodern, and the third a hybrid combining archaic with modern and postmodern features.

Collapsing the inside and outside

What has become abundantly clear through the 1990s is that one cannot understand war without transcending the traditional framework of International Relations (IR) theory.

For our present purposes, R.B.J. Walker's elaborate deconstruction of the conception of the State and the international system of which it forms a constituent part is especially relevant. According to Walker, IR orthodoxy (and especially Realism) is founded on a distinction between an 'inside' and an 'outside'. The inside was originally a Hobbesian *bellum omnium contra omnes*, but it was subsequently pacified in a national order dominated by the State, whether conceived of as the Leviathan of Hobbes himself or as a contractual social construction as envisaged by Rousseau.[3] The outside, however, was predestined to remain anarchic, since this was the realm of the States, depicted as sovereign entities operating as individuals in the state of nature, only 'writ large'. By implication, it was futile to look inside states, since states were unitary actors; but it was also unpromising to look beyond the system of states, say to transnational or supranational actors, since there was no way the states would ever relinquish their sovereignty.

This was, indeed, a 'grand narrative', according to postmodern authors, only a wrong and profoundly a historic one. In truth the state is a historical construct that has been under constant evolution ever since its emergence – and it is, at best, 'peaceful', within in the narrowest possible sense, and often the latent conflicts may develop into violent struggles or even civil wars.[4] Furthermore, several (categories) of actors other than states have made their appearance on the international stage, only remain excluded from orthodox/Realist analysis, e.g. via its terminological closures. By (presumed) implication, if only IR theory can escape the Procrustean bed of these closures, nothing would speak against analyzing possibilities for various forms of global (or regional, for that matter) governance.[5] This might result in a relegation of the state to merely one among a heterogeneous group of actors alongside, for instance, international organizations, transnational civil society etc. Some of these forms of governance may, in fact, hold some promise of solving ethnic conflicts, a matter to which I shall return in due course.

Figure 1.1 Modern and postmodern inside/outside

Modern   Postmodern

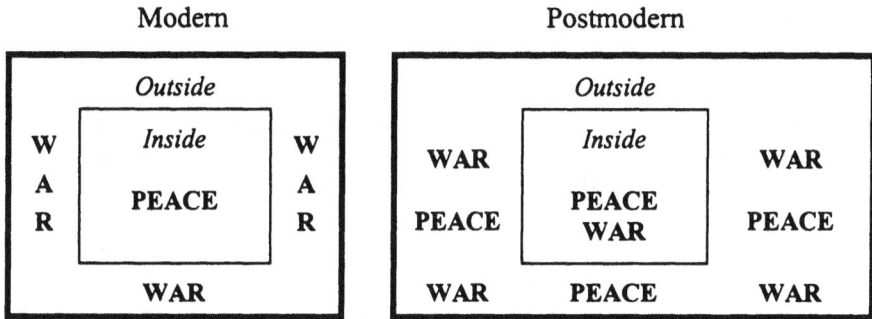

This deconstruction also allows for a clearer picture of the phenomenon of war: Neither is the inside as pacific nor the outside as anarchic and conflictual as traditionally assumed, but the peace within is intermingled with conflict and the war without is (or at least might be) blended with peace or 'peaces'.

Postmodern war and the postmodern military

The focal shift from the State to other actors has also had profound implications for the meaning of 'war'.

Quite a few authors (including non-postmodernists) have written about the 'postmodern military', analysing the evolving social position and/or tasks of the military in postmodern society. In this connection authors have coined chivalric neologisms for the 'new' military such as '*miles protector*' or 'knights in white armour' for the land warriors. The postmodern military men, according to these conceptions, are not so much fighters as protectors, peacekeepers and technicians; usually professionals rather than conscripts; and a very large proportion of them are not actually soldiers but civilians. Finally, postmodern soldiers may be 'post-heroic', i.e. no longer expected to put their lives at stake, for whatever cause – to the extent that they nevertheless have to fight, but they would do so in a risk-free way, i.e. by fighting 'wars without tears'.[6]

However, the application of postmodern theories to the study of war as such is a fairly recent phenomenon, and what has been produced to date does not by any means add up to any coherent theory.[7] Most postmodernists, in line with their deconstructivist predisposition, have confined themselves to analysing the 'language games' entailed by the dominant discourse on deterrence and war, as well as the phenomenon of simulacre and 'wars of make-believe'. Postmodern observers do have a point when they warn against the blurring of distinctions between games and 'the real thing', as video games become increasingly realistic, actual war increasingly 'stage managed', and the media coverage more and more massive and instantaneous:

> With this war, cyberspace came out of the research labs and into our living rooms. The written word lost out to the video of a video of a bomb that did not need books to be smart ...; to a hyperreal Gulfspeak that 'attrited' all critics ... For six weeks and one hundred hours we were drawn into the most powerful cyberspace yet created, a technically reproduced world-text that seemed to have no author or reader, just enthusiastic participants and passive viewers.[8]

Thus envisaged as unreal, i.e. a game, postmodern war lends itself nicely to all forms of 'critical analysis', e.g. to being analysed as a '(body) language game'. Similarly, the entire Cold War could be seen as a gigantic chess game, where the contestants competed via potential next moves that none of them wished to make, i.e. where military moves (alignments, deployments, mobilizations, arms acquisitions etc.) were really nothing but signals, a form of 'body language writ large'.[9]

The bright side of this form of postmodern war is that it is relatively bloodless, because nothing happens: nobody gets killed (or, at worst, there are only very few fatalities), since the bombs are never detonated, or if some are (as in the Gulf War) they are so surgically precise that collateral damage is minimal. Not only do We (the good guys) not suffer any casualties, but neither do They (the bad guys) – not because they do not deserve it, but thanks to Our magnanimity. However, there is a darker side even to this form of postmodern war: first of all, something might have gone wrong with nuclear deterrence, in which case it would most likely have gone catastrophically wrong, i.e. brought about a thermonuclear conflagration, perhaps even 'nuclear winter'.[10] But it did not. Secondly, beyond the confines of the central conflict the two superpowers fought each other by means of proxies in wars that were far from sanitary or bloodless – even though they were made to look trivial by means of terms such as 'peripheral wars', 'small wars', 'low-intensity conflict' or 'regional conflicts'.

The last point brings us to the really dark side of postmodern warfare, namely new forms of violent conflicts that are all too real, encompassing phenomena such as guerilla and civil wars – occasionally also featuring 'ethnic cleansing' and other atrocities of genocidal proportions. These are violent armed conflicts fought (for the most part, or exclusively) within state borders, by non-regular warriors (sometimes kids), and often against civilian targets – or at least in a way that ensures that the casualties are predominantly civilians.

This type of war is also known as 'nontrinitarian war' (Martin Van Creveld) or 'transitional war' (William R. Thompson).[11] What may warrant the label 'postmodern' are the following features:

- such wars are predominated by flux and uncontrollability;
- they are 'about' something entirely different from the objectives of 'modern' wars;
- they are often non-binary, i.e. they pit more than two sides against each other, which opens up possibilities for shifting alignments as well as risks of regressing to a situation of 'everybody against everybody else';
- the political setting is distinctly 'non-Westphalian';
- the war has shed its last 'duel-like' (i.e. Clausewitzian) features and become asymmetrical to the point of incommensurability;
- the warring sides use both modern and 'postmodern weapons'; and
- the characteristic vulnerabilities of postmodern/postindustrial society are exploited to their fullest.

What one might call the 'Clausewitzian paradigm' of war has thus lost its universal applicability (if it ever had one). Clausewitz conceived of war as a means to political ends, i.e. as a continuation of politics by other means, and as clearly subordinate to the political logic, even though it might have its own 'grammar'.[12] 'Postmodern wars' are different.

Premodern, modern and postmodern war

The best way of understanding the new and emerging may be to compare it with the past and present. To this end, I have in the following compared postmodern with premodern and modern war, generalizing to an outrageous (but in this context inevitable) extent.[13]

As set out in Table 1.1, I have divided the distinguishing features according to the questions: who does the fighting?, on whose behalf?, against whom?; why?; where?; how?; to which extent?; and by which means? (weapons and other).

Table 1.1 Premodern, modern and postmodern war

	Pre-modern	Modern	Post-modern	
			Collective	Intrastate
Who?	Mercenaries 'Amateurs'	Conscripts Professionals	Conscripts Professionals	Militias Terrorists Mercenaries Children
On whose behalf?	Clan or tribe Feudal rulers Warlords	The State	Global or regional organizations	Nation, ethnic, religious group Warlords
Against whom?	Soldiers	Soldiers Civilians	Soldier/ civilians	Civilians
Why?	Economic ends: booty	Political ends: territory, sovereignty	Political ends: international law, human rights	Individual and group ends
Where?	Inside/Outside	Outside	'Outside as Inside'	Inside/Outside
How?	Disorderly	Principles of war	Principles of war	Guerilla warfare Terrorism
To what extent?	Low intensity No rules, but chivalry	High intensity Laws of war	High/low intensity Laws of war	High intensity 'Anything goes'
By which means?	Primitive weapons	Conventional weapons WMD	Non-lethal weapons Info-systems	Small arms Computer viruses

This analysis is also based on the assumption that 'war' may have ceased to be a single phenomenon, if it ever was. A trifurcation seems to have occurred into the following categories, which have very little in common:

- 'Modern wars', i.e. international wars of aggression and national defence (which one might also call 'Clausewitzian wars'). This category used to be the main one, but has been practically empty for several years, even though it would probably be premature to declare it obsolete.[14]
- 'Collective wars', i.e. wars waged by inter- or even supranational institutions, e.g. in the form of collective security campaigns or humanitarian interventions.
- Intrastate wars, for which I reserve the label 'postmodern wars'. To the extent that others get involved, they tend to be waging what is euphemistically called 'operations other than war' (OOTW), e.g. in the form of peacekeeping or humanitarian assistance. For the participants, however, they are all too war-like, and labels such as 'low intensity conflict' or 'small war' are clearly misnomers.[15]

Who?

Whereas archaic wars were fought primarily by professionals (*Landsknechte*, musketeers etc.), i.e. what we would today call mercenaries or soldiers of fortune, 'modern' war has tended to assume the form of an orderly *levée en masse*. Most countries have thus relied on conscription based on universal (and with the exception of Israel only male) compulsory military service. The goal has, however, been to make the army an integral, yet at the same time distinct, element of society: 'Civilized' in the 'like everybody else' sense, yet performing a specialized task for which the military has been trained, like everybody else;[16] and the task being not so very different from those of most other professions, since actual fighting is quite rare.

The latter is even more true for post-modern wars of type A, i.e. peacekeeping and similar military operations. Here the soldiers are usually more akin to craftsmen or technicians than to warriors, and it is no longer a matter of 'defending the motherland'. Hence, conscription is no longer really appropriate, and hence the clear trend is towards an abolition of conscription in favour of professionals.

Postmodern warfare type B, on the other hand, tends to be waged by whoever is around, including women and children – and is fought in a highly irregular, sporadic and spasmodic fashion, where occasional acts of war blend in with everyday life. The division of labour between warriors and the productive segments of society has thus broken down. Another reappearing phenomenon is that of various forms of mercenaries, i.e. 'guns for hire'. These phenomena to some extent reflect a tendential 'privatization of security': if, as a consequence of its general crisis, the State loses its credibility as a provider of individual security, its citizens may resort to self-help, as in the Hobbesian 'state of nature'.[17]

Whose?

As elaborated upon by Martin Van Creveld, modern war is 'trinitarian', i.e. waged by armies on behalf of the trinity of people, army and government, and it became even more symbiotically so with the advent of nationalism, democracy and universal conscription.[18] Some have even argued that the evolution of the State and war were inextricably intertwined, to the extent that one was inconceivable without the other.[19]

Postmodern wars of type A are, almost by definition, waged on behalf of the international community (i.e. the United Nations and/or regional organizations). Type B postmodern wars, on the other hand, are waged on behalf of very diverse entities, such as clans, ethnies, religious communities, warlords or the like – and in some cases on behalf of nobody at all, except the lone warrior himself, operating in a post-apocalyptic 'Mad Max' setting. This is, for instance, the tragic fate of many of those child soldiers (especially widespread in Africa) who constitute one of postmodern war's darkest features.

Whom?

In premodern war, the weapons were usually directed against the other side's troops. Civilians suffered, of course, if only because of the pillaging (and occasional rape) that followed in the trail of the armies moving about, mainly in order to avoid engagements (*sic!*). This was, however, 'collateral damage' rather than direct war damage; mostly paid in the coinage of material values rather than blood; and usually of a limited and/or very localized scale.

Modern war, in contrast, became increasingly directed against civilians, with the Allied (conventional and nuclear) bombings of Hamburg, Dresden, Tokyo, Hiroshima and Nagasaki standing out as prototypical examples. Nothwithstanding the occasional planning for city avoidance and counterforce targetting, nuclear war planning pointed in the same direction, only with even more pronounced genocidal implications. The scale of mobilization, on the other hand, also multiplied battle deaths, with the carnage in the trenches along the Western front in the First World War as the best known example, described so graphically in Erich Maria Remarque's novel, *Im Westen Nichts Neues* (*All Quiet on the Western Front*).

In postmodern warfare type A, the number of combatant and civilian casualties is usually rather low, while in type B the death toll may be very high, at least on a local scale. Most casualties and fatalities are civilians, for at least two reasons: because the distinction between combatants and civilians has been blurred, and because of the location of the war, which is often fought in densely populated areas ('concrete jungle warfare', for instance), with massive collateral damage as the inevitable result. With the intention of crippling the enemy economically and socially, rather than defeating him militarily, agriculture and/or infrastructure are often targetted, e.g. by means of landmines. In some cases, moreover (particularly when ethnicity are involved), war regresses into genocide or other forms of 'ethnic cleansing', e.g. by means of rape.[20]

Why?

Modern wars are typically fought for political ends, as most succinctly put by Clausewitz in the quote above. Such use of military means for political ends was originally entirely possible and instrumentally rational: there were certainly political goals worth fighting for, i.e. which warranted risking whatever the use of the military means might entail, even in the worst of cases. However, with the First and Second World Wars and, even more so, with the nuclear revolution, a point was reached where the destructive (and indeed suicidal) potential embedded in the means was out of proportion with the ends: was the possible annihilation of the entire society of not only the vanquished, but also the victor (the prospect of global thermonuclear war) really a reasonable price to pay for any political goal? Surely not.

The steady growth of global interdependence (trade etc.) only magnified this unbridgeable gap between ends and means, since states now had even more to lose from a severance of trade routes as would result from even minor wars – as well as more to gain by staying at peace with each other. Some have even argued that war has become so utterly dysfunctional among 'trading states' as to make it well nigh inconceivable.

A further factor pointing in the same direction is the global spread of democracy. This form of government is inherently peaceful, at least in the sense that democracies very rarely, if ever, go to war against other democracies. By implication, the number of state dyads among which war remains conceivable is rapidly shriking, while the global 'zone of peace' expands.[21] Finally, the very fact that states have previously waged (trinitarian or Clausewitzian) wars to no avail, and at mind-boggling costs, may in itself serve as a powerful inhibition against any repetition thereof. War-weariness may thus have proliferated and intensified to such an extent as to make large-scale war obsolete.[22]

Postmodern wars (type B) are different, however. They are not fought for political goals, at least not exclusively, and they are thus no longer (only or mainly) a continuation of politics. War as such may thus serve a purpose, regardless of who wins, at least at the level of individual warriors, but perhaps also at that of collectives, e.g. nations (*vide supra*). Having lived the life of a warrior for some time is often tantamount to having lost whatever one owned or cherished before the fighting started: home, land, possessions, family, job etc. There may thus be no normalcy to return to, and no improvement of one's condition to hope for, unless one's side prevails and can divide the spoils of conquest among themselves. So the fighters might just as well carry on the struggle.

Emotionally, there are sunk costs as well, on all sides of the conflict, such as relatives and kinsmen who have been killed by the enemy and are now crying out for revenge; or atrocities committed that are best kept secret and not thought about. Also, some may even have grown accustomed to 'living on the edge' as warriors do, with all the excitement and 'male bonding' it involves.

One of the postmodern features of ethnic conflicts is that they are about identity, in more than one respect.

- The very act of fighting, with the accompanying putting one's life at stake, may be a precondition for the development of a 'we-feeling', and for separating 'us' from 'them', i.e. 'Self' from 'Other'. Combat duties (however irregular) may thus help emergent nations in their

(Andersonian) 'imagination of their community'. In some cases, an actual history is at hand which may be resurrected from oblivion in order to provide (preferably heroic) symbols for nation building. When there are no such collective memories, new ones may be created by war.

- Putting up a struggle may be a precondition for recognition as an identity by the Other, hence indirectly also for self-identification. The taking of lives may thus be as important as winning.
- Open, and preferably violent, heroic and spectacular, conflict may force third parties to take a stand, whereby they may also have to acknowledge both sides as political entities.[23]

Where?

While archaic wars, at least in the Middle Ages, were rather fluid wars of disengagement because of deliberate battle avoidance, modern wars have tended to be fixed and of an ever-expanding spatial scope and magnitude, albeit with a twist: the expanding size of armies, on the one hand, intensified destruction and expanded the battlefield; on the other hand, the increasing destructive power embedded in the weapons used forced a gradual dispersion of forces – pointing towards the 'empty battlefield',[24] which would indeed be a postmodern phenomenon. Nevertheless, modern war has tended to remain fixed in the sense that a significant distinction remained between front and rear, albeit eroded by the introduction of long-range bombers and ballistic missiles.

Postmodern wars of type B are mostly civil wars that take place within state borders – even though the mismatch between nation and state borders, or the involvement of external actors may lead to a spread across borders.[25] The very concepts of front and rear tend to loose their meaning – along with the distinction between combatants and civilians. Some such wars already feature urban guerilla fighting; others are (semi)-'post-territorial' by being directed against another country's citizens or possessions, regardless of their location – e.g. airlines and their passengers or embassies.[26]

Other varieties of postmodern wars are assuming increasingly virtual and post-territorial features, i.e. have almost entirely shed their territorial garments. Everybody acknowledges the growing importance of 'information dominance', i.e. of being able to see without being seen and hear without being heard by the enemy, all in real time. Some have argued that this is, in fact, the distinguishing feature of the heralded 'Revolution in Military Affairs' (RMA), the first glimpses of which we saw during the Gulf War.[27] In the future, one might envision wars fought entirely in cyberspace (i.e. in an electromagnetic no-mans-land without any spatial coordinates),[28] between 'hacker terrorists' and states (or firms); or wars featuring a race between information and disinformation attempts, that might be called 'epistemic wars'.

How?

Modern war is orderly, and modern European strategists have all along envisaged war as proceeding according to plan, in some cases even in a 'geometrical fashion',[29] hence, for instance, the Principles of War of Antoine de Jomini that were presumably of perrenial validity.[30] Some strategic thinkers allowed room for 'the fog of battle',[31] but basically war was an activity to plan for, and one that was expected to proceed (largely) according to plan.

Postmodern warfare type B, on the other hand, is disorderly. There may be tactics of cyberwar or urban guerilla warfare, but a strategy thereof is hardly conceivable. At most, it would be a 'grand strategy' envisaging disorganization of the respective adversary. Moreover, against enemies who wage war in a postmodern fashion, conventional strategy leads nowhere. This phenomenon was already visible in the Vietnam War, where Robert MacNamara's 'technowar' (based on the systems analyses of his Harvard 'wizz kids') was to no avail, simply because the enemy was too intangible and refused to play 'by the rules'.[32] Indeed, the same had already been the case in the desert warfare described by Lawrence of Arabia who likened the use of conventional means against the intangible guerilla to 'eating soup with a knife'.[33] Postmodern warfare waged against modern adversaries might thus be seen as an 'ultra-indirect' approach to strategy, taking Liddell Hart further than he envisaged venturing himself.[34] Postmodern guerilas might attempt to turn the technological sophistication and complexity of their modern adversaries into liabilities rather than assets. Just consider how immensely vulnerable (post)modern societies are to any severance of their power supplies, or to computer viruses. Even though numerous technical safeguards may be devised, it will remain a measures-versus-countermeasures game in which that side which possesses the structural advantage will prevail; and to disrupt is simply structurally less demanding than to protect. The modern protectors may thus be fighting a losing battle against the postmodern disruptors.

Postmodern wars may also become increasingly fictional, yet with all too real implications. As was illustrated by Stanley Kubrick's *Doctor Strangelove*, the worst 'doomsday bomb' is the one which does exist, but is unknown by the enemy. The ideal bomb would not exist at all. However, the respective enemy would believe it did (or even that it might), which would produce all the deterrent and/or compellent (e.g. blackmail) effect one could wish for. To the extent that 'cyber warriors' could disseminate disinformation to such an effect, they would possess very powerful weapon indeed – without actually having any.

To what extent?

Contrary to some readings of Clausewitz, modern war is not the absolute war with a boundless escalatory momentum that he described in *Vom Kriege*.[35] It is limited, above all by the political ends as a means to which war is conceived. First of all, a war for political ends thus has to observe certain limitations, beyond which it ceases to be a rational endeavour. Secondly, politics (and the underlying ethics) have proscribed an increasingly broad range of conceivable *casus belli* as well as ways and means of waging war: the *jus ad bellum* and *jus in bello* bodies of international law.[36]

What is left is a rather narrow range of reasons for which a state may go to war, which boil down to (national or collective) self-defence and collective security operations; and a rather circumscribed range of permissible forms of warfare and legitimate weapons: no warfare against civilians, no use of chemical or biological (or, after the World Court ruling, nuclear) weapons at all, etc.

It is, of course, debatable to what extent (if at all) such regulations are mere window-dressing or actually contribute to 'civilizing war'.[37] The question of what belligerents refrain from doing out of respect for the regulations is counter-factual and hence impossible to answer with any certainty. In any case, strong states seem to be a necessary, even if they are no sufficient condition for the 'civilization of war'.

Postmodern warfare (type B), in comparison, is unregulated and therefore tendentially boundless, if only because of who is waging it. The laws of war are laws for states, whereas there are few, if any, laws regulating the behaviour of individuals or bands of mercenaries that are roaming wild.[38] Moreover, the above-mentioned psychological factors tend to imbue postmodern warfare with a rage that may transcend all bounds – and which may degenerate into vicious circles of blood-feud-like revenge. To the extent that political leaders want to limit fighting, they often lack the authority to do so.

By which means?

It is not so much the invention of individual weapons that determines the evolution of warfare as their introduction on a mass scale. Moreover, the decisive factor is usually not weapons at all, but rather society's general technological state, as reflected, *inter alia*, in its infrastructure (in the widest sense of the word).

Archaic and medieval war featured weapons based on quite primitive technologies, with limited lethality and fairly short range. The resultant limitation on the scale and intensity of warfare was reinforced by other technological and societal factors such as the limited transport capacity and difficulties with mobilizing large forces for more than very short periods.

Modern war, in contrast, is preconditioned on a higher level of productivity that makes sizable numbers of otherwise productive people dispensable from their productive duties without this having serious detrimental effects on overall production. Not only did industrialization accomplish this feat, its cost-effective methods of production also allowed states to equip mass armies with state-of-the-art weapons possessing a growing range and destructive power – culminating in the combination of long-range missiles and thermonuclear weapons.

In postmodernity all the benefits that were to be reaped from the above developments have already been reaped: distances have ceased to be insurmountable obstacles and have become, at worst, mere impediments; and, in a curious post-Einsteinian way, space and mass are being mirrored in time. The only sensible measure of space (e.g. distance) may now be the time required to traverse (or otherwise 'cover') it. This is even more true when what is transported is not material objects (such as projectiles or aircraft carriers) but immaterial stuff such as information, as is the most characteristic feature of postmodern 'information war'.

While in modern war what mattered was 'who gets there the fastest with the mostest', in the postmodern age it has become more important who knows what first, i.e. who is best at gathering, analysing and disseminating information. All data on the disposition of the respective enemy are available in 'real time'; the most important weapons are no longer those that are best at killing the enemy, but those that blind, deafen or otherwise confuse the enemy the most thoroughly, thereby incapacitating him. The time has thus come to make the most of Liddell Hart's indirect approach:

> To cut an army's lines of communication is to paralyze its physical organization. To close its line of retreat is to paralyze its moral organization. And to destroy its lines of intercommunication − by which orders and reports pass − is to paralyse its sensory organization, the essential connection between brain and body. [...] To paralyse the enemy's military nerve-system is a more economical form of operation than to pound his flesh.[39]

It may even have become undesirable to kill the enemy, hence the attraction of such 'non-lethal' weapons as are presently being researched in the Pentagon and elsewhere − including computer viruses and weapons intended to sever power grids.[40] An optimistic reading thereof might be that we are rapidly approaching a 'war without tears', i.e. one in which neither We (the good guys) nor They (the bad guys) come to any serious harm. If believed in, such as (hyper- or) postmodernist vision would go a long way towards removing the inhibitions against going to war in the first place. War might actually be fun, or at least harmless.

The optimists are almost certainly wrong, however, first of all, because the non-lethality of the aforementioned non-lethal weapons is debatable. They may produce fewer direct battle fatalities, but some of them produce just as many indirect, and mostly civilian, casualties and fatalities. Secondly, once a war has started (say, because of a sanguine view about how it would be waged), the 'fog of war' may set in. In this fog, it is highly likely that temporary military setbacks would be responded to with the introduction of 'old-fashioned', i.e. deliberately lethal, weapons. In conclusion, war may become more likely as well as equally destructive.

The even darker side of postmodern weaponry is that its lethality is undiminished, while its production costs are falling, making them available in meaningful quantities to both minor military powers and to non-state warring parties. Even disregarding the weapons that are presently being sold at dumping prices or otherwise 'leaking' from the ex-Soviet Union, the weapons supply may also be rising from clandestine production.

All of the above types of weaponry are distinctly modern or postmodern, which have led some observers to characterize postmodern wars such as those in the former Yugoslavia as 'medieval wars fought with modern weapons'.[41] However, another frequent phenomenon in postmodern wars is the use of modern or even premodern weaponry, above all various forms of small arms. What is disturbing about this is the fact that they are proliferating so widely and uncontrollably, and hence are available in such quantities that the supply itself contributes to the aforementioned 'privatization of security'.[42]

Conclusion

We have seen in this chapter that the phenomenon of war has become even more complex than in the past. The Clausewitzian paradigm probably retains its validity for 'modern' interstate wars, while other theoretical approaches are needed to comprehend the two varieties of 'postmodern war' described in this chapter.

Notes

1 On postmodern IR 'theory' see George, Jim: *Discourses of Global Politics: A Critical (Re)Introduction to International Relations*, Boulder: Lynne Rienner, 1994. Various approaches are presented in Smith, Steve, Ken Booth and Marysia Zalewski (eds): *International Theory: Positivism and Beyond* Cambridge: Cambridge University Press, 1996. For a critique see Vasquez, John A.: 'The Post-Positivist Debate: Reconstructing Scientific Enquiry and International Relations Theory After Enlightenment's Fall', in Ken Booth and Steve Smith (eds): *International Relations Theory Today*, Cambridge: Polity Press, 1995, pp. 217-240; or Østerrud, Øyvind: 'Antinomies of Postmodernism in International Studies', *Journal of Peace Research* 33(4) (November 1996), pp. 385-90.

2 See, for instance, Gellner, Ernest: *Postmodernism, Reason and Religion*, London: Routledge, 1992; Lapid, Yosef and Friedrich Kratochwill: 'Revisiting the "National": Toward an Identity Agenda in Neorealism', in Lapid and Kratochwill (eds): *The Return of Culture and Identity in IR Theory*, Boulder: Lynne Rienner, 1995, pp. 105-126; Wæver, Ole, Barry Buzan, Morten Kelstrup, Pierre Lemaitre *et al.*: *Identity, Migration and the New Security Agenda in Europe*, London: Pinter, 1993.

3 Walker, R.B.J.: *Inside/Outside: International Relations as Political Theory*, Cambridge: Cambridge University Press, 1993.

4 Spruyt, Hendrik: *The Sovereign State and Its Competitors*, Princeton, NJ: Princeton University Press, 1994.

5 On 'governance' see Camilleri, J.A. and Jim Falk: *The End of Sovereignty? The*

Politics of a Shrinking and Fragmenting World, London: Edward Elgar, 1992. On alternatives to the State see Lapidoth, Ruth: *Autonomy. Flexible Solutions to Intrastate Conflicts*, Washington, D.C.: United States Institute of Peace Press, 1996.

6   Bellamy, Christopher: *Knights in White Armour. The New Art of War and Peace*, London: Hutchinson, 1996; Däniker, Gustav: 'The Guardian Soldier: On the Nature and Use of Future Armed Forces', *Research Paper*, no. 36, New York and Geneva: UNIDIR, 1995, UNIDIR/95/28. See also Moskos, Charles C. and James Burk: 'The Postmodern Military', in James Burk (ed.): *The Military in New Times. Adapting Armed Forces to a Turbulent World*, Boulder: Westview, 1994, pp. 141-162; Luttwak, Edward N.: 'A Post-Heroic Military Policy', *Foreign Affairs* 75(4) (July-August 1996), pp. 33-44.

7   See, for example, Coker, Christopher: *War and the 20th Century. The Impact of War on the Modern Consciousness*, London: Brassey's, UK, 1994; Gray, Chris Hables: *Postmodern War. The New Politics of Conflict*, London: Routledge, 1997.

8   Der Derian, James: *Antidiplomacy. Spies, Terror, Speed and War*, Oxford: Polity Press, 1992, pp. 173-202, quotation from pp. 174-175. See also Baudrillard, Jean: *The Gulf War Did Not Take Place*, Bloomington: Indiana University Press, 1995; Norris, Christopher: *Uncritical Theory. Postmodernism, Intellectuals, and the Gulf War*, Amherst: University of Massachusetts Press, 1992; Campbell, David: *Politics Without Principle. Sovereignty, Ethics, and the Narratives of the Gulf War*, Boulder: Lynne Rienner, 1994.

9   Klein, Bradley S.: *Strategic Studies and World Order. The Global Politics of Deterrence*, Cambridge: Cambridge University Press, 1994; Luke, Timothy W.: 'On Post-War: The Significance of Symbolic Action in War and Deterrence', *Alternatives* 14(3) (July 1989), pp. 343-362.

10 For an early, i.e. 'pre-postmodern' critique of nuclear deterrence see Green, Philip: *Deadly Logic. The Theory of Nuclear Deterrence*, Columbus, Ohio: Ohio State University Press, 1966; or Rapoport, Anatoli: 'Critique of Strategic Thinking', in Naomi Rosenbaum (ed.): *Readings on the International Political System*, Englewoood Cliffs: Prentice-Hall, 1970, pp. 201-227.

11 Van Creveld, Martin: *The Transformation of War*, New York: The Free Press, 1991, pp. 57-62; Thompson, William R.: 'The Future of Transitional Warfare', in Burk (ed.): *op. cit.* (note 6), pp. 63-92; Snow, Donald M.: *UnCivil Wars: International Security and the New Pattern of Internal War*, Boulder: Lynne Rienner, 1996; idem: *Distant Thunder. Patterns of Conflict in the Developing World*. 2nd edn, Armonk, NY: M.E. Sharpe, 1997.

12 Clausewitz, Carl von: *Vom Kriege. Ungekürzter Text nach der Erstauflage (1832-1834)*, Frankfurt a.M.: Ullstein Materialien, 1980, pp. 34, 677.

13 Based, *inter alia*, on the following; Howard, Michael: *War in European*

History, Oxford: Oxford University Press, 1976; Dupuy, Trevor N.: *The Evolution of Weapons and Warfare*, London: Jane's, 1980; McNeill, William H.: *The Pursuit of Power. Technology, Armed Force, and Society since A.D. 1000*, Oxford: Basil Blackwell, 1983; Jones, Archer: *The Art of War in the Western World*, London: Harrap, 1988; Creveld, Martin Van: *Technology and War from 2000 B.C. to the Present*, New York: Free Press, 1989.

14 Wallensteen, Peter and Margareta Sollenberg: 'The End of International War? Armed Conflict 1989-95', *Journal of Peace Research* 33(3) (August 1996), pp. 353-370.

15 On the various terms see Beaumont, Roger: 'Small Wars: Definitions and Dimensions', in W.M.J. Olson (ed.): 'Small Wars', *Annals of the American Academy of Political and Social Science*, vol. 541, London: Sage, 1996, pp. 20-35. On OOTW see Taw, Jennifer Morrison and Bruce Hoffman: 'Operations Other Than War', in Paul K. Davis (ed.): *New Challenges for Defense Planning. Rethinking How Much is Enough*, Santa Monica: RAND, 1994, pp. 223-250.

16 Diamond, Larry and Marc F. Plattner (eds): *Civil-Military Relations and Democracy*, Baltimore: John Hopkins University Press, 1996.

17 Cock, Jacklyn: 'The Cultural and Social Challenge of Demilitarization', in Gavin Cawthra and Bjørn Møller: *Defensive Restructuring of the Armed Forces in Southern Africa*, Aldershot: Dartmouth, 1997, pp. 117-144.

18 Posen, Barry R.: 'Nationalism, the Mass Army, and Military Power', *International Security* 18(2) (Fall 1993), pp. 80-124.

19 Krippendorff, Ekkehardt: *Staat und Krieg. Die historische Logik politischer Unvernunft* (Frankfurt: Suhrkamp Verlag, 1984); Giddens, Anthony: *The Nation-State and Violence*, Oxford: Polity Press, 1995; Porter, Bruce: *War and the Rise of the State*, New York: The Free Press, 1994.

20 Rotberg, Robert I. and Thomas G. Weiss (eds): *From Massacres to Genocide. The Media, Public Policy, and Humanitarian Crises*, Washington, D.C.: The Brookings Institution and The World Peace Foundation, 1996; Melvern, Linda: 'Genocide behind the Thin Blue Line', *Security Dialogue* 28(3) (September 1997), pp. 333-346; Tétreault, Mary Ann: 'Justice for All: Wartime Rape and Women's Rights', *Global Governance*, vol. 3, no. 2 (May-August 1997), pp. 197-212.

21 Singer, Max and Aaron Wildawsky: *The Real World Order. Zones of Peace / Zones of Turmoil*, Chatham, NJ: Chatham House Publishers, 1993. See also Mansfield, Edward D.: *Power, Trade and War*, Princeton, NJ: Princeton University Press, 1994; Brown, Michael E., Sean Lynn-Jones and Steven E. Miller (eds): *Debating the Democratic Peace*, Cambridge, MA: The MIT Press, 1996. For a contrary view see Galtung, Johan: *Peace by Peaceful Means: Peace and Conflict, Development and Civilization* , London: Sage, 1997, pp. 49-59.

22 Mueller, John: *Retreat from Doomsday: The Obsolescence of Major War*, New

York: Basic Books, 1989.

23 Middleton, Hugh: 'Some Psychological Bases of the Institution of War', in Robert A. Hinde (ed.): *The Institution of War*, New York: St. Martin's Press, 1992, pp. 30-46; Leslie E. Sponsel and Thomas A Gregor (eds): *The Anthropology of Peace and Violence*, Boulder: Lynne Rienner, 1994, *passim*; Berkowitz, Leonard: 'Biological Roots: Are Humans Inherently Violent?', in Betty Glad (ed.): *Psychological Dimensions of War* (London: Sage, 1990), pp. 24-40; Kull, Stephen: 'War and the Attraction to Destruction', *ibid.*, pp. 41-55; Kellett, Anthony: 'The Soldier in Battle: Motivational and Behavioral Aspects of the Combat Experience', *ibid.*, pp. 215-235; LeShan, Lawrence: *The Psychology of War. Comprehending its Mystique and its Madness* (Chicago: Noble Press, 1992); Gelven, Michael: *War and Existence. A Philosophical Inquiry* (University Park, Pennsylvania: Penn State Press, 1994); Ehrenreich, Barbara: *Blood Rites. Origins and History of the Passions of War*, London: Virago Press, 1997.

24 Dupuy: *op. cit.* (note 13), pp. 309-15.

25 Midlarsky, Manus I. (ed.): *The Internationalization of Communal Strife*, London: Routledge, 1992; Brown, Michael E. (ed.): *The International Dimensions of Internal Conflict*, Cambridge, MA: MIT Press, 1996.

26 Derian, James Der: 'The Terrorist Discourse: Signs, States, and Systems of Global Political Violence', in Michael Klare and Daniel C. Thomas (eds.): *World Security. Trends and Challenges at Century's End*, New York: St. Martin's Press, 1991, pp. 237-65; Gilbert, Paul: *Terrorism, Security and Nationality. An Introductory Study in Applied Philosophy*, London: Routledge, 1994; Laqueur, Walter: 'Postmodern Terrorism', *Foreign Affairs* 75(5) (September-October 1996), pp. 24-36.

27 Keaney, Thomas A. and Eliot A. Cohen: *Revolution in Warfare? Air Power in the Persian Gulf*, Annapolis, Maryland: Naval Institute Press, 1995; McKitrick, Jeffrey *et al.*: 'The Revolution in Military Affairs', in Barry R. Schneider and Lawrence E. Grinter (eds): *Battlefield of the Future. 21st Century Warfare Issues*, Maxwell Air Force Base, Alabama: Air University, 1995, pp. 65-97.

28 Stein, George: 'Information War – Cyberwar – Netwar', *ibid.*, pp. 153-179. The ideas are based on Toffler, Alvin and Heidi Toffler: *War and Antiwar: Survival at the Dawn of the 21st Century*, Boston: Little, Brown & Co., 1993.

29 Gat, Azar: *The Origins of Military Thought. From the Enlightenment to Clausewitz*, Oxford: Clarendon Press, 1989, pp. 56-135.

30 Jomini, Antoine-Henri de: *Traite des grandes operations militaires*, 2nd edition, Paris: Magimel. Librairie pour l'art militaire, 1811, vol. 4, pp. 275-286. On the subsequent evolution see Schneider, Barry R.: 'Principle of War for the Battlefield of the Future', in Schneider and Grintner (eds.): *op. cit.* (note 27), pp. 1-42.

31 Clausewitz: *op. cit.* (note 12), pp. 77-79.

32 Gibson, James William: *The Perfect War. The War We Couldn't Lose and How We Did*, New York: Vintage, 1988.

33 Lawrence, Thomas Edward: *The Seven Pillars of Wisdom. A Triumph*, London: Jonathan Cape, 1935, pp. 192-193.

34 Hart, Basil Liddell: *Strategy. The Indirect Approach*, 2nd edition (1967, reprint), New York: Signet Books, 1974, *passim*. See also Luttwak, Edward N.: *Strategy. The Logic of War and Peace*, Cambridge, MA: Harvard University Press, 1987.

35 Clausewitz: *op. cit.* (note 12), pp. 18-21.

36 Elshtain, Jean Bethke (ed.): *Just War Theory*, Oxford: Blackwell, 1992; Nardin, Terry (ed.): *The Ethics of War and Peace. Religious and Secular Perspectives*, Princeton, NJ: Princeton University Press, 1996.

37 Santoni, Ronald E.: 'Nurturing the Institution of War: "Just War" Theory's "Justifications" and Accomodations', in Hinde (ed.): *op. cit.* (note 23), pp. 99-120; Greenwood, Christopher: 'In Defence of the Laws of War', *ibid.*, pp. 133-147.

38 O'Brien, William V.: 'The Rule of Law in Small Wars', in Olson (ed.): *op. cit.* (note 15), pp. 36-46.

39 Hart: *op. cit.* (note 34), pp. 183, 219.

40 Morehouse, David A.: *Nonlethal Weapons. War Without Death*, Westport, CT: Praeger, 1996; Lewer, Nick and Steven Schofield: *Non-Lethal Weapons: A Fatal Attraction?*, London: Zed Books, 1997.

41 Tromp, Hylke: 'On the Nature of War and the Nature of Militarism', in Robert A. Hinde and Helen E. Watson (eds): *War: A Cruel Necessity? The Bases of Institutionalized Violence*, London: I.B. Tauris, 1995, pp. 118-131, quote from p. 122.

42 Boutwell, Jeffrey, Michael T. Klare and Laura W. Reed (eds): *Lethal Commerce: The Global Trade in Small Arms and Light Weapons*, Cambridge, MA: American Academy of Arts and Sciences, 1995.

2 From Inter-State War to Warlordism: Changing Forms of Collective Violence in the International System

DIETRICH JUNG AND KLAUS SCHLICHTE

Introduction

Since the end of the Second World War the forms of violent conflicts in the international system have undergone a tremendous change. The classical war between states accounted for less than 25% of the 196 wars between 1945 and 1996. Violent intra-state conflicts have become the major feature of warlike events in this period. According to these findings, theories of both the realistic school and liberal institutionalism do not provide a sound explanation of the current status of war and peace in the international system. While Realism is focused on an interpretation of war as the outcome of international relations modeled around a state-centristic view in which only states occur as actors, liberal institutionalism is captured by the dream that a global civil society emerges able to mitigate the negative results of state power and to foster international relations on the basis of mutually shared norms and values.

While both theories may help to explain historical developments and political events characterizing international politics at the moment, the form and occurrence of violent conflicts, however, is gradually escaping the grip of both of them.[1] And while Realism tends to become blind concerning the changing forms of war, liberal institutionalism tends to focus only on one side of the coin of global development. However, the spread of NGOs and other nonstate actors in international politics is not just a step towards more inter- and transnational cooperation, but also is accompanied by an increasing number of non-state actors using the means of violence without any superior control, and somehow fueling their means of warfare by making use of the spread of NGOs.[2]

This article attempts to answer the following questions: which direction have wars, as a major phenomenon in the field of international relations, taken since the end of the Second World War? Second, how we can reach for an explanation of this development? To this end, the first part will give a brief description of some general statistical trends and patterns of war development since 1945. These observations are based on the data gathered by the Arbeitsgemeinschaft Kriegsursachenforschung (AKUF), the Study Group on the Causes of War at Hamburg University.[3] As statistical findings have to be interpreted in the light of theoretical devices, the second chapter presents some basic assumptions of the so-called 'Hamburg Approach', the theoretical framework developed by the AKUF.[4] The Hamburg Approach draws rather more on works of classical sociology than theories of international relations. Against the background of the statistical findings and the theoretical framework, in a third step the development of so-called 'war economies' and the emergence of warlordism will be presented as one field of further research.

Statistical Trends of War Development since 1945

How wars have developed over time is one of the most frequently asked questions in the area of peace research. The scientists involved in the academic study of war and peace have assembled a mass of material and data about the main trends of war development, of types and kinds of organized violence in history. Furthermore, the numerous academic efforts to quantify organized mass violence differ in their general orientation, specific questions and their operational definitions. Thus, in this chapter an account of the state of the art cannot be given, because a complete overview about all efforts made in this direction or even about all current research projects deserves a study for itself.[5] The aim of this chapter is rather to present some results of the long-standing research project undertaken by the AKUF and to stimulate critical comments and remarks on results which have not yet been published in English.

The academic effort to quantify organized mass violence demands first a precise definition of the phenomena referred to as war. Thus, the understanding of war has to be limited to an operational definition as opposed to other phenomena of collective violence, like banditry, rebellions, mutinies, organized crime, coup d'etats, etc. It is exactly with this definition that the dispute within the discipline starts. Therefore we must begin by giving the definition of war used by the AKUF. In contrast to many other projects, the AKUF does not use strict quantitative criteria and defines war in the following manner:

A war is a violent mass conflict, fulfilling the following three characteristics:

1. two or more armed forces are involved in the fighting, where at least one of them is a regular armed force of a government in power (military, police forces, paramilitary forces);
2. both sides show a minimum of centrally directed organization of the battles even if this means only organized defense or strategically planned attacks; and
3. the armed operations show a certain degree of continuity and are not simply spontaneous, occasional confrontations. The involved actors are acting according to a recognizable strategy.

This definition – war as a state-related, organized and continuous violent mass conflict – still has many disadvantages, but includes, unlike so many other definitions, the increasing number of intra-state conflicts without relying on questionable indicators such as the number of battle related deaths etc. The AKUF does not use quantitative criteria like numbers of victims or battle related fatalities, since these data must be considered to be highly unreliable. In numerous cases of wars the AKUF counts as such, these data are even not at hand. Apart from this, there are no good reasons to decide whether just battle related deaths should be considered or whether combat fatalities or death tolls caused by famine and diseases should be considered as well. How many wounded persons can count as a dead one? These questions can not be solved by strict quantification. Rather, we must take more or less arbitrary decisions. So this definition tries to avoid the appearances of quantitative exactness and in practice each case which seems to be questionable has to be discussed within the study group. Because of this very soft definition, the scope of organized violence the AKUF takes into consideration is much larger than that of others. Certainly there are a lot of cases in the data of the AKUF which other scholars would argue do not meet their definition of war.

Based on this definition of war, the AKUF counted 196 wars in the period between the end of World War II and new year's eve 1996. In 1996 the AKUF registered 28 wars of which two, in Chechnya and Mali, definitely ended in the same year.[6] With some more differentiation we can observe five major trends in war development since 1945.[7]

First observation: The number of wars per year has steadily increased

The number of wars fought per year has steadily increased until the year 1992, which marks, with 52 wars, the peak since 1945. According to our analysis, this increasing number of wars per year is largely due to the fact that wars last longer and longer. Taking into account the numbers of wars that begin each year and the number of wars ending per year, the increase can not be traced to a growing number of new wars.

Second observation: The overwhelming majority of wars since 1945 are intra-state wars

In the period of time under scrutiny 129 out of 196 wars were intra-state wars, while only in 43 cases did wars in the classical sense of inter-state wars occur. The remaining cases are mixed types, showing components of both intra-state and inter-state war. A closer examination shows that this development is due to two phenomena: firstly, in the period in question the importance of inter-state wars has decreased in comparison to other epochs. And secondly, there is a constant decrease of inter-state wars within the period since 1945.

Civil wars and other forms of collective violence involving only one party which could be considered as a state actor, have been the most frequent forms of violent mass conflicts since 1945. Thus, the classical usage of the term war, referring only to violent conflicts between states, would cover only a small and decreasing proportion of warlike events. It is the growing amount of armed intra-state conflict that causes the growth in the period after 1945. Anti-regime wars and other intra-state wars waged about secession or autonomy of regions have been the most frequent types of war in the last few decades. The classical inter-state war has become the exception among violent mass conflicts.

Third observation: More than 90 per cent of the 196 wars between 1945 and 1996 took place in countries of what used to be called the Third World

The geographical spread of wars indicates that the causes of war since the end of the Second World War must obviously be sought in the social and political dynamics of the so called Third World.[8] In the developing countries a growing amount of armed mass violence can be observed.[9] In contrast to this belligerency of the Third World, there are just a few intra-state wars to be registered in the industrialized capitalistic countries of the West and no inter-state war took place between them in the period under scrutiny. In other words: while developing societies normally show a certain amount of organized violence within their boundaries and among each other, the developed capitalist democracies can be labeled as a war-free zone. This empirical fact is to be discussed in the discipline of International Relations under the conception of 'democratic peace'. Or as we would rather put it: the peace between developed capitalist societies.

Nevertheless, the so called great powers were involved in a large number of violent conflicts. In particular, the former colonial powers, Great Britain and France, the US and the former USSR took part most frequently in the wars since 1945. According to the ranking of states involved in warfare, Britain leads with 18, the US (12) and France (11) are number three and four.[10] But they almost exclusively took part as interveners, that is to say they engaged in ongoing wars on behalf of one party or as members of UN missions, rather than starting wars. Mainly, these interventions occurred to back a certain regime in power which was contested by a sub-state actor. But we have to emphasize that most wars after 1945 took place in the regions of the Third World. And the Middle East, Sub-Saharan Africa, South and Southeast-Asia were the most war-torn regions.

Fourth observation: All through the period since 1945, intra-state wars last significantly longer than wars between states

Whereas the majority of wars between states are finished within one year, intra-state wars tend to become protracted conflicts. The wars in Angola, Cambodia, on the Philippines, in Kurdistan or in Columbia are examples of such protracted conflicts which last more than 20 years. The longest lasting war we have in our list of ongoing wars is the war in Myanmar (Burma) which started in 1948. So the history of independence of Myanmar is a history of war. On the other hand, the brief war between Peru and Ecuador in 1994 illustrates how internal protest and pressure from the international community can be more successful in bringing war to an end when the case in question is an inter-state war.

There is ample speculation about this observation. One could refer to the tendencies of ever growing interdependencies between states and political actors. In the perspective of the stream of liberal thought on international relations one could argue that international institutions can deal better and better with interstate-violence, because the norms of peaceful behavior increasingly dominate the interaction between states. This is an argument belonging to the old tradition of liberal thought on international relations.[11] An alternative interpretation, out of the realist perspective, would refer to a hierarchy in international relations which ensures the control of inter-state conflicts by the great powers because they are interested in maintaining the status quo of the international order.[12] This is not the place to add to these speculations. But it is worthwhile to underline the fact that we do not yet have a really satisfactory explanation for the decreasing importance of international war.

Fifth observation: 65 wars since 1945 were ended by mediation of a third party

In asking the question how wars have come to an end in the period under consideration, only 28 wars ended with a military victory for the aggressive side. Out of 161 wars being considered as ended, in 42 cases it was the defending side that could repulse the aggression, and 65 wars were ended by mediation of a third party.[13] If we differentiate these findings further, the chance of the defending party in repulsing the aggressor in intra-state wars is higher than in inter-state wars. Moreover, there is a significantly lower percentage of intra-state wars that could be finished through the mediation of a third party. Mediation seems to be more successful in inter-state wars and in around 62 per cent of all cases ended by mediation between 1945 and 1992, the UN (40.5 per cent) or regional organizations acted as mediators.[14]

Obviously there is an increasing number of wars ended by mediation, and supra-national organizations and non-state actors are the most prominent mediators. This observation too could be used as a confirmation of liberal institutionalism. In other words, the ever growing interdependencies between states seem to enforce the building of institutions which can be used to control conflicts and in order to avoid the use of violence.

Let us close this brief presentation of statistical findings with a glance at the most recent developments: The early 1990s have shown a greater number of violent conflicts than ever seen before in the period since 1945. But when we look at the curve for the period after 1992, we can see an obvious decrease in the number of wars led per year. There have been other regressions and when compared with other decades the level of wars today is still high. Nevertheless, the decline is dramatic and needs a precise explanation.[15]

Part of this explanation might be what happened in the former Soviet Union and its zone of influence. Until 1989 this zone was almost warfree, despite its public image. The dramatic increase which led to the record of 52 wars in 1992 is largely due to the demise of the state-socialist system which brought 12 new wars along, of which 10 had come to a precarious end by 1996. Apart from the events in the former Soviet Union, which can be held responsible for the rapid increase and the following decline, no new trend of war development is observable which separates the period after the Cold War from the decades before.

Thus, the main findings based on the research by the AKUF can be summarized as follows: the increasing number of wars since 1945 is largely due to an increasing number of intra-state wars in Third World states. These intra-state wars tend to last longer than inter-state wars and are more difficult to end by classical political efforts and mediation of third parties. These findings apply equally to the period after 1989 when the area of formerly state-socialist countries became plagued by wars.

War Development and the 'Great Transformation'

From the perspective of a political scientist it is perhaps most astonishing that the discipline of international relations has so far not developed a coherent explanation of why wars have developed in this way over the last decades. According to some scholars of the discipline, this lack of explanation may be due to the fixation on conceptions of statehood and political forms that date from the classical era of the European state system. On the one hand, these conceptions of European state-building from the 16th century onwards have little in common with the historical realities of our time. Furthermore, a transhistorical explanation of war is neither possible nor would it make sense, not to mention a mathematical one. On the other hand the fact that most wars in the period considered are intra-state wars in the Third World leads us to reflect on the processes of state-building and social change in these regions which have inherited their political and economic structures from their former European colonial powers. The form and the social bases of most of these wars indicate that the emergence of violent mass conflicts in developing countries is linked with the 'Great Transformation', as Karl Polanyi called the process of imposition of capitalist modernity.[16]

According to the Hamburg Approach, the origins of most ongoing wars can be found in this fundamental transformation of traditional societies, the successive spread of elements of modern capitalist society in a global dimension. This transformation is a non-linear process in which traditional modes of production, forms of social organization and political domination as well as traditional ideas and values are gradually superseded by patterns of modern capitalistic societies. Since all developing societies are affected by this transformation, it gives us in a historical and systematic perspective the general standard for comparative studies. With respect to violent conflicts, the Great Transformation shows thereby two contradictory faces: while developed capitalist societies are characterized by internal peace politically based on democracy and the rule of law, the developing process itself is characterized by a series of violent conflicts and wars. Therefore the peaceful development of western states based on a network of the rule of law, democratic participation, the state monopoly of physical force, social justice, interdependencies, and the control of passions – the so-called 'Hexagon of Civilization' – is a late and still precarious result of this social transformation.[17]

As in European history, the transformation of traditional societies in the Third World is confronted with a break-down of traditional forms of conflict regulation. The Great Transformation has first and foremost to be considered as the complete destruction of previously valid forms of life and social reproduction. Therefore, the modernization process becomes the central conflict generating variable for the explanation of global war development. A regionally and historically comparative perspective could reveal that the structural aspects of the state-building processes in Third World regions is not so much different from what happened in the so-called developed world over the last few centuries. Rather, the differences must be found in the historical conditions and in the ways this transformation leads to mass violence.

The modern nation-state in the former colonial world is not the outcome of a long-lasting process of integration, characterized by the struggle of different political units, but the imposed form of integration guaranteed from outside – by the international system. Not the formation of the state monopoly of the legitimate use of physical force, but the struggle for this formally granted monopoly characterizes the political development. Whereas the process of state-building in Europe was accompanied by a huge amount of violence, both between and within states, in contemporary Third World regions mass violence is almost exclusively a phenomenon within states.

The dominance of intra-state wars reveals a characteristic specific to developing societies: the institutions of the modern state in these countries are usually not capable of mediating the social conflicts resulting from society's transformation to capitalism. The state is not the crystallization point of collective identity, but only a formal framework acquired during the colonial past and guaranteed by world state order and international law. The modern state, described by Max Weber by the claim to monopolize the use of force, by compulsory jurisdiction and continuous operation within a certain territory, exists in many Third World countries as a mere territorial and legal cover, as an imposed form whose social content has yet to consolidate itself. In this consolidation process violence is still a rational option for self-enrichment or for gaining political power. Only in fully fledged capitalist societies has physical violence become dysfunctional. Here, the general rule of civic-capitalist forms of behavior and social organization even determines the external behavior of states. The balance of powers, the constitutional state, the rule of law, democracy and general welfare obviously constitute a bulwark against the emergence of warlike conflicts within and between developed societies. Thus, the undeniable violent trail of capitalism in history cannot be understood as quality of capitalism itself, but as a condition of its emergence and advancement.

Against this background, two general structural features are discernible explaining the war development in the Third World:

1. The attempt at an inner consolidation of formally established statehood. In most developing societies a huge gulf between the political and social integration of their people is discernible. This leads to a chronic deficit of legitimacy of state rule. Not the postcolonial state but tribal, ethnic or religious groups are the points of reference for identity and political loyalty. The modern state only exists as a territorial frame, whose internal institutional setting has still to be consolidated, guaranteed by the world state system and by international law.

2. A tendency towards diffusion and privatization of physical force. The essential point of this consolidation process of the state is the

formation of a legitimate monopoly of the use of physical force. However, wars like in Afghanistan, Somalia or Columbia show that the historical development can also follow an opposite path. Not the monopolization of violence and the establishment of the rule of law, but a tendency of diffusion of physical force can be observed. Physical force becomes a power resource of regionally, religiously, ethnically or ideologically mobilized militias and their 'warlords', of various groups of organized crime or of independently acting state organizations, so-called antinomic violence, following their particular political and economic interest. Against the theoretical background of modern statehood, these are all phenomena which can be labeled as privatization of physical force.

To sum up this brief description of some of the theoretical assumptions of the Hamburg Approach: the Global Transformation offers in a historical and systematic perspective the general standard for comparative research; the dichothomic ideal types of tradition and modernity and the sociological conceptions attached to them provide us with a conceptional apparatus grounded in social theory; the understanding of the modernizing process as a contradictory whole of integrating, civilizing and pacifying developments on the one hand and as a process characterized by disintegrating, destructive and violent phenomena on the other; the inner consolidation of formally established statehood and the tendency of diffusion and privatization of physical force as two general structural features of war development since 1945.

Nevertheless, this structural analysis based on social theory is not sufficient to answer the question why in a specific case actors are willing to use the means of violence in conflicts. The conflictive developments of social transformation must not necessarily lead to violent conflicts. Modernization and war development are in an explanatory connection but they don't determine each other. In the end, the concrete actors decide about the form of conflictive action in conflicts triggered by social transformation. But social action is not structurally determined, but historically contingent. Therefore, research on causes of war has to confront the problem of indeterminacy in social action and to explain in case studies how the use of physical force is legitimated by the resort to the world of symbolic representation of the groups involved in war.[18]

War Economies and Warlordism

As intensive case studies are not the subject of this article we would like to finish with a topic which has been hitherto almost neglected, but indicates a field for future research efforts which do not only want to reach for explanation but also to contribute something to the political agenda. Despite the brilliant book – 'Economie des guerres civiles' – of the research group around Jean-Christoph Rufin and Francois Jean the economic side of ongoing wars is an almost neglected aspect.[19] When we look at the most prominent wars in the last few years, where the outlooks to end them are the darkest, we have to realize that wars have begun to live on themselves. In Colombia as in Afghanistan, in Liberia as in Myanmar, war has become a system of social reproduction. On the one hand costly for the population, on the other profitable for a small minority.

While there is a correlation between developed capitalism and the pacification of conflicts, war and trade are not mutually exclusive. War does not mean an end of economic exchange but that the economy becomes a means of warfare. Under the conditions of classical inter-state war the control of the national economy by an authoritarian state was often decisive for the outcome of a war. During the Cold War period the supply of armament, foreign military advisers and financial aid by the super powers became an important aspect of regional wars. Since the end of the bipolarity of the international system at the latest, actors in regional wars are more and more compelled to secure their material reproduction beyond politically inspired foreign support. In many of the protracted violent conflicts in the Third World violence meanwhile has become for itself a means of economic power. In those cases the use of violence is no longer aiming at political goals, but to secure the material base of militias and to enrich their leaders. The 'warlord', as a political and military leader, has become an 'entrepreneur' whose economic activities are grounded in military power and the use of force.

With the total collapse of the state, violence became the essential resource to gain economic profits and political and economic power were in one hand. It would be erroneous to believe that these war economies only live on the dark sides of the world market. Not only weapons and drugs are exported from war areas. Timber, iron ore, diamonds and even human labor force are export goods of societies at war. However, the purchasers of these 'commodities of war' are not at all obscurant organizations only involved in black market deals. The British African Mining Consortium as well as the French Sollac company were purchasing iron ore from Liberian warlords. Also many European companies are engaged in the so-called 'arms-for-nature-swaps', for example the exchange of tropical timber against weaponry. During the civil war in Liberia this country became the third most important supplier of timber to France.[20] The white zones of the world market know how to profit from the existence of war economies too, and so the international community has not shown serious efforts to bring these links under control.

The ongoing wars in Cambodia, Myanmar and Sri Lanka are other cases in point showing how the appropriation of resources by the use of violence has become an independent force in protracted conflicts. The war in Cambodia was and is accompanied by an extensive exploitation of national resources such as tropical timber, mineral resources, precious stones and antiques. The number of Thai companies, which are in the north-western frontier zone of Cambodia dealing with the Khmer Rouge in timber, has been estimated around fifteen. The Thai economy is linked with the war economy of the Khmer Rouge by cross-border transportation lines. Beside their political and military organization, the Khmer Rouge also established centrally controlled forms of economic organization.[21]

In Myanmar too, the appropriation of national resources plays a central role in the strategies of the warring parties. In addition Myanmar is considered to be the worlds biggest producer of opium and heroin. Its production of raw opium doubled between 1982 and 1988 from 400 to 800 tons per year, and the control of drug production and trafficking plays a major role in the war development in Myanmar. One of the most prominent warlords in Myanmar, the so-called 'king of drugs' Khun Sa, had around 40 per cent of the drug business under his control and established between 1993 and 1996 with his 'Mon-Thai-Army' an independent 'Shan state' in the north east of the country. At the same time, however, almost 60 per cent of the areas for opium cultivation were in the hands of the official army and the military regime in Rangoon is suspected of playing an increasing role in the drug business of the country.[22]

Diasporas providing warring militias with economic means is another feature of long-lasting intra-state wars which can be observed in the wars in Sri Lanka, Lebanon, Kurdistan or the former Yugoslavia. The Tamil diaspora in Western Europe and the US, for instance, can be considered as both a result and a guarantee for the continuation of the civil war in Sri Lanka. Between 1983 and 1992 almost 40 per cent of the Tamil population of the Jaffna peninsula, the central war zone in Sri Lanka, left for Europe and the US. Organized by the 'World Tamil Coordinating Committee' the Tamil Tiger militia is levying war-taxes under the migrant population to finance their war for the establishment of a Tamil state in Sri Lanka.[23]

Despite agricultural raw materials, mineral resources, drugs and war-taxes, human aid given by NGOs is increasingly becoming an important resource for internal warfare. Warlords and militias are organizing the supply of foreign aid into the regions under their control and functioning thereby as racketeers, as 'someone who creates a threat and then charges for its reduction'.[24] It is peculiar that by foreign aid, resources out of the international system are imported directly into the local conflict scene. It makes one apprehensive that an analysis of the relations between humanitarian assistance and intra-state wars comes to the result that: 'it represents...a resource which political and economic actors are looking for to appropriate and use for their interests'.[25]

According to Waldmann, the differences between inter-state wars and intra-state wars are somehow institutionalized in the figure of the warlord. He emerges after the collapse of state structures and as racketeer he and his militia provide state functions at a low level. As a product of war and with the use of force as his power base, a warlord is not interested in a peaceful solution of the ongoing conflict.[26] While being a leader of a locally based militia the warlord is acting in the international realm as entrepreneur connecting the local war economy with the world market. A shift in the power relations of the warring militias, the disarmament of his troops or the cut of his economic ties to the outer world would lead to an end of his powerful position. Warlords and their war economies are therefore a major obstacle to finding peaceful conflict solutions.

Conclusion

The statistical findings of the AKUF clearly show a shift from inter-state to intra-state wars since the end of World War Two. This trend is accompanied by a tendency of intra-state wars to last longer and be more difficult to end through the mediation of a third party. This is due to the fact, that protracted violent conflicts tend to develop a kind of self dynamic which is closely linked with the institution of the warlord and the emergence of war economies. Based on the theoretical assumption that the underlying conflicts are triggered by the social transformation happening in

Third World countries, the main causes of these wars must be found within the changing societies of the countries at war. According to these findings Realist explanations of war, still concentrated on inter-state wars, seem to be odd, or as Holsti has put it: there is no anarchy between Third World states but within them.[27] This anarchy within Third World states must be analyzed in comparison to the process of state formation in Europe. Charles Tilly, for instance, showed in his work the interrelation between state-formation, social change and wars in Europe.[28] Thereby one can find structural analogies to what is happening in our times in the Third World. Furthermore, the dissolution of state structures in protracted conflicts like in Afghanistan, Liberia, Myanmar, Somalia etc. could be subordinated under the category of feudalisation, used by Norbert Elias to explain the decay of political authority in Europe before the advent of the absolutist state.[29]

However, the political and economic environment in which these wars are taking place is completely different from what was to happen in European history, as the example of the 'modern' warlord shows. We are at present confronted with a picture of an inner consolidation of formally established statehood, guaranteed from outside by the international state system. A process of state formation which, nevertheless, sometimes leads internally to the complete destruction of what can be called a state. The 'billiard ball' state of the Realist construction of the international system turns than out to be a fragmented society falling apart from within.

Regarding the presented statistical trends of war development since 1945, the other thing we should bear in mind is the fact that they only show the peak of organized violence in the period considered. By definition, we excluded all forms of organized violence which show no direct involvement of governmental forces or which are lacking our criteria of mass-character and continuity. But the closer we look at developments in various world regions, the more we are confronted with changes in the forms of violence. In Latin America, in Africa, as well as in parts of the former Soviet Union a tendency towards the privatization of violence can be observed. Whether we talk of organized crime, terrorism, youth-gangs or so-called antinomic violence, all of them may be indicators that 'violence will trickle down' in the politically uncontrolled spheres of world society. Results which are not only a threat for societies with a yet unfinished process of state-building, but also for developed capitalistic societies which take the once arduously acquired democratic state under the rule of law as granted. Therefore warlordism, war economies, the privatization of violence and their complex linkages to the international system mark an important field for future research. In a time when we are being told that the coming epoch will face a 'clash of civilizations' we must emphasize that wars and violent conflicts are among the most complex social phenomena and their explanation needs a reflected and critical approach. Buying into simplistic interpretations may otherwise turn out to be self-fulfilling-prophecies.

Notes

1 In a recent example Fearon is giving a 'rationalist explanation for war' based on the 'ideal case of rational unitary states' and showing 'how war could occur given the assumption of rational and unitary ('billiard ball') states', Fearon, James D. 1995: 'Rationalist Explanations of War', *International Organization* 49(3), pp. 379-414 (p. 410).

2 How NGO's providing foreign humanitarian aid could also become a ressource for war-waging militias: Jean, Francois 1996: 'Aide humanitaire et économie de guerre', in: Jean/Rufin (eds.): *Economie des guerres civiles*, pp. 543-589.

3 The Study Group on Causes of War in Hamburg was founded in the late 1970s and has built a data base on wars beginning with the year 1945. The group combines empirical study with theory-building and established a data base with data gathered by Istvan Kende, a Hungarian scientist (1917–1988). As work has progressed, revisions to Kende's original data have been made several times. The group consists of nearly forty graduate students and research associates and is led by Prof. Klaus Jürgen Gantzel.

4 The 'Hamburg Approach' has been elaborated in a series of three monographs: Siegelberg, Jens 1994: *Kapitalismus und Krieg. Eine Theorie des Krieges in der Weltgesellschaft*, Münster und Hamburg; Jung, Dietrich 1995: *Tradition – Moderne – Krieg. Grundlegung einer Methode zur Erforschung kriegsursächlicher Prozesse im Kontext globaler Vergesellschaftung*, Münster und Hamburg; Schlichte, Klaus 1996: *Krieg und Vergesellschaftung in Afrika. Ein Beitrag zur Theorie des Krieges*, Münster und Hamburg.

5 For an overview on the state of the art, cf. Vasquez, John A. 1988: 'The Steps to War: Toward a Scientific Explanation of Correlates of War Findings', *World Politics* 40(1), 108-145; Mendler, Martin/Schwegler-Rohmeis, Wolfgang 1988: *Weder Drachhentöter noch Sicherheitsingenieur – Bilanz und kritische Analyse der sozialwissenschaftlichen Kriegsursachenforschung* (HSFK Forschungsbericht), Frankfurt a.M. According to our knowledge there are currently at least five large research projects which try to register armed

conflicts over longer historical periods: COSIMO (Heidelberg), LORANOW (Boulder), COW (Ann Arbor), the group around Wallensteen (Uppsala) and the AKUF (Hamburg).

6 The 28 registered wars took place in the following countries: *Africa:* Algeria, Burundi, Liberia, Mali, Sierra Leone, Somalia, Sudan, Chad, Uganda, Zaire; *Middle East:* Afghanistan, Iraq (Kurdistan), Lebanon, Chechnya, Tajikistan, Turkey (Kurds); *Asia:* Cambodia, India (Kashmir), Myanmar (Burma), Papua New Guinea (Bougainville), Philippines (NPA and on Mindanao), Sri Lanka; *Latin America:* Columbia (FARC, ELN), Guatemala, Mexico (Chiapas, EPR) and Peru (Sendero Luminoso, MRTA), see: Rabehl, Thomas/Trines, Stefan (eds.) 1997: *Das Kriegsgeschehen 1996. Register der Kriege und bewaffneten Konflikte*, Arbeitspapier 6/1997, Research Unit of Wars, Armament and Development, University of Hamburg.

7 The following data are all taken from the data base of AKUF which is published in Gantzel, Klaus Jürgen/Schwinghammer, Thorsten 1995: *Die Kriege nach dem Zweiten Weltkrieg 1945–1992. Daten und Tendenzen*, and Gantzel, Klaus Jürgen 1997: 'War in the Post-World War II World: Some Empirical Trends and a Theoretical Approach', in: Turon, David (ed.): *War and Ethnicity. Global connections and Local Violence*, San Marino.

8 We are well aware how questionable the term 'Third World' is and we use it therefore only as a residual category to subordinate those regions in which capitalistic modernization was rather an imposition from outside than an internal development.

9 It might well be that the increasingly intensive observation has led to the growing number of registered armed conflicts and wars in the last two decades. The history of most of the peripheral societies has not yet been examined so painstakingly that one could be sure about the exact number of conflicts. Nevertheless, it is highly improbable that these corrections would reverse the general trend, i.e. a growing number of violent mass conflicts since 1945 and that they are geographically located in the Third World. Other scholars come to similar results, cf. Holsti**Error! Bookmark not defined.**, Kalevi J. 1992: 'International Theory and War in the Third World', in: Job, Brian L. (ed.): *The Insecurity Dilemma. National Security of Third World States*, Boulder and London.

10 Second ranking is India (16).

11 Cf. Rosenau, James N. 1994: 'Neue Perspektiven in der Weltpolitik: Anmerkungen zur Antiquiertheit zwischenstaatlicher Kriege', in: Krell, Gert/ Müller, Harald (eds.): *Frieden und Konflikt in den internationalen Beziehungen. Festschrift für Ernst-Otto Czempiel*, Frankfurt a.M./New York, pp.116-132; Mueller, John 1989: *Retreat from Doomsday*, New York.

12 Cf. Waltz, Kenneth N. 1988: 'The Origins of War in Neorealist Theory', *Journal of Interdisciplinary History* XVIII/4, pp. 615-628.

13 In 26 cases the end of the war is not yet classified or the war was fading out.
14 The Arab League (9,5 per cent), the OAS (7,1 per cent) and the OAU (4,8 per cent) were engaged in regional mediation.
15 Other scholars agree with these findings, see Wallensteen, Peter/Sollenberg, Margareta 1995: 'After the Cold War: Emerging Patterns of Armed Conflict 1989–1994', *Journal of Peace Research* 32(3), pp. 345-360.
16 Polanyi, Karl 1957: *The Great Transformation. The Political and Economic Origins of Our Time*, Boston.
17 According to Dieter Senghaas the peaceful development of the western industrialized states is based on this Hexagon of Civilization, Senghaas, Dieter 1994: *Wohin driftet die Welt? Über die Zukunft friedlicher Koexistenz*, Frankfurt a.M. p. 20.
18 For an example of a case study based on the Hamburg Approach, see Endres, Jürgen/Jung, Dietrich 1998: 'Was legitimiert den Griff zur Gewalt? Unterschiede im Konfliktverhalten islamistischer Organisationen in Ägypten', *Politische Vierteljahresschrift* 39(1), pp. 91-108.
19 Jean, Francois/Rufin, Jean Christophe (eds.) 1996: *Economie des guerres civiles*, Paris
20 Cf. Schlichte, Klaus 1997: 'Das Chaos der Gewalt und die Regeln des Marktes: Zur Behinderung von Friedensprozessen durch Kriegsökonomien', in: *Jahrbuch Frieden 1997*, München, pp. 140-148 (p. 145).
21 Cf. Lechervy, Christian 1996: 'L'économie des guerres cambodgiennes: accumulation et dispersion', in: Jean/Rufin (eds.), 1996, pp. 189-232.
22 Boucaud, André/ Boucaud, Louis 1996: 'Burma: Verließ mit goldenem Boden', *Der Überblick* 3(96), pp. 35-38.
23 Angoustures, Aline/Pascal, Valérie 1996: 'Diasporas et finanncement des conflits', in: Jean/Rufin (eds.) 1996, pp. 495-542 (p. 501).
24 Tilly, Charles 1985: 'War Making and State Making as Organized Crime', in: Evans, Peter/Rueschemeyer, Dietrich/Skocpol, Theda (eds.) 1985: *Bringing the State Back in*, Cambridge, p. 171.
25 Jean, Francois 1996, p. 567.
26 Waldmann, Peter 1997: 'Bürgerkrieg – Annäherungen an einen schwer faßbaren Begriff', *Leviathan* 25(4), pp. 480-500 (p. 497).
27 Holsti, Kalevi J. 1991: *Change in the International System. Essays on the Theory and Practice of International Relations*, Aldershot/Brookfield, p. 19.
28 Tilly, Charles 1990: *Coercion, Capital and European States, AD 900–1900*, Cambridge, Mass.
29 Elias, Norbert 1989: *Über den Prozeß der Zivilisation, Bd. 2, Wandlungen der Gesellschaft, Entwurf zu einer Theorie der Zivilisation*, Frankfurt a.M., p. 76.

3 Towards a Comprehensive Analysis of Ethnicity and Mass Violence: Types, Dynamics, Characteristics and Trends

CHRISTIAN P. SCHERRER

Abstract

Analysis of intra-state conflict, its types, causes and possible peace strategies, is highly topical. However, research deficits prevail regarding many issues and problems in this vast field. Research on the causes of wars was mainly concerned with *classic* types of conflicts between states but does not easily apply to intra-state conflicts. Compared to the tremendous increase in intra-state warfare and non-military types of mass violence such as genocide and mass murder, the Clausewitzean type of inter-state conflicts was in recent decades an exceptional phenomenon. In two-thirds of all contemporary conflicts the *ethnic factor* (e.g. ethnic nationalism) is a dominant or influential component.

The struggles of ethnic and national groups for survival, rights or recognition dominate contemporary warfare to an increasingly large extent and result in 'anarchy' in the state system. In the South there are a growing number of states which cannot claim to have an effective monopoly on violence. Depending on the criteria employed about half of those states are *failed states* and potentially become *dangerous states* (repression, war, genocidal policy).

The lacunas of global surveys on mass violence can be identified. Present war registers overlook certain categories and types of violence such as genocide, mass murder, communal violence and post-modern types of conflicts that do not necessarily involve state actors, e.g. gang war. Most registers are constructing static entities instead of expressing the permanent mutation of conflicts in the real world. There are very few 'pure types'. Conflicts develop over time and may change in quality, with a new type becoming dominant over the other(s).

The high frequency and huge potential of ethnic types of conflict are decisive factors in regard to the possibilities of structural prevention of violence, conflict management and transformation as well as regarding the role of multi-lateralism in preventing violence. State failure and violent ethnic conflict are closely linked.

Introduction: intra-state conflicts as structural feature of the new world order

In the *grand design* the suggestion is to look at ethno-political conflict constellations as a structural feature of the *new world order*. Since the 1980s macro-trends have increasingly suggested that the world system is rapidly evolving into a complex multi-polar order.[1] Regional conflict scenarios make sense. Even more so if they are determined not only by geographical but also by macro-cultural (*civilizational*) and political criteria. To give an example: the collapse of the USSR and the subsequent outburst of ethnic conflicts on the periphery of that former 'empire' were closely linked. Some elements significantly differ from the situation in other world regions, particularly in the South. Ethno-nationalism in the East grew almost institutionally. This resulted from a form of administrative *ethnicization* which was one of the main constitutive elements of the Soviet experience.

A sort of 'Third World War' is in full swing. Warfare and mass violence is not going on between East and West, nor between North and South, but occurring at this very moment inside some 60 states in four continents. The regional distribution of contemporary violent conflicts shows a clear global trend: warfare and mass violence are infrequent in the North and West but part of the *normality* in the South and some areas of the East. Many wars in the South would not be fought without the involvement of the North.

According to the ECOR register, two-thirds of the violent conflicts from 1985 to 1996 had a dominant or influential ethnic character. There were some disturbing changes in the general trend in recent years. Foreign military intervention has been exceptional and has lately increased significantly. Complex emergency cases led to an alarming increase in conflict-induced mortality. Warfare and mass violence are becoming increasingly chaotic at a conceptual and practical level, with inter-ethnic wars increasing at the cost of both inter-state and ethno-nationalist wars, and gang wars nearly doubling in a ten-year period. State failure, warfare and mass violence are inextricably linked. One of the most dangerous sources of armed conflicts is the assertion of all powers by nation states in their relations to what they call *minorities*.

According to ECOR's global survey, *nation states* are exceptions to the rule: only a very small fraction of the world's population lives in what could be called an ethnically homogenous state. Just 20 countries with a population average of 500,000 can be called nation states. Only very few states with considerably more than 10 million citizens are homogenous nation states. In some cases minorities are a 'secret'.[2] Most states pretend to be nation states but in reality have a multi-ethnic and multi-cultural composition. This fiction is kept up at a high cost. In the USSR, the very coining of the term 'titular nation' points at the fact that there is no single nation state that has taken the place of the former Soviet Union.

Since 1945 more than 250 major wars have taken place, mostly in the Third World, and recently in the CIS and Yugoslavia. Very few of these wars were interstate conflicts. The last *classic* interstate wars were fought for some weeks in 1995 (Peru vs. Ecuador) and in May 1998 (Eritrea vs. Ethiopia). In both cases mediation was rapidly in place and hostilities ceased. Today, all wars are so-called *internal* conflicts, yet many are fought with outside assistance. Research to identify the root causes of the tremendous upsurge of ethno-nationalism in the global framework leads to questions linked with the nature of ethnicity and the ethnic basis of nations. Often these categories are not very adequately used. If we look underneath the structure of some 200 states there is an extraordinary multitude of perhaps 6,500 up to 10,000 nations, nationalities, and peoples as ethnic *entities* of diverse size. Groups rank from 900 Rama Indians in Nicaragua to 25 or 30 million Oromo at the Horn of Africa and up to 1.1 billion Han Chinese.

This diversity represents a tremendous richness of different cultures for most people but a threat to others. Characteristics given to identify an ethnic group or a nationality are by no means an academic exercise but will gain more political relevance as relations between nationalities, nations and states are increasingly seen as an important element of what is called *international politics* and *international relations*. The legacies of colonialism and other external conditions contributed to separate nations from nationalities. The *invention* of the nation state, its official nationalism and false expectations raised by development ideologies in the former colonies are basic sources for past and future conflicts.

Taking into account the fairly recent discovery of the ethnic phenomenon by the mass media since the end of the Cold War and considering a general research deficit concerning these 'forgotten wars' being fought in many Third World countries, a number of deficits have prevailed. The attempt here would be to propose an actor-oriented typology only indirectly related to root causes but directly linked to the main driving forces and manifestations of violent conflict world-wide.[3]

Practically all wars are nowadays intra-state wars. Since 1945 *internal* conflicts within the borderlines of a single state are by far more numerous than interstate conflicts (international armed conflicts) between two or more states. Distinguishing *internal* and *external* conflicts – even though politically as well as analytically relevant – tend to become invalid. The sacrosanct principle of non-interference in the *internal affairs* of states has always been a shaky rule as the high number of foreign state interventions shows: states of the North have been actively involved since 1945 in over 390 wars fought by state actors in the South. Compilations concerning the period 1945–91 go as high as 690 foreign overt military interventions.[4]

The principle of non-interference was respected or violated according to political or economic interests at stake. Interference traditionally takes place by supporting insurgencies with arms and equipment, providing safe haven (*hinterland*) for rebels in neighbouring states or through direct involvement of foreign states with combatant troops. Non-interference was never really applied to economic activities and fully contradicts the trend of globalization. In economics the principle of autarchy has long been obsolete.[5] Or let us take migration or ecological disruption. It does not stop at borders and could induce more conflict issues and threats in the near future. In the past non-interference was only exceptionally honoured, according to political preferences – on a case-by-case basis.

The debate should best be linked with particular conflict issues and threats. The term *internal conflict* became invalid in regard to a number of issues and threats that can no longer be considered as falling under the competence of the state. Thus the scope of what are 'internal affairs' of states has to be redrawn.[6]

Definitions of mass violence, ethnicity and main actors

Wars and non-war types of mass violence (such as genocide or large-scale massacres) have to be clearly defined and distinguished as follows.

Major wars and mass violence may be distinguished from other armed conflicts or massacres by various degrees of medium or high intensity, claiming usually more than an estimated 1,000 victims per annum or as an average during the course of the conflict (see, for instance, CoW, SIPRI and others). In many cases the numbers of victims are contested or otherwise questionable. Governments tend to reduce the number of victims while rebels tend to inflate the numbers. Additionally, in most wars the adversaries exaggerate enemy casualties. Verification of numbers of battle-related deaths and (even more so) of massacre-related deaths are an awesome task.

War is defined as a violent mass conflict involving two or more armed forces as combatants/actors in warfare. In not all cases are regular state armed forces (such as military, police forces, militias and other paramilitary troops) involved. Not-state actors are mainly so-called liberation movements having regular guerrilla or partisan armies, often recruiting along ethnic, national or social class lines. Tribal militias, gangs and other irregular forces have different agendas; they have less or no centralized control, nor identifiable lines of command. In most types of contemporary warfare violent clashes and combat between the warring parties take place with some degree of continuity. Ethno-nationalist wars especially tend to become *protracted conflicts*.

Non-war types of mass violence are characterized by a separation of perpetrators of mass murder and their victims. In most cases the victimization and aggression are organized, supported or tolerated by state actors. Contrary to asymmetries in many types of wars (concerning quality of weaponry, use of resources and level of training) in non-war mass violence there is a clear difference to be made between armed perpetrators and the victimized non-armed civilians which are by definition defenceless. The worst type of mass violence is genocide.

Genocide is defined as state-organized mass murder and crimes against humanity characterized by the intention of the rulers to exterminate individuals because of belonging to a particular national, ethnic, 'racial' or religious group. *Mass murder* committed against members of a particular political group (called *politicide* by Barbara Harff) or social group (called *democide* by Rudolph Rummel) are equally horrifying but do not legally fall under the Anti-Genocide Convention of 1948. The *most deadly regimes* in the twentieth century have all committed total genocide against domestic groups, mainly the barbarian attempt to exterminate *their* minorities.

Dominant groups got into position of command over the so-called monopoly of violence. Their assertive relationship towards ethnically distinct nationalities (*nations without own state*) became the most important dangerous source of violent conflict since 1945, increasingly so with each cycle of decolonization.

Ethnic communities can be defined as historically generated or (in some cases) re-discovered communities of people that largely reproduce themselves. An ethnic or *communal group* has a distinct name, which often simply signifies 'person' or 'people' in the ethnic community's language, a specific, heterogeneous culture, including, particularly, a distinct language, and a collective memory or historical remembrance, including community myths (myths of foundation or emergence relating to shared ancestry). This is producing a degree of solidarity between members, generating a feeling of belonging.

Ethnicity as a term is used to describe a variety of forms of mobilization which ultimately relate to the autonomous existence of specifically ethnic forms of socialization. No clear-cut distinction can, however, be made between struggles by social classes and struggles by ethnic groups. To talk about the politicization of ethnicity seems tautological. Different types of actors such as states, transnational companies, liberation movements, migrants' organizations, political parties, pressure groups, strategic groups, military leaders and populists all seek to make political capital out of 'ethnic identity'. Some actors deliberately try to influence and manipulate the ethnic-identity set-up.

Conflict causes, driving forces and colonial legacies

In two-thirds of all contemporary conflicts the *ethnic factor* (ethnicity) is a dominant or influential component. Ethnicity is mostly negatively charged in political discourse, having connotations such as 'primitive', 'backward', or 'irrational'. Contrary to the prognoses of political and social sciences in regard to the development of modern societies, ethnicity has lost none of its importance in recent decades. On the contrary, the importance of the ethnic dimension and its politicization have increased – influencing issues of status and categorization in violent conflicts as well as processes of civilian disputes, social demarcation and exclusion.

Identification of the driving forces of ethnic nationalism in the global framework leads to questions linked with the nature of ethnicity and the ethnic base of nations. Often these categories are not very adequately used. Underneath the structure of nearly 200 states there is an extraordinary multitude of perhaps 6,500 up to 10,000 ethnic *entities* of diverse size – from nations, nationalities and peoples to *minorities* and other distinct groups.[7] This diversity represents a tremendous richness of different cultures for most people but a threat to others. Characteristics given to identify a ethnic group or a nationality are by no means an academic exercise but will gain more political relevance as relations between nationalities, nations and states are increasingly seen as an important element of what is called *international politics* and *international relations*.

The legacies of colonialism and other external conditions contributed to separate nations from nationalities. The *invention* of the nation state, its official nationalism and false expectations raised by development ideologies in the former colonies are some of the basic sources for past and future conflicts. The European nation-state project created large-scale disorder after having been exported to the colonies. The official nationalism failed to satisfy its own aspirations of achieving an acceptable degree of development. State failure to safeguard internal peace and security created extreme problems.

Typology of contemporary violent conflicts

Typologies of conflicts are indispensable for any survey of conflicts. In order to register violent conflict comprehensively we need to re-evaluate typologies and to develop a sophisticated methodology to codify conflicts in such a way that changes are indicated and become visible.

Lacunae of global surveys on mass violence

Four main lacunae of global surveys on mass violence can be identified.

1. Present war registers overlook or deliberately ignore certain categories and types of mass violence, such as genocide, mass murder, communal violence, and post-modern types of conflicts, such as interethnic conflicts and gang wars.
2. Some conflict types do not necessarily involve state actors.
3. Most registers are constructing static entities instead of expressing the permanent mutation of conflicts in the real world. Conflicts develop over time and may change in quality, with a new type becoming dominant over the other(s).
4. External factors can not be ignored.[8]

Such shortcoming and gaps have serious implications: a critical limitation occurs if compilations exclude non-war types of mass violence. This necessarily results in limited explanatory power since the latter account for a higher number of casualties than wars in recent decades. For instance the war starting 1990 in Rwanda served as only a smokescreen for a much larger crime, the extermination of an entire population group, killing more people than all wars in FSU and Europe since the end of the Cold War.[9]

Drawing from over ten years of fieldwork and conflict analysis, ECOR developed what is presently the most advanced survey, based on a typology and codifying conflict cases according to a dynamic model featuring multiple components, thus reflecting both complexity and change in contemporary mass violence. Analysis illustrates that conflicts change over time and can have two or more different layers. Secondary and tertiary components have to be identified in order to understand changes and provide analytic insight for responses to conflict. This of course makes conflict analysis a complex task. In order to allow comparison with other compilations the ECOR register more or less follows (in types A–D) standards set by AKUF, corrected by Nietschmann's early works.[10]

Overcoming the exclusion of ethnicity and non-war mass violence

The problem is that *ethnicity* was seen in much of the academia a sort of taboo, and this has only changed recently.[11] Regarding conflict actors the main criteria can not be described adequately by the *ownership* of the state in all cases. The typology has been extended to include wars between non-state actors (E and F). Not only wars but also organized mass murder such as genocide (G) have to be included. However, most present registers and 'war lists' (such as the AKUF, SIRPI, CoW) exclude non-war types of violence.[12] My emphasis on inclusion of non-war types of mass violence is not an 'armchair idea'.[13]

Another emphasis concerns ethnic conflict. The challenge is to introduce a clear-cut distinction in different *types* of ethnic conflicts. Furthermore it has to be recalled that the newly discovered byword 'ethnicity' is in some cases (such as in Rwanda and Yugoslavia) used with the intent to divert attention away from 'real' causal processes and issues at stake. For many scholars 'ethnicity' is not an object of genuine attention but relegated as 'epiphenomenon' compared to the 'real' underlying issues or even referred to as something that ought not to be. The virtual 'taboo' concerning ethnicity – never honoured by some scholars but still held in good faith in much of the scientific community – has its consequences. The notion of ethnicity is still largely missing in most registers and 'war lists'.

A third emphasis concerns the notion of non-state actors. All registers and 'war lists' exclude the category of gang wars. To elaborate on this: why exclude it and on what grounds? The phenomenon is of increasing importance, as can be seen from the findings based on the ECOR register. If violent conflict by non-state actors were to be excluded then, according to the findings presented here, about a fifth of contemporary mass violence (most of type E and all of F) would be excluded. The much-discussed post-modern warfare and its various new actors such as warlords, gangs, mercenaries and commercial private armies (e.g. the *Executive Outcomes*) cannot be ignored.[14]

Typology of mass violence (A–G)

The resulting typology permits an analysis of global trends in warfare and non-military types of mass violence which otherwise would remain invisible. The methods and techniques applied to read the database of traditional registers would not be able to detect the most disturbing trends and extreme problems that the victims of conflict and the international community are facing today.

A: Anti-regime-wars or political and ideological conflicts: State versus Insurrection (SvI). There are different forms: liberation movements vs. colonial powers; popular movements and/or social-revolutionary movements vs. authoritarian state; destabilization or re-establishing a *status ante*. The aim is to replace the government of the day or to change the social-political system. Destabilization conflicts started in the framework of the Cold War can be very violent and have long duration; exemplary cases are RENAMO in Mozambique or UNITA in Angola, Mujaheddin (until 1991) and Taliban in Afghanistan, *Contras* in Nicaragua. Today some former destabilization conflicts mutated to become dominantly ethno-nationalist or ethnic-*tribalist* (e.g. in Afghanistan and Angola).

B: Ethno-nationalist conflicts in diverse forms, mostly as intra-state conflicts opposing states and national groups (State versus Nation, SvN); sometimes as interstate conflicts (MSvN). Ethno-nationalist SvN-conflicts are the most frequent type of contemporary armed conflicts and wars; such conflicts are generally of long duration (decades) even conflict resolution would only in a few cases afford to create new states. The aim is self-defence; in extreme cases as struggle for survival against aggressive state policies and outright threats of extermination. Possibilities for conflict resolution range from concessions regarding cultural autonomy and diverse degrees of autonomy to (con-) federal solutions and sovereign statehood.

C: Interstate conflicts, State versus State (SvS), earlier seen as the 'classic type' of warfare. Cases: war at the Persian Gulf between Iraq and Iran (1980-88), the 11-days-war between Mali and Burkina Faso (12/1985) or the invasion of USA in Panama (12/1989). The number is limited; according to the ECOR-Register during the decade 1985-94 there were 12 cases only (of 102 wars). The latest cases were minor: 1995 a brief war occurred between Peru and Ecuador and in 1998 between Eritrea and Ethiopia; in both cases the incompatibility was about (mutual) territorial claims. Application of the Geneva Conventions is unproblematic. Coalitions or war alliances are seldom: multi-state versus state (MSvS); multi-state vs. nation/nationality (MSvN); several states vs. several other states (MSvMS). This latter constellation was the classic World War coalition. There were a few MSvS or MSvN cases since 1990, all opposing Western powers and smaller states or nations. Examples: USA, UK, France, and others vs. Iraq 1990/91 (second Gulf war) and the NATO intervention against Serbs in Bosnia 1995 (as well as the latest NATO intervention threat against Serbia in Kosovo/a in 1998).

D: Decolonization wars or Foreign-State-Occupations (FSO): There are still a few Afro-Asiatic cases: Western Sahara, East-Timor, West-Papua and Palestine; Eritrea became a sovereign state in 1991/92. Most examples of type D have a dominant ethno-national character. Because of its privileges in international law type D is different from B (which is of decisive influence for a possible conflict resolution). Essentially former European colonial territories were occupied or annexed by non-European regional powers; the occupied peoples have a case in the UN.

E: Inter-ethnic conflicts: Type E is, together with B and D, part of the ethnic conflicts in a broad sense, but is different concerning its actors and aims. They act according to particular collective (non-private) interests. The issues are manifold but usually sectarian and sectorial: particular interests, *tribalism*, clan conflicts, chauvinism and *narrow nationalism*. Economic aspects play a role but cultural and political aspects predominate. As in B the militants use their own group as a recruiting and support base; actors are not forced to develop a war economy above normal levels. Such conflicts are often fought without a state actor taking part.

F: Gang wars: Non-state actors (mixed with criminal elements), especially in situations of state collapse. They act according to particular or even private interests. Economic aspects seem to predominate and a particular type of war economy is developed. Gang wars are fought about valuable resources (diamonds, gold, precious stones, drugs etc.), land or control of markets. Actors are village militias, demobilized soldiers or mercenaries (*contras, re-contras, re-compas*), so-called death squads, the Mafia, (drug) syndicates (e.g. in Columbia or in the Golden Triangle of SE Asia), professional groups (e.g. *Garimperos* vs. Indians in the Amazon), private armies of war lords (in Afghanistan, Liberia, Somalia, etc.) or big landowners (in Latin America vs. landless *campesiños*), settlers or migrants vs. indigenous peoples (e.g. in the mountain areas of Bangladesh, Tripura and Assam; in the Kenyan Rift Valley etc.).[15]

G: Genocide: State-organized mass murder and crimes against humanity characterized by the intention of the rulers to exterminate individuals because they belong to a particular national, ethnic, 'racial' or religious group (genocide). Genocide is the worst type of mass violence and has to be clearly distinguished from warfare. Target and victims are civilians (non-combatants) including old people, children and even babies. Recent cases of large-scale genocide were the extermination committed by states. From 1975 to 1979 the Khmer Rouge regime in Cambodia exterminated the Vietnamese, Cham and Chinese minorities; mass murder was also committed against ethnic Khmer (*auto-genocide*).[16] Rwanda's Hutu power regime wiped out the entire Tutsi branch of the Banyarwanda in 100 days (7 April–15 July 1994); massacres have been repeatedly committed against the Tutsi since 1959 and against two other minorities (Gogwe and Hima).[17] Sudan's NIF-regime has committed genocide against the Nuba in Central Sudan and Dinka civilians in Southern Sudan from the early 1990s up to the present day.[18]

On the basis of these seven core types of conflicts diverse mixed forms can be identified.[19] Their characteristics and main impulses shall be analysed, starting with their historical and regional background. The task of conflict research remains a Herculean one: to detect the roots, genesis and dynamics of intra-state conflicts. The aim is to give a survey of conflict potentials, to identify belligerent actors and their goals, to analyse characteristics of rebel forces, to research the course of a particular conflict and its means (own resources, external support), as well as possible foreign involvement. Furthermore the task for peace research is to think about ways of structural prevention, transformation and resolution.

Registers of contemporary violent conflicts, 1985-96

Registers of contemporary wars often blur the high proportion of ethnically determined or induced types of conflicts. Such conflicts appear in combination with other types and forms of intra-state conflicts; this blurs a clear categorization. Today the category of *ethnic conflict* has gained broad acceptance. A few years ago this category was generally avoided, for different reasons: in many Third World countries because of the connotation of ethnicity carrying 'backwardness', 'primitive culture' and 'pre-modernity'; in Europe (especially in Germany) because of political implications or historic reasons somewhat 'value-neutral' official and camouflage terms were used. Usually the findings or results of a register have to be analysed and interpreted carefully where the outcomes for the same period can show a high degree of divergence concerning the over-all number of conflicts, the proportion of a particular type, e.g. ethnic conflicts or substitute categories.[20] Some authors underestimate the potential for ethnic conflicts. Most experts agree that their number is increasing. One out of six individuals belongs to a minority at risk.[21]

Trends and perspectives

The heterogeneous dynamic character of contemporary violent conflicts has to be expressed adequately. In ECOR's evaluation this has been solved as follows: besides pointing at a dominant type, a secondary and tertiary component was codified.

In order to exclude multiple counting of particular components only the last phase of a war was relevant. In the register the composition of the seven types of wars (A–G) features a dominant component followed by a secondary or tertiary. Results regarding the seven types of violent conflict are shown in Table 3.1.

Table 3.1   The seven types of violent conflict in per cent, 1985-94

Conflict types 1985–94	A Anti-regime	B Ethno-nationalism	C inter-state	D decolo-nization	E inter-ethnic	F gang wars	G geno-cide	B+D+E+G ethnic conflicts
Dominance	19.6	44.1	11.8	4.9	13.7	3.9	2.0	64.7
Mentioning	30.7	29.3	8.0	5.3	17.3	7.6	1.8	52.9

All conflicts with dominant ethnic-induced or ethnicized character (types B, D, E and G) account for nearly two-thirds (64.7%) of all contemporary conflicts. According to the number of appearances, ethnic components received 53.7% of all those mentioned. That means that there is a significant trend: the ethnic factor bears a higher dominance than other conflict components such as the anti-regime component. Compared with ethnic-induced conflicts the anti-regime conflicts would be half as dominant.

The result shows some clear trends: in the 12-year period (1985-96) ethno-nationalist wars and genocide became more dominant than anti-regime wars or gang wars. Dominance and frequency are roughly balanced regarding interstate wars, decolonization wars and interethnic wars.

- Most significant is the result concerning the two most frequent types of war (A and B): conflicts from 1995 and 1996 contain most frequently an anti-regime component (31.5%) and an ethno-nationalist component (28.1%). Significantly the ethno-nationalist character of contemporary violent conflicts predominates twice as frequently as the character of anti-regime conflicts (38.75 to 22.5). This result is almost in line with the result from the decade 1985 to 1994 (see Table 3.2).

Table 3.2   Types of conflict in per cent, 1985-94

Conflict types 1985–1996	A Anti-regime	B Ethno-nationalism	C Inter-state	D Decolonization	E Inter-ethnic	F Gang wars	G Genocide	B+D+E+G ethnic conflicts
Dominance:								
1985–94	19.6	44.1	11.8	4.9	13.7	3.9	2.0	64.7
1995–96	22.5	38.8	3.8	5.0	21.3	6.3	2.5	67.5
Influence:								
Secondary	31.5	28.1	3.9	5.1	21.3	8.4	1.1	55.6
tertiary	30.7	29.3	8.0	5.3	17.3	7.6	1.8	52.9

Reduction of interstate wars and increase of foreign interventions

Shocking for mainstream security studies and conflict research is the fact that the Clausewitzean type of inter-state conflicts has practically disappeared. The most significant trend in recent years shows a progressive decline in the absolute number (and proportion) of inter-state conflicts. Today there are less than 1 in 20 conflicts (3.75%, 1985–1996). Currently there is only one case of a pending interstate conflict. The provocative assessment is that interstate conflict character may increasingly become a component of other types of conflicts.

Even worse, today interstate conflicts increasingly mutate into a sub-component or an extension of intra-state wars. In Africa this pattern can be demonstrated in several recent cases occurring in the years 1996–98. The military involvement of eight African states and a dozen non-state actors in the new war in the Congo between the Kabila regime and the RCD-rebels since August 1998 is the latest and most complex case.[22] Contrary to the *classic* type of interstate conflict, different types of ethnic conflicts/disputes could be compared to rhizome plants growing for decades, nearly impossible to uproot and growing 'everywhere', always surfacing where and when you would not expect it.

In the last two years the amount of foreign state participation increased to 17 cases (of 80 conflict cases). Compared to 1985–94 there had been 27 cases of foreign state intervention; in 15 of those 27 cases the intervention occurred in the last phase of the conflict, while in 12 cases the former state intervention took place in the 1980s. In the two-year period 1995–96 the number of foreign state interventions was 23 cases where in six cases the foreign intervention started before the mentioned period. Hence recent foreign state intervention is with 17 cases for 1995 and 1996 extraordinary high. Rarely interventions occur in types B and E.[23] The question of foreign state intervention is to be distinguished clearly from support by foreign states for one or more conflict actors (e.g. by providing hinterland or weapons).[24]

Regional distribution of conflicts: decrease in Asia versus increase in Africa

The distribution of conflicts according to world regions is shown in Table 3.3. Today 45% of all violent conflicts are taking place in Africa, which is more than 50% more than during the decade 1985-94.

Table 3.3   Distribution of conflicts according to world regions in percent, 1985-94, 1995-96

World region	1985–94 (decade)	1995–96 (2 years)
Asia	42.2	33.7
Africa	29.4	45.0
Europe	14.7	7.5
Americas	13.7	13.7

During the period of 1985 to 1996 the regional distribution of violent conflicts was largely modified. While the proportion of Latin America remained constant, those of Asia and Europe were declining. On the other hand the proportion of violent conflicts in Africa was increasing dramatically. According to both the number and mortality of violent conflicts, Africa has become the most war-torn continent in recent years, ahead of West Asia and South Asia.

Table 3.4   Sub-regional distribution and change in percent

Number of conflicts	1985–94	% of total	1995–96	% of total	change %
Central America	7		4		–
South America	7		7		+
Latin America total	14	13.7	11	13.7	0
Western Europe	3		3		+
Eastern Europe	5		2		–
SE: Caucasus	7		1		–
Europe total	15	14.7	6	7.5	– 49
N Africa	5		8		+
W Africa	5		8		+
Central Africa	5		7		+
E Africa	10		11		+
Southern Africa	5		2		–
Africa total	30	29.4	36	45.0	+ 53
West Asia	11		6		–
Central Asia	3		3		+
S Asia	7		5		–
SE Asia	15		7		–
E Asia	1		0		–
Island Asia/Pacific	6		6		+
Asia total	43	42.2	27	33.7	– 21
World's conflicts	102	100	80	100	–/+

In Africa the civilian population suffered heavy losses by exterminatory mass violence, warfare and war-induced famine. Five African countries were in 1996 among the nine countries affected by major armed conflicts claiming more than 1,000 lives:[25] Algeria, Burundi, Congo-Zaire, Sudan and Uganda (besides Afghanistan, Chechnia/RF, Sri Lanka and Turkey/Kurdestan). In 1997 the number of African countries with major conflicts claiming more than 1,000 violence-related deaths rose to eight (Angola again, Rwanda again and Congo-Brazzaville) compared to three other cases with more than 1,000 violence-related deaths in the rest of the world.

After 1990 Europe became temporarily once again one of the major theatres of war. The talk about 'Europe as an island of peace' in the midst of a war-torn world was abruptly silenced in 1991. The most peaceful world regions were East Asia and North America (the latter without taking into account high rates of urban violence and criminality).

Six years later violent conflicts in Europe were reduced to half and conflicts in Asia decreased by one-fifth. Only in Africa did conflicts increase dramatically by more than 50%.

Table 3.5 Correlates of frequency and dominance high for ethno-nationalism

Period	Dominance/frequency		Quota	
	1985–94	1995–96	1985–94	1995–96
Anti-regime conflict	19.2 : 30.7	23.7 : 31.8	0.63	0.75
Ethno-nationalism	44.1 : 29.3	38.7 : 28.4	1.51	1.36
Inter-ethnic conflicts	13.7 : 17.3	20.0 : 20.4	0.79	0.98

The most frequent dominant conflict type was the ethno-nationalist, with 38.75% of all cases (28.1% of mentioning). In clear distance the concerning dominance the type of anti-regime wars (23.75%) and inter-ethnic wars (20%), the latter with a strong increase, followed by gang wars (7.25%), decolonization wars (5%) and interstate conflicts (3.75%). Genocide (2.5%) remains the most rare type of violent conflict but the one with the highest mortality.

Those conflicts in 1995 and 1996 that acquired a dominant ethnic character (types B, D and E) account for two-thirds (66.25%) of all contemporary violent conflicts in this period. According to the number of mentioning per type of conflict the ethnic conflict components appeared in over half of all cases.

Recent trends: increasing complex crisis and state collapse

Genocide and mass murder of defenceless victims account for 2% and 2.5% of all conflicts in the respective periods. This is an alarming sign and a matter for the most serious concern. The number of victims of genocide and mass violence in the period 1985–96 is much higher than the frequency would suggest. The small number of genocide and mass violence shows a higher mortality then all other conflicts put together! The state-organized genocide in Rwanda 1994 alone took 1 million lives in a period of 100 days. This incredible number of victims is more than twice the number of victims caused by all violent conflicts taking place from 1988 to 1996 in the former Soviet Union and the former Yugoslavia put together.

In the 1990s a dramatic increase of extreme crisis situations and complex emergency cases led to an alarming increase in conflict-induced mortality in cases of protracted conflicts. The most deadly contemporary case of mass violence – in a cumulative count since 1954 – ravages Sudan. An estimated 2.5–3 million people became the victims of genocide, war and famine, as a consequence of the successive Sudanese regimes' onslaught in southern Sudan. This conflict goes on unabated.[26]

Another matter for concern is the proportion of gang wars that have nearly doubled in a period of only ten years (from 3.9% to 6.25%). So far chaotization and warlordism only characterize a small number of all conflicts (one-sixteenth), but their number might increase even further. This concern is based on evidence since the higher proportion of mentioned cases compared to the proportion of dominance of this type of post-modern conflict indicates further increase in dominance and frequency.

In the case of most ethnic nationalist type of conflict the silence of Western mass media is even more suspicious; such conflicts account for 40% of all violent conflicts. The ethnic nationalist character tends towards becoming the dominant component of contemporary conflicts. One of the conflict impacts is the relatively low chance for peaceful conflict settlement. This is one of the main reasons for the steady increase (up to 1995) of such durable protracted conflicts. This again contributed significantly to the increase of the total number of wars since 1945. The related type of decolonization conflict continuously accounts for one in twenty wars. Such conflicts are also a reality that receives only little attention by the Western media.

Another cause for alert is the rising number of inter-ethnic conflicts – in other words, conflicts between ethnic groups without participation of state actors in most cases. This type of conflict increased by nearly one-third. The trend points to a further fragmentation within existing states. This has resulted in a rising loss of hegemony of state actors in many countries in the South. State failure, protracted warfare and other forms of mass violence are inextricably linked.

Appendix – Register of contemporary major wars and mass violence

Definitions

Wars and genocide have to be clearly defined and distinguished.

War is defined as a violent mass conflict involving two or more armed forces as combatants/actors in warfare. Regular state armed forces are not involved in all cases. Non-state actors are mainly so-called liberation movements having regular guerrilla or partisan armies, often recruiting along ethnic, national or social class lines. Militias, gangs and other irregular forces have different agendas; they have less or no centralized control or identifiable lines of command. Combat takes place with some degree of continuity.

Major war and mass violence are distinguished from other armed conflicts or massacres by various degrees of medium or high intensity, claiming usually more than an estimated 1,000 victims per annum as an average during the conflict period. In many cases the numbers of victims are contested or otherwise questionable.

Impure types/different components: Combining the basic types can adequately solve the inherent difficulty of all the 'impure' types we find in the real world. Thus we get closer to the 'mixed types' encountered in the field.

Dynamics and change: To illustrate the dynamics and the changing composition of contemporary wars a second method was used. The diachronic development was cut in phases of warfare. Contemporary wars do not resemble football games any more. For a given phase the register shows the primary or dominant type followed (if necessary) by a secondary or tertiary characterization of a particular conflict, hence describing the heterogeneous and dynamic nature of most *modern* non-Clausewitzean types of conflicts.

Typology and legend

A *Anti-regime-wars* (politico-ideological conflicts): State versus Insurrection (SvI).
B *Ethno-nationalist conflicts*: in diverse forms, mostly as intra-state conflicts (State versus Nation, SvN), sometimes as interstate conflicts (MSvN).
C *Interstate conflicts*: State versus State (SvS), earlier seen as 'classic case' of warfare.

D *Decolonization wars* or *Foreign State Occupations* (FSO): mostly Afro-Asiatic cases.
E *Inter-ethnic conflicts*: together with B and D part of the ethnic conflicts in a broad sense; differences concern actors (mainly non-state) and aims (sectorial).
F *Gang wars*: Non-state actors (mixed with criminal elements), especially in situations of state collapse.
G *Genocide*: State-organized mass murder and crimes against humanity.

Mixed types: AB, BA, BC, CB, AC, CA, AE, EA, ABC, BAC etc. The first mentioned type in a given period is the dominant type in combination with a less influential secondary and/or tertiary type.

+ *Foreign actor*: direct interference/engagement of an outside power with combatants being not only military 'advisors'.

/ *Phase/periods*: slash between types or periods of time indicate different phases or paradigmatic changes in the course of warfare/violence:

   1. different periods of a conflict, e.g. in some cases interrupted by period of peace (as in Sudan 1972–93);
   2. changes of intensity, caused by changes of the course of violence, qualitative changes of strategies by one or several actors, qualitative change in availability of weapons (e.g. introduction of heavy artillery of weapons of mass destruction);
   3. paradigmatic change of character (by which one type/component becomes dominant over another), as a result of important political changes, change of objectives, new alliances, fall of the regime etc.

... *Periods of time*: war is continued after the registered period 31 December 1994 or 31 December 1996.

(?) *Termination*:   the date or the termination of warfare is questionable.

Table 3.6   Register of violent conflicts, 1985–94*

World region	No.	Country	Nation(alitie)s/actors	Conflict types	Period/phases
Central America	1	Guatemala	Maya-Kiché, Ixil, EGP, others	B / GBA / BA	1954 / 78–1985 / 86–...
	2	Guatemala	URNG	AB	1960 / 80–92 (?)
	3	Nicaragua	FDN-Contras/Re-Contras	A+ / AF	Apr 1981–90 / ...
	4	Nicaragua	Miskitu/Sumu, Rama	B+ / B	Feb 1981–87 / 90
	5	El Salvador	FMLN, Pipil	AB	1980 / 81–Feb 1992 (?)
	6	USA	Panama (LD-RP)	C	20–24 Dec 1989
Caribbean	7	Haiti	Tonton Macoutes, FRAPH; US	FA / FA+	Sep 1991 / Sep 1994– ...
South America	8	Brazil	Gold searchers vs. Yanomami	FE	1986 (?)–...
	9	Columbia	FARC, EPL; ELN; M-19	AB / A / A	1964 / 65 / Jan 74–Mar 90 / ...
	10	Columbia	Drug syndicates, death squads.	AF	1970 (?)– ...
	11	Columbia	Guajiro	BA	1975 (?)– ...
	12	Suriname	Busi Nengee/Kalinja, Lokono	BA/B	21 Jun 1986–7 Jun 1989
	13	Peru	Sendero Luminoso, militias	ABF	May 1980– ...
	14	Peru	Aymara, Quichua, MRTA	BA	Nov 1987– ...
North Africa	15	Morocco	West Sahara: Sahrawi	DB	18 Nov 1975–1992 (?)
	16	Sudan	South Sudan: SPLA	BGA	Sep 1983–...
	17	Sudan	SPLA-Dinka, SPLA-Nuer	BE+	Aug 1991–...
	18	Algeria	GIA, AIS (Armée Isl. du Salut)	AF	1991– ...
	19	Egypt	Moslem fundamentalists	A	1992– ...
West Africa	20	Senegal	Diola, MFDC	BA	Apr 1990– ...

World region	No.	Country	Nation(alitie)s/actors	Conflict types	Period/phases
	21	Liberia	NPFL, INPFL	EA / EA+	Dec 1989 / Aug 1990–...
	22	Sierra Leone	RUF, NPFL, ULIMO	AEC	Jan 1991–...
	23	Mali	Burkina Faso	C	21–31 Dec 1985
	24	Mali/Niger	Tuareg: MFUA, MPA, FIAA	BCE / BC	May 1990–92 / Jun 1994 ...
Central Africa	25	Chad	FAN, FAP, MPS	E / BAC+ / BA+ / B	June 1966/ 79 / 90/ 91– ...
	26	Rwanda	Bahutu, Tutsi, FPR/RPA	BA+	Oct 1990 / 92– Jul 1994
	27	Rwanda	Interahamwe/CDR/GP vs. Tutsi	GEF+	6 Apr 1994–15 Jul 1994
	28	Burundi	Tutsi (army), Bahutu (militias)	G / EAC	1972–... / Aug 1993– ...
	29	Zaire	Luba; Hunde, Nyanga, Hutu	EA / GEA	Aug 1992 / Mar 1993– ...
East Africa	30	Ethiopia	Eritrea: ELF, EPLF	DB / DAB	1962 / 1976– May 1991
	31	Ethiopia	Tigrai, TLF, TPLF, EPRDF	B / BA	1975–May 1991
	32	Ethiopia	Oromo: OLF, IFLO, UOPL	BAD / BDA	1976 / May 1991– ...
	33	Ethiopia	Gojjam, Gondar: EPRP, EDU	A / AB / BA	Mar 1974 / Dec 1975 / May 91– ...
	34	Ethiopia	EPRDF: EPDM, OPDO, u.a.	AB	Jan 1989–May 1991
	35	Djibouti	Afar (FRUD, others.)	BEA / BAE	1981 / Oct 1991–...
	36	Eritrea	ELF-Idriss, Jihad, ELF-GC	EA+	1993(?)–...
	37	Somalia	Somaliland: Isaaq, SNM	BA+ / BA	1980 / 1990– May 1991
	38	Somalia	Marehan, SSDF, SDM, USC	EA / E / E+	1988 / Jan 1991 / Dec 1992– ...
	39	Uganda	NRM, Acholi, Langi, Bari	AB / EA	Feb 1981 / Feb 1986 / – ...

World region	No.	Country	Nation(alitie)s/actors	Conflict types	Period/phases
South Africa	40	Angola	MPLA; FLNA, UNITA	D / BAC+ / BAE	1961–75 / 20 Jun 1991–...
	41	Namibia	SWAPO, Herero, !Khoi; TA	BD	1966–22 Dec 1988
	42	Zimbabwe	ZANU, Ndebele-ZAPU	AB / EA	Jan. 1983 / 1987–May 1988
	43	Mozambique	FRELIMO; RENAMO	D / AC / AE+	1991 / 75–Oct 1992 (?)
	44	South Africa	ANC, PAC/Inkatha, Boers	DA / DAE / EAD	1962 / 76 / 90–...
Europe West	45	Spain	Euskadi, ETA, HB	BA	1937– ...
	46	France	Corsica, FLNC	BA	1950– ...
	47	N-Ireland	IRA, UVF, UFF	DB / DEA / EDA	1961–69 / 1986–10 / 94(?)
Europe East	48	Yugoslavia	Slovenia/Croatia	AB / CB	Jun–Jul 1991 / Oct 1991
	49	Croatia	Serbs (Krajina, Slavonia)	G / BF+ / EA	1940–44 / mid 1991–93 / May 1995
	50	Bosnia:	*Tshetnik*i, Muslims, HOS, others	EFB+	Mar 1992–...
	51	Moldavia	Russians, Ukrainians, Kosaks	EF+	Mar–Aug 1992
	52	Rumania	Securitate, Timisoara Magyar	AE	17–28 Dec 1989
Europe SE	53	Georgia	Gamsachurdia rebels	A / AEF	Sep 1991 / Jan1992–Nov 1993
	54	Georgia	S-Ossetia	B	Dec 1990–Jul 1992
	55	Georgia	Abchasia; alliance, Russians	BC / BC+	Aug 1992 / July 1993–Dec 1993
	56	Chechnia	Inguschi, North Ossetians	BE	Dec 1991–Mar 1992
	57	Aserbaijan	Nagorny-Karabach	BE / CBE	1988–90 / 1992–May 1994 (?)

World region	No.	Country	Nation(alitie)s/actors	Conflict types	Period/phases
	58	Armenia	SW-Aserbaijan	CBEF	Mar 1993– May 1994
	59	Chechnia	Russian Army vs. Chechen	BEAF	11. Dec 1994–...
West Asia	60	Libanon	Maronites/Druse, Shiites/Hesb	AE / CEA / EAC	Apr 1975 / 78 / 82–93 (?)
	61	Israel	Palestine: PLO/Hamas; Druse	DB	1968– ...
	62	S-Jemen	Tribes, clans, JSP	AEF	13–29 Jan 1986
	63	N-Jemen	South Jemen	ABC / BAC	Dec 1991 / Mar 1994–Jul 1994
	64	Turkey	Kurds, PKK, HRK	B / BADF	1970 / 1984–...
Persian Gulf	65	Iran	Aseri, Kurds, Turkmen	BA	Jul 1979–88 / ...(?)
	66	Iraq	Kurds, PUK, KDP	BA / BAC / BA+	1976 / Feb 1991 / Mar 1991–...
	67	Iraq	Iran (1st Gulf war), Kurds	CB	Sep 1980–20. Aug 1988
	68	Iraq	Kuwait	CD	2–4 Aug 1990
	69	USA/GB a.	Iraq (2nd Gulf war)	C	17 Jan–27 Feb 1991 /...
	70	Iraq	Shiites	AB / CAB	1990–2 Mar 1991–...
Central Asia	71	Tajikistan	CP, clans, Russian troops	EAF+	Aug 1992–Jun 1993 (?)
	72	Afghanistan	CP, Pathanen, Tajik, Usbek, a.	ABE / BAE+ / EB	1973 / Oct 78 / Apr 92– ...
	73	Pakistan	Sindhi, SNA, Muhajir, Paschtun	BEF	Nov 1986– ...
South Asia	74	India	Pakistan (Siachen glacier)	C	Apr 1984–1989 (?)
	75	India	Kashmir: Muslim/Jamu/Ladakh	BE / BAE	1986 / 90– ...
	76	India	Punjab: Sikhs, KLF, KCF	BAE	Jul 1982–...
	77	India	Bihar: Naxaliten	A	1988–... (?)

World region	No.	Country	Nation(alitie)s/actors	Conflict types	Period/phases
	78	Sri Lanka	LTTE, EPRLF, Tamils, Muslims	B / BA+ / BAE+	Jul 1983 / Sep 1987 / Mar 1990– ...
	79	Sri Lanka	JVP, Singhalese Youth	AE	Jul 1987–Nov 1989 (?)
	80	Bangla Desh	CHT-Tribes, Chakma, SB, a.	BAF	1973– ...
	81	NE-India	Tai-Asom, ULFA, Boro/Bodo	BEA	1990– ...
	82	NE-India	West Begal/Himalaya: Gorkha	BA	1987–88 (?)
SE-Asia	83	NE-India	Naga: RGN, NNC, NSCN	BD / BEA / AB / BA	1954 / 63 / 72 / Nov 75– ...
	84	NE-India	Manipur: KNA, NSCN, Meitei	BA / BEA / BAE	1960 / 75 / 84 / May 92– ...
	85	NE-India	Mizo: MNF, u.a.	BAE	1966–Jun 1986
	86	Burma	Karen: KNDO, KNU	BEA / B / BA	1947 / 50 / 88– ...
	87	Burma	CPB (PVO, Red Flag), DPA	A / A+ / AB	1948 / 62 / Mar 1989– ...
	88	Burma	KIO, Mon; NDF; Pa-O, KNPP	B / BAE / BA	1962 / 76 / Nov 1988– ...
	89	Burma	Shan, Da'an, ALF, Wa, a, a.	EA / EBA	1970 (?) / 88– ...
	90	Burma	DAB: NDF, ABSDF, PPP, a.	AB	Nov 1988– ...
	91	Burma	opium guerrilla: KKY, MTA, Wa	EA+ / EFA / FE	1950 / 76 / Mar 1989– ...
	92	Thailand	Laos	C	Nov 1987–Feb 1988
	93	Laos	Hmong, LLA, drug wars	FEC+ / FEA	1970 / 75– ...
	94	Cambodia	Khmer Rouge, ANS, Sihanouk	A / CA / G / AB+ / A+	1968 / 70 / 71– 75 / 79 / 85– ...
	95	Vietnam	Montagnards, KPNLA, FULRO	B / BA+ / B	1964 / 1970 / 75– Oct 1992 (?)

World region	No.	Country	Nation(alitie)s/actors	Conflict types	Period/phases
East Asia	96	China	Vietnam	C	Feb / Mar 1979–88
Island Asia	97	Philippines	NPA, Cordillera, CPA, Bontok	AB	1970– ...
	98	Philippines	Mindanao: Moro, MNLF, MILF	BA+ / BA	1970 / 89– ...
	99	Indonesia	Aceh, others	B	May 1990– ...
	100	Indonesia	East Timor	DBA	Aug 1975– ...
	101	Indonesia	West Papua, OPM	DGB	1965– ...
Asia Pacific	102	New Guinea	Bougainville	BAD	Feb 1989– ...

* Copyright © by Christian P. Scherrer/ECOR, 1995

Sources: Scherrer, 1988, 1997; ECOR, 1991, 1992, 1994a., 1995, 1996, 1997, div.; AKUF, 1996, 1997; Heidelberger Institut für Internationale Konfliktforschung, 1996; SIPRI, div.; Gantzel/Schlichte, 1994; Gantzel/AKUF, 1992; Nietschmann, 1987; SEF 1996, 1997; Wallensteen/Axell, 1993.

Table 3.6 registered violent conflicts including genocide (Rwanda, Central Sudan), wars, armed conflicts, rebellions etc., taking place in 1985–94 in 16 regions of the world. Table 3.8 registered violent conflicts taking place in 1995–96 in 15 regions of the world (no major conflict in East Asia). Already in 1993/94 a slight reduction in the number of ongoing violent conflicts but no reduction of mortality at all occurred. A reason for the slight numeric reduction was the termination of most wars in the former USSR – after the explosion of violence from 1989/90 to 1994.

The number of conflicts remained high through 1995 and 1996. The absolute number of conflicts was not sharply decreasing as other sources suggest.[27] Concerning the virulence of violent conflict in the Third World there is no reason to talk about a relaxation. Many *endless* civil wars are still being continued. In 1994 the worst genocide since the Holocaust claimed up to 1 million lives. In 1995 two new armed conflicts were started, in 1996 three, and 1997 two. Some of the new wars are linked to older wars (Niger, Liberia, Eastern Zaire/Rwanda), others are truly new.

Table 3.7   **Result: frequency and dominance of seven types of conflicts 1985-94 (types/components mentioned in the respective most recent phases of violent conflicts fought during the decade 1985-94)**[*]

Types of conflict	All regions 1985–94							
	A	B	C	D	E	F	G	Cases
Lat America 13.7%	6-4-0	5-4-0	1-0-0	0-0-0	0-1-0	2-2-1		14
Central America	3-2-0	2-2-0	1-0-0			1-1-0		7
South America	3-2-0	3-2-0	0-0-0		0-1-0	1-1-1		7
Europe 14.7 %	2-2-2	7-3-1	3-1-0	0-1-0	3-3-2	0-3-1		15
Western Europe	0-2-1	2-0-0	0-0-0	0-1-0	1-0-0			3
Eastern Europe	1-0-0	1-1-1	1-0-0	0-0-0	2-1-0	0-3-0		5
SE: Caucasus	1-0-1	4-2-0	2-1-0	0-0-0	0-2-2	0-0-1		7
Africa 29.4 %	5-16-2	13-1-2	1-1-2	2-2-1	7-6-2	0-1-1	2-1-0	30
North Africa	2-1-0	2-0-1	0-0-0	1-0-0	0-1-0	0-1-0	0-1-0	5
West Africa	1-2-0	2-0-0	1-1-1	0-0-0	1-1-0			5
Central Africa	0-3-0	2-0-0	0-0-1	0-0-0	1-3-0	0-0-1	2-0-0	5
East Africa	1-7-2	5-1-1	0-0-0	1-1-0	3-0-1			10
Southern Africa	1-3-0	2-0-0	0-0-0	0-1-1	2-1-1			5
Asia 42,2 %	7-19-4	20-8-2	7-0-2	3-1-2	4-6-5	2-0-4	0-1-0	43
West Asia	1-6-0	4-2-1	4-0-2	1-1-1	1-1-0	0-0-1		11
Central Asia	0-1-0	1-1-0			2-1-0	0-0-2		3
South Asia	2-4-0	4-0-0	1-0-0		0-1-3	0-0-1		7
SE Asia	3-6-3	8-3-0	1-0-0		1-3-2	2-0-0		15
East Asia	0-0-0	0-0-0	1-0-0					1
Island Asia/Pacific	1-2-1	3-2-1	0-0-0	2-0-1			0-1-0	6
World's conflicts in the decade 1985–1994	20-41-8	45-16-5	12-2-4	5-4-3	14-16-9	4-6-7	2-2-0	102
Number of appearances, 1985– 94	69	66	18	12	39	17	4	225

[*] Copyright © by Scherrer/ECOR, 1995

Table 3.8   Register of violent conflicts, 1995–96[*]

World region	No.	Country	Nation(alitie)s/ actors	Types of conflicts	Period/phases
C America	1	Mexico	EZLN (Chiapas), Tzeltal, Tzotzil	BA / AB	Jan 1994 / 2 / 1995– ...
	2	Mexico	EPR/ELN (Guerrero, Oaxaca)	BA	Jun 1996–... *(new)*
	3	Guatemala	URNG	GAB / AB	1960 / 1980–Dec 1996 (?)
	4	Nicaragua	(Re-) Contras, recompas, gangs	A+ / AF	1981–90 / ...
S America	5	Brazil	settler, gold rush vs. indigenous	GE / FE	1986 (?) / 89–...
	6	Columbia	FARC, EPL; CGSB	AB / A / A	1964/65 / Jan 74–Mar 90 / ...
	7	Columbia	ELN vs. S, TNC	AB / A / A	1965 / 74– ...
	8	Columbia	drug syndicates, death squads	F	1970 (?)– ...
	9	Peru	Sendero Luminoso/Rojo; militias	ABF	1980–Mar 1995 / ...
	10	Peru	MRTA; Aymara, Quichua	AB	Nov 1987–1992 / ...
	11	Ecuador	Peru	C	Jan–Feb 1995
N Africa	12	Morocco	W-Sahara; Polisario; MINURSO	DB	Nov 1975–1992 / ... (?)
	13	Sudan	South Sudan: SPLA	BA+	Sep 1983– ...
	14	Sudan	SPLA vs. SSIA, Nuer u.a.	F / BE+	Aug 1991– ...
	15	Sudan	Arab militias vs. SPLA	F / FE	1983 / 91– ...
	16	Sudan	Central Sudan: Nuba genocide	BGA / GBE	1989 / 91– ...
	17	Sudan	NDA; Northern Sudanese+SPLM	AB+	Oct 1989 / 95– ...
	18	Algeria	Muslim fundamentalists AIS, GIA	AF	1991– ...
	19	Egypt	Muslim integrists/M. brotherhood	AF	1992– ...

World region	No.	Country	Nation(alitie)s/ actors	Types of conflicts	Period/phases
W Africa	20	Senegal	Diola, MFDC	BAD / BA	1990–94 / Jan 1995– ...
	21	Liberia	NPFL, ULIMO (K+J), LPC	EF / EA+ / A	1989 / 95 / Apr 96– ...
	22	Sierra Leone	RUF, NPFL, ULIMO	EC / AE+	Jan 1991– ...
	23	Mali	Tuareg: MPA, FIAA; militias	BAE / BCE	1990–92 / 1994– ... (?)
	24	Niger	Tuareg: FLAA	BAE / BCE / BC	May 1990–91 / Oct 94– ...
	25	Niger	Arabs, others; FDR	BE	1995– ... *(new)*
	26	Ghana	Konkomba vs. Nanumba, Gonja	EA	Feb 1994– ...
	27	Nigeria	Ogoni (MOSOP), others	BA	1990/
C Africa	28	N Chad	MDD, Frolinat, FNT	B / BAC+ / BA+ / E	Jun 1966 / 79 / 90 / 91– ...
	29	S Chad	CSNPD, FARF	BA / BEA	1985 / 91 / Aug 94– ...
	30	Rwanda	post-genocide/destabilization	EFC+ / G / BA+	Oct 90 / Apr–Jul 94 / ...
	31	Burundi	Tutsi/Hutu: Army vs. FDD others	G / EAC	1972– ... / Aug 1993– ...
	32	Zaire-South	Luba; Katanga-Shaba; Lumumbist	EA / AE	Aug 1992 / Mar 93– ...
	33	Zaire-East	Hutu, FAZ; Tutsi, Hunde	GEF	Summer 1994–...
	34	Zaire-East	Hutu+FAZ; AFDC, Banyamulenge	EA / A	Sep 96 / 96–... *(new)*
E Africa	35	Ethiopia	Oromo: OLF, IFLO, UOPL	BAD / BDA	1976 / May 1991–...
	36	Ethiopia	Somali, div.	BEA	1974 / 1992–...
	37	Ethiopia	Gojjam, Gondar: EPRP, EDU	A / AB / BA	Mar 74 / Dec 75 / May 91–...
	38	Ethiopia	Somalia: ONLF, WSLM, others	CE	Aug 1996–... *(new)*
	39	Djibouti	Afar (FRUD others.)	BEA / BAE	1981 / Oct 1991–...
	40	Eritrea	ELF-Idriss, Jihad, ELF-GC	EA+	1993 (?)–...

World region	No.	Country	Nation(alitie)s/ actors	Types of conflicts	Period/phases
	41	Somalia	clans; SNA, USC, UNOSOM	EF / EA / EF	1988 / Jan 91 / Dec 92– ...
	42	Somaliland	Issa/other clans	EF	1992–...
	43	Uganda	LRA+HSM, WNBF; Acholi, Langi	AB / EA	Feb 1981 / Feb 86 / –...
	44	Uganda	MIR (Islamic), UDFM	EA+	1995–... *(new)*
	45	Uganda	Sudan; div. guerrilla groups	ECA	1991 / 1996–...
S Africa	46	Angola	FLEC-FAC, FLEC II	AE / AEF	1975 / 1993 / 1994–...
	47	South Africa	Kwa-Zulu: Inkatha IFP	EA	1990–...
W Europe	48	Spain	Euskadi, ETA, HB	BA	1937–...
	49	France	Corsica, FLNC	BA	1950–...
	50	N-Ireland	IRA; UVF, UFF	DB / DEA / EDA	1961-69 / 86–10 / 94 / 95–...
E Europe	51	Croatia	Serbs (Krajina, Slavonia)	G / BF+ / EA	1940–44 / mid 91–93 / May 95
	52	Bosnia:	Chetniks, Muslims, HOS, others.	EFB+	Mar 1992– Oct 1995 (?)
SE Europe	53	Chechnia	Russian intervention vs. Chechen	BEAF	11 Dec 94–22 Aug 1996
W Asia	54	Lebanon	SLA, Hisb-Allah, Amal, PFLP	EC / CE	1982–93 / 93– ...
	55	Israel	Palästina: PLO/Hamas	DB	1968– ...
	56	Turkey	Kurds, PKK	B / BADF	1970 / 1984– ...
	57	Iran	Kurds, KDPI; Aseri	BA / BAD	Jul 1979–88– ...
	58	Iraq	Kurds, PUK, KDP	BA / BAC / BA+	1976 / 88 / Mar 90– ...
	59	Iraq	Shiits/Shia	AB / CAB / AB	1990 / Mar 1991 / 1991– ...
C Asia	60	Tajikistan	CP, Clans, CIS/Russian troops	EAF+ / EA+	Aug 92–Jun 1993/93– ...
	61	Afghanistan	CP, Pathans, Tajik, Usbek, a.	ABE / BAE+ / EB	1973 / Oct 78 / Apr 92– ...

World region	No.	Country	Nation(alitie)s/ actors	Types of conflicts	Period/phases
	62	Pakistan	Sindhi, MQM, Muhajir, Pashtun	BEF / EF	Nov 1986–1990 / 90– ...
S Asia	63	India	Kashmir: Muslim/Jamu/Ladakh	BE / BAE	1986 / 1990– ...
	64	India	Bihar: Naxalits	A	1988– ...
	65	Sri Lanka	LTTE, Tamils	B / BA+ / BAE+	Jul 83 / Sep 87 / Mar 90–...
	66	Bangla Desh	CHT: Chakma, Shanti Bahini	BAF	1973– ...
	67	NE-India	Tai-Asom, ULFA, Bodo BSF	BEA	1989– ...
SE-Asia	68	NE-India	Naga: RGN, NNC, NSCN	BD / BEA / AB / BA	1954 / 1963 / 1972 / Nov 75 –...
	69	NE-India	Manipur: KNA, NSCN, Meitei	BA / BEA / BAE	1960 / 75 / 84 / May 92– ...
	70	Burma	Karen: KNDO, KNU	BEA / B / BA	1947 / 1950 / 1988– ...
	71	Burma	Mon, NMSP	B / BAE / BA	1962 / 76 / Nov 88–Jun 95
	72	Burma	opium guerrilla: MTA, Wa	EA+ / EFA / FE	1950 / 76 / Mar 1989– ...
	73	Laos	Hmong, LLA, drug war lords	FEC+ / FEA	1970 / 75– ... (?)
	74	Cambodia	Khmer Rouge/Ieng Sary; ANS	A / CA / G / AB / A+	1968 / 70 / 71–75 / 1979– ...
Island Asia	75	Philippines	NPA, Cordillera, CPA, Bontok	AB	1970– ...
	76	Philippines	Mindanao: Moro, MNLF, MILF	BA+ / BA	1970 / 1989–Sep 1996 (?)
	77	Indonesia	Aceh others.	B	May 1990– ...
	78	Indonesia	East-Timor	DBA	Aug 1975– ...
	79	Indonesia	West-Papua, OPM	DGB / DB	1965– ...
Asia-Pacific	80	New Guinea	Bougainville, BRA, BTG	BAD	Feb 1989–Dec 95 / ...

Table 3.9 Number of conflicts by type, divided as primary, secondary, tertiary and as total, 1995–96

Type	A	B	C	D	E	F	G	total
No. of conflicts as dominant type	18	31	3	4	17	5	2	80
No. of conflicts as secondary and tertiary influence	29-9	18-1	3-1	2-3	16-5	7-3	1-0	98
Total	56	50	7	9	38	15	3	178

In the years 1995-96 some 80 conflicts were fought (75 violent conflicts still continued and 5 new conflicts were started); 27 violent conflicts were settled within the 12-year period (in 1985–94 some 102 violent conflicts occurred); in some of these conflicts the end of the war or the ceasefire remained precarious.

Notes

1 Compare: 'Neue Weltordnung: "Dialektik zwischen Orient und Okzident". Ein Gespräch mit Johan Galtung. Groningen. Juli 1990'; in *ECOR Papers* Series no. 3.

2 The two Koreas are the best cases for homogeneity. Japan is also relatively homogenous, with indigenous Ainu, former Korean slave workers, so-called Asian 'comfort women' and migrant communities as relatively small non-Japanese communities. The 'sex slaves' issue had been kept secret, as a result of 'the warrior-macho logic of governments that the suffering of women was outside the responsibility discourse' (Galtung, 1997, 28), ignored by the Tokyo Tribunal, the 1952 Peace Treaty and Peace Treaty with South Korea.

3 A three-volume handbook on ethno-nationalism attempts to avoid the systematic distortion of facts by most belligerent parties through participatory observation (Scherrer, Christian P.: *Ethno-Nationalismus*. Vols 1-3. Münster: *agenda* 1996, 1997, 1998/99, forthcoming). Most case studies are based on first-hand information and field experience. Case studies determined the approach of the Ethnic Conflicts Research Project (ECOR), a research project on ethnicity and conflict resolution started in 1987.

4 Northern states' direct intervention in the South was carried out mostly as (former) colonial power or as intervention power. The country with the highest amount of war involvement was Great Britain (19) followed by France and USA (14 each), USSR/Russia (7) and Turkey (5). Stiftung Entwicklung und

Frieden, SEF: *Global Trends*, 1998. Frankfurt: Fischer, 1997, 369. Tillema compiled interventions for the period 1945–91 (Tillema, Herbert, K., '690 foreign overt military interventions, 1945–1991', in Duyvesteyn, Isabelle: *Wars and Military Interventions since 1945*. *WP* 88/95. Hamburg (AKUF) 1995).

5   Some 38.000 transnational corporations made a turnover of more than 5.500 billion US-$. World trade grew from 10% of world-wide production of goods in 1970 to 25% in 1995 (SEF, 1995, 2).

6   The term *internal conflict* became invalid concerning conflicts about asymmetric resource distribution, economic under-development and ecologically induced conflicts. The latter may well escalate because of global and regional disruption of the natural environment (*green house effect*) or sudden large changes of climate caused by hydro-dams. Dams can be the issue in wars for water in the Middle East (Turkey vs. Syria and Iraq; Israel vs. Lebanon, Syria and Jordan) and in Western Africa (Senegal vs. Mauritania) where there is considerable mixing of ecological issues with ethnic issues.

7   6,267 ethnic groups in 159 countries (1979), numbers given by: Boulding, Elise, 'Ethnic Separatism', in Kriesberg, Louis (ed.), 1979, 276. The *Ethnologue* of SIL/Grimes *et al*. (eds) 1996 listed 6,700 language groups.

8   States of the North were 88 times (of 363 cases) directly involved in wars. SEF, *Global Trends*, 1993, 181.

9   Scherrer, 1997. In this century the number of war-related victims is estimated equal to victims of slaughter. For the period from 1900 Rummel estimated twice the number of 38.5 million victims. Rummel, R.J., 'Power, genocide and mass murder', *Journal of Peace Research* 31(1), 1994, 2-3. A solution which has proved unviable is to register (for the sake of a narrow definition of war) non-war violence such as 'massacres' only if they constitute 'mass murder or exterminatory actions occurring during a war or in close relation to a war' (Gantzel, 1997, 259). As examples Bosnia (1992) and Rwanda (1994) were mentioned!

10 The AKUF data is not collected in field research. Criteria of their compilation are partly outdated and non-operational. The AKUF-register excludes whole sections of contemporary violent conflicts (already analysed by Nietschmann more than a decade ago). See Nietschmann, Bernard: 'Militarization and indigenous peoples', in *Cultural Survival Quarterly* 11(3), Cambridge MA, 1987, 1-16.

11 The AKUF-typology needs further revision and modification to indicate other dominant actors or decisive factors. Ethnicity is seen (by Gantzel) as a 'secondary construct' (*sic*!). In Wiberg's ironic critique Gantzel runs the risk that his 'definition of ethnic conflicts becomes so restrictive that their absence becomes nearly tautological' (Wiberg 1997, pp. 308-12, 311). Lately a research deficit concerning *ethnic* conflicts was acknowledged, and after critics AKUF revised its typology (Gantzel, 1997, 321; Rabehl/Trines, 1997). The definition

of war is still state-centred and expects legitimate state monopolies of violence in force almost everywhere. In the era of state collapse such an approach suffers a loss of credibility.

12 The major difference with the Uppsala/SIPRI list is the issue of including/excluding non-war violence in a list of mass violence. I am not interested in a 'list of armed conflicts'. Concerning the magnitude and salience of non-war mass violence, it is hard to believe that excluding genocide and mass murder would be viable: many of those conflicts which are named 'armed conflicts' are in reality outright slaughter of civilians. I can only repeat again that a critical limitation occurs if compilations exclude non-war types of mass violence. This necessarily results in limited explanatory power! The most obvious reason for that would be that the latter accounts for a higher number of casualties than wars in recent years. For instance, limited warfare starting in 1990 in Rwanda served as a smokescreen for a much larger crime: the extermination of an entire population group.

13 As UN Special Investigator I experienced the consequences of the world's fastest genocide very personally and directly (see Scherrer 1997: *Ethnicization and Genocide in Central Africa*. Ffm/N.Y.: Campus). Statements as the ones that 'the Rwanda genocide ... was part of the war' or 'part of the war aim' (*JPR*, review process 3/1998) are outrageous. This is based on a deeply erroneous definition of genocide as part of warfare, and it banalizes the Rwandan Holocaust. One can only imagine the outcry if the same were claimed to be applicable to the *Shoah* (the Nazi Holocaust against the European Jews).

14 Private armies and *post-modern warfare*: see Shearer 1998. The new journal *Civil War* dedicated a good part of its first issue to that type of warfare (see Jones, C. and C. Kennedy-Pipe, 'Thinking about civil wars'; Nossal, K.R., 'Roland goes corporate: mercenaries and transnational security corporations in the post-Cold War era'; Cerny, P., 'Neo-medievalism and civil war'; and Duffield, M.: 'States and private protection'). But most scholars are still failing to grasp the essence of Non-Clausewitzean warfare. ECOR's typology and conflict list constitutes a substantial improvement compared to most current typologies and 'war lists'. The PIOOM map of conflicts and the mapping based on the ECOR list of violent conflicts are nearly identical, even though elaborated in different ways. Self-reflection and re-evaluation of methods/theories are needed.

15 Some of the frequent clashes between settlers and the indigenous do not have to include criminal elements (at least with no higher participation of criminal actors as in other types of conflicts). However, such conflicts become gang wars and not 'normal' inter-ethnic conflicts because the settlers would often not be grouped together and armed without the support of the state they belong to. Individual settlers conceive indigenous territories as *terra nullius*, as settler states have done for centuries.

16 See Kiernan, Ben (1996) *The Pol Pot Regime: Race, Power, and Genocide in Cambodia under the Khmer Rouge, 1975–79*, New Haven, London: Yale University Press.

17 Regarding genocide in Rwanda, compare: Scherrer, Christian P., *Ethnisierung und Völkermord in Zentralafrika: Genozid in Rwanda, Bürgerkrieg in Burundi und die Rolle der Weltgemeinschaft*. Frankfurt: Campus, 1997; African Rights/Omaar, Rakiya/Waal, Alex de, *Rwanda: Death, Despair and Defiance*, London (African Rights) 9/1994 (revised edition 8/95). Joint Evaluation of Emergency Assistance to Rwanda (JEEAR)/Millwood, David (chief ed.), *The International Response to Conflict and Genocide: Lessons from the Rwanda Experience*, 5 vols, Copenhagen (JEEAR) 3/1996.

18 The perpetrators of genocide in South and Central Sudan are the Sudanese Army and tribal Arab militias. Irregular forces have been armed and recruited by the central governments since the reign of Sadiq al-Mahdi.

19 Mixed types such as AB, BA, BC, CB, AC, CA, AE, EA, ABC, BAC etc. The first mentioned letter indicates the type which in a given period is the dominant type in combination with a less influential secondary type and an even less influential tertiary type.

20 1992 for the first time in history (AKUF, 1993) 50 wars were fought. In 1993, the UNDP register listed 52 *major armed conflicts*. In the same year there were wars in 42 states and violent political conflicts in another 37 states. Gurr's 'Minorities-at-risk' Project identified 50 conflicts for the same year with 70 ethno-political actors involved. According to the ECOR-register, 1985–94, 102 wars were fought; 80 of them continued 1995–96. In the course of 1997 a couple of new conflicts broke out.

21 Gurr identified for 1990 233 minorities at risk in 93 countries, representing nearly a billion people or 17.3% of the world's population (Gurr, 1993, 11). In 1945–49 26 *ethno-political* groups were in conflict; in 1950–59 there were 36 groups; in the 1960s the same number; in 1970-79 the number rose to 55, in the 1980s it reached 62 and 1994 70 ethnic groups were in armed struggle (Gurr, 1994). If all parties and involved ethnic groups were to be counted, their number would be higher. In Burma alone some 20 ethnic groups and other actors are in conflict with the military regime.

22 Cases in Africa: Angola, Zimbabwe, Sudan (unofficially), Namibia and Chad propped-up the faltering government army (dominated by Kabila's Lubakat officers and the Katanga gendarmes as troops) while Uganda, Rwanda, Burundi and the SPLA supported the RCD rebels (dominated by the Banyamulenge). Some of the involved states are only interested to clear the hinterland of their respective insurgencies, e.g. Angola vs. UNITA, Uganda vs. LRA, ADF, and WNB, Rwanda vs. FAR-Interahamwe and Burundi vs. FDD. Some of the dozens of militias and gangs in Congo-DRC struggle in changing alliances with state actors.

In 1996 and 1997 there were several cases: The Angolan military involvement 10/1997 has been giving decisive support for Sassou Nguesso's 'cobra' militia who tried since 6/1997 to seize control over Congo-Brazzaville from the Lissouba government. The intervention of Rwanda and Uganda in 11/1996 helped AFDL-rebels to topple the Mobutu regime in May 1997. Fresh Rwandan troops were last crossing 10/1997 into Congo-Zaire to quell continuing but sporadic warfare. Sudanese State army battalions are fighting an 'endless' civil war in South Sudan and occasionally crossing the borders Northern Uganda 'in hot pursuit' since 1996. The same is true of the Ethiopian EPRDF-army when fighting Ethiopian Somali rebels (Ogadeni) across the border in stateless Southern Somalia 1996/97.

23 In all rules no Third Parties may take immediate part in combat in the case of ethnic conflicts. Exceptions from the rule are such ethno-national conflicts that have earlier been named 'regional conflicts' or proxy wars during the Cold War period (escalated by the intervention of super powers).

24 All successful rebel organizations have or had their hinterland in one or more neighbouring states. This fact will be officially denied by the respective states out of diplomatic necessity. A few states provide resistance movements of neighbouring countries with hinterland depending on political conjuncture and the current state of interests. Such support has a long tradition and even includes criminal organization (organized crime, e.g. drug cartels; terrorist groups; normal delinquency).

25 Quantitative criteria such as 1,000 victims per annum remains a tentative criterion. Contrary to the *Correlates of War Project* and others, AKUF/Gantzel refuse to apply (mechanic) quantitative criteria and followed Istvan Kende's definition of warfare. Indeed, the way Small/Singer apply their criteria shows some inconsistencies of a marked quantitative approach (Gantzel, 1997, 259). Wallenstein/Sollenberg use the 1,000 victims criteria to distinguish *intermediate armed conflicts* (1,000 'battle-related deaths' for the entire course of conflict) and *wars* (during a particular year). The cardinal problem: genocide-related deaths can not be classified as battle-related and are by definition excluded! Victims of the Rwanda genocide (1994) are mentioned but not recorded. In the case of Burundi, large-scale mass violence (massacres 1993 onwards, 50,000 victims in 1993 alone) remains unmentioned and not recorded. To separate figures of battle-related death and slaughter of civilians is in this case extremely problematic and difficult to verify. An appendix contains 'unclear cases'. (Wallenstein/Sollenberg 1997, 339-58; 339; 352, fn 22; 350, fn 18; 355-6).

26 In this century the number of battle-related victims is less than the number of victims of genocide and mass murder. For the period 1900–87 Rummel estimates twice the number of 38.5 million victims. See Rummel, 1994, 2-3.

27 According to Wallensteen/Sollenberg (1997, 340) there was since 1992 an

overall downward trend of armed conflict (excluding non-war types). After the increase to 55 in 1992 (from 51 in 1991 and 49 in 1990) the number of armed conflicts was generally decreasing: first sharply in 1993 to 46, 42 in 1994 and 35 in 1995, finally again slightly increasing to 36 armed conflicts 1996.

PART IIa

ISSUES AT WAR: SOME MAIN KINDS OF ISSUES

4 Terrible Territoriality? Issues in Recent Literature on Conflict over Territory

Tuomas Forsberg

Introduction

Territory, writes William Connolly, derives from the same etymological origin as 'terrible' and 'terror'.[1] Such a view points to the negative aspects of territoriality. Territories are often seen as manifestations of violence, exclusion and power. At the same time, however, territoriality has also traditionally been seen as a solution for the problems of war and violence and its role is essential to the positive values of security and identity.

Indeed, the relationship between territoriality and conflict seems paradoxical. This is why it is not possible to advance any simple account of territoriality. Not only are the etymological roots of 'territory' unclear, but its relationship to conflict still causes many opposing arguments and unexplored questions. In particular, considering the main theme of this volume, we have only a vague understanding of the role of territoriality in intra-state conflicts. At one level the role of territoriality is clear and acknowledged: it is the central stake in secessionist conflicts. But territoriality is an issue in various kinds of intra-state conflicts ranging from boundary disputes between administrative units to territorial gang wars and from competition over marketing areas between firms to gendered conflicts in urban planning over how to create 'secure' or 'functional' places. In this sense, almost every actor has some kinds of territorial interests and almost every conflict has some kind of territorial dimension. Wars – if not territorial – are at least spatial. As Colin Gray has reminded, '[armed] conflict cannot occur beyond geography'.[2] We can quarrel with distant people, but in most cases we can only fight with those who are in our proximity.

In the following I hope to pave the way for future analysis of territoriality in various types of conflicts through a consideration of some central issues in the recent literature on territorial conflict in the field of international relations and international law. I will start with noting the renewed scholarly interest in territorial questions. I will then present some empirical patterns of the relationship between territoriality and conflict. Thirdly, I will consider some theoretical attempts to explain territorial conflict. Finally, I will present the debate over the moral justification of secession. In due course, I will consider what the implications of this literature are for intra-state disputes. In particular, I will discuss the importance of territory for ethnic groups.

The growing interest in space, territory and boundaries

Space, territoriality and boundaries have become an increasingly popular subject. After a relatively silent period during the Cold War geopolitical themes have found their way back to the study of international relations as with many other social sciences as a part of discussions on globalization, neo-nationalism and the collapse of empires. This revival is also distinct from the earlier geopolitical schools and behaviouralist approaches as it is based on the realization that space and social processes are mutually dependent. The view that space is social rather than natural has reminded social scientists that the study of space cannot be left to (physical) geographers.

This earlier lack of interest in territoriality may at first be astonishing when one thinks of the centrality of territoriality for the state-system. As John Ruggie in his infamous article has put it, the neglect of territoriality is 'akin to never looking at the ground that one is walking on'.[3] The body of literature is still deficient in many respects. Conceptually, territoriality has been too closely attached to state sovereignty and nationalism. In David Jacobson's words, 'the association of nations and states with fixed, clearly demarcated territories has been presumed to be so given or even natural that until recently, scholars left the issue of territoriality as implicit, constant like the weather that did not need to be discussed'.[4]

As Ruggie also pointed out, part of the problem with current writings on territoriality is that we lack adequate vocabulary. In fact, the growing amount of literature on territoriality has often contributed to more ambiguous uses of the term than to any consensual understanding of it. In many cases territoriality metaphorically refers to all kinds of restrictions, exclusions or attempts to establish sovereignty without any specification that the basis of restriction, exclusion or sovereignty would be geographical.[5] Among various definitions of territoriality, perhaps the most useful derives from Robert Sack, according to whom territoriality is not any relationship between human beings and their environment but an attempt to affect, influence or control actions by enforcing control over a specific geographical area.[6] Thus ethnic groups, for example, have several kinds of boundaries – both territorial and symbolic that are controlled and which can be exclusive.

In a lot of recent literature, the view is also widespread that territoriality is a mode of governance that stems from the peace of Westphalia. Although the Westphalian system is a paramount case of a territorial organization of power, territoriality is by no means distinctive of modern times, or of advanced modern states. In Grosby's view, it is rather a fundamental feature of all human societies.[7] Against the view that eroding state sovereignty means eroding territoriality, he argues that the significance of territoriality remains a fundamental constitutive element of contemporary societies. Territoriality is a strategy to organize power that goes far beyond the current state system.

Empirical patterns

Are territorial disputes particularly dangerous? Recent literature on conflict and territorial dispute has given empirical support to the view that territorial disputes have been a main reason for inter-state wars. The literature also points to another typical aspect of territorial disputes: they tend to be more long standing than other kinds of disputes.

According to the war statistics of Kalevi Holsti, militarized conflict during the past four centuries has evolved around territorial disputes and another quarter of wars were closely linked to territorial issues.[8] Similarly, Stephen Kocs has found that war initiation depends heavily on the presence or absence of a never-resolved territorial dispute.[9] Hensel points to the same tendency when he argues that disputes over territorial disputes have been much more escalatory than non-territorial disputes.[10] Perhaps even more powerfully, John Vasquez has made the point that territorial disputes are the main issue that has contributed to power politics and wars.[11]

The general finding that territorial disputes are warlike, however, needs some important qualifications. First, although territory has been a main reason for conflict in the past, the share of territory as the cause of violent conflict is in decrease. In Holsti's view there is less willingness to use force to solve territorial disputes than previously. Secondly, some other issues, such as ethnic issues, can be more war-prone than territorial disputes. Moreover, some other characteristics of territorial disputes can be more typical, such as the durability of such disputes. Indeed, many territorial disputes do not escalate into violent conflicts and there are many successful examples of peaceful settlement of territorial conflicts.[12] Finally, because the organization of power in general and the uses of military force are territorial, it is difficult to separate pure territorial conflicts where the point of contest is about territories *per se*. Every issue may become territorial through processes of territorialization that occur when disputes escalate towards military conflict.

There is little literature that would draw a comparable empirical picture of the role of territoriality in intra-state disputes. To name one recent prominent example, the otherwise excellent article by Daniel Byman and Stephen van Evera on the causes of civic violence does not deal with territoriality as a separate factor.[13] In their view the main cause of civic violence is communal hegemonism, which means the aspiration of ethnic, religious, clan or class groups for hegemony over other groups. Although the aspiration for communal hegemony does not necessarily rely on territorial priniciples, it is sometimes strikingly territorial. For example in South Africa an important part of that communal hegemony was the territorial segregation of races or the attempt of it through creating homelands and establishing pass control.

The general view is that disputes over internal boundaries – although they can be contested as often as external boundaries – are considerably easier to solve. For example, in his classic piece on boundaries Eric Fisher makes the point that unlike state borders 'it is relatively easy to change internal boundaries before they have crystallized'.[14] Shared norms, especially the unchallenged respect of the decisions by authorities and common beliefs in administrative effectiveness facilitate the resolution of such conflicts.

Ethnic borders constitute quite a different case as they tend to be much more violent than other kinds of borders. The issue is burning because the number of secessionist conflicts has been steadily increasing since the end of the Cold War while military conflict between states over territory has been rare.[15] Against this background it is important to try to explain why some territorial disputes that emerge are violent. What is it that makes some types of territorial disputes more violent than others?

Ethnicity as a cause of territorial disputes

There are several competing accounts of why territorial disputes emerge and escalate into wars. The first family of explanations likens the explanation of territorial disputes to a rational explanation of conflict in general. At the heart of such explanations is the view that politics consists of a continuous struggle over power. Enlarging one's territory is rational because territories are strategic and economic assets. Changes in power relationships also affect the tendency to claim territories because the stronger one is, the more likely it is that the claim will succeed. In the classical geopolitical paradigm, changes in borders reflected the changes in power relations. This account of the reasons for territorial disputes can also give a plausible explanation as to why the number of severe territorial disputes has been decreasing. The explanation is that the strategic and economic value of territories has radically diminished due to technological development and changes in the modes of production.

The second account of territorial disputes is based on socio-biological assumptions about human beings. The socio-biological view of human territoriality is that human beings have a genetic tendency to mark territories as their own and defend them against intruders. Although many scholars regard such theories as discredited, they are very much alive and in their more sophisticated forms should certainly not be rejected outright. For example, John Vasquez has argued that the predisposition to kill over territory cannot be explained fully without taking into cognizance the similarity of this behaviour with the behaviour of other territorial animals.[16] The socio-biological explanation, however, can only with difficulty explain why certain kinds of territorial disputes are more violent than others or why there are clear historical changes in the number and nature of territorial disputes.

The third way to explain territorial conflicts focuses on the meaning that is given to the territory by the participants of the dispute. As many scholars have underlined, territoriality implies not only the physical but also the social and psychological aspects of space. In order to understand the importance of territory for human beings one must take into account how the land is conceived by the people who live within the territory and the shared significance attributed to these bounded patterns of relationships.[17]

This group of explanations is by no means unitary but refer to a variety of cultural, normative or other ideational factors. For example, because territory is a vital constituent of the identity of a state, states value territory beyond its 'rational' strategic and economic value. Because territory is conceptualized as private property, it has to be protected. A normative explanation of territorial disputes thus holds that territorial claims are often motivated by the sense that a piece of territory rightly belongs to 'us' rather than to those who occupy it at the present. Due to the emphasis that is laid on territorial integrity in international law, territorial issues have a central place in our understanding of what is right and wrong in international politics. Indeed, David Welch suggests that disputes over territory are among the issues that are likely to trigger a sense of injustice most often in international affairs.[18] International norms and subjective views of justice may thus well explain the rise of territorial disputes.[19]

Nevertheless, accurate theoretical models should consider the simultaneous impact of different factors. Paul Huth has recently tried to combine two accounts when he has stated that material and financial resource demands of national security policy do not have a privileged position in comparison to domestic policy needs that are grounded in nationalist sentiments. In his view, while domestic needs often launch and keep the territorial issue on the agenda, material factors constrain decision-makers from escalating the dispute into militarized conflict. In other words, state leaders do not think of strategic gains or are not constrained by the balance of power when they start a dispute over territory, but they act strategically in their decisions as to when and to what level they will escalate a conflict. Domestic political needs will lead them to consider trade-offs and possible conflicts of interest with strictly military security concerns.[20]

The socially constructed aspects of territory have been of special importance for ethnic groups. Anthony Smith argues that *ethnie* always possess ties to a particular locus or territory which they call their own. Territory is important as a point of origin and the object of allegiance. In his view territory is relevant to ethnicity not because it is actually possessed nor even for its 'objective' characteristics of climate, terrain and location but because of an alleged and felt symbiosis between a certain piece of earth and 'its' community. If the people constitute the soul, territory is the body of the collective self. It is the mythical and poetic character of territory described in family narratives, songs, paintings and pieces of literature that are important for ethnic groups. As a result, no direct personal experience is required for a strongly felt tie of identity. Furthermore, although homelands typically entail ideas of 'sacred' places and centres, sites of historical memory or natural beauty, even ordinary landscapes can become significant in the consciousness of ethnic groups.[21] As Yi-Fu Tuan notes, deep attachment to homeland may come 'simply with familiarity and ease', with the memory of sounds and smells or of communal activities and homely pleasures accumulated over time.[22] Although social constructions are always historically changing, ethnic meanings that are attached to territories have proven to be relatively durable.

In particular, territory has been central for many indigenous people over centuries. Often the significance of territory for indigenous people depends on similar reasons than for the ethnic groups. Territory is often very closely linked to their traditional livelihood. They also refer to ideas that the land has been wrongfully taken away or colonized. Yet, in addition to that, they often have an ancient spiritual relationship with land that contains many religious sites.[23] There may be more general sympathy for the land claims of indigenous people than those of ethnic groups in general because the former seldom put forward secessionist claims. Yet the basic issue of whether such apparently mythical value put on territory can be given a legitimate status by other groups who also have interests in the territory remains basically the same.

It has often been the uniting aspect of territoriality that has helped to constitute the feeling of togetherness of an otherwise dispersed ethnic group in the past. At the same time the concept of homeland nevertheless bears seeds of a protracted conflict. Territorial disputes arise when homelands and sacred places are not controlled by the ethnic group that regards them as such. The problem is that ethnic boundaries only seldom coincide with state boundaries and the same place can often be equally sacred for two or more ethnic groups. If another group has a right to reign over the area, it is feared that access to the historical sites can be denied, or they can be destroyed. The mere practice of ethnic rituals on one's territory can be viewed as a hostile act because it is seen as a symbolic occupation of the territory of the other side. For example, the division of Belfast according to ethnic lines denies the Orange order to march their traditional parade through a Catholic neighbourhood, but giving them such a right would leave the Catholic population with the impression that they are not at home where they live.

For aforementioned reasons territory is valuable for most if not all ethnic minorities but the role of territory becomes crucially important when ethnicism develops into (ethno-)nationalism. As Colin Williams and Anthony Smith argue, for 'whatever it may be, nationalism always involves a struggle for land, or an assertion about rights to land'. If nations aim at building a state of their own, they have to focus on territory. Hence, 'the nation, almost by definition, requires a territorial base in which to take root and fulfil the needs of its members'. Nationalist ideologies put emphasis on many issues that have a strong emotional loading, but the trouble with the nationalist concept of territories is that it often serves as a rhetorical justification for territorial expansion and 'ethnic cleansing' – the positive attitude towards a particular territory becomes a negative attitude towards other people. Nationalist state building also leads to the 'hardening' of space as it involves attempts to eliminate all twilight zones and interstices between compact, clearly bounded national states.[24] This imagined homogenization of space in nationalist ideology has thus led to the situation where changes in external boundaries are extremely crucial from a number of perspectives, whereas changes in internal boundaries bear only a minor significance.

Although the relationship between nationalism and territorial conflict is well established, it is nevertheless not necessarily that simple. Some nationalist movements put more emphasis on culture than on territory.[25] And it is futile to interpret all territorial aspirations as a manifestation of some belligerent and exclusive nationalist ideology. Indeed, it is not entirely clear why territorial rights should be more difficult to accept than cultural rights. Territories can not be stripped of all the meanings that people have given to them. The question is rather how territorial identities can be accommodated with other needs.

Self-determination and the right to secede

The international community has devoted a great amount of attention to territorial disputes and to consideration of what is the best way to deal with them. The main issue at stake – which has usually overridden other concerns has been the preservation of stability. In the post-Second World War era the trend has been clearly in favour of the status quo and against peaceful changes of territories. Decolonization was an exemption – clearly restricted by the salt water principle; otherwise attempts to change boundaries of current states have been discouraged. The trend has been to create ways that get the challenger to drop the territorial claims rather than building mechanisms that would facilitate peaceful change of territories.

Justifications of territorial changes do not have any widely shared source. The apparent problem in dealing with different nationalist claims on territorial control is not the denial that territorial injustices would not have happened, but the practical difficulties that are involved in every attempt to restore historic borders. Moreover, the ideology of historic homelands is often based on flimsy historical evidence. Furthermore, any doctrine of natural frontiers of a nation or ethnic group is often regarded as even more suspect. It is often argued that the problem with democratic theory is that it does not propose any solution to the question as to how the boundaries of the unit of democracy should be determined.[26] This view gives a basis for the argument that no redrawing of territorial boundaries can be defended by democratic values.

Among the three main bases of territorial claims natural borders, history and self-determination it is the last that has been given most attention recently. Self-determination is a contested principle, the status of which has varied in the course of the history from reluctant acceptance to anxious promotion.[27] In the Cold War era the prevalent view was that the right of self-determination should have strict limits of application. By the same token, international law has given only little if any support to secessionist claims. Yet, in the view of Lawrence Eastwood, secessionist rights have been developing in the post-Cold War era due to the dissolution of the Soviet Union and Yugoslavia.[28]

The scepticism of the international community and the majority of scholars towards secession has nevertheless remained strong. The right to self-determination has been in vogue, but the point of contest has been the question of whether self-determination can be extended to territorial claims. For some, any idea of self-determination is only a hollow shell if it excludes the possibility of secession but for others there is no necessary link between self-determination and territorial secession. As Allen Buchanan and Diana Orentlicher have stated, there is an urgent need for coherent international principles and procedures concerning secession as the international community has failed to develop a principled response to secessionist movements.[29]

Liberalism is often seen as a political philosophy that gives a robust right to secede that is grounded in the idea of political self-determination.[30] According to its logic authority must be based on consent: state is a social contract and not an organism. It follows that if there is a right for individuals to exit, there must be a right for a group to secede. Logically, this liberal view of the voluntary agreement of the group means that such groups can have many reasons for their wish to secede and it can be heterogeneous as to its characteristics. Another competing view of self-determination is that it can be promoted only on the basis of certain characteristics that the seceding group must have, such as a common history or distinctive culture. Such ideology makes a clear distinction between national self-determination that includes a right to territory and independent statehood and cultural self-determination that includes only a right to certain autonomy in cultural matters. Few people can enjoy the former whereas many the latter.

The opposition to self-determination refers typically to the negative consequences of such a right – not to the inherent moral character of the principle. For example, Amitai Etzioni's view is that it is time to withdraw moral approval from most of the separatist movements, as they are destructive. He expects that the principle of self-determination hinders economic development by increasing fragmentation instead of integration and undermines democratic principles by strengthening national extremist forces.[31]

The right to secede does not, however, mean that all possible groups would secede. On the contrary, Dietrich Murswiek has argued that the best precaution against secession is a right to secession.[32] Indeed, in Christopher Wellmann's opinion, it is difficult to deny such a fundamental right merely on the basis of projected detrimental consequences. He argues that consequences are detrimental only if the right is unlimited. Therefore he suggests that any group may secede as long as it and its possible state are large, wealthy, cohesive and geographically contiguous enough to form a government that effectively performs the functions necessary to create a secure political environment. Precisely what the size and nature of the group must be can be determined only on a case-by-case basis. Nevertheless, such groups have a primary right to secede even in the absence of past injustices.[33]

For others, however, secession should be considered only a possibility of last resort, instead of a primary right it is a remedial right. In Daniel Philpott's view any group of individuals has a prima facie right to self-determination. Yet, secession should be endorsed only when a people would remain exposed to great cruelty, if left with a weaker form of self-determination.[34] Buchanan argues that a group has a right to secede only if the physical survival of its members is threatened by actions of the state or if its previously sovereign territory was unjustly taken by the state. A regime of international law that recognized a right to secede in the absence of any injustices would encourage even just states to act in ways that would prevent groups from becoming claimants to the right to secede. This might thus lead to the perpetration of injustices.[35]

The mainstream proposal for solving ethnic conflicts is that self-determination should and can be promoted without changing borders or creating new ones.[36] For example Patrick Thornberry thinks that it is more productive to start from the rules of basic human rights.[37] Gidon Gottlieb argues that the principle of self-determination must be supplemented by a new scheme that is less territorial in character and more regional in its scope. Such an approach would, however, entail granting of functional spaces and national home regimes in historical lands but it would not be based on sovereign geographical units delimited by single lines.[38]

Agreement on the right to secede does not yet determine the territorial boundaries within which a group may secede. If territorial secession seems inevitable or has become an actuality, the international community has supported the principle of *uti possidetis*, according to which the borders of the new state should be the same as the borders of the prior administrative unit. This seems to pose least problems. Steven Ratner has recently argued that this principle is nevertheless highly suspect, because of the differences between internal and international borderlines. Internal boundaries have been drawn in order to unify the polity whereas external borders are meant to separate them. Moreover, in his view the principle of *uti possidetis* is at odds with current principles of international law. He suggests that there are rational reasons for line-drawing, such as the age of the border, the process by which it has been drawn and the creation of viable entities. Moreover, peaceful settlements based on an agreement between the participants should be respected by the third parties. Finally, despite a number of problems related to the execution of plebiscites, such models could be reassessed.[39] Contrary to the prevalent received wisdom, Lawrence Fairley has argued that when plebiscites have been executed, they seldom fail.[40]

The empirical record concerning secession and partition, or mechanisms and principles upon which they are based, such as plebiscites, is ambivalent and can be interpreted in many ways. Analysing such historical cases in greater depth and systematizing these findings is certainly one field where more work needs to be done as current discussion often has only a thin empirical basis. The Quebecois question, for example, certainly does not have the same background and implications as, say, the Kurdish question or the question of Russian minorities in the former Soviet republics.

Finally one has to bear in mind that territorial issues – although they are distinctive are seldom the only reason for violent conflicts nor is their solution alone sufficient to resolve such conflicts. Violent conflict does not emerge when new states are created, nor does partition stop it. For example Eritreans had border clashes with the Tigrean nationalist movement before they gained their independence. On the other hand the partition of Czechoslovakia did not lead to any severe territorial conflict. Although principles are needed, they have to be contextual. It is inevitable that borders always both create and solve problems, and there are different ways of defining their course and functions.

To sum up, the principle of self-determination and its secessionist implications remain a difficult and contested issue within the liberal political theory. A broad consensus exists that there should be a right to self-determination and that secession cannot be regarded as an unlimited right, but there is no consensus when secessions should be acceptable and when not. On the one hand, promoting secessionist movements causes fragmentation and instability, on the other hand, denying such a right is difficult considering the liberal normative framework upon which international politics otherwise rests.

Conclusions

Disputes that revolve around territorial issues involve considerable risks. The received wisdom is that inter-state territorial disputes are often violent but that intra-state territorial disputes are warlike only when they are supported by ethno-nationalist arguments and entail claims of secession. Such disputes are difficult to solve by peaceful means because the mythical and sacred elements of homelands are extremely pivotal to the identity of ethnic groups. There are a number of ways to solve territorial conflicts, but scepticism of territorial changes has been the prevalent tendency. The dilemma is, however, that sharing territorial rights is not possible when territory is seen in terms of sovereignty. Yet, attempts to convert territorial rights to general human rights or extended cultural autonomy does not do full justice to the territorial needs many ethnic and other groups have.

Notes

1 William Connolly, *The Ethos of Pluralization*, Minneapolis: The University of Minnesota Press, 1995, p. xxii. According to Ayto territory derives from a different Indo-European origin than terror, namely from *tersa* which simply means dry land as opposed to sea and is the same root word thirst. Terror in turn derives from the Indo-European word *tre* which means to shake. John Ayto, *Dictionary of Word Origins*, London: Bloomsbury, 1990, p. 525
2 Colin S. Gray, 'The Continued Primacy of Geography', *Orbis* 40(2), 1996, pp. 247-259.
3 John Ruggie, 'Territoriality and beyond: Problematizing Modernity in International Relations', *International Organization* 47(1), Winter 1993, pp. 139-174.
4 David Jacobson, 'New Frontiers: Territory, Social Spaces, and the State', *Sociological Forum* 12(1), 1997, 121-133.
5 See e.g. the concept of territoriality in Gilles Deleuze and Felix Guattari, *A Thousand Plateaus*, London: The Athlone Press, 1988.
6 Robert Sack, *Human Territoriality*, Cambridge: Cambridge University Press, 1986. See also Tuomas Forsberg, 'Beyond Sovereignty, Within Territoriality. Mapping the Space of Late-Modern (Geo)Politics', *Cooperation and Conflict* 31(4), 1996, pp. 355-386.
7 Steven Grosby, 'Territoriality: The Transcendental, Primordial Feature of Modern Societies', *Nations and Nationalism* 1(2), 1995, pp. 143-162.
8 Kalevi Holsti, *Peace and War: Armed Conflict and International Order 1648–1989*, Cambridge: Cambridge University Press, 1991.
9 Stephen A. Kocs, 'Territorial Disputes and Interstate War 1945–1987', *The Journal of Politics* 57(1), 1995, 159-175.
10 Paul Hensel, 'Charting a Course to Conflict: Territorial Issues and Interstate Conflict, 1816–1992', *Conflict Management and Peace Science* 15(1), 1996, pp. 43-73.
11 John Vasquez, *The War Puzzle*, Cambridge: Cambridge University Press, 1993.
12 See e.g. Gudrun Schwarzer, 'Friedliche Konfliktregulierung: Saarland – Österreich – Berlin', *Zeitschirft für internationale Beziehungen* 1(2), 1994, pp. 243-277.
13 Daniel Byman and Stephen Van Evera, 'Hypotheses on the Causes of Contemporary Deadly Conflict', *Security Studies* 7(3), 1998, pp. 1-50.
14 Eric Fisher, 'On Boundaries', *World Politics* 1(2), 1949, pp. 196-222.
15 Alexis Heraclides, 'Secessionist Conflagration. What Is to Be Done?', *Security Dialogue* 25(3), 1993, pp. 283-293.
16 Vasquez, *The War Puzzle*, p. 294.
17 See e.g. Grosby 'Territorialaity', and Friedrich Kratochwil, Paul Rohrlich and Harpreet Mahajan, *Peace and Disputed Sovereignty. Reflections on Conflict*

over Territory, Lanham: University Press of America, 1985, p. 53.

18 David Welch, *Justice and the Genesis of War*, Cambridge: Cambridge University Press, 1993.

19 Tuomas Forsberg, 'Explaining Territorial Disputes: From Power Politics to Normative Reasons', *Journal of Peace Research* 33(4), 1996, pp. 433-450; see also Masato Kimura and David Welch, 'Specifying "Interests": Japan's Claim to the Northern Territories and Its Implications for International Relations Theory', *International Studies Quarterly* 42(2) 1998, pp. 213-244.

20 Paul K. Huth, *Standing Your Ground. Territorial Disputes and International Conflict*, Ann Arbor: The University of Michigan Press, 1996.

21 Anthony D. Smith, *The Ethnic Origin of Nations*, Oxford: Basil Blackwell, 1986, p. 28.

22 Yi-Fu Tuan, *Space and Place. The Perspective of Experience*, Minneapolis: The University of Minnesota Press, 1977, p. 159.

23 David Knight, 'Self-Determination for Indigeneous Peoples: The Context for Change', in R.J. Johnston, David Knight and Eleonore Kofman (eds), *Nationalism, Self-Determination and Political Geography*, London: Croom Helm, 1988.

24 Anthony D. Smith, 'States and Homelands: the Social and Geopolitical Implications of National Territory', *Millennium* 10(3), 1981, pp. 187-201; Colin Williams and Anthony D. Smith, 'The National Construction of Social Space', *Progress in Human Geography* 7(4), 1983, pp. 502-517.

25 Yael Tamir, *Liberal Nationalism*, Princeton: Princeton University Press, 1993.

26 Frederick Whelan, 'Prologue: Democratic Theory and the Boundary Problem', in J. Roland Pennock and John Chapman (eds), *Liberal Democracy* XXV, New York: New York University Press, 1983.

27 Morton Halperin and David Scheffee with Patricia Small, *Self-Determination in the New World Order*, Washington: Carnegie Endowment for Peace, 1992.

28 Lawrence Eastwood, 'Secession: State Practice and International Law after the Dissolution of the Soviet Union and Yugoslavia', *Duke Journal of Comparative and International Law* 3(2), 1993, 299-349.

29 Allen Buchanan, 'Self-Determination, Secession, and the Rule of Law', in Robert McKim and Jeff McMahan (eds), *The Morality of Nationalism*, New York: Oxford University Press, 1997; Diana Orentlicher, 'Separation Anxiety: International Responses to Ethno-Separatist Claims', *Yale Journal of International Law* 23(1), 1998, pp. 1-78.

30 For a liberal analysis of territorial rights see, Hillel Steiner, 'Territorial Justice', in Simon Caney, David George and Peter Jones (eds), *National Rights, International Obligations*, Boulder: Westview Press, 1996.

31 Amitai Etzioni, 'The Evils of Self-Determination', *Foreign Policy* 89, 1992–93, pp. 21-35.

32 Dietrich Murswiek, 'The Issue of a Right of Secession – Reconsidered', in

Christian Tomuschat (ed.), *Modern Law of Self-Determination*, Dordrecht: Martinus Nijhoff, 1993, p. 39.

33 Christopher Wellman, 'A Defense of Secession and Political Self-Determination', *Philosophy and Public Affairs* 24(2), 1995, pp. 357-372.

34 Daniel Philpott, 'In Defense of Self-Determination', *Ethics* 105, 1995, pp. 352-385.

35 Allen Buchanan, 'Theories of Secession', *Philosophy and Public Affairs* 26(1), 1997, pp 31-61.

36 See e.g. John Coakley, 'Approaches to the Resolution of Ethnic Conflict: The Strategy of Non-territorial Autonomy', *International Political Science Review* 15(3), 1994, pp. 297-314.

37 Patrick Thornberry, 'Self-Determination, Minorities, Human Rights: A Review of International Instruments', *International and Comparative Law Quarterly* 38(4), 1989, pp. 867-889.

38 Gidon Gottlieb, *Nation Against State. New Approaches to Ethnic Conflicts and the Decline of Sovereignty*, New York: Council of Foreign Relations Press, 1994, pp. 44-47.

39 Steven Ratner, 'Drawing a Better Line: Uti Possidetis and the Borders of New States', *American Journal of International Law* 10(4), 1996, pp. 590-624.

40 Lawrence Fairley, *Plebiscites and Sovereignty. The Crisis of Political Illegitimacy*, Boulder: Westview Press, 1986.

5 The Role of Development and Environmental Change in Conflict Processes

WENCHE HAUGE

Introduction

Civil wars have become increasingly common ever since the end of World War II. Up to the mid-1970s this tendency could be explained as mirroring the expansion of independent states in the international system, but from then on the number of civil wars has increased much faster then has the number of newly independent states. True, since 1993 there has been a decrease in civil wars.[1] On the other hand, the 1990s seem likely to emerge as the worst decade for a full two centuries, in terms of civil war, because of the extremely high level during the first half of the decade.[2]

There is also another clear pattern: most civil wars after World War II have taken place in poor and developing countries. Although there were many internal conflicts active during the Cold War, it is only recently that the world's attention has been directed fully towards the many long-lasting, painful and recurrent conflicts in the developing countries. Some of the developing countries are oil-rich, but most of them are low- or lower-middle income countries, by World Bank criteria,[3] with agriculture responsible for a relatively high share of their GDP. A few high- and upper-middle income countries, which are oil-rich states, are still considered as developing by the UN criterion, which is that they are not industrialized.

Latin America was the most war-prone region from 1945 to 1960. In the 1960s and 1970s the picture changed, as most of the intrastate wars took place in South and East Asia, only to be surpassed by Africa in the period from 1980 to 1992. In this regional distribution of civil wars, based on a criterion of 1,000 battle-related deaths, Europe is almost totally absent.[4]

There is a vast and diverse academic literature on the study of conflict causation and conflict processes. However, given the clear pattern of upsurge of conflicts in the Third World after World War II, we should question the relevance of some of this literature. Much of it fails to address properly, if at all, the crucial issue of the role of development and natural resources in conflict processes.

Missing Links in Conflict Research

Most conflict researchers acknowledge the principle of multicausality in theory, but few adhere fully to the principle in their practical research. Thus much of the literature on causes and dynamics of conflicts is constructed around one or two dimensions of the societies in focus, such as political system and regime type or ethnic cleavages and ethnic politics. More recently, studies of the role of renewable resources in internal conflicts have come to constitute another such type of literature. Studies of domestic inequality and income distribution would be yet another one.

While this literature has contributed much to our understanding of civil conflicts, it also has obvious weaknesses. One of these weaknesses has been noted above: that the fields of research are not well enough integrated with each other. Another weakness is that some important dimensions are almost totally absent – and one of these dimensions is development. Whereas several studies address the implications of income inequality and internal distribution for political violence, there are very few that analyze the role of countries' economic frameworks for development and how this affects conflict propensities and conflict processes.

Environmental Change and Conflict

Stretching the security concept to include the environment has received considerable attention and resulted in a vast literature. The debate became particularly intense with the end of the Cold War and the ensuing search for a new security paradigm.[5] Much of this literature is, not surprisingly, politically motivated, focused on international relations and interstate conflicts. It has little to offer the study of internal armed conflicts.

However, there is also a growing academic literature focusing on links between environmental stress and internal conflicts/civil war. Numerous statements and findings within this literature have indicated that struggles over access to and control over natural resources have been an important cause of tension and conflict.[6]

Still, there is no consensus on this issue. Much of the criticism, targeted in particular against the work of Thomas Homer-Dixon and his colleagues, has centered around concepts, methodology, and lack of theoretical framework.[7]

The Concept of Environmental Scarcity

The work of Thomas Homer-Dixon and his colleagues has been central in recent academic debates about the relationship between renewable resources and conflict. On the basis of a series of case-studies – among them South Africa, Chiapas (Mexico), Rwanda, Pakistan and Gaza – Homer-Dixon concludes that degradation and depletion of renewable resources contribute to domestic armed conflict. The clearly defined methodology as well as the development of new concepts and models in the case-studies has created a new basis for debate within this field.

Environmental scarcity is the core concept in Homer-Dixon's work. This concept has three dimensions: supply-induced scarcity, demand-induced scarcity, and structural scarcity.[8] Supply-induced scarcity exists when resources are being reduced and degraded more rapidly then they are renewed. Demand-induced scarcity is created by population growth or increased per capita activity. Finally, an inequitable distribution of resources may take place when the resources are concentrated in the hands of a few people while the rest of population suffers from resource shortages.

Increased environmental scarcity, viewed in terms of some or all the above mentioned dimensions, is argued to have several consequences, which in turn lead to civil conflict. Important intervening variables between environmental scarcity and conflict are decreased agricultural production, decreased economic activity, migration and weakened states.

Homer-Dixon is also concerned with the context in which environmental scarcity operates, referring for example to ecosystem vulnerability and in general to political, social and economic context. However, his main focus is on how environmental scarcity affects economy and politics, not vice versa. Thus there is a lack of questioning about possible spurious effects, or of the relative importance[9] of environmental change, compared to for example economic and political factors.

The concept of environmental scarcity has obvious weaknesses. A post-modern criticism, as carried out by Ronnie Lipschutz,[10] is critical to the notion of 'scarcity' when it, as here, is linked to environmental resources. *Nature* is not 'scarce'. Scarcity is a matter of definition and a man-made phenomenon, linked to factors such as power politics and distribution as well as to the drawing of boundaries and to international conditions and politics.

Lumping together environmental degradation, population issues and politics of distribution into a concept labeled 'environmental scarcity' may serve to distract attention from poverty, from economic structures, and from politics. Why? Both because much depends on which of these dimensions are focused most intensely on in the case-studies, and also because of possible spurious effects, for example from economic conditions. The tendency to an unbalanced focus can be seen in Homer-Dixon's work. Whereas population growth is referred to frequently in all the case-studies, little mention is made of, for example, their generally low energy consumption. Low energy consumption usually indicates a poor country. Thus, in analyzing the role of environmental change in conflicts of these countries, we will also need to address the role of their general economic framework for development.

The lack of questioning about the relative importance of environmental scarcity as well as the use of methodology has given rise to the sharpest criticisms against the work of Homer-Dixon and his colleagues.[11] In the case-studies there is no variation, in the independent nor in the dependent variable. The cases chosen are countries which experience both environmental stress and civil conflict. Thus there is a lack of control.

The Relative Importance of Environmental Change

Seeking to address some of the challenges noted above, Hauge & Ellingsen[12] carried out a quantitative study which covers the period 1980–92 and includes economic, environmental, political and population variables. The independent variables included were as follows: deforestation, land degradation freshwater per capita, population density, regime type, regime stability, GNP per capita, and income inequality. The analysis was carried out with two different dependent variables or datasets on conflict/civil war.[13] For civil war, the Correlates of War dataset was used.[14] The Correlates of War project operates with a threshold of at least 1,000 battle-deaths per year for a war to be registered, whereas the other conflict dataset, Wallensteen & Sollenberg,[15] operates with a threshold of 25 battle-deaths in the course of one year.

What are the main conclusions to be drawn from our logistic regression analysis? In relationship to civil war and to small-scale conflict, soil degradation and freshwater scarcity are found to have an effect, also when we control for economic development, income inequality, regime type, regime stability and population density. Of these two environmental variables, soil degradation has the strongest and clearly most significant effect. Deforestation also has an effect on armed conflict, but this is significant only when small-scale conflicts are included. High population density has a significant effect on civil war, and the effect becomes more pronounced when small-scale conflicts are included.

Although both degradation of renewable resources and high population density have an effect on small-scale conflict as well as on civil war, also when economic and political variables are controlled for, it is GNP per capita that has the strongest and most significant effect on both of the dependent variables. The lower the GNP per capita, the greater the propensity both to small-scale conflict and to civil war. GNP per capita is followed in importance by land degradation, which also has a strong effect on small-scale conflict and on civil war. However, when we turn to low freshwater availability per capita, we find it has a greater effect than regime type on small-scale conflict, but not on civil war. Also the effect of deforestation exceeds that of regime type for small-scale conflict. In general, we see that the environmental variables have greater effect on small-scale conflict than on civil war.

The results of the logistic regression indicate first and foremost that links between various indicators of economic development and conflict/civil war should be further explored. Many developing countries also share characteristics such as a high commodity concentration in export and a high external debt; moreover, many of them have undergone periods of liberalization and economic reform programs. However, the result of the statistics also underlines the complexity of the problm. It is necessary to analyze the relationships between and among economic, political, environmental, and population factors in the process that leads to conflict and civil war.

Economic Development and Civil War

Whereas there are several studies of links between income inequality, internal distribution and political violence, little work has been done on the relationship between economic development (as defined earlier) and armed conflict. And despite the many analyses of links between internal distribution patterns and conflict, there is no consensus on the issue.[16]

Part of the problem with these analyses as well as with Homer-Dixon's model, where distribution of land is included, is that they are not seen in relation to the economic structure and level of development of the country/ies in question. When focusing on distribution, for example, we need to know how important agriculture is to the national economy, how large a portion of the population is employed in agriculture, and what other employment possibilities exist within a particular country.

A country's export structure may have implications for the use of land, and thus also for the distribution of land. Subsistence peasants, small-scale farmers, and indigenous populations often lose out in the fight for good arable land, when a country needs foreign exchange from export and the authorities pursue an agricultural policy favoring large and productive landholdings/cash-crops, logging, mining and cattle industry. Mexico (Chiapas) and Brazil are two examples of this.[17]

Within the academic literature on conflict, development is a missing link. Some quantitative studies on the relationship between economic development and conflict have been carried out, but without a well-founded theoretical framework.[18] Economic growth is often used as a control variable in statistical analyses, but without comprehensive theoretical reasoning to back it up.

An important part of the problem is that the field of development studies and the field of conflict studies have been relatively isolated from each other. Furthermore, there has been a general crisis or a vacuum in development theory since the period of modernization theory and dependency theory, which represented the most important schools and also the two extremes within development theory. The vacuum concerns the more holistic and coherent theorizing on development, since there has not been a lack of partial and more fragmented theories.[19] Any serious effort to link development studies with conflict studies therefore will have to include some of the theories related to modernization, dependency and underdevelopment, where these theories offer conclusions relevant to political stability and violence.

A Dynamic Model

Not all of the theorists who stress the importance of socio-economic change to civil conflict can be placed within the modernization tradition. Theories of modernization, however, have played an important role in the academic debate on development and to a certain degree also in the academic debate about political violence and internal war.

One central feature of modernization theory is the firm belief in the direction of the development process: it is seen as starting with traditional societies and ending with modernized (i.e. industrialized) societies. For the study of civil conflict, the interesting aspect concerns the theory arguments about the consequences of this process.

The Feierabends[20] classify nations into three groups: modern societies, traditional societies and modernizing societies, in which the latter are seen as passing through the stage from traditional society to modernity. The period of transition is regarded as a period of considerable strain and tension and thus is the period most likely to bring about political violence and civil conflict. This view is also held by Huntington.[21] In contrast to some of the optimism among other modernization theorists, Huntington underlines the destabilizing effects of transition and indicates the contrasting stability of both underdeveloped and developed societies. Whereas both traditional and modern societies are stable, transitional societies are seen as highly unstable. Huntington's principal thesis is that major violence and instability is 'in large part the product of rapid social change and the rapid mobilization of new groups into politics coupled with the low development of political institutions'.[22]

Socio-economic change and social mobilization are closely linked in the modernization process. Huntington describes the economic aspects of modernization as 'Diversification of activities as a few simple occupations give way to many complex ones; the level of occupational skill rises significantly; the ratio of capital to labor increases; subsistence agriculture gives way to market agriculture; and agriculture itself declines in significance compared to commercial, industrial and other non-agricultural activities'.[23] Social mobilization comes as a consequence of changes in people's attitudes, values and expectations, from those associated with the traditional world to those common to the modern world. This again comes as a consequence of increased literacy, education, communications, mass media exposure and urbanization – processes closely linked to economic development.

Huntington holds a positive view of modernity itself. Rather, it is the *process* of modernization that is problematic. Whereas modernity breeds stability, modernization breeds instability. Poverty, or low level of economic development as such, is not a cause of instability and violence. With reference to the 1960s, Huntington thus argues that the causes of violence in modernizing nations lay not in their 'backwardness', but in the modernization process itself. 'Wealthier nations tend to be more stable than those less wealthy, but the poorest nations, those at the bottom of the international economic ladder, tend to be less prone to violence and instability than those countries just above them.'[24]

A Static Model

In contrast to the modernization theorists, who focus on the process of change towards modern societies, other scholars have focused more on relatively permanent structures and the level of development. Rapkin & Avery[25] have constructed a model of world markets and domestic political instability which sees domestic political instability as produced by sudden shocks and gradual effects originating in world commodity and capital markets. The effects of instabilities originating in world markets are mediated by levels of domestic economic and political development in Third World countries. In monocultures for example, or in countries depending on export income from just a few commodities, falling prices on the world market may have major consequences for the economy.

In Rapkin & Avery's research, linkages between economic and political instabilities serve as an umbrella concept under which a variety of more specific relationships are hypothesized to be active. They identify two broad categories of linkage: (1) domestic consequences – both economic and political, issuing from exposure to volatility in world markets for the goods and commodities which developing countries export and import. (2) domestic consequences – stemming from participation in world markets for capital, technology, and other factors of production.

The authors distinguish between the different manifestations of political instability on the part of the masses and on the part of the elites. This distinction is useful, they argue, because certain types of economic instabilities may catalyze a mass response, whereas other types may trigger an elite response.

External Factors, Domestic Dynamics and Civil Conflict

Rapkin & Avery have managed to incorporate the interaction between world markets (both commodity and capital) and domestic structures (both political and economic) in their model, which gives it credibility – but their model fails to focus on the interaction between the domestic structures in the process that leads to conflict. This is a problem that Rapkin & Avery are aware of: 'Nor are we postulating deterministic external causes to the point of excluding or under-emphasizing internal causal factors. A complete explanation of political and economic instabilities will have to account for both internal and external causes, as well as for *the interaction between the two*'.[26]

Huntington, by contrast, is concerned with the mismatch between socio-economic change and the development of political institutions in response to growing social mobilization, but does not consider external factors at all. This is a major weakness in his theory. The developing countries have gradually become more and more integrated into the world economy. Domestic socio-economic change is very much linked to international economic structures and how these behave. Suffice it here to mention falling prices on primary commodities – still crucial to the economy of many developing countries – such as coffee, cotton and rice; the debt crisis with ensuing payment difficulties for many poor countries and consequently also dependence on the international financial institutions, the IMF and the World Bank for new credit and for postponing of debt repayment.[27]

In a quantitative study covering the period 1980–92, Hauge & Hegre[28] tested out Huntington's dynamic model and Rapkin & Avery's static model on outbreaks of civil war. The Correlates of War dataset[29] was used for outbreaks of civil war. Agriculture's annual share of GDP (in percent) was used to measure the level of economic development, and the annual change in agriculture's share of GDP was used to measure change in economic development (alternatively modernization/industrialization). Stable political rights was used as a control variable, and fall in income from primary commodities was included to account for the external factors in Rapkin & Avery's model.

The result of the logistic regression gave no support to Huntington's theory but supported Rapkin & Avery's model. Fall in export income from primary commodities was found to have a very clear and significant effect on outbreak of civil war. Although this analysis needs to be rerun with more data, the result creates a basis for some preliminary research questions.

Huntington's modernization theory from 1968 seems to have little explanatory relevance for the civil wars of the 1980s and 1990s. This is contrary to theoretical directions which stress the importance of change, both economic and social, to political violence. Are there any plausible explanations for this finding? And why are, on the other hand, low levels of economic development so highly correlated with conflict?

Part of the explanation might be that, even when there is growth and socio-economic change in many of the developing countries, this is seldom enough to change economic structures and bring them out of the vicious circle of high commodity concentration, low sectoral diversification, high external debt and the comcomitant pressure on and degradation of natural and renewable resources – which in the next round strikes back at the economy. Most African and Asian countries are still low- and lower-middle income countries by World Bank criteria, whereas the Asian NICs and some Latin American countries are more of an exception than the rule. Moreover, recent developments in parts of Asia and particularly in Indonesia seem to indicate that the economic future in this region is not overly bright.

Rapkin & Avery focus both on commodity markets and capital markets and their relationship to armed conflict. Whereas conflict research has paid scant attention to links between international commodity markets and domestic conflict, the linkages between participation in markets for capital, technology and other factors of production and conflict have been subjected to some study. Walton & Seddon[30] have examined the relationship between widespread popular unrest in the cities of the developing world and the process of economic and social transformation which is associated with a renewed emphasis on liberalization and the promotion of free markets on a global scale over the past two decades. Walton & Seddon use the concept 'austerity protests', which they define as large-scale collective actions including political demonstrations, general strikes, and riots, which are animated by grievances over state policies of economic liberalization implemented in response to the debt crisis and market reforms urged by international agencies through the structural adjustment programs.[31] They find that several of these riots have been directly triggered by food and transport prices rising almost overnight.

Mass layoffs of civil servants have also triggered off riots and strikes on several occasions. Cuts in official expenditures is among the central conditionalities in the economic reform programs of the IMF and the World Bank. Walton & Seddon find that so far most of the austerity riots have taken place in cities of Latin America and North Africa, although they have registered some in Asian and in Central and Eastern European cities as well. The recent economic crisis in Indonesia, which forced President Suharto to resign, indicates that these problems are now also becoming serious in parts of Asia.

Walton & Seddon's work concentrates on riots, a clearly urban phenomenon. Auvinen[32] has looked into the relationship between several socio-political and economic indicators and various types of political conflict in an early warning context. While he found that the link between IMF intervention and political conflict in general was weak, he also found that 'a history of IMF intervention' was associated with all forms of political conflict in his nine year average dataset. This means that the number of former IMF arrangements and high conditionality are crucial for the occurrence of both political protest and civil conflict.

In general, both Walton & Seddon's conclusions and Auvinen's findings indicate that more work needs to be done in this field as well as on the relationship between commodity markets and domestic conflict. The theory basis for this work also need to be elaborated further and linked to other fields of conflict research.

Separate Research Fields and Lack of Control

In this chapter I have sought to link the role of environmental change to the role of economic development in the analysis of armed conflict. Although the principle of multicausality is widely accepted, research fields within this area still lead largely separate lives. In the future, studies on links between economic and environmental conditions and conflict will have to be placed within the larger context of conflict research. One obvious related field here is research on the relationship between political conditions and conflict.

There is a vast literature studying links between regime types, regime change, democratization and conflict. Most theories on the relationship between democracy and political violence lean towards the view that democracies are less likely to experience violent conflict and rebellion than autocracies and regime types in-between, also called semi-democracies.[33] Another approach within the same field of studies is the analysis of the democratization process. Whereas the above studies suggest that relatively stable democracies discourage violent conflict, the democratization process itself is by other researchers held to be rather violent.[34]

Much of this literature fails to take proper consideration of the economic context and the level of development. This concerns also the environment. The democratic peace might thus be mainly a *peace of the wealthy*, since most of the well-established democracies are found in the industrialized and rich world. The study by Hauge & Hegre[35] points in that direction. The result of their quantitative study indicate that whereas in industrialized countries stable democracy decreases the likelihood of conflict, in non-industrialized countries stable democracy actually increases the probability of conflict. The well-established democracies in India and Colombia, two rather conflict-ridden countries, may be mentioned as examples.

Future Research

The topic of this chapter has been research on the relationship between development, environmental change and armed conflict. A central problem has been that the various fields of conflict research are not well integrated. A related problem is that also development research and conflict research have been two very separate fields of research.

Despite these problems, interesting work is being done both on the role of renewable resources in conflict causation and on the role of some aspects of economic development. Let me conclude by identifying several challenges with reference to future research on development, environment and conflict:

- Conflict research and development research needs to be better integrated.
- More attention needs to be given to the relationship between economic development and degradation of renewable resources in the process that leads to conflict.
- The role of economic and environmental factors in the conflict process needs to be analyzed within a framework that acknowledges the principle of multicausality.

- There is a need for more quantitative studies on links between environmental degradation and conflict, with additional data on some of the environmental variables.
- More control variables could be brought into quantitative studies of the environment, development and conflict, such as land distribution and ethnic fragmentation.
- Series of case-studies could be done on the basis of quantitative findings within this field.
- There is a need to develop the theory framework on the relationship between economic development and intrastate war.

Notes

1 Gleditsch, Nils Petter, 1996, 'Det nye sikkerhetsbildet: Mot en demokratisk og fredelig verden?' *Internasjonal Politikk* 3, 1996.
2 Smith, Dan, 1997, *The State of War and Peace Atlas*. London: Penguin; Wallensteen, Peter and Margareta Sollenberg, 1997, 'Conflicts, Conflict Termination and Peace Agreements, 1989–96' *Journal of Peace Research* 34(3), August, pp. 339-358; Wayman, Frank Whelon; David Singer and Meredith Sarkees, 1996. 'Inter-State, Intra-State, and Extra-Systemic Wars 1816–1995'. Paper presented at the annual meeting of the International Studies Association, San Diego, April 16–21, 1996.
3 The World Bank operates with thresholds of GNP per capita, given in USD. The thresholds divide countries into four categories: high-income, upper-middle income, lower middle-income and low-income. The thresholds are adjusted every year, but the changes are usually very small.
4 Hauge, Wenche and Håvard Hegre, 1977, 'Economic Development and Civil War'. Paper presented to the 38th Annual Conference of the International Studies Association, Toronto, 18–22 March.
5 Brown, Neville, 1989, 'Climate, ecology and international security', *Survival* 31(6), November/December, pp. 519-532; Ullman, Richard H., 1983. 'Redefining Security', *International Security* 8 (Summer), pp. 129-153; Mathews, Jessica Tuchman, 1989. 'Redefining Security', *Foreign Affairs* 68 (Spring), pp. 162-177; Buzan, Barry, 1991. *People, States and Fear*, 2nd Ed. Boulder, CO: Lynne Reinner Publishers, Inc; Pirages, Dennis, 1991. 'Social Evolution and Ecological Security', *Bulletin of Peace Proposals* 22(3), pp. 329-334; Lodgaard, Sverre, 1992. 'Environmental Security, World Order and Environmental Conflict Resolution', in Gleditsch (ed.), *Conversion and the Environment. Proceedings of a Seminar in Perm, Russia, 24–27 November 1991. PRIO Report*, no. 2, pp. 115-136; Myers, Norman, 1993. *Ultimate*

Security: The Environmental Basis of Political Stability. New York: W.W. Norton & Co.

6 Brock, Lothar, 1996, 'The Environment and Security: Conceptual and Theoretical Issues', in Nils Petter Gleditsch, ed. *Conflict and the Environment.* Dordrecht, Boston and London: Kluwer Academic Publishers. Published in cooperation with NATO Scientific Affairs Division, pp. 17-35; Bächler, Günther, Volker Böge, Stefan Klötzli, Stephan Libiszewski and Kurt R., Spillmann, 1996, *Kriegsursache Umweltzerstörung: Ökologische Konflikte in Der Dritten Welt und Wege ihrer friedlichen Bearbeitung,* Zürich: Verlag Rüegger; Brundtland, Gro et al., 1987, *Our Common Future. World Commission on Environment and Development,* Oxford: Oxford University Press; Galtung, Johan, 1982, *Environment, Development and Military Activity: Towards Alternative Security Doctrines,* Oslo: Norwegian University Press; Gleick, Peter H.,1993, *Water in Crisis: A Guide to the World's Fresh Water Resources,* New York and Oxford: Oxford University Press, for Pacific Institute for Studies in Development, Environment and Security & Stockholm Environment Institute; Homer-Dixon, Thomas F., 1991, 'On the Threshold. Environmental Changes as Causes of Acute Conflict', *International Security* 16(2), pp. 76-116; Homer-Dixon, Thomas F., Jeffrey H. Boutwell and George W. Rathjens, 1993, 'Environmental Change and Violent Conflict', *Scientific American* 268(2), pp. 38-45; Renner, Michael; Mario Pianta and Cinzia Franchi, 1991, 'International Conflict and Environmental Degradation', in Raimo Väyrynen, ed. *New Directions in Conflict Theory. Conflict Resolution and Conflict Transformation.* London, etc.: SAGE, in association with the International Social Science Council, pp. 108–128.

7 Deudney, Daniel, 1991, 'Environment and Security: Muddled Thinking', *Bulletin of the Atomic Scientists* 47(3), pp. 22-28; Levy, Marc A., 1995, 'Is the Environment a National Security Issue", *International Security* 20(2), pp. 35-62; Gleditsch, Nils Petter, 1998, 'Armed Conflict and the Environment: A Critique of the Literature', *Journal of Peace Research* 35(3), May, pp. 381-401.

8 Homer-Dixon, Thomas F., 1994, 'Environmental Scarcities and Violent Conflict: Evidence from Cases', *International Security* 19(1), pp. 5-40; Percival Val and Thomas Homer-Dixon, 1998, 'Environmental Scarcity and Violent Conflict: The Case of South Africa', *Journal of Peace Research* 35(3), May, pp. 279-299.

9 The relative importance here refers to the frequency of environmental degradation occurring as a cause of domestic armed conflict globally, compared with other factors, and not its relative weight or importance in any particular domestic armed conflict.

10 Lipschutz, Ronnie D., 1997, 'Environmental Conflict and Environmental Determinism: The Relative Importance of Social and Natural Factors', in Gleditsch, ed. *Conflict and the Environment,* pp. 35-51.

11 Hauge, Wenche and Tanja Ellingsen, 1998, 'Beyond Environmental Scarcity: Causal Pathways to Conflict', *Journal of Peace Research* 35(3), May, pp. 299-319; Levy, 1995; Deudney, 1991; Gleditsch, 1997.

12 Hauge and Ellingsen, 1998.

13 Civil war has been defined by three dimensions; internality, type of participants and the degree of efficient resistence. In short, Small and Singer (1982, pp.31-47; pp. 203-222) define civil war as 'a military conflict within a state where the national government is one of the active parties and where both parties in the conflict can and intend to struggle despite any costs'. A quite similar definition can be found in Wallensteen and Sollenberg (1997, p. 354) ' An armed conflict is a contested incompatibility which concerns government and/or territory where the use of armed force between two parties, of which at least one is the government of a state, results in at least 25 battle-related deaths.'

14 Small, Melvin and David J. Singer, 1982, *Resort to Arms International and Civil Wars 1816–1980.* Beverly Hills, London and New Dehli: SAGE Publications.

15 Wallensteen and Sollenberg, 1997.

16 Lichbach, Mark Irving, 1989, 'An Evaluation of Does Economic Inequality Breed Political Conflict' *World Politics* XLI(4), pp. 431-70.

17 Harvey, Neil, 1994, *Rebellion in Chiapas: Rural Reforms, Campesino Radicalism and the Limits to Salinismo*, San Diego: Center for U.S.-Mexican Studies; Schöneberg, Regina, 1996, 'Environmental Conflicts in the Amazon Region of Brazil' in Günther Bächler and Kurt R. Spillmann (Eds.) *Kriegsursache Umweltzerstørung (Environmental Degradation as a Cause of War: Country Studies of External Experts).* Vol. 111. Verlag Rüegger.

18 Hibbs, Douglas A., 1973, *Mass Political Violence: A Cross-National Causal Analysis*, New York: John Wiley & Sons; Auvinen Juha Y., 1995, 'Socio-Political and Economic Indicators for Conflict Early Warning'. Paper prepared for the 36th Annual ISA Convention, 21–25 February 1995, Chicago, IL.

19 Hettne, Björn, 1995, *Development Theory and the Three Worlds*, Essex: Longman Scientific & Technical.

20 Feierabend, Ivo K., Rosalind L. Feierabend and Betty Nesvold, 1972, 'Social Change and Political Violence: Cross-National Patterns', in Ivo K. Feierabend, Rosalind L. Feierabend and Ted Robert Gurr (eds), *Anger, Violence and Politics*, Englewood Cliffs, NJ: Prentice Hall, pp. 107-125.

21 Huntington, Samuel P., 1991, *The Third Wave: Democratization in the Late Twentieth Century*, Norman, OK and London: University of Oklahoma Press.

22 Huntington, 1968, p. 4.

23 Huntington, 1968, p.33.

24 Huntington, 1968, p. 41. Huntington realizes that there is little statistical evidence of links between rapid economic growth and political instability. On the basis of that he suggests that the relationship between economic growth and

political instability varies with the level of economic development. His hypothesis is that at low levels, a positive relationship exists, at medium levels no significant relationship exists and at high levels there is a negative relationship.

25 Rapkin, David P. and William P. Avery, 1986, 'World Markets and Political Instability within Less Developed Countries', *Cooperation and Conflict* XXI, pp. 99-117.

26 Rapkin and Avery, p. 102.

27 United Nations Conference on Trade and Development, Annual, *UNCTAD Handbook on International Trade and Development Statistics*, Geneva: United Nations Publication.; The World Bank, Annual, *World Development Report*, Washington: Oxford University Press; International Monetary Fund, Annual, *Annual Report*, Washington D.C.

28 Hauge and Hegre, 1997.

29 Small and Singer, 1982. See note 13 for definition.

30 Walton, John and David Seddon, 1994, *Free Markets and Food Riots: The Politics of Global Adjustment*, London: Basil Blackwell.

31 Walton and Seddon, p. 39. There are different types of structural adjustment loans given by the IMF and the World Bank, but the conditionality attached to them in general tends to be the same. The main content of these conditionalities are cuts in official expenditure, devaluation, liberalization of import and investment in export-led growth. Although structural adjustment loans given, for example by the IMF under SAF (Structural Adjustment Facility) are supposed to last for three years, a SAF loan is often renewed or followed by an ESAF (Enhanced Structural Adjustment Facility) loan (IMF, 1987–94). Whether it is the IMF, the World Bank or both that gives the loan, the adjustment period tends to last for in average 6-10 years.

32 Auvinen, 1995.

33 Riggs, 1994, *Ethno-National Rebellions and Viable Constitutionalism*, Paper presented at the XVI Congress of Political Science, Berlin, 21–25 August, 1994; Rummel, Rudolph J., 1995, 'Democracies ARE more Peaceful', *European Journal of International Relations* 1(4), December, pp. 457-479; Eckstein, Harry and Ted Robert Gurr, 1975, *Patterns of Authority: A Structural Basis for Political Inquiery*, New York: Wiley.

34 Huntington, Samuel P., 1991, *The Third Wave: Democratization in the Late Twentieth Century*, Norman, OK and London: University of Oklahoma Press; Jowitt, Ken, 1991, 'The New World Disorder', *Journal of Democracy* 2(4), December, pp. 11-20; Rupesinghe, Kumar, 1992, 'The Disappearing Boundaries between Internal and External Conflicts, pp. 1-26 in Kumar Rupesinghe, ed. *International Conflict and Governance*, New York: St. Martin's.

35 Hauge and Hegre, 1997.

PART IIb

ISSUES AT WAR: ETHNONATIONAL ISSUES

6 Socially Constructed Ethnic Identities: A Need for Identity Management?

TARJA VÄYRYNEN

Introduction

The end of the Cold War closed four decades of military confrontation between East and West. Yet the end of this struggle has not brought relief from armed conflicts. Rather, violence has shifted from inter-state relations to inter-community relations. What kind of conflicts are there, then, in a turbulent world which is no longer organized by the bipolar conflict of East and West? The dominant conflict type is ethnopolitical [1] conflict which includes politicized identity concerns. Resolving ethnopolitical conflicts, therefore, requires understanding both of the processes through which the identities of the actors are constructed and of the relationship between the processes of identification and conflict management.

This chapter intends to study the logic of identity-formation, and especially the construction of violent ethnic identities. The aim is to suggest a conceptual and theoretical framework within which vital questions related to ethnic identification and ethnic conflict can be asked. Furthermore, the argument aims at justifying the dialogic mode of conflict resolution. The first section studies some of the main themes shared by the literature on ethnic conflict and points out the lack of several important discussions. The second section examines both at micro and macro levels the context and the logic of identity-formation, and argues that the understanding of these is vital for an understanding of ethnopolitical conflict. The last section of the chapter establishes a link between identity-formation and the practices of ethnopolitical conflict resolution.

The state of art in the study of ethnic conflicts

Violence, assimilation and identities

Three observations seem to underlie most parts of the recent study on ethnopolitical conflict. First, there is an agreement that political violence does not exist any more in the place the modern study of international relations assumed it to exist, namely in inter-state relations. The location of violence started to shift from inter-state relations to intra-state relations after the Second World War, but was recognized with a sense of urgency after the disintegration of the Cold War international system.

Secondly, the assumption that different cultural, religious and ethnic groups will assimilate into the majority group of the state when the modernization project reaches a mature stage is largely neglected. There have always been scholars who have studied critically the assimilation thesis which was prominent in the study of multi-ethnic societies especially in the 1960s and 1970s. The thesis, which largely dismissed the possibility of conflicts of identity – among them ethnopolitical – was challenged, for example, by Walker Connor. He argued that improvements in the quality and quantity of communication and transportation media curtails the cultural isolation of identity groups. Advances in communication and transportation increase the cultural awareness of the minorities by making their members more aware of the distinction between themselves and others, and, therefore, more prone to identity politics.[2]

Thirdly, the influx of studies which employed social constructionists frameworks in social sciences thirty years ago paved the way for the acceptance of the notion of multiple identities. It is argued that we do not have just one identity, but an 'identity budget' from which we draw an identity or an aspect of an identity according to the social context in which we find ourselves. In a similar vein, the relational nature of identity, namely, the idea that the creation of an identity is based on the drawing a border between the 'self' and 'other', was convincingly introduced to the study of ethnic groups. For example, Fredrik Barth argued that actors use ethnic identities to categorize themselves and others for the purposes of interaction. Organization along ethnic lines implies boundary-maintenance between those who belong to the group and those who do not.[3]

In sum, the acknowledgement of the novel locations of violence, the failure of assimilation in multi-cultural societies and the constructionist ways of theorizing identity-related issues are the themes which inform the most recent study on ethnic conflict. The new locations of violence are thought to be demonstrated by collecting data;[4] the refutation of the assimilation thesis is founded on case studies on conflicts in multi-ethnic societies;[5] and the understanding of identity-formation is largely derived by emphasizing the contextual or instrumental nature of identity and by rejecting extreme modes of essentialism.[6]

Ethnicity and ethnic relations

The study of ethnic conflict draws largely from the study of ethnicity and ethnic relations of which there is an abundance in the sociological and anthropological literature. A variety of studies attempts to explain why ethnic identification takes place.[7] For example, according to Michael Hechter, ethnic identification arises from 'internal colonialization' in which some parts of the country exploit others. Ethnic mobilization is an unavoidable consequence.[8] According to Paul Brass, on the other hand, ethnic communities are created and transformed by particular élites. Modernizing and post-industrial societies which are undergoing dramatic changes are especially prone to community creation and transformation.[9]

The sociological and anthropological literature on ethnicity also pays attention to the multiple forms of ethnic identification and the relationship between identification and the type of society. It is argued that ethnic identification in pre-modern societies is different from that in post-industrial societies. For example, Martin Heisler points out four settings within which ethnicity and ethnic relations should be studied: primitive, preindustrial, nationalist and post-nationalist. In small, primitive societies ethnicity is derived from kinship type of contacts between the members of the society as a 'natural' element of everyday life, whereas in the post-nationalist context ethnic community is 'imagined',[10] because 'modern, industrialised societies are often psychologically unsatisfying, inhospitable, or worse' – they 'tend to fragment the persona and lead to alienation'.[11] Similarly, it is acknowledged that ethnic identification has different stages which range from the formation of ethnic community to the politicizing of the community, to the ethnonationalistic stage.[12]

Ethnopolitical conflict in peace and conflict studies

There is still surprisingly little literature on ethnicity, ethnic relations and ethnic conflict in the field of peace and conflict studies. The core literature, on the other hand, on ethnopolitical conflict largely dismisses the processes and logic of identification. It follows that it misses some important aspects of ethnopolitical conflict resolution. The studies take as their starting point the simple dichotomies set by primordialist and instrumentalist as well as objectivist and subjectivist categories. In the primordialist view, ethnic groups are taken as givens. It is, thus, an essentialist approach to human identification. The instrumentalist view is based on the rational choice theory which in its extreme form reduces ethnic identification to cost-benefit-oriented economic choices. Objectivist accounts try to establish 'objective' (e.g. language, colour, religion) criteria according to which an ethnic group can be identified. Subjectivist views rely on the groups' own definition when acknowledging the existence of an ethnic group. The following examples demonstrate the approaches.

Donald Horowitz argues that ethnic identity is established at birth; people are born into an ethnic group in which they will die. In other words, ethnic groups consist mostly of those who have been born into them. Individuals may alter their ethnic identity, but even in that case the meaningfulness of identity derives from acceptance by an ethnic group *as if* born into it. Ethnic identity of the group is based, according to Horowitz, on a myth of collective ancestry. In short, ethnic group is a form of extended kin-group and as such fulfils certain individual needs (e.g. a need for security).[13] Stephen Ryan asks the vital question 'why an identification in terms of ethnicity has become so important in contemporary politics?' He gives ethnicity a subjectivist definition by stating that an ethnic group is a 'group of people who define themselves as distinct from other groups because of cultural differences'.[14]

The understanding of conflict, after the introduction of the basic dichotomies, is based on either the theories of group behaviour or on attempts to delineate the preconditions for ethnopolitical conflict. Horowitz studies the role economic interests, modernization, cultural pluralism and colonial policies have in ethnic conflict. He examines also the cognitive elements which accompany conflictual behaviour. For him, the fundamental question is 'what fosters ethnic conflict as a particular form of group behaviour?'[15] Ryan, on the other hand, wonders whether multi-ethnic societies are violent, how to establish stable relations and what happens to communities when they engage in violent conflict with each other.[16]

A call for 'scientific' study of ethnopolitical conflicts is presented by some authors. For example, Michael Brown claims in a paternalistic tone that 'serious academic studies of the causes of ethnic conflict develop explanations at three main levels of analysis: the systemic level, the domestic level and the perceptual level'.[17] 'Serious academic studies' examine causes and test hypotheses. Ted Gurr has produced exactly what would qualify, by Brown's definition, as a 'serious academic study'. Gurr tests the likelihood of ethnopolitical conflicts with data on more than 200 ethnopolitical groups. The following four hypothesis are tested in his study: the influence of the breakdown of the bi-polar international system, of economical disparity, of encounters between cultures and civilizations and of transitional periods (e.g. the creation of a new state, revolution and democratization) on the likelihood of conflict. According to Gurr's findings, only the last hypothesis gets a significant amount of support from data. In other words, it seems that states going through a major transitional period are prone to ethnopolitical conflicts.[18]

The expression 'communal conflict', under which ethnic conflicts can be seen to fall, is employed by the scholars who write within the tradition of 'integrative conflict management'.[19] The writers do no emphasize the specific nature of ethnopolitical conflicts. Rather, they use the term 'identity conflict' to describe all conflicts which either arise from a need for identity or revolve around identity issues. The literature approaches the formation of identities from two distinct angles. The authors rely either on human needs theories or on (socio)psychologically oriented theoretical frameworks.[20]

For John Burton, who exemplifies human needs thinking, identity-formation relates to the need for identity. He considers the need for identity to be a biologically based drive. If the need and, thus, the drive underlying it, are not satisfied, conflict emerges. The need satisfaction may be hindered for several reasons (e.g. élites and social structures may prevent needs satisfaction), but the result is always conflict, because human beings are conditioned, if not determined, to gratify their needs regardless of the consequences for the self or the society.[21]

At the psychological end of the spectrum is Vamik Volkan's approach which emphasizes the psychology of group relations. According to Volkan, issues of 'enemies and allies' are inherent both in human evolution and the development of human mind. The psychoanalytic conception of 'projection' plays an important role in his theory. Volkan claims, on the basis of child development theory, that groups also project certain aspects of themselves onto other people. The feeling of 'we-ness', which is a core of ethnicity, arises from positive projections, whereas the ideas and images of 'other-ness' and 'enemies' arise from negative projections. Ethnic identity can be expressed both peacefully (e.g. through rituals and artefacts) and violently. Violent expression comes to the fore when the group identity is somehow disturbed.[22]

The question of whether there is something in the process and logic of ethnic identification which relates them to conflict is largely dismissed in the literature. The literature discusses identification in a very restricted manner by employing the continuum set by primordialism (essentialism) and instrumentalism (voluntarism), and by complementing it with theories of group behaviour. An exception seems to be the (socio)psychological strand exemplified by the 'integrative conflict management' approach. Furthermore, theorizing, for example in international relations – which examines the logic of political identification has not yet penetrated to the study of ethnopolitical conflict in peace and conflict studies.[23] The theorizing on political identification employs late modern theoretical and critical frameworks and vocabulary against which the field has immunized itself.[24]

Ethnic conflict resolution

Given that the dynamics of identity-formation are not fully examined, important elements of the study of ethnopolitical conflict resolution are missing. The strengths of different conflict management techniques are assessed mainly from an instrumentalist point of view. The focus is on cost-benefit-oriented actors whose conflict resolution behaviour is assumed to be based solely on (instrumentally) rational choices.

Ryan claims that there are three phases of ethnic conflict resolution: peace-keeping, peace-building and peace-making. He is not satisfied with approaches which simply aim at managing conflicts (e.g. peace-keeping) and, thus, recommends the integration of conflict management and resolution. He notes that the conventional approaches to ethnopolitical conflict management do not address the psychological issues ('destructive processes') in conflict and, therefore, grass-roots action is needed to complement official negotiations. Ryan believes that psychological issues cannot be dealt with management approaches. He does not, however, discuss how ethnic identification affects these psychological issues which may turn into 'destructive processes'.[25]

In Horowitz's study the main focus is on ethnic group behaviour. He examines ethnic accommodation, partition, internal integration, equal distribution of resources and structural changes as a means of reducing tension in behaviour. He introduces structural techniques (e.g. federalism and regional autonomy) for ethnic conflict management without relating them to ethnic identity.[26] John McGarry and Brendan O'Leary broaden Horowitz's agenda by setting up a general taxonomy of ethnopolitical conflict resolution. They categorize eight macro-methods of ethnic conflict regulation. The methods for eliminating differences are: genocide, forced mass-population transfers, partition and/or secession (self-determination) and integration and/or assimilation. The ways for managing differences, on the other hand, are: hegemonic control, arbitration (third-party intervention), cantonization and/or federalism and consociationalism or power-sharing. The taxonomy derives, thus, from an assumption that there are two distinct ways to deal with actual or potential ethnic conflicts, namely, there are structural methods for eliminating and managing differences. Although McGarry and O'Leary do recognize the role that difference has in conflict management, they do not explore it in relation to identity-formation, and especially to ethnic identification.[27]

The techniques of conflict resolution employed by the 'integrative conflict management' approach have promising features when examined from the point of view of ethnopolitical conflict management. Although many scholars/practitioners theorize and practice conflict resolution within simplified human needs or psychological frameworks, there are elements in the approach which deserve to be studied further and re-articulated.

The theorists – who also work as conflict resolution practitioners – suggest problem-solving conflict resolution, which takes place in workshops which are academically based, with unofficial small group discussions. Workshops bring together representatives of parties in conflict for direct communication. A panel of scholars which facilitates and promotes communication between the parties is an essential part of this mode of conflict resolution. Unlike many traditional mediators, facilitators do not propose or impose solutions. Rather, the function of the third party in the problem-solving workshop is to produce an atmosphere where innovative solutions can emerge from the interaction between the parties themselves. The objective of the workshop is both to create analytical communication and to generate inputs into political processes. A strength of the approach lies in its informality, which allows discussions on ethnic identification during the conflict resolution process. However, in order for this to actualize, the processes of identification need to be understood both at the micro and macro levels.

The process of identification: life-world, modernity and global social practices

One needs to identify with something, because there is an original and insurmountable lack of identity. The lack is thus truly inherent in any identity. Two features of identification are fundamental: the failure in fully constituting any identity and the relationship of identification to the 'other'. First, as noted, there is always a void in identification which is open to distortions and excesses, and which produces anxiety and uncertainty. The failure of full identification triggers new acts of identification which aim at mastering those disturbing effects. Secondly, there is a constitutive dialogical relationship between the fictional 'self' and the 'other'. Despite the fundamental void from the point of view of the 'self', subject is counted as a unity in the field of the 'other'.[28]

Micro level: ethnic identification in the life-world

We are born into a world that existed before our birth. This world is from the outset not merely a physical but also a sociocultural one. The sociocultural world is a preconstituted and preorganized world whose particular structure is the result of a historical process and is therefore different for each culture and society. The social world is experienced by us as a web of social relationships, of systems of signs and of institutionalized forms of social organization.[29]

The meaning of the elements of the social world is largely taken for granted by those living in the world. There are cultural patterns which are peculiar to social groups and which function to a member of a group as unquestioned schemes of reference. In Alfred Schutz's words,

> any member born or reared within the group accepts the ready-made standardised scheme of the cultural pattern handed down to him by ancestors, teachers, and authorities as an unquestioned and unquestionable guide in all situations which normally occur within the social world.[30]

Our identification takes place, thus, within this taken-for-granted framework of cultural patterns.

We approach the world through typifications. Typifications are fundamentally intersubjective and formed in the main by others, by predecessors or contemporaries, as appropriate tools for coming to terms with things and people. The knowledge of typifications and of their appropriate use is an inseparable element of the sociocultural heritage handed down to the person and stored in a person's 'stock of knowledge'. In sum, the knowledge included in the individual stock is largely socially derived, distributed and approved.[31]

From the point of view of the society, any society considers itself as a little cosmos, and the maintenance of the cosmos requires symbols to keep it together. Societies, social groups, need their central myths, or dominating ideologies, to justify and to establish foundations for self-interpretation. The central myth as a scheme of self-interpretation itself belongs to the relative natural conception of the world which the in-group takes for granted.[32]

Ethnicity guides interpretation and action in the social world. It is, thus, a part of the frame of reference of the social group in terms of which both the physical as well as sociocultural world is interpreted. It is an element of the frame of reference which consists of the sum-total of the various typifications. In other words, ethnicity is a way to typify the world, others and oneself, and as such it implies roles and ways to act. As Max Weber argues, the existence of a marriage or a state means nothing but the mere chance that people will act and will act in a specific way. Similarly, following Schutz's terminology, the existence of an ethnic group means nothing but the mere likelihood that people will act in accordance with the general framework of typifications in which ethnicity, as a reference to certain criteria of communality (e.g. language, history, 'race'), is considered to have high relevance.[33]

Although ethnicity can be a part of the relative natural conception of the world of the social group and form a foundation for individual identification, it is not a stabile element. On the contrary, its meaning is constantly negotiated in social interaction between the social actors. In other words, it is continuously negotiated in encounters which are political and involve power.[34] As Hannah Arendt notes, 'power springs up whenever people get together and act in concert'.[35] Furthermore, ethnicity is employed in order to draw boundaries regarding who belongs to the group and who does not. As argued earlier, the ethnic group is about boundary-maintenance: ethnicity is a way to structure interaction which allows the persistence of differences. Ethnic communality is, therefore, always an artefact of boundary-drawing activity: always contentious and contested, glossing over some differentiations and representing other differences as powerful and separating factors.[36] In sum, there is nothing in the structure of the stock of knowledge and the logic of typification themselves which gives ethnic communality and identification a particular importance. Activated ethnicity as a boundary-drawing resource of the social group, and politicized community-building criteria thought to be related to ethnicity (e.g. language and religion), are, however, crucial from the point of view of violent ethnic identification.

Modern instrumentality

Modernity shapes the contents of our stocks of knowledge and thereby our ways to typify the world. The question arises whether there is something in the 'modern' content of our stock of knowledge which relates particularly to violent ethnic identification. The intent is not to claim that violent ethnic identification did not take place in pre-modern settings. Rather, the aim is to examine the modern conditions under which violent ethnic identification happens in the capitalized and globalized world. A fundamental account of modernity is provided by Martin Heidegger when he discusses the notion of 'technological'.

It should be noted before examining technology that modernity is a historical period which matured into a cultural project with the growth of the Enlightenment and into a socially accomplished form of life with the growth of industrial society. One of the tasks modernity sets for itself is to bring order into chaos. Ordered existence requires nature, the unordered, to be mastered, subordinated and remade to meet 'human needs'. The unordered needs to be held in check, restrained and contained. The struggle for order is essentially a fight against ambiguity, ambivalence and fuzziness. Order is, thus, continuously engaged in a war of survival, its enemy being chaos and chaos being understood to be pure negativity. In order to be effective, modern mastery requires (and produces), in its will to design, manipulate and engineer, sovereign agencies aiming at accomplishing the task.[37]

Technology, in the Heideggerian view, is neither the application of science nor does it refer to the mere instruments we associate with technology. Rather, technology is a mode of thought being characteristic of the Western metaphysical tradition and manifest through the way we bring things to presence. Technology has become fruition in modern times in the form of calculative and instrumental reasoning which characterizes modern rationality. Instrumental reasoning brings things into presence as calculable matter. In other words, by enframing things in a certain manner things are held readily available in effect as a kind of objectivized and homogenized form. Things are standing in reserve to be employed and re-deployed in continuous exercise of instrumentally propelled production and consumption. Technology is a mode of thought which is also a mode of practice, a way of being in the world: we do not have technology, we are had by it. Heidegger argues that all aspects of modern life are becoming determined technologically: also politics and social life are largely technologized.[38]

David Campbell and Michael Dillon develop the Heideggerian notion of technology further and argue that violence has become the *ultima ratio* of modern politics, because 'subjectivation' liberated political understanding and framed the world in a 'technological', instrumental, manner. The basic political subject is violent by virtue of its very composition. According to Campbell and Dillon, security is the foundational value around which the political subject of violence revolves. Security is not merely the main goal of the political subject of violence, it is, rather, the principle of the formation of the subject. The political subject of violence, invoking constantly security, comes in a variety of forms: God, rational subject, nation, state, people, class, race etc.[39] Ethnic group can be added to Campbell's and Dillon's list. The issue of violent ethnic identification is, thus, fundamentally a question of modern political subjectivity. The roots of violent ethnic identification lie in the ontological insecurity of the subject.

Macro level: territorial state, de-territorialization and assumed unity

If technology conditions the way we are in the world by forming a part of the content of our stock of knowledge, the question arises at the macro level: what kind of social and political practices can emerge within the framework created by technology? Seen from the angle of ethnic conflict, three social practices are fundamental: sovereign territorial state, globalization and media practices. They create 'identity spaces' within which ethnic identification takes place, and they are the social practices which make parochial 'ethnic subjects' possible. The study of ethnic identification and conflict needs, thus, pay attention both to global processes and their local manifestations.

The sovereign territorial state and its assumed coexistence with the nation is of vital importance in understanding ethnopolitical conflict. The sovereign state has traditionally tried to offer the instrumental solution for the challenge set forth by different forms of identity politics (e.g. class, gender and ethnic claims). In other words, the state has aimed at providing a shared domain of meaning for groups located within its sovereign control and territory. The state, as a social and political practice and as a system of inclusion and exclusion *par excellence*, has tried to solve the problem of conflicting identity claims by producing precise distinctions between citizens and aliens, by domesticating particular identities and by creating a coherent sovereign identity. In short, it is a social practice from which modern ethnic identification emerges.[40]

As Zygmunt Bauman describes modern state:

> National states promote 'nativism' and construe its subjects as 'natives'. They laud and enforce the ethnic, religious, linguistic, cultural *homogeneity*. They are engaged in incessant propaganda of *shared* attitudes. They construct *joint* historical memories and do their best to discredit or suppress such stubborn memories as cannot be squeezed into shared tradition – now redefined in the state-appropriate quasi-legal terms, as 'our common heritage'. They preach the sense of *common* mission, *common* fate, *common* destiny. They breed, or at least legitimise and give tacit support to, animosity towards everyone standing outside the holy union.[41] [emphasis by Bauman]

State has become more and more contested space. According to Arjun Appadurai, 'nation-state' is a battle of imagination with 'state and nation seeking to cannibalise each other'. Groups with ideas about nationhood seek to capture or co-opt states power, and states simultaneously seek to capture and monopolize ideas about nationhood. Here is, thus, a platform for separatism and micro-identities to become political projects within nation-states. Ideas of nationhood appear to be steadily increasing in scale and regularity crossing often existing state boundaries. Kurds, Sikhs, Tamils, Sri Lankans, Quebecois represent 'imagined communities' which seek to create states of their own or carve pieces out of existing states. States, on the other hand, are seeking to establish the monopoly of producing distinctions and differences, a task in which they are never fully successful.[42] From the perspective of the 'nation-state', thus, an ethnic group claiming a right to produce difference and make distinctions which transcend the official state ideology is an 'enemy within'.

Globalization is also embedded in technology and in its instrumental rationality. Globalization implies accelerated processes, growth of global institutions and increased flows of information. It is closely connected with global capitalism, which is in an interesting contradiction with the maintenance of states and sovereignty for the political organization of international relations. Capital flows clearly across national borders and is multinational and transnational by nature.

Global capitalism produces, with growing internationalization of production and finance, global divisions of labour. Global division of labour has its local counterpart, namely, segmenting of labour force along 'race' and 'ethnic' lines. As Jindy Pettman puts it, 'the increasingly global economy shapes the new international division of labour along state, national, racialized, ethnicized, and gender divides'.[43] The international political economy of, for example, migrant labour is a part of this division, and a motive of huge population movements, 'movement of bodies'.

The movement of bodies – for whatever reason and among other global flows – deterritorializes the world assumed to be divided along territorial lines by shifting labouring populations into relatively wealthy societies or populations from poor into little less poor societies. Deterritorialization creates a version of 'ethnoscape' (Appadurai's term) which has sometimes an exaggerated and intensified sense of criticism or attachment to politics of home-state. In other words, identity-formation becomes deterritorialized and assumes an increasingly symbolic character in a nomadic world. According to Appadurai, deterritorialization, whether of Hindus, Sikhs, Palestinians or Ukrainians, is now at the core of a variety of global fundamentalism. Invented homelands can become fantastic and one-sided to an extent that they provide material for new 'ideoscapes' (concentrations of images which have often to do with ideologies of states and their counter-ideologies) in which ethnic conflict can begin to erupt. Search for identity is at its most intense in the de-territorialized world when identity is located in the not-yet-accomplished future.[44]

Media contributes to ethnic identification as well as to the creation of assumed unified nation-states. As argued above, ethnic identification consists often in a utopia as a construction of the future state of affairs in which all differences are reconciled around an unified body politic. Media works towards the utopia by producing networks of signs and images representing 'oneness' and 'otherness'. 'Mediascapes' provide large and complex repertoires of images, narratives, and 'ethnoscapes' to viewers throughout the world. They help to constitute narratives of the 'other' and proto-narratives of possible lives which produce a platform for the desire for acquisition and movement. Furthermore, media helps groups spread over vast and irregular spaces stay linked together and create political sentiments based on intimacy and locality.[45]

Deterritorialization and dislocation of peoples do not remove the need for overcoming separation. Instead they enforce the search for unity. Aesthetic experiences of community which allow experiences of unity or community become more and more important when 'the self seeks to overcome its separation and the extreme differentiation of modern societies by mirroring itself in signs that facilitate the illusion that the very difference that establishes the sign is overcome in the experience of the sign'.[46] For example, a state flag is a sign which stems from sovereign state as social practice establishing differences between citizens and aliens. Differences are, thus, constitutive of the sign. The experience of the sign, on the other hand, gives an illusory experience of national unity and even of a community of citizens which overcomes obvious 'internal' differences.

Foundations for conflict resolution: void in identification and dialogical social practices

It should be noted that ethnic conflict or violent ethnic identification does not stop the process of identification. In other words, identification continues into and through the conflict. However, in conflict situation narratives on ethnicity (e.g. ethnic origin, group membership) tend to become fixed, and this is often wrongly seen to imply fixed identities. Ethnic narratives in conflict situations do seal off alternative ways of typifying the world.[47] They seal off alternative interpretations which could destabilize the dominant interpretations. Ethnic narratives seal off, for example, alternative self-definitions of the group and therewith exclude alternative identifications, roles and modes of action. In the conflict situation ethnic narratives, thus, become rigid and readily reenacted. However, as Sara Cobb notes, 'narrative closure is never complete and contestation is inevitable', for example, 'in mediation as disputants refute, deny, and elaborate the discursive context in which they are located by self and other'.[48]

Neither does any political and social practice fully encompass society. There is always excess both in social practices and in the spaces of identification they create. As the Lacanian theory states, every signifier fails to represent the subject and leaves, therefore, a residue: linguistic disruption (present in metaphors and metonyms) 'determines the indeterminacy of the subject'. Excess leaves a residue on the basis of which a continuous constitution of identity takes place.[49] Similarly, the social world is not entirely defined in terms of repetitive and sedimented practices, because the social always overflows the institutionalized frameworks. It follows, that the fullness of society in which the subject finds its true identity is never finally achieved. Despite the modern technological enframing of the world, a dimension of construction and creation is inherent in all social practice. This constructive moment which exceeds the sedimented social practice creates a space for innovation.[50]

The void created by excess and the lack of full narrative closure should be employed in conflict resolution practices. The void in identification, the 'unfinished' political subjects the void creates, the failure of any social practice fully to encompass a society and the openness of all narratives bring about space in which conflict resolution can produce change. It should be emphasized that conflict resolution is a social and political practice itself among other practices in which space for identification is created. Conflict resolution can create a new, less violent, identification and political sphere *only* if it is based on the creation of 'alternative' social practices and therefore 'new political subjects'.

Discursive/dialogic institutions and communities are an alternative to instrumental institutions and therefore can form a platform for novel social practices.[51] The dialogic community:

> ... anticipates non-violent strategies of conflict resolution as well as encouraging cooperative and associative methods of problem-solving. It is a matter of political imagination as well as collective fantasy to project institutions, practices and ways of life which promote non-violent conflict resolution strategies and associative problem-solving methods.[52]

The dialogic community is a moral conversation in which the capacity to reverse perspectives, that is, the willingness to reason from others' point of view and the sensitivity to hear their voice, is paramount. The dialogic community in which dialogic relations are established is, thus, broader than dialogic speech in the narrow sense of the word. The aim of dialogue is not consensus or unanimity, but the 'anticipated communication with others with whom I know I must finally come to some agreement'.[53] In such a conversation, which is also called 'enlarged thinking' by Benhabib, the identity of the moral self becomes reconceptualized by virtue of the nature of community.

Since there are no standpoints which are not dependent upon socially produced, shared and approved ways to typify the world and subject positions, the aim of the establishment of the dialogic community cannot be the finding of a set of universal moral principles, values or rationales. Rather, the emphasis should be on 'sustaining those normative practices and moral relationships within which reasoned agreement as a way of life can flourish and continue'.[54] An inability to come to a shared understanding is not a final outcome, but indicates that one has been unable to bring the process of understanding to a conclusion. Dialogue is, by its nature, repeatable and, by being repeated, it can be moved forward.

Official and formal attempts to resolve ethnopolitical conflicts through negotiations seldom give birth to a dialogic framework, for they aim at reaching agreement on an exchange or on the realization of a common interest in the context created by technology. Negotiations which rely solely on instrumental bargaining on interests – or rather, interests turned into utilities – do not produce 'new subjects' or new points of identification. Neither does the bargaining structure with the manipulative (biased) mediator generate the dialogic community, because the biased third party operates in a context of power politics and, therefore, in a context of instrumental cost-benefit calculations. Official negotiations and biased mediation tend to re-enforce ethnic structures by appealing to a limited set of negotiable interests and utilities which necessitate the existence of an assumed coherent and sovereign identity; they require an agency which is entitled to resort to instrumental reason and institutions.

Problem-solving workshop conflict resolution can be seen in the light of the creation of the dialogic community. It does not need to be based on instrumental bargaining or the involvement of the biased mediator. Rather, it can aim at establishing a framework for the solutions arising from the interaction of the parties themselves. However, the workshop conflict resolution should be re-interpreted and re-conceptualized in order for its full capacity for ethnic conflict resolution to actualize. It should free itself from the socio-biological discourse dominating the theorizing and workshop practices and see itself as a social practice intended to produce new social and political agency through dialogue in a way suggested above.

Notes

1 Although the terms 'ethnopolitical' and 'ethnic' are used interchangeably in the text, it should not be taken to imply that conflicts are non-political or that ethnicity as such leads to conflicts.

2 Connor, Walker (1972), 'Nation-Building or Nation-Destroying?', *World Politics* 24, pp. 319-355.

3 Barth, Fredrik (ed.) (1969), *Ethnic Groups and Boundaries, The Social Organization of Culture Difference*. Boston: Little, Brown and Company.

4 See, for example: Sollenberg, Margareta and Wallensteen, Peter (1997), 'Major Armed Conflicts', in *SIPRI Yearbook 1997: Armaments, Disarmament and International Security*, Oxford: Oxford University Press, pp. 16-30.

5 Montville, Joseph (ed.) (1990), *Conflict and Peacemaking in Multiethnic Societies*, Lexington, M.A.: Lexington Books.

6 Barth (1969), *op. cit.* Eriksen, Thomas (1995), 'We and Us: Two Modes of Group Identification', *Journal of Peace Research* 32(4), 427-436. Roosens, Eugeen (1989) *Creating Ethnicity: The Process of Ethnogenesis*. London: Sage Publications.

7 For summaries see: Eriksen, Thomas (1993), *Ethnicity and Nationalism: Anthropological Perspectives*. London: Pluto Press. Pieterse, Jan (1996), 'Varieties of Ethnic Politics and Ethnicity Discourse', in Edwin Wilmsen and Patric McAllister (eds), *The Politics of Difference, Ethnic Premises in a World of Power*, Chicago and London: The University of Chicago Press, pp. 25-44.

8 Hechter, Michael (1975), *Internal Colonialism: The Celtic in British National Development 1536-1966*, London: Routledge and Kegan Paul.

9 Brass, Paul (1991), *Ethnicity and Nationalism: Theory and Comparison*, New Delhi: Sage.

10 On 'imagined communities' see Anderson, Benedict (1983), *Imagined Communities: Reflections on the Origins and Spread of Nationalism*, London: Verso.

11 Heisler, Martin (1990), 'Ethnicity and Ethnic Relations in the Modern West', in Joseph Montville (ed.), *Conflict and Peacemaking in Multiethnic Societies*, Lexington, M.A.: Lexington Books, p. 36.

12 Brass (1991), *op. cit.*

13 Horowitz, Donald (1985), *Ethnic Groups in Conflict*, Berkeley, Los Angeles, London: University of California Press, pp. 52-57, 74.

14 Ryan, Stephen (1990), *Ethnic Conflict and International Relations*, Aldershot: Dartmouth, pp. xiii-xvii.

15 Horowitz (1985), *op. cit.*, pp. 95-228.
16 Ryan (1990), *op. cit.*, pp. 1-22. Ryan, Stephen (1996), 'The Voice of Sanity Getting Hoarse?: Destructive Processes in Violent Ethnic Conflict', in Edwin Wilmsen and Patric McAllister (eds), *The Politics of Difference*, Chicago and London: The University of Chicago Press, pp. 144-161.
17 Brown, Michael (ed.) (1993), *Ethnic Conflict and International Security*, Princeton, New Jersey: Princeton University Press, p. 6.
18 Gurr, Ted (1994), 'Peoples Against States: Ethnopolitical Conflict and the Changing World System', *International Studies Quarterly* 38(3), pp. 347-377.
19 See: Azar, Edward (1990), *The Management of Protracted Social Conflict, Theory and Cases*, Aldershot: Dartmouth. Burton, John (1997), *Violence Explained*, Manchester: Manchester University Press. Doob, Leonard (ed.) (1970), *Resolving Conflict in Africa: The Fermeda Workshop*, New Haven, London: Yale University Press. Kelman, Herbert (1991), 'Informal Mediation by the Scholar/Practitioner', in Jacob Bercovitch and Jeffrey Rubin (eds), *Mediation in International Relations, Multiple Approaches to Conflict Management*, Basingstoke, London: Macmillan Press, pp. 64-96. Mitchell, Christopher and Banks, Michael (1996), *Handbook of Conflict Resolution: The Analytical Problem-Solving Approach*, New York and London: Pinter. Volkan, Vamik and Itzkowtz, Norman (1994), *Turks and Greeks, Neighbours in Conflict*, Huntington: The Eothen Press.
20 For alternative approaches see: Broome, Benjamin (1993), 'Managing Differences in Conflict Resolution: The Role of Relational Empathy', in Dennis Sandole and Hugo van der Merwe (eds), *Conflict Resolution Theory and Practice, Integration and Application*, Manchester and New York: Manchester University Press, pp. 97-111. de Reuck, Anthony (1990), 'A Theory of Conflict Resolution by Problem-Solving', in John Burton and Frank Dukes (eds), *Conflict: Readings in Management and Resolution*, London: Macmillan, pp. 183-198. Väyrynen, Tarja (1995), 'Going Beyond Similarity: The Role of Facilitator in Problem-Solving Workshop Conflict Resolution', *Paradigms* 9(2), pp. 71-85.
21 Burton (1997), *op. cit.*
22 Volkan and Itzkowtz (1994), *op. cit.* See also Aho, James (1994), *This Thing of Darkness: A Sociology of Enemy*, Seattle and London: University of Washington Press.
23 See, for example: Campbell, David (1993), *Writing Security*, Minneapolis: University of Minnesota Press. David Campbell and Michael Dillon (eds), *The Political Subject of Violence*, Manchester and New York: Manchester University Press. Connolly, William (1991), *Identity/Difference: Democratic Negotiations of Political Paradox*, Ithaca, NY: Cornell University Press. Dillon, Michael (1996), *Politics of Security*, London and New York: Routledge. Feldman, Allen (1991), *Formations of Violence, The Narrative of the Body and*

Political Terror in Northern Ireland, Chicago and London: The University of Chicago Press. Laclau, Ernesto (1996), 'Universalism, Particularism, and the Question of Identity', in Edwin Wilmsen and Patric McAllister (eds), *The Politics of Difference*, Chicago, London: University Chicago Press pp. 45-58. Shapiro, Michael (1997), *Violent Cartographies*, Minneapolis, London: University of Minnesota Press. Walker, R.B.J. (1993), *Inside/outside: International Relations as Political Theory*, Cambridge: Cambridge University Press.

24 See the following discussion: Østerud, Øyvind (1996), 'Antinomies of Postmodernism in International Studies', *Journal of Peace Research* 33(4), pp. 385-390. Smith, Steve (1997), 'Epistemology, Postmodernism and International Relations Theory', *Journal of Peace Research* 34(1), pp. 330-336.

25 Ryan (1990), *op. cit.*, pp. 50-93. Ryan (1996), *op. cit.*, p. 160.

26 Horowitz (1985), *op. cit.*, pp. 563-680. See also: Hannum, Horst (1990), *Autonomy, Sovereignty, and Self-Determination*, Philadelphia: University of Pennsylvania Press. Kaufman, Chaim (1996), 'Possible and Impossible Solutions to Ethnic Civil Wars', *International Security* 20(4), pp. 136-175.

27 McGarry, John and O'Leary, Brendan (1993), 'Introduction. The Macro-political Regulation of Ethnic Conflict', in John McGarry and Brendan O'Leary (eds), *The Politics of Ethnic Conflict Regulation*, London, New York: Routledge, pp. 1-39.

28 For a full description of the Lacanian identification theory, see Laclau, Ernesto and Lilian Zac (1994), 'Minding the Gap: The Subject of Politics', in Ernesto Laclau (ed.), *The Making of Political Identities*, London, New York: Verso, pp. 11-39.

29 Schutz, Alfred (1964), *Collected Papers I*, The Hague: Martinus Nijhoff, pp. 226-231.

30 Ibid., p. 49.

31 Ibid., pp. 120-134. Schutz, Alfred and Thomas Luckmann (1974), *The Structures of the Life-World*, Vol. 1, London: Heinemann, pp. 261-262.

32 Schutz (1964), *op. cit.*, pp. 95-129, 227-255.

33 For a full account see Väyrynen, Tarja (1998), 'Ethnic Communality and Conflict Resolution', *Cooperation and Conflict* 33(1), pp. 59-80.

34 On the political nature of human encounters see Arendt, Hannah (1958), *The Human Condition*, New York: Doubleday & Company, pp. 178-184.

35 Arendt, Hannah (1970), *On Violence*, San Diego, New York and London: Harcour Brace & Company, p. 52.

36 Barth (1969), *op. cit.*, pp 9-38. Bauman, Zygmunt (1992), 'Soil, Blood and Identity', *The Sociological Review* 40(4), pp. 675-701.

37 Bauman, Zygmunt (1991), *Modernity and Ambivalence*, Ithaca, New York: Cornell University Press, pp. 7-8.

38 Campbell and Dillon (1993), *op. cit.*, pp. 20-24.

39 Ibid., pp. 1-47.
40 For the sovereign state see: Ashley, Richard (1989), 'Living on Border Lines: Man, Poststructuralism, and War', in James Der Derian and Michael Shapiro (eds), *International/Intertextual Relations*, Lexington: Lexington Books, pp. 259-322. Campbell (1993), *op. cit.* Linklater, Andrew (1990), *Men and Citizens in the Theory of International Relations*, London: Macmillan. Linklater, Andrew (1994), 'Dialogue, Dialectic and Emancipation in International Relations at the End of the Post-War Age', *Millennium: Journal of International Studies* 23(1), pp. 119-131. Walker (1993), *op. cit.*
41 Bauman (1991), *op. cit.*, p. 64.
42 Appadurai, Arjun (1990), 'Disjuncture and Difference in the Global Cultural Economy', *Theory, Culture and Society* 7(2-3), pp. 295-310.
43 Pettman, Jan Jindy (1996), 'Border Crossing/Shifting Identities: Minorities, Gender, and the State in International Perspective', in Michael Shapiro and Hayward Alker (eds), *Challenging Boundaries: Global Flows, Territorial Identities*, Minneapolis, London: University of Minnesota Press, p. 264.
44 Appadurai (1990), *op. cit.* Bauman (1992), *op. cit.*
45 Appadurai (1990), *op. cit.* Schulte-Sasse, Jochen and Schulte-Sasse, Linda (1991), 'War, Otherness, and Illusionary Identification with the State', *Cultural Critique* 9, pp. 67-95.
46 Schulte-Sasse and Schulte-Sasse (1991), *op. cit.*, p. 78.
47 On narrative closure see Cobb, Sara (1994), 'A Narrative Perspective on Mediation: Toward the Materialization of the 'Storytelling' Metaphor', in Joseph Folger and Tricia Jones (eds), *New Directions in Mediation*, Thousand Oaks, London, New Delhi: Sage Publications, pp. 54-56.
48 Ibid., p. 56.
49 Aoki, D. S. (1995), 'Using and Abusing of French Discourse Theory: Misreading Lacan and the Symbolic Order', *Theory, Culture and Society* 12(4), pp. 47-70.
50 Feldman (1991), *op. cit.*, p. 5. Laclau, Ernesto (1994), 'Introduction', in Ernesto Laclau (ed.), *The Making of Political Identities*, London, New York: Verso, p. 3. For more on Lacan's symbolic order and its indeterminacy see Aoki (1995), *op. cit.*
51 On dialogue see: Bakhtin, M. M. (1986), *Speech Genres and Other Essays*. Austin: University of Texas Press. Benhabib, Seyla (1992), *Situating the Self*, Cambridge: Polity Press. Gadamer, Hans-Georg (1991), *Plato's Dialectical Ethics*, New Haven and London: Yale University Press.
52 Benhabib (1992), *op. cit.*, p. 49.
53 Ibid., p. 9.
54 Ibid., p. 38.

7 Identity and Intra-State Ethnonational Mobilization

RALF RÖNNQUIST

According to most social scientists in the 1950s and 1960s, developments in modernized societies, particularly an ever-increasing economic internationalization and interdependence, would in time make ethnonational identities more or less politically irrelevant and the nation-state obsolete. In the late 1960s, however, the so-called 'ethnic revival' in the West indicated that this form of identity had not lost its mobilization potential.

Scholarly interest in the subject grew steadily during the 1970s and 1980s, but mushroomed with the rapid and dramatic dissolution of multinational states east of the former Iron Curtain in the 1990s, which seemed to confirm that the stability and viability of political communities still to great extent depended on how well they complied with cultural and historical divisions of territories. In that part of Europe, the conflicts between different groups who have claimed the right to control territories on the basis of ethnonational identification have in several cases escalated to a level of civil war with horrible costs in human suffering as a result. The worst manifestations of intra-state ethnonational conflicts in Western Europe have been terrorist campaigns. Corsica in France, the Basque countries in Spain and the British province of Northern Ireland are the most notorious examples.

To say that there are divergent opinions on the nature and causes of this undercurrent in the tide of international integration would be an understatement, but regardless of the differences that are to be found between specific cases of intra-state ethnonational conflicts they are fundamentally alike in the respect that they all focus on the discrepancies between the extension and the character of territorial governance and the ethnic composition of the area in question. They are all essentially about incompatible claims of rights to enforce control over access to a territory and the activities and things within it.

Although this type of conflict always constitutes a challenge to the authority and legitimacy of the territorial regime, there are cases where none of the directly involved conflict parties dominates the body politics of the state which, instead, is controlled by a separate party. Northern Ireland is one example. The province's Protestant majority (approximately two-thirds of the population) has had a reputation for being 'more British than the British', but being British does not mean the same thing to them as it does to the larger population of the 'British Isles'. In the eyes of most people, in spite of the rhetoric of political and paramilitary actors, 'the Troubles', the euphemism commonly used for the conflict, concerns British Protestants as well as Irish Catholics, the relations between what the Anglo-Irish peace initiative in December 1993, the Downing Street Declaration, neutrally called 'the two traditions of Northern Ireland'. In other words, the conflict is to a significant extent intra-regional.[1]

Territoriality, attachment to a given geographical area, is recognized as a central factor in human activity and human relations, since territories, for groups as well as individuals, are a resource to secure basic needs as survival and reproduction and constitute an important power base. Territoriality has for this reason been the focus of much attention in various scientific disciplines, often in conjunction with the concept of 'region'. Of course, various disciplines have made use of different divisions depending on the types of questions posed, but here the concept of region will have a rather specific meaning and refer to the usage of the term made in cultural geography. It concerns specific territories in which social and socio-economic processes, such as the division of labour, have given rise in the course of history to a particular identity shared by the population of that region. Understood in this theoretical sense, a 'region' can in practical terms vary greatly in size, and need not necessarily comply with boundaries of states. Regional identities may be attached to spatial entities transcending existing states as well as to territories within states.[2]

In this context it is necessary to focus on the institutionalization of regions. Institutions, defined as 'standardized, quite permanent modes of behaviour which are controlled by expectations, connected with various roles', reflect and reproduce a collective history of the area, and the process of institutionalization is therefore of decisive importance for the emergence of a common regional identity. This identity is spread and reinforced by means of the cultural processes of communication within the region and which under given circumstances can survive from generation to generation.[3]

In general, governments of states have made considerable efforts to develop a common identity among the citizens, and to make that identity the only politically relevant territorial identity, since it is a central element in the cohesion of the state in periods of external and internal pressure. Such an identity-building process involves the transmission of institutions (social, cultural, economic and political), but has often proved difficult to control, and depends, among other things, on the cultural inclusiveness of the institutions of the state and on the existence of competing bases of identification.[4] One of the important factors in this context is the connection between territoriality and ethnicity.

The term ethnicity refers to a set of common characteristics for a given group of people. In this respect ethnicity does not differ from culture defined as 'acquired patterns of thought and actions and their products, based on values which are common to groups of people who are or who have been in contact with one another'.[5] An individual's awareness of being a bearer of a specific identity may be more or less developed, as well as more or less obvious to an outside observer, and relates to the conditions determined by his or her surroundings. This concerns both how clearly the cultural pattern of his or her group manifests itself and how far the cultural distance to other groups is. When it comes to the group as such, the identity is in general socially defined.[6]

As with the case of cultural groups in general, there are a great variety of possible bases for designing ethnic groups and the borders between them. Religion and language belong to the most predominant, but ethnic groups may be distinguished from one another on less obvious grounds and the perception of characteristics of a certain group may also differ depending on if it is internally or externally defined. In other words, the collective identity of a specific group of people can mean something to them, which it might not mean to others, and groups that by others are treated as a homogenous entity may find it rational to act like one. Fredrick Barth has cogently argued that it is at the boundaries of ethnic groups that ethnicity becomes meaningful. The cultural stuff that they enclose is of less importance. It is, however, common to distinguish ethnic groups from other cultural groups by the emphasis the former places on descent, which implies that members of an ethnic group are normally born into the group and the shared cultural heritage. The common descent may very well be a fiction, but what is important is that the group perceives itself as having undergone a long historical development which is distinct from that of other groups.[7]

Ethnic groups need not have any territorial attribution. However, considering that the emergence of common cultural features is to a large extent a product of processes evolved over a long period of time, and that these processes have affected groups of peoples which have been in contact with each other, it is natural that cultural identity-building, in general, has been territorially delimited. Various ethnic groups may also inhabit a specific territory and associate themselves with it. One may here speak of ethnoterritorial groups. In the case of such groups, the territory normally becomes a symbol for social kinship and an inalienable part of the common ethnic identity. For the individual members of the ethnic collective, the attachment to the territory in question also implies an emotional link, since the land is part and parcel of the collective identity and thereby also of the individual identity. An external threat to the territory, on the other hand, tends to reinforce the sense of kinship and unity within the ethnic group. Empirically speaking, there are few, if any examples of groups that have voluntarily renounced a part of the territory to which they consider themselves to have a historical claim.[8]

In the case of ethnonational groups, the attachment to the territory is linked with a perception of a possessive relationship between people and space. The territory in question is imagined as a historic 'homeland', as a rightful inheritance from past generations. In the case of ethnonational groups, the attachment to the territory is linked with a perception of a possessive relationship between people and space. The territory in question is imagined as a historic 'homeland', as a rightful inheritance from past generations. Ethnonationalism could thus be seen as an ideology built on the belief that there is a group of people who qualify to be regarded as an ethnonation, that its interests and values are superior to all other interests and values, and that the nation should be as independent as possible, which presupposes control over the territory it associates itself with.[9] The geographical boundaries may, however, have an elastic quality. Expansion or contraction does not necessarily have any major consequences to national consciousness or identity, since the conception of the homeland may as well be based on a symbolic as a physical delimitation of space.[10] Even if the external conditions for ethnonational identities and perhaps even for territorial divisions in general are changed, these identities have proved to retain a strong emotive force and have in several cases been revived and reinforced in conjunction with changes, structural as well as situational, which have rightly or wrongly been perceived as unfavourable to the group in question.

Ethnonational identity can thus be said to be closely related to an aspect of historical consciousness which is particularly alive – the collective memory. This may be far from a very 'true' or 'realistic' recollection of the group's past experiences and could perhaps best be described as a half-remembered but never forgotten history. Nevertheless, it can be both an existentially and politically relevant perception of history, not least so since different groups refer to it as part of a contest for power.[11] Conceptions of ethnic and national communities are, however, as has often been pointed out, humanly produced and as such also humanly changeable. The historian Eric Hobsbawm has, among many others, made a good point when stressing that images of ethnic distinctiveness and national traditions usually lack the deep historical roots that are commonly ascribed and in general are 'inventions' in order to serve the interests of social and political actors. In this context historians, lay as well as professional, have often played a very important role, not only by being in most cases the originators and promoters of the most prevailing myths about origins of peoples and stereotypes of popular culture, but also by reinterpreting the past and mediating new perspectives on group relations in a spatial context.[12]

On the other hand, the argument has often been overstated and the perspective has in general been restricted to one side of the process to communication, to the propagandists. Any invention or reinterpretation of the components of ethnicity must in one way or the other comply with the existing collective memory and established social understandings within the group to which the message is directed.[13] One may therefore assume that transformations cannot radically deviate from previous articulations, and that they at every given point of time can only be manipulated to a certain extent.

Although significant changes in the conceptions of ethnic identities are a relatively time-consuming process, it is nevertheless necessary to take them into account. They affect the group members' frames of reference and structures of expectation, i.e. the way people organize their knowledge of the world around them and use it to interpret new information, and thereby the preconditions for political mobilization. However, neither the structural nor the actor-oriented explanations that have been put forward to explain the revival of ethnonationalism have paid much attention to people's perceptions of the significance of ethnic and territorial identity. A great majority of scholars have regarded other structural factors as the dynamic ones, and when taken into consideration, these forms of identities have seldom been treated as more than locational referents and static background variables.[14]

Like all collective identities, however, ethnic and territorial identities have to be communicated, which is done in a specific but at the same time changing societal environment. They are influenced by the experiences of the group and should therefore be seen as dynamic variables, both in relation to content and in relation to the individuals that carry the identity. A good argument could thus be made for a more balanced approach, not least considering that the fundamental precondition for intra-state ethnonational conflicts is that a group, or part of it, identify itself on the basis of ethnic affinity and territorial affiliation.

Ethnonational identities *per se*, however, do not necessarily have any direct impact on political behaviour, but there is a subjective aspect of identity that may have such implications. In this context it is relevant to distinguish between identity and identification. The former can be described as a passive awareness of a condition, while the latter refers to an active consciousness of belonging to a group. Identification implies a perception of separation between groups, and it is often coupled with a readiness to safeguard the collective identity and to defend the group's real or perceived interests. This is the kind of identification that can acquire political importance, either by giving legitimacy to a regime, or by providing the basis for political mobilization.[15] It is not, however, a sufficient condition. The question of identification has first to become a political issue and the group, or parts of the group, see itself as a party in a contest with at least one other group of people concerning the distribution of power, material resources, status and values. Without a distributional element, identity will not be a motivation for conflict; without an identity element the question of distribution will remain unfocused and not be a valid base for political mobilization.[16]

Compared to the multiplicity of explanations of the causes and nature of ethnonational conflicts, the agreement regarding the pattern for this type of conflict to arise may appear to be striking. The stages of conflict development could be summarized under the headings: politicization of identity; articulation of conflict objects and demands; mobilization and choice of conflict methods; and, at the end of the scale, resolution – hopefully at the negotiation table. However, since governments are usually one of the parties in a conflict, these conflicts are normally characterized by an asymmetrical power-relationship, which is generally considered unfavourable for negotiation and is one of the explanations as to why they so often manifest themselves in violent forms. In terms of legitimacy, access to resources and military power, governments are, in general, the strongest party in the conflict. Ethnonational groups that challenge the authority and legitimacy of the state have to fight for all of these and are, at least to begin with, the weaker parties. On the other hand, ethnonational actors are normally fixed on the conflict and redress the asymmetry with their intensity of engagement, their commitment to a 'just cause', while governments are distracted by many other interests and have to weight its devotion to the particular conflict in relation to both domestic and international considerations.[17]

Although these stages of conflict development follow in logical order, ethnonational conflicts can move back as well as forward along the full scale of conflict development. They can in this respect be regarded as moving targets, and many of their dynamics have to do with attempts by the parties to push it in one direction or the other. The first stage, politicization, can take place against the background of various structural and situational circumstances, but is most often seen as a result of societal modernization processes, such as the development of capitalism, industrialism or state penetration into wider spheres of the 'civil' society. This initial phase is normally associated with members of the group's intellectual elite who try to make the group conscious of its own individuality, to turn identity into identification, and is usually characterized by agitation rather than organization.[18]

Intra-state ethnonational conflicts are as a rule multidimensional. Each dimension can contain a particular value or conflict object, and the second stage of conflict development, articulation, is characterized by several organizations that present different types of demands, representing different parts of the disaffected population. Together these dimensions constitute the conflict, but they may vary in their impact and the most important dimensions relate to political and administrative influence, economic power and cultural standing which are perceived to be unevenly or unjustly distributed among the parties of the conflict. The conflicts within the dimensions are in principle relative and of a variable-sum character even if they are often perceived by the parties to the conflict as absolute and as zero-sum conflicts, which explains the high degree of polarization that is to be found in so many cases of ethnonational conflicts.[19]

As the conflict continues into the stage of mobilization, disparate groups come under pressure to bring this diversity under one roof, and to unite behind a few overriding demands in order to assert legitimacy as a representative voice of the ethnonational group and to exert maximum pressure on the counter party. The primary function of what might be called ethnonational movement discourse is to constitute the subjects and objects of the conflict, and it is in the mobilization stage that the consolidating nationalist message comes out as uniting ideology. Hereby, mobilization becomes a factor of some importance in itself for the identification process.[20] It is also at this stage of conflict development that the chances to find a political solution to the conflict become significantly reduced. The actors who mobilize tend to be inward-looking and preoccupied with the building of solidarity within the movement and are therefore less inclined to negotiate.[21]

To the study of intra-state ethnonational conflicts, as well as to group conflicts in general, mobilization is also of particular interest since it is one of the three closely inter-related dimensions by which conflict intensity is judged. The other two are demands and conflict behaviour. Demands may be of varying scope and lie on a scale between, at one end, symbolic claims and, at the other end, radical demands which, to the counter-party, may appear to be non-negotiable and as performative threats. Conflict behaviour refers to methods employed, ranging from bilateral negotiations to unilateral resort to violence. Those two dimensions are essentially qualitative indications of the seriousness of a conflict.[22] Mobilization, on the other hand, is usually seen as a quantitative dimension. The political impact of the support given to the demands and methods of the conflict parties often depends, however, less on the size of the mobilized group than on the influence and resources of those who are mobilized, their degree of commitment, and their preparedness for action. Thus, mobilization contains important qualitative aspects.

But, mobilization is not only a question of content. It is also a question of form, and the concept will in this context overlap with conflict behaviour. Ethnonational mobilization has taken place both outside established political structures, including a wide range of actions from organizing demonstrations, civil disobedience and passive resistance, to armed struggle, and within the framework of existing political systems, which in western democracies has either been in the form of an all-party or single-party approach. The advantage of the all-party strategy is that different social strata have the opportunity to act on the basis of their own social values. The drawback is that it may be difficult to make ethnonational demands political priorities. The separate political party approach has, on the other hand, the disadvantage that the party will find difficulty in creating an own political profile in all questions which are not related to the ethnonational conflict and party members as well as the possibility that potential supporters may find themselves in a cross-pressure situation.[23]

The methods of mobilization do not exclude each other. The choice depends to a large extent on the actors' perceptions of possibilities – their assessments of the relationship between existing barriers and available resources, an evaluation of the mobilization potential in different approaches. In other words, kinds of cost-benefit analyse.[24] Also the immediate aims of conflict actors usually shift in the course of campaigns as the political opportunities change, as is well illustrated by the propaganda war for the hearts and minds of the Irish minority in Northern Ireland. In order to build support and prestige, the Provisional Irish Republican Army (PIRA) initially provided community defence and avoided overt offensive actions against the British Army. When the latter lost its credibility as a neutral peacekeeping force in the eyes of the minority, the 'Provisionals' exploited this support by launching an urban guerrilla campaign with the traditional objective to end British rule in Ireland. In the early 1990s, the possibilities of forming a pan-nationalist front between PIRA's political wing, Sinn Fein, and the leading party of minority, the Social Democratic and Labour Party, started a debate on whether a political or armed struggle best served the purpose of realizing the unification of 'the Six Counties' in the north and the Irish Republic in the south. The same actor may even use several alternatives for action at the same time. To quote a prominent member of Sinn Fein, Danny Morrison, at the party's 'Árd Fheis' (congress) 1981; 'will anyone here object if with the ballot box in this hand and an Armalite in this hand we take power in Ireland?'[25]

The choice of mobilization strategies is not always, however, a free one. Strong and repressive governments can effectively close the door to the political arena, but the possibilities to mobilize an ethnonational group can also be restricted by less obvious circumstances, such as the actors' access to, and ability to make use of, information and communication structures, and their capacity to provide a functional organizational framework. Also the degree of urbanization and the group's level of education and employment are factors of relevance in this context.[26] Of fundamental importance is, however, the group members' perception of the validity of an ethnonational perspective on the distribution of power and resources and the perceived significance of conflict objects. Discontent with the group's position in relation to other groups is not necessarily seen as ethnically conditioned or it may only be felt by certain sub-sections. The demands of ethnonational actors may coincide with interest of societal categories, such as class, profession or status group, and amplify the perception of the political relevance of ethnonational identification. On the other hand they may not, in which case potential supporters will find themselves in a situation where they have to choose between different possible identification objects. How ethnonational demands relate to other societal divisions and conflicts – a relational aspect – are often decisive for the possibilities to attract mass support.[27]

Another factor of importance is that the relationship between ethnonational actors' measures and aims is perceived as balanced, which in its turn depends on predominant social values and on what might be called a legacy of history. Previous exposure to discrimination on grounds of ethnic or territorial identity will increase the tendency to interpret a current uneven resource distribution as an intentional policy from the group who control government, and the methods used to protest in the past will influence, if not determine, future mobilization strategies and conflict behaviour. Consequently, support behind actors who are trying to promote ethnonational demands with violent means can to some extent depend on a deeper form of political culture.[28] In Northern Ireland, armed actors have been a part of political life since long before its foundation in 1921, and in the consciousness of the minority, Irishmen have constantly been maltreated under British rule.

To the ongoing process to make peace and social stability in the province, almost thirty years of paramilitary terrorism and open hostility between the two communities constitute a serious problem in itself. Locally, violence has to some extent become self-generating. Especially in cities and larger towns, there have been few families who have not suffered from action by paramilitaries, less organized extremists or regular security forces. In parts of Belfast and Londonderry, two generations have been brought up in an environment where violence or threats of violence have been a 'natural' part of daily life, with the result that normal psychological barriers against physically aggressive behaviour have broken down.[29]

The Troubles have also significantly reinforced urban residential segregation. In order to avoid harassment and to secure property and health, thousands of families have moved out of mixed areas, and in 1991 half of the population lived in areas where one of the groups were in a majority of at least 90%. This development has, of course, meant an overall reduction in everyday cross-community contacts, but by gathering in predominantly Catholic or Protestant areas, attitudes and values within the groups have become more homogeneous and the polarization between the groups accentuated.[30]

On this intra-regional level of the conflict, the ceasefire of the major paramilitary actors in the autumn of 1994 did not reduce the tensions. Contrary to the Berlin Wall, which was torn down at the end of the Cold War, the Peace Wall that divided Catholic and Protestant areas in central Belfast, was extended in the first year of peace. The riots in connection with 'the marching season' (April to September) in the following years were the most severe since the early 1970s, and institutions and buildings symbolizing the groups' respective identities were attacked to an unprecedented extent.[31] To build not only a political system that creates a balance between minority and majority, but also structures and regulations that lay the foundation to equal social, economical and cultural opportunities, can against this background prove to be a complicated process. What 'they' gain will easily be seen as 'our' loss as in a zero-sum game.

The peace process is also endangered by what the Irish historian James Beckett once called 'the tyranny of the dead'. The sacrifices of past and present 'freedom fighters' make it harder to accept negotiated compromises as a reasonable outcome in relation to the invested human capital. In the words of Bernadette Sands-McKevitt commenting on the all-party (and, by a majority in referendums both north and south of the border, democratically sanctioned) Good Friday Agreement in May 1998: 'My brother didn't give his life for cross-border bodies'.[32] Sands-McKevitt was a high-profile member of the Continuity IRA, a faction of militants who had left the PIRA to continue the armed struggle for a United Ireland. The brother in question was Bobby Sands, the PIRA prisoner who in 1981 starved himself to death for 'Ireland's freedom' and in protest at being deprived of the status of political prisoner. By this ultimate demonstration of Irish republican eschatology, Bobby Sands secured a place for himself among the most prominent of national martyrs and changed in the eyes of both a broad Irish and international opinion the relationship between subject and object of political violence, between victim and victimizer. Sands's death was seen as being caused by a rigid and inhumane attitude on the side of British authorities, and the reaction led to a peak in the support behind the Republican movement.[33]

The possibilities of mobilizing people in a given conflict situation are, however, not only dependent on place-specific conditions, activities and understandings. External coalition partners, which ethnonational actors, in general, are eager to find in order to strengthen their position, may profoundly affect both mobilization and conflict development. These may be found among interest groups and similar movements within the state or abroad, among international organizations and foreign governments – perhaps with an interest in destabilizing the state where the conflict takes place. In the worst of cases, intra-state ethnonational conflicts have turned into proxy wars for distant powers. Examples are abundant in modern Africa, but are also to be found in European history.[34]

Outside support may also be drawn from a government or other actors in a neighbouring state of the same ethnonational identification – as in the case of irredentism – or where the group in question constitutes a substantial minority. In this context, it is not only the fact that the territory inhabited by an ethnonational group may be divided by state boundaries that creates a potential for external influence. Migration may be of equal importance, and in some cases emigration has made it possible to find coalition partners in very distant states and has affected both the domestic and foreign politics of those states. The massive influx of Irishmen in the USA during the second half of the nineteenth century has, for example, created an important source of economic, political and moral support for the nationalist movement in Ireland before 1921 and in Northern Ireland since. The size of the group of voters who have a hyphenated Irish-American identity has also forced American administrations, especially when led by the Democratic Party, to make the conflict in Northern Ireland a relatively significant foreign policy issue.[35]

Large-scale institutional and political developments (ideological as well as geopolitical) are other types of forces transcending state boundaries that may have significant effects on the conditions for mobilization. To many Scots, for example, the British state has lost its *raison d'être* altogether by the development of the European Union at the same time as the risks of separation have been perceived as reduced to insignificance. In Ireland the political impact of the American and French revolutions on the emergence of a revolutionary Republican movement in the late eighteenth century can hardly underestimated, but a so-called demonstration effect was also very important in the first phase of politicization and protest in Northern Ireland in the late 1960s. The arguments of the civil rights movement, and especially the ambition to make the streets the proper place for politics, were heavily influenced by the example set by Martin Luther King's campaign for equal rights in America. However, while leading civil rights activists articulated the conflict in terms of social class and tried to mobilize on cross-community basis, when developing into a mass movement, the support was almost exclusively drawn from members of the Catholic community who were motivated by a traditional discontent with discrimination on the basis of ethnic identity. What the civil rights movement accomplished – besides more concessions to the demands of the minority in a few years than had been possible during the whole period since the foundation of Northern Ireland in 1921 – was to raise the tension and act as the catalyst for an open conflict between the two groups. Hereby the civil rights movement paved the way for a mobilization behind militant actors on both sides.[36]

Notes

1   *The Independent* 16/12 1993. It is in the local context that the terms Protestant and Catholic first and foremost have their meaning. In spite of the religiously inspired rhetoric of such politicians as Ian Paisley, in modern Northern Ireland few Protestants have found their personal faith politically important *per se*, and on the Catholic side no political actor have put forward religion as a source of conflict. The terms Protestant and Catholic are perceived by most people in the province as badges recognized by all as standing for particular traditions and historical experiences, and they should rightly be regarded as names of group identities with only intra-regional relevance. The Protestant majority's political control over Northern Ireland came to an end when direct rule by central government was introduced in 1972. Rönnquist, R. (1997), 'The Troubles – tidsperspektiv på en samtidshistorisk konflikt,' in L. M. Andersson and U. Zander (eds), *In med historien*, Lund, pp. 64-66, 74; Rönnquist, R. (1998),

'God Save Britain', in S. Tägil (ed.), *Europa – historiens återkomst*, Hedemora, pp. 19-20, 128-133, 153, 158-159.

2 See Johansson, R., Rönnquist, R. and Tägil, S. (1998), 'Territorialstaten i kris?', in *Europa historiens återkomst, op. cit.*, pp. 15-17; Sack, R. (1986), *Human Territoriality. Its Theory and History*, Cambridge, pp. 7-14, 19-21, 26-27, 32-34, 216-219. On different perspectives of territoriality, see also Grosby, S. (1995), 'Territoriality: The Transcendental, Primordial Feature of Modern Societies', *Nations and Nationalism* 1(2), *passim*. Concerning the concept of regions in different sciences, see Claval, P. (1987), 'The Region as a Geographical, Economic and Cultural Concept', *International Social Science Journal* 112, *passim*. Borders between regions are discussed in Tägil, S. *et al.* (1977) *Studying Boundary Conflicts*, Lund, pp. 150-152.

3 According to the Finnish geographer Anssi Paasi one can differ between four stages of regional institutionalization: '1) assumption of territorial shape 2) development of conceptual (symbolic) shape 3) development of institutions and 4) establishment as part of the regional system and regional consciousness concerned. The order between those stages does not, however, necessarily follow a historical line of development.' Paasi, A. (1986), 'The Institutionalization of Regions: a Theoretical Framework for Understanding the Emergence of Regions and the Constitution of Regional Identity', *Fennia* 164(1), pp. 111, 121. On the definition of institutions, see p. 139. Cf. Deutsch, K. (1969), *Nationalism and Social Communication*, London, pp. 86-88, on processes of cultural communication.

4 Cf. Knight, D. (1982), 'Identity and Territory: Geographical Perspectives on Nationalism and Regionalism', *Annals of the Association of American Geographers* 72, pp. 514-517. See also the discussion in Seton-Watson, H. (1977), *Nations and States. An Enquiry into the Origins of Nations and the Politics of Nationalism*, London, pp. 143-191.

5 This definition takes into account both attitudes and behaviour, based on common values. In general the qualification must be made that more than one criterion must be used. A clear demarcation may thereby be drawn excluding different forms of sub-cultures. Cf. Johansson, R. (1976), *Kulturella beroenden. Sverige – världen – framtiden*, Stockholm, p. 13.

6 Tägil, S. (1984a), 'Ethno-regionalism as a Problem of Conflict Theory', in in S. Tägil (ed.), *Regions in Upheaval*, Lund, pp. 17-18.

7 See Barth, F. (1969), 'Introduction', in F. Barth (1969), *Ethnic Groups and Boundaries. The Social Organization of Culture Difference*, Oslo, pp. 13-16; Chapman, M., McDonald, M. and Tonkin, E. (1989), 'Introduction', in E. Tonkin, M. McDonald and M. Chapman (eds), *History and Ethnicity*, London, pp. 11-17; Rönnquist, R. (1990), *Historia och nationalitet. Skotsk etno-territorialitet i ett historiskt perspektiv*, Lund, pp. 23-24. Concerning ethnic myths, see e.g. the discussion in Smith, A. D. (1986), *The Ethnic Origins of*

Nations. Oxford, pp. 174-209 and in G. Hosking and G. Schöpflin (eds), *Myths and Nationhood.* London, *passim.* It has to be stressed, however, that conceptions of ethnic affinity can be more or less inclusive. Scots is an example of on an ethnically defined group of people composed of two once cultural distinct and regionally separated groups, anglized Lowlanders and clan-bound Gaels in the Scottish Highlands. Rönnquist (1990), *op. cit.*, pp. 81-91.

8 Johansson, Rönnquist and Tägil (1998), *op. cit.*, pp. 18-19; Smith, A.D. (1981), 'War and Ethnicity: the Role of Warfare in the Formation, Self-images and Cohesion of Ethnic Communities', *Ethnic and Racial Studies* 4, pp. 375-384.

9 See Rönnquist (1990), *op. cit.*, pp. 29-30. Nations and nationalism are, needless to say, concepts that have been applied to other territorial communities apart from ethnonational ones. Nations can refer to states and their citizens, and nationalism to a rallying to the state and its welfare, but also to groups over and under that level who cultivate a vision of forming an autonomous entity on the basis of common cultural or territorial identification. However, in spite of the differences, it is common to stress the idea of having a legitimate right through ancestral ties to control a defined territory when these concepts are discussed. Cf. Williams, C.H. and Smith, A.D. (1983), 'The National Construction of Social Space', *Progress in Human Geography* 7, *passim* (especially p. 509). For a discussion on the varieties of nationalism and different perspectives on the phenomena, see e.g. Connor, W. (1995), *Ethnonationalism: The Quest for Understanding*, Princeton, NJ, chs 3-4; Hutchinson, J. and Smith, A.D. (1994), *Nationalism*, Oxford, *passim*; Smith, A.D. (1971), *Theories of Nationalism.* London, chs 7-9; Smith, A.D. (1973), 'Nationalism', *Current Sociology* 21, pp. 47-94.

10 See Gottman, J. (1973), *The Significance of Territory.* Charlotteville, pp. 134-143.

11 Cf. Connerton, P. (1989), *How Societies Remember.* Cambridge, chs 1-2; Le Goff (1992), J. *History and Memory.* New York, pp. 3-4, 55-58, 81-151; Smith, A.D. (1992), 'Chosen Peoples: Why Ethnic Groups Survive', *Ethnic and Racial Studies* 15, pp. 436-441, 446-452.

12 See Hobsbawm, E. (1983), 'Mass-Producing Traditions: Europe, 1870–1914', in E. Hobsbawm and T. Ranger (eds), *The Invention of Tradition.* Cambridge, *passim.* Good examples of historians as mythmakers are given in the studies collected in *The Invention of Tradition.* See also Rönnquist (1990), *op. cit.*, pp. 43-51, 56, 100-101.

13 Cf. Murphy, A. (1991), 'Regions as Social Constructs: The Gap between Theory and Practice', *Progress in Human Geography* 15, pp. 24, 28-30.

14 Paasi (1986), *op. cit.*, pp. 12-23; Rönnquist (1990), *op. cit.*, pp. 28, 30-40.

15 See Johansson, Rönnquist and Tägil (1998), *op. cit.*, pp. 14-15.

16 See Tägil, S. (1984b), 'The Conditions for Ethno-Regional Conflict: Conclusions', in S. Tägil (ed.), *Regions in Upheaval.* Lund, pp. 242, 244, 247;

Zartman, W. (1995), 'Dynamics and Constraints in Negotiations in Internal Conflicts', in W. Zartman (ed.), *Elusive Peace: Negotiation an End to Civil Wars*, Washington DC, p. 5.

17 Zartman (1995), *op. cit.*, pp. 1, 7-9. While more than half of the conflicts between states during the 20th century have been transferred from fields of battle to the negotiation rooms, about two-thirds of internal conflicts have ended with surrender or total defeat by one of the parties involved. Ibid., p. 1.

18 Most scholars seem to accept that there have been societal phenomena related to ethnonationalism before those processes of societal modernization – patriotism, xenophobia, ethnocentrism etc. Some would even agree that there have been earlier historical examples of ethnic groups that have attached their ethnic identity to a homeland and on this basis claimed a right to political control over the defined territory. However, these phenomena have not been considered as the real thing. Protonationalism is a term that is often used to dismiss them, but on what grounds are sometimes less than clear. See e.g. Newman, S. (1991), 'Does Modernization Breed Ethnic Political Conflict?', *World Politics* 43, *passim*; Rönnquist (1990), *op. cit.*, pp. 29-32.

19 Cf. Tägil (1984b), *op. cit.*, p. 244.

20 Blain, M. (1994), 'Power, War and Melodrama in the Discourses of Political Movements', *Theory and Society* 23, p. 830.

21 Zartman (1995), *op. cit.*, p. 14.

22 Tägil (1984a), *op. cit.*, pp. 38-40.

23 Tägil (1984b), *op. cit.*, pp. 242-243.

24 Cf. Blain (1994), *op. cit.*, pp. 808, 812-813; Tägil, *et al.* (1977), *op. cit.*, pp. 46-48, 131-133.

25 Rönnquist (1998), *op. cit.*, pp. 154-158, 160-161. In the winter of 1969/70 the original Irish Republican Army had split into an 'official' and a 'provisional' branch. The 'Official IRA' stopped its offensive operations in May 1972 and transformed into a political party in 1984.

26 Cf. Nyström, K. (1985), 'Institutionaliseringens betydelse för nationalistisk mobilisering', *Sociologisk Forskning* 1; Rönnquist (1990), *op. cit.*, pp. 26-28. In Northern Ireland, a high level of unemployment, especially among the youth, has facilitated recruitment to the paramilitaries on both sides. While youth without work in many other Western societies have tried to find a way to self-realization through sport, gang crime and drugs, the illegal armies of Northern Ireland have offered an alternative. They have provided a purpose, an identity, a form of career and income. Bell, D. (1990), *Acts of Union: Youth Culture and Sectarianism in Northern Ireland*. London, p. 22-24; Burton, F. (1978), *The Politics of Legitimacy: Struggles in a Belfast Community*. London, pp. 81-110.

27 Rönnquist, R. (1984), 'Class versus Ethnicity. Social Conflict and Political Mobilization: The Case of Scotland', in S. Tägil (ed.), *Regions in Upheaval*. Lund, pp. 106-109, 135-140.

28 Political culture can be seen as relatively fast changing societal phenomenon, in terms of left- or right-wing tendencies influencing a wider spectrum of political actors and the electorate, but it might be given a deeper meaning and relate to collective political behaviour that tends to repeat itself over time. Cf. Blain (1994), *op. cit.*, p. 819.

29 Kelley, J. and McAllister, I. (1986), 'Economic Theories and Political Violence in the Northern Ireland Conflict', in Y. Alexander and A. O'Day (eds), *Ireland's Terrorist Dilemma*. Dordrecht, pp 77, 88-92; Poole, M. (1983), 'The Demography of Violence', in J. Darby (ed.), *Northern Ireland. The Background to the Conflict*. Belfast, pp. 168-174.

30 Rönnquist (1998), *op. cit.*, pp 159-168. Cf. Butler, D. and Stokes, D. (1974), *Political Change in Britain*. London, pp. 130-140.

31 See the Northern Ireland Office's report 'Security, Crime and Policing in Northern Ireland' (1996), and 'The North Report on Parades' (1996), both published on Internet: http://www.open.gov.uk/index.htm. See also *Belfast Telegraph*, 15 April 1997.

32 *Irish News*, 14 April 1998. In May 1998 another group of former members of the PIRA reorganized under the name the Real IRA. The Irish National Liberation Army, a break-away from the Official IRA in 1976, had never declared a ceasefire and was, of course, together with the minor groups of active loyalist paramilitaries yet another threat to a peaceful solution to the conflict.

33 Cf. Blain (1994), *op. cit.*, pp. 812, 817-825; Feldman, A. (1991), *Formation of Violence: The Narrative of the Body and Political Terror in Northern Ireland*. Chicago, pp. 238-244, 254-256, 264.

34 The most notable example in a British context is the French involvement in Scottish insurrections in the first half of the 18th century. See e.g. McLynn, F. (1981), *France and the Jacobite Rising of 1745*. Edinburgh, *passim*.

35 Gulke, A. (1997), *Northern Ireland: the International Perspective*. Dublin, ch. 7; Rönnquist (1997), *op. cit.*, pp. 72-73.

36 Rönnquist (1998), *op. cit.*, pp. 155, 176-177, 189-196. On the demonstration effect, see Lijphart, A. (1977), 'Political Theories and the Explanation of Ethnic Conflict in the Western World', in M. Esman (ed.), *Ethnic Conflict in the Western World*. Ithaca and London, pp. 63-64.

PART III

CAUSES OF PEACE AND CONFLICT TRANSFORMATION

8 Conflict Management and the Process of Escalation: Timing and Types of Responses

CHRISTIAN P. SCHERRER

Introduction

This chapter will correlate peace strategies such as the possibilities for the structural prevention of violence, conflict management and transformation with six stages of conflict. The role of different actors in preventing violence will be explored, including governments, development agencies, non-governmental organizations (NGOs) and the UN system. The question 'What to do in a particular situation?' is both linked with the type of conflicts we are dealing with as well as with the stage of escalation of the conflicts at the particular time of intervention. The focus will be on the importance of the right timing in response to conflict. Types of responses are clearly related to different types of conflicts. In my view peaceful responses – and peace strategies in general – should learn from existing schemes and aim at long-term structural and interactive prevention of violent conflict rather than plunge into activism producing short-term bandages. Proven mechanisms range from minority protection, affirmative action to autonomy regulations, power sharing, nationality policies, and (con-)federal schemes. Procedures and instruments would include standard setting for international laws and rules, such as schemes for the protection of non-dominant groups, as well as regimes for controlled partition/secession.

The crucial question of the right timing for peaceful responses to conflict

Let us think about conflicts in a very general way. In daily social life conflicts make sense. Conflict is an essential form of social interaction.[1] To argue with someone brings problems out. Problems should be expressed (not suppressed) – only in this way can solutions be found. To have it out with a person makes arrangements possible, with due respect for different interests and positions. Therefore we should not talk about preventing conflicts but about preventing destructive ways of dealing with incompatibilities, contradictions, disputes, and different interests and positions. Interaction becomes destructive by use of violence.

In processes confronting social groups or larger sections of society the option of using violence should be prevented from the onset. Some may argue that pacifism in interethnic or international relations is a questionable position. For instance they might claim the right to self-defence. Here things already start to get difficult. Others think about revolutionary violence, which should be characterized as *controlled* violence against oppression. The ideal typical case would be a so-called 'natural right of resistance' against tyranny. But we all know that there are no ideal typical cases in social life nor in the real world. It may only be consequent and genuine *common sense* to say that violence breeds violence and that prevention is better than cure.

Collective memory and dormant conflict

Conflicts are a natural thing and mere differences *as such* are not conflictive and therefore do not usually carry or provoke violence. Cultural or ethnic differences can be interesting or attractive and make social life more colorful – as long as such differences were not politicized and exploited for particular interests. Even worse, if states engage in such activity. Immanuel Kant's questions about sustainable peace by banning wars on a global scale 'for all time', thus establishing *eternal peace*, seemed not from this world. Kant wrote his piece about *eternal peace* some 200 years ago – after the French Revolution and at the height of the era of enlightenment. Common sense maintains that wars have always been fought. Therefore there is always a past full of memories of hostilities and despair. Past violence itself is a source for traumatizing memories.

A constitutive element for each and every society, community or ethnic group is what has been called the *collective memory*. Other elements would be a common language, being part of a common culture, living in a particular place or territory as a space of communication and social interaction and feeling some kind of solidarity of belonging to a particular group. It is the collective memory before all other elements making up a community of people which is the most decisive element regarding conflict.

The collective memory is a kind of living history book, giving a record of past traumatic experiences. Like official or written history it is full of myths. Common memories about the past reflect all kinds of events, including disputes, past injustice and traumas, violence and victimization, wars, and mass violence. In some cases the worst memory is about genocide. Psychologists talk about internalization such as 'sleeping memories' that can suddenly be reactivated. Peace researchers should know very well that memories of past horrors are still virulent after generations of peace and stability.

Adequate choice of procedures and use of instruments at the right time

Like memories conflicts can also be pending in a sub-conscious or *sleeping* stage, waiting to be suddenly reactivated. That is why this stage is the best time for prevention. Even weak preventive measures would have an effect. Targeted measures against renewed violence should be aware of the root causes of a *dormant conflict* (stage 1).

The adequate choice of procedures and use of instruments is important. Galtung made concrete proposals for conflict prevention, transformation or resolution in 35 conflict cases. To prevent conflicts from emerging the alternative options would be either *reliving the tragedy* (Galtung) in order to stop traumatization or to neutralize trauma by confidence building and *empowerment* – in order to prevent it from emerging again. In a post-conflict situation we would deal with the '3R' for Reconstruction, Reconciliation, Resolution.[2]

The weakness of many of the attempts made by peace and conflict research to respond to the ethno-national challenge has been due to a variety of factors. The way in which, up to now, almost all research capacity has been geared to classical, inter-state situations of conflict, and the general fixation on the activities of the superpowers and big powers, have proved totally inadequate. Endogenous causes of conflict, most notably the virulence of the ethnic factor, have been systematically underestimated. The global phenomenon of violent internal conflicts has, it is true, assumed a higher profile in research terms since 1989–90, but there continues to be serious research-related deficiencies.

Considerable deficiencies exist in regard to: (1) diagnosis, especially of the causes and dynamics of various types of violent conflict; (2) anticipatory capacity – that is, the ability to identify and respond to signs of potential conflict with foresight, on the basis of a thoroughgoing knowledge of the major causes of dissension (early warning/early action); (3) the structural prevention of conflicts; (4) therapeutic measures, especially in the form of constructive conflict management and peaceful intervention; and, finally, (5) 'peace search' – in other words, influencing the macro-political framework conditions.

A typology of responses to conflict would have essentially to include all kind of procedures and instruments for prophylactic peace-building and peace-keeping at the stage of *sleeping conflict*. A typology for crisis prevention and conflict management would first characterize institutions, procedures and instruments for peaceful coexistence (see Table 8.1). In a more specific typology for local and global peace building (see Table 8.2) instruments for violence prevention and inter-ethnic balance would be listed.

Stages of conflict escalation and possible constructive responses

Let us now look into conflict stages and possible constructive responses in an abstract way. The Herculean task of peace-building would most effectively be approached by various ways of structurally preventing violence on different levels. This would include different actors or institutions and can be achieved by various means. In the following general survey of types of crisis prevention and conflict management I have tried to specify some aspects of my typology of peace in order to give a historic and structural view of existing institutions, procedures and instruments for peaceful coexistence (cf. Table 8.2). In much the same way the procedures and instruments for violence prevention and inter-ethnic balance are given in a systematic overview (cf. Table 8.1 Typology for crisis prevention and conflicts management).

Structural prevention at the stage of dormant conflict

Realistically, peaceful coexistence would be approached by a minimal level effort. Before creating new instruments the application of existing instruments has to be guaranteed or enforced. International law is to safeguard international security as well as internal peace. The critical factor in International Law – in general, and in regard to human and minority rights in particular – is the lack or fragmentary nature of mechanisms and procedures for enforcing legal instruments such as declarations, conventions, covenants and treaties. Enforcing International Law is the real problem. It can be done in three ways:[3]

1. by comprehensive review processes and checks and controls, as in the case of the European Convention on Human Rights or in the case of the Convention for Indigenous Peoples of the International Labour Organization (ILO convention 169);
2. by institution building, as in the case of OSCE and its institution of a High Commissioner for Minorities, or the latest case, the establishment of an International Criminal Court (ICC), in order to outlaw gross human rights violations such as genocide and crimes against humanity, still meeting strong resistance by large states such as USA and France;
3. by refining an arsenal of sanctions, which would hurt the non-complying regimes and not the people.[4]

The total or almost total absence of sanctions is a phenomenon common to all contractual arrangements in International Law. There is simply no world government that ensures that International Law is observed. The United Nations are not a 'World Republic' (Kant) that could engage in global governance in this sense.

Structural prevention has many options regarding the multitude of 'new wars' and conflict characterized by ethnic factors. The best timing for it would be intervention at the stage of *dormant conflict*. This is where/when the obstacles would be few but the choice of possible approaches would be fairly broad. The scope would be large and open. Duplication is not a problem. A range of different actors and institutions could participate to take up their own initiatives.

The most effective forms of structural prevention are those built-in state structures, and combine elements such as autonomy for non-dominant groups, self-governance and (con-)federal schemes with power sharing. Peaceful coexistence and inter-ethnic balance can be achieved by a number of models for power sharing. The cases to be mentioned as examples – as you may see at once (Table 8.1) – can not be all that ideal. Other approaches for the realization of free association and internal self-determination of all peoples can be undertaken by way of autonomization – with a range of cases to be studied and compared. More systemic schemes for self-governance were realized by the nationality policies of large multi-ethnic states such as the former Soviet Union, China or India. Some cases might be considered as incomplete models. Nevertheless, many lessons can be learned from these long-term experiences. A last type of preventive response is still somewhat utopian. It would consist of regimes for secession and rules for the creation of new states or their international recognition.

There are other types of peace building, for instance the minority rights approach, undertaken on different levels ranging from international standard setting in the framework of the UN Human Rights Commission and at conferences of the OSCE to the creation of domestic laws. Legislation is best done in an interactive process involving different actors directly or at least consulting those groups, which are to profit from it. An ideal case for the latter could have been the elaboration of the Universal Declaration of the Rights of Indigenous Peoples at UN Geneva. Annual sessions of the Working Group on Indigenous Populations included hundreds of delegates from all over the world. The remarkable process of drafting such a declaration was suddenly interrupted – after 10 years of hard work!

Table 8.1 Typology for crisis prevention and conflict management: institutions, procedures and instruments for peaceful coexistence*

Peace building/types	Scope, realm	Principle	Period	Models and processes/ deficits/needs	Aims/objectives/ expectations
Peaceful coexistence by *structural prevention* of destructive interaction.	UN, regional regimes, states, societies, NGOs.	Interactive preventive rule of law.	Increasingly since 1945; still to be enforced.	Application of existing instruments/laws (international pacts, conventions, declarations) as well as development of new instruments in international law; problem: how to break passive/active resistance of states?	New instruments to combat destructive interaction between states and nation(alitie)s; rapid establishment of international criminal justice in high demand; lack of enforcement.

Peace building/types	Scope, realm	Principle	Period	Models and processes/ deficits/needs	Aims/objectives/ expectations
Peaceful coexistence by granting comprehensive *minority rights*.	States, multilateral regimes.	Active preventive internal rule of law.	Since 1980s; increasingly since 1990.	Protection of the rights of non-dominant groups (OSCE HCNM); standard setting by UN-CHR towards *Universal Declaration of the Rights of Indigenous Peoples*.	Internal peace and external security through inter-ethnic balance and protection of new minorities; application of international law.
Peaceful coexistence by *power sharing*.	States/ regimes/ civil actors.	Active preventive innovative.	For many centuries; more cases still to be established.	Lessons to be learned from experiences with different existing models of power sharing, representation, ethnically mixed elites and their co-operation (CH, Lebanon, Malaysia, Benin); models of limited attractivity.	Comparison of existing models and their performance; development of new instruments to promote con-structive interaction and balance of different ethnic and national groups.
Peaceful coexistence by granting *internal right to self-determination and free association* for all peoples.	Co-operation of involved state(s) and peoples; facilitation by UN, regional regimes, INGOs/NGOs.	Interactive preventive innovative.	Increasingly since 1945; still to be established on larger scale.	'Lessons learned?' from experiences with autonomy regulations and self-governance in all continents; models: *korenisazia* and autonomization in FSU and China; creation of new states in India, quotas for scheduled castes/tribes; autonomy regulations in Europe; lack of implementation.	Comparison of existing models and their performance; development of new instruments to promote con-structive interaction between states and nation(alitie)s; establishment of international regimes in high demand.
Peaceful coexistence by establishing *(con-) federal schemes*.	Co-operation of multi-ethnic state and people(s); facilitation by relevant actors.	Interactive preventive.	Increasingly since 1945; still to be established.	Lessons to be learned from experiences with federal schemes in all continents; models (also incomplete): FSU/RF, India, Nigeria, Tanzania, Ethiopia, new South Africa, Switzerland, Spain etc.	Comparison of existing models and their performance; development of new models to promote (con-) federal and regional schemes.

Peace building/types	Scope, realm	Principle	Period	Models and processes/ deficits/needs	Aims/objectives/ expectations
Peaceful coexistence by rules for the realization of the *full right to self-determination*.	Co-operation of involved state(s) and international community.	Interactive preventive innovative.	Still to be established.	Consequences to be drawn from experiences with destructive ethno-nationalist civil wars in all continents; deficit of shared norms/standards for secession; global governance.	Rules for the creation of new states; regimes for recognition of claims; new instruments to promote con-structive transition.
Preventing/ transforming violent conflict by *preventive diplomacy*.	State system primary; civil actors such as INGOs.	Reactive/ active; state-centred regime building.	On the rise since 1990; medium term.	Multi-ethnic societies/states; actionistic activities/power mediation, conflict regulation/agreements between the parties to the conflict; little impact.	*Protection*/minimal rights for non-dominant groups; security through respect for others, recognition of multiplicity.
Preventing violence by *early warning linked to early action*.	UN, INGOs, regional regimes, states local civil actors.	Active preventive.	Still to be established.	Increasing capabilities of early warning; full use of conflict prevention networks to be built-up jointly by multilateral regimes, research institutes and INGOs/NGOs.	Top priority for bridging the gap between early warning and early action.
Peace by peaceful intervention: *mediation/fac ilitation*.	Civil society actors, NGOs/ INGOs, some states.	Reactive-activist interactive (mainly internal) preventive.	On the rise since 1980s; short to longer term.	Multi-ethnic societies/states; actionistic mediation/facilitation, conflict regulation/solutions through agreements between in-side parties facilitated by out-side parties.	*Empowerment* for non-dominant groups; security through respect for others, recognition of multiplicity/ promotion of minorities' issues.
Peace building by *constructive dialogue*.	States external and local civil actors.	Active/ reactive processual preventive force innovative.	On the rise since 1990s; medium term.	Improvement of overall relationships in multi-ethnic societies/states; recognition and awareness about hidden perceptions/agendas of involved parties.	Discovering shared needs; focusing on the future; translating common needs into 'joint actions as stepping stones to agreements' (D. Weeks).

Peace building/types	Scope, realm	Principle	Period	Models and processes/ deficits/needs	Aims/objectives/ expectations
Peace building by constructive *conflict resolution* approaches.	States external and local civil actors.	Active/ processual preventive innovative.	Still to be established.	Facilitation of conflict resolutions through negotiation about binding agreements as constructive medium and long term approaches.	Shared needs and joint plans for the future; securing accountability of all parties and building sustainability.
Peaceful inter-ethnic coexistence by *enforcing accountability and compliance* of/by the states.	UN/regimes under monitoring and watch by NGOs/ INGOs.	Interventive; rule of national and international law.	Long-term approach; still at point zero.	Enlightened civilized state leaders and civic organizations pushing for change; over-all promotion of standard-setting in international law in order to force states to obey to the rules and comply with international law.	Humanitarian minimum and respect of human and minority rights; no double standards; clear-cut sanctions to be introduced against deviation/crimes by repressive and intransigent state governments.
Peace by peaceful means: education, *culture of peace* by lively cross-cultural communi-cation.	Civil society civilized states.	Active, interactive preventive innovative.	Medium periods.	Enlightened libertarian sectors of societies/civilized states pushing for change; prevention of violence by getting to know each-other (*multikulti* vs. daily racism; travelling, cultural contacts, arts, etc.).	Conflict regulation through rights for non-dominant groups (citizenship for 2nd generation migrants); respect for other societies and different cultures/life styles.

* Copyright 1997 © by C.P. Scherrer/ECOR

Table 8.2   Typology for local and global peace building: violence prevention and inter-ethnic balance[*]

Peaceful coexistence	Scope, realm	Principle	Period	Characteristics/ phenomena	Aims/ objectives/ results
Negative peace by *threat of aggression*; *pax americana/ sovietica*/etc.	Global state system globalize economy.	Deterrence (external) and internal control.	Short and medium-term.	Northern states or regional powers against weaker Southern states; exception: mutual deterrence of the super powers (Cold War).	Imposition of interest/containment/ economic interest; result: hegemony.

Peaceful coexistence	Scope, realm	Principle	Period	Characteristics/ phenomena	Aims/ objectives/ results
Negative peace by *military intervention* named *'humanitarian'*.	State system (often against civil society); UN.	External; state-centred; powered by legacy of Euro-colonialism/ imperialism.	Short-term since colonialism.	Usually colonial powers, Northern states or regional powers against weaker states at the peripheries; expression of (post-) colonial dependency (*dependencia*); toppling of unfriendly governments, eg. US-interventions in Latin America since Monroe.	Often ultimate with no agreement proposed; control/imposition of 'solutions'; result: conflict of interests; partial and non-sustainable effect, perpetuation of dependency.
Coexistence/ peace by *arbitration and settlement of disputes*.	State system.	External potentially also internal.	Since 1899 First Hague Peace Conference.	Establishment of the *Permanent Court of Arbitration* (PCA) 1899 and the Convention for the *Peaceful Settlement of International Disputes* (CPSID) provide for legal base.	Peaceful settlement of disputes is an good old idea (reaffirmed by the UN-Charter 1945, Article 33c); result: PCA had little impact.
Coexistence by *agreements*.	State system (primary); TNCs.	Internal/ expansive state-centred; *colonialism*.	Since the early 19th century.	Settlers vs. indigenous nations/weak settler states; conflict reduction by treaties, mostly broken after changes of the balance of power.	First territorial invasion; control of lands and resources; population control.
Coexistence through welfare state policies and agreements.	State system (primary); economy civil society.	Internal state-centred; expansive, *internal colonialism*.	Longer periods since the early 20th century.	*Mainstream*-societies vs. indigenous groups/strong settler states; attempted reduction of conflict, post-colonial *trusteeship* ideology; limited agreements with indigenous groups; reservation-type of system complemented by affirmative action (USA, Australia, NZ).	Alien control of most indigenous lands and resources; population control.

Peaceful coexistence	Scope, realm	Principle	Period	Characteristics/ phenomena	Aims/ objectives/ results
Internal peace and coexistence by means of modern treaties.	State system economy civil society.	Internal and state-centred; softened *internal colonialism*.	Undefined periods since the 1980s.	*Mainstream*-societies, indigenous and other minorities/strong settler states; conflict prevention through treaties and agreements with indigenous peoples; partial to full self-governance (Canada, Denmark, Sweden).	Control and internal peace as aim; result: hopeful beginnings in Kalaallit Nunaat, Nunavut, Dené NWT, Saami Land.
Coexistence by means of *autonomy/ conservation* (in Southern neo-liberal states).	State system (primary); civil society (only corporate).	Internal state-centred; internal colonialism by other means.	Shorter and longer periods.	*Mestizo* societies vs. manifold indigenous communities/weak states (periphery); agreements with selected communities; type: *comarca* (Panama since 1920s), *resguardo;* non-integration often broken by attempts of assimilation; self-rule in Eastern Nicaragua, flawed by neglect/ paternalism.	Traditional institutions (*caciques/congreso*-system); control by concession of self-rule; aim to avoid structurally induced conflicts by territorial autonomy regulations (by law or constitutional, often *ad hoc*); real autonomy needs an economy.
Peaceful coexistence by *self-rule and free association* (based on Northern welfare states).	State system and civil society.	Associative non-expansive internal/ external.	Medium and longer periods after 1945.	Enlightened/libertarian societies, indigenous minorities/social welfare states; structural conflict avoidance, conflict regulation or solution through rights and concessions, self-governance (Føroyar or Faroe Islands' home rule 1948).	Security through respect for others; high degree of organization; development and prosperity for many; few solid models for indigenous and minority self-governance realized (traditional institutions etc.).
Peaceful coexistence by *neutrality and welfare*.	State (primary) civil society.	External/ internal.	Austria, Malta a/o for 50 years.	Liberal social-democrat societies, protection for minorities/welfare states; structural conflict avoidance (Austria: federal elements), prosperity for many in crisis.	Conflict regulation through welfare state; proportional representation in parliamentary democracy; non-allied policy in crisis.

Peaceful coexistence	Scope, realm	Principle	Period	Characteristics/ phenomena	Aims/ objectives/ results
Peaceful coexistence by *neutrality and (con-) federation.*	State system and civil society.	Stable self-centred.	Swiss model 400 years (?).	Decentralization in multi-ethnic pluri-cultural Switzerland: confederation since 1848, linked with big-party concordiality in the central · government; respect for other indigenous languages/cultures, but no inclusion of migrants; prosperity for many in crisis.	Conflict regulation/solution by self-rule (canton system) and proportional/regional representation; elements of direct democracy over-powered by corporatist interests; serious abuse of federalism.
Peace through *involvement/ peaceful intervention.*	State system/UN-System OSCE, OAU, etc.	Reactive/ active civil society actors only marginally incl.	Since 1945, on the rise since 1990 Short term.	Divided societies/states; UN-operations; OSCE-missions; in between intervention and mediation/facilitation.	Conflict regulation/solution through agreements between parties to the conflict; security through inter-ethnic balance and protection of national minorities.

* Copyright 1997 © by C.P. Scherrer/ECOR

Emerging conflict setting the stage for peace workers and NGOs

Most people in crisis areas never get involved in violent acts, and most do not support violence. They are potentially welcoming any initiative for peace-keeping and peace-building. In every society and sub-group one will always find peace-loving people who are struggling for mutual understanding. The more intensively a conflict is going to escalate the more such brave people will be forced to be silent. In certain situations they will not be able to expose themselves without running high risks. A second group of people only gets involved if a conflict is already in an *emerging stage* (stage 2). They may get involved because of persuading memories of past threats and horrors confronting their group, people or party with another/other parties to the conflicts. Many people may get involved only *halfway.* First they do not want 'to have something to do with that savagery'. In many cases they don't even know to which party or group they should belong.

In an emerging stage of conflict there are usually plenty of public threats by the aggressors and early warnings from the side of targeted groups and local NGOs. But often little or no action is taken from the side of the international community, at least no comprehensive action. The case of Rwanda showed this in the most shocking way. Rwanda 1994 was the most striking example exposing the gap between Early Warning and Early Action.[5]

In many cases non-governmental local organizations such as popular associations, churches and politicians try to mediate and facilitate dialogue. International NGOs might get involved. Preventive diplomacy would also include other states and multi-lateral organizations. The aim is to calm the waves and work for a peaceful settlement and constructive resolution approaches. In the non-violent emerging stage of a conflict most options for reactive, active and even inter-active responses are still open. The structural prevention approach might already face more obstacles and difficulties to find broad-based political support in order to press for implementation and realization – often controlled by intransigent state bureaucrats. Adequate responses at this stage would be early actions by manifold actors and constructive peace building/keeping such as dialogue, go-between mediation, and facilitation of conflict transformation or sometimes resolution.

Escalation sets increasing limits for constructive responses to conflict

In the *stage of escalation* to violent conflict (stage 3) there will be a serious limitation of options as well as a reduction in the types of responses and numbers of actors involved. While at an emerging stage many actors are non-governmental, governments would now take over and try to control possible responses to conflict. State actors would increasingly try to monopolize the public sphere. Especially in ethno-nationalist conflicts this could mean that collaborators of INGOs would meet hostility, be harassed or kicked out of the country. Local NGOs would be banned or framed. The main conflict actors will not hear appeals for constructive dialogue any more. Most parties to the conflict now find it impossible to compromise. The ideological battle is in full swing. In the omnipresent propaganda the *enemy* will be dehumanized, thus preparing the ground for full-scale violence soon to follow.

The *severe phase* (stage 4) is characterized by a now fully violent and militarized conflict. Most doors will be closed. Civil actors are out of the picture for the most part. No other than combatant parties (governments and rebels), rarely multilateral actors would have any say. The vested interests of those intervening would become clearer. The possibilities for responses other than military interventions are now totally restrained. All parties to the conflict find it impossible to do anything else than fight it out.

In the *phase of de-escalation* (stage 5) combatant parties would sign ceasefire agreements. All conflict actors are looking for *repair* and seek assistance and equipment to be prepared in case of renewed violence. Some NGOs are welcome again, mostly those bringing in humanitarian aid and assistance. Here the classic peace-keeping efforts would be started. The case of headline conflicts as depicted by Western mass media – which acquires the status of an additional involved actor since the media has great influence on local and international conflict actors – has its own externally induced dynamics. Sometimes peace-keeping would include deployment of troops from major powers or UN blue helmets. In this case an eventual military intervention would be named 'humanitarian'. As we have witnessed, the number of personnel in UN operations fell from its 1994 peak of 76,000 blue helmets to barely 15,000 today. This was the result of the Rwanda shock and several failed Chapter VII operations to enforce peace on warring parties

As many examples might show, the danger at this stage is that the cycle of violence turns back and the conflict relapses to stage 3, only to start escalating again. Power mediation, as state-centred response to conflict, could also be a possibility again. INGOs would try to push for peace-building. They would start confidence-building measures (often including sugar, which means material assistance for elites and bureaucracy), and try to initiate dialogue between the parties to the conflict.

Peace building and consolidation in post-conflict situations

Peace building in the *post-conflict phase* of rebuilding and reconciliation (stage 6) would have short- to medium-term perspectives. War-torn societies need rehabilitation and reconstruction efforts. This is the time for the 'big rush'. The bulk of the NGOs will come in now. They will be accredited swiftly and allowed to bring in tax-free any amount of material they may need for their work – including whatever luxury they need for their collaborators, e.g. expensive four-wheel-drive cars for circulation in the capital city.

Some of the critical skills of INGOs are in high demand by now, such as constructive conflict resolution approaches and co-operative planning. Arbitration by neutral outsiders or partial insiders would be taken up, in order to settle the conflict in a peaceful manner. Building a culture of peace at all levels would also include the grass roots level. Local capacity building will be crucial in order to make peace efforts sustainable.

Conventional conflict management approaches would only deal with the leadership of the former adversaries now searching for a longer-term solution. This would then best be accomplished in way of binding agreements or even spectacular peace treaties – signed under the spotlight of the international media. Donor countries will be promising a lot of aid. Rehabilitation and development projects will be set up in order to consolidate the still shaky negative peace. However, most donors are still not sensitive enough to grasp the influence of development aid on conflict and to use incentives and disincentives skilfully. Lessons learned from the Rwanda shock?

NGOs in conflict situations

Non-governmental organizations only became a mass phenomenon in the last decade. Three reasons for the rise of NGOs to become key players on an international level:

1. The first condition was set when neo-liberalism became state policy in France, under Giscard d'Estaing, as well as in Britain, under the rule of Margaret Thatcher, and in the USA after Ronald Reagan came to power in 1980.
2. Governments created NGOs for intelligence purpose or instrumentalized them for activities they could not carry out themselves, especially when intervening in situations of intra-state conflict. To avoid the embarrassment of possible violations of the principle of non-interference, states use NGOs.
3. Civil society building in Western countries, as a result of the 1968 rebellions, created an increasingly more complete network and a parallel infrastructure of civil society institutions, which were partly substituting state institutions.

During the 1980s 'conflict resolution' became an issue and developed into a burgeoning industry first in the USA. Before the mid-1980s assistance in conflict situations – especially in the case of intra-state conflicts – was bound to strict rules. Assistance in war situations was only given after the adversaries agreed to a ceasefire. In the mid-1990s 'conflict prevention' became more and more important. This is basically a result of large-scale failures of the international system. Effective prevention would make many (I)NGOs jobless. NGOs were increasingly operating in conflict areas under ill-defined and self-appointed multi-task mandates that included virtually everything, starting from humanitarian assistance up to conflict resolution.[6]

The Rwanda shock was among the most noticeable events in a period of time, which witnessed mounting activities of NGOs worldwide. The genocide in Rwanda resulted in an unprecedented loss of lives. Above one million Rwandans became the victims of the genocidal state machinery. This is more than the double causality recorded for all violent conflicts in eastern countries such as the former Soviet Union and Yugoslavia. The genocide in Rwanda sent shock waves through the international community. The very role of NGOs in conflict situations came under scrutiny.[7] Some of these organizations were said to have been actively contradicting UN policies.[8] Some NGOs were precipitating the government's policy, especially the official policy concerning the internally displaced persons (IDPs).

Since the electronic media became more and more important for funding of non- governmental organizations the role of media has to be reassessed. During the period of April and May 1994 some NGOs such as *Caritas*, *Oxfam* or *Care International* received donor money of up to 1.2 million US-Dollars per day, based on images of refugees brought into their living rooms by the international news media. The result of these developments is highly ambiguous: in some Third World countries humanitarian aid accounts for up to 50% of the value of the Overseas Development Assistance (ODA). The long-term perspective of development as an instrument for conflict prevention is increasingly challenged by short-term NGO activism.

Low chances for peaceful settlement of protracted conflicts

In protracted conflicts, negotiation or outside party (*Third party*) mediation are generally very difficult and rarely successful. In an analysis of (potential) *success* of ongoing mediation efforts in 22% of 284 wars and crisis in the period 1945–90 Bercovitch *et al.* concluded with a negative assessment: the longer the duration of a conflict the lower are the chances to reach any settlement.[9]

The principle of self-determination is a focal point of the programmes of most insurgencies and ethnic resistance movements. The *multiplication of states*, a substantial growth in the number of independent states (presently close to 200) has already started to become a real scenario. Secessionist movements contributed to many deadly conflicts, but secession also brought the resolution of a few protracted conflicts, as the case of Eritrea might prove.

Rules, procedures and regimes for secession, federation and inter-ethnic power sharing need to be developed. These issues may soon be ranking high on the agenda of the United Nations and regional organizations such as OSCE, OAU, OAS, and ASEAN. Resolving conflicts in Afghanistan, Somalia, Rwanda or Bosnia asked for more comprehensive UN-interventions. Increasingly since the *Rwanda-shock* – caused by the worst genocide since 1945 and the total failure of the international community to respond in time – prevention of violent conflict was put on the agenda of national, supranational and multilateral actors. However, the talk is mainly about acute prevention and crisis management.

To prevent or even 'solve' conflicts is an awesome task. By the time they got the attention of the mass media and (with that) the political class in the West, the targeted conflicts have for the most part already escalated and reached various stages of violence. Reactive approaches are likely to overwhelm the capacities of conflict research and conflict management – and necessarily so. The acute-prevention approach is bound to become just another failure. More constructive approaches have to be discussed. Most of the latest conceptions are still in a somewhat embryonic stage. The inherent danger is that integral approaches escape the short-term logic of policy-makers or do not usually deal with headline conflicts. Their success does not seem measurable.

Today there is much talk about crisis control and responding to crisis. These are basically reactive responses. On the other hand there is not much talk about structural and proactive prevention. Examples of different forms of national self-administration from all parts of the world should be scrutinized and analyzed. There seems to be no mechanic link between conflict intensity and degree of ethnic heterogeneity in a given territory. In many regions of the world distinctly different ethnic groups have for centuries coexisted peacefully.

In traditional societies ethnic heterogeneity and cultural diversity were not *per se* sufficient reasons for inter-group conflicts. External intervention or asymmetric relationships – and, in reaction, the politicization of ethnicity – brought disorder and violation of rules which often led to conflictive escalation. In the societal realm – in order to secure survival – every society had to produce its own mechanism of various scales to effectively calm down, moderate, mitigate, regulate and solve internal conflicts. Here many lessons could be learned.

Only recently has there been an intensification of research efforts in regard to ethno-nationalism (as the main type of internal conflict). The lack of political and institutional consultation in peaceful conflict-settlement initiatives is particularly lamentable. In the area of peace-building, externally directed, coercive mediation (power mediation) aims more at producing direct effects in ongoing violent conflicts – ceasefires, for example, or negotiations; medium-term 'go-between' actions, meanwhile, or third-party interventions, work towards the broader transformation of such conflicts through a process of (re)conciliation aimed at securing lasting peace. The tradition of arbitration exists in many societies. Autochthonous or other long-established forms of conflict settlement offer a potential source of inspiration.

Notes

1 Conflicts are a natural thing. What we may understand under the term conflict is a representation for energies and an expression of an emotional or rational way to get down to a problem.
2 Galtung, Johan (1997), *Conflict Experience 1952–97*. www.transcend.org/ Ibid 1998. After Violence: 3R, Reconstruction, Reconciliation, Resolution. Coping With Visible and Invisible Effects of War and Violence. Download from website www.transcend.org/. Galtung (1994), questioned the triangle of diagnosis, prognosis and therapy, asking, 'Why should anyone relive a trauma? – To demystify the past ...'. He correlated the time dimension with peace work (analysis and practice). For a typology for conflict intervention compare: Galtung, J. (1994), 'Conflict Interventions', in Calließ, J. and Merkel, Ch. (eds), *Peaceful Settlement of Conflict*, Evangelische Akademie Loccum: Protokolle 24 (1 and 2); Loccum, 1994: 13.
3 The status of some instruments is essentially that of a declaration of human-rights principles. In International Law, a declaration of principles has mainly political-cum-moral force and implies legal obligations. See Scherrer, C.P.

(1998), 'Fundamental Human Rights must be Protected'. *Working Paper*, Copenhagen: Copenhagen Peace Research Institute.

4   It became clear that ad hoc international tribunals such as the ones for Former Yugoslavia (in The Hague) and for Rwanda (in Arusha) were important steps towards a permanent Criminal Court. However, it also became clear that some states want the ICC to be closely connected to the UN Security Council, in order to give the old 'nuclear aristocracy' among the permanent members of this Council the possibility to use their veto and try to seize the definition power on what would be considered as crimes to be persecuted by the ICC. This seems unacceptable and contrary to the very idea of an independent court. It should also be guaranteed that individuals and citizen groups (as in the case of the European Convention on Human Rights), as well as the Court's prosecutors and governments, are allowed to bring cases to the Court.

5   After the testimony given by General Romeo Dallaire (commander of UNAMIR II) in Arusha 1998 we know that the details of the planned extermination of a vulnerable minority group were known in the headquarters of UN and Western governments well in advance. In this case there was no early action at all, even in the wake of state organized mass murder. Nothing was done when government leaders announced violence and incited the people by means of radio emissions; this was even reported by several foreign TV-stations.

6   NGO fields of labour are manifold (according to Ropers, 1997) including: monitoring, fact finding, advocacy etc.; empowerment of disadvantaged groups (e.g. most discriminated groups) resulting in possible reactions against cutbacks and against the excessive privileges of privileged groups; measures to mitigate conflicts and accommodate just demands etc.; peace education, e.g. school textbooks about what happens/happened in conflicts; crisis management activities in general; combining humanitarian assistance with conflict transformation (danger of prolonging conflict by providing humanitarian assistance); strengthening information exchange between actors; mobilizing the media and public opinion for peaceful solution of conflicts; working directly on the conflict: negotiation and mediation to be introduced (no social engineering); track 2 does not reach top leadership level; reconciliation and cohabitation, integration of combatants, reconstruction; training and capacity building; development of institutions linked to conflict resolution, working for conflict prevention and linking it to early action (Ropers, Norbert, 'The Role of NGOs in Conflict Situations'. Paper. Moscow: IFPR-RAS, 1997).

7   Under the title of 'Humanitarism Unbound' the London-based human rights organization African Rights has criticized the behaviour of NGOs in the case of the Rwanda crisis. For instance, when I came to Rwanda there were about 120 NGOs. When I left four months later there were about 500 NGOs present in Rwanda.

184 *Christian P. Scherrer*

8   The United Nations created UNREO, a specialized body to co-ordinate NGOs in Rwanda, to deal with the issue. On the Rwanda disaster and the response of the international community see Scherrer, C.P., *Ethnicization and Genocide in Central Africa*, Ffm, New York: Campus.
9   Bercovitch, J. *et al.* (1991), 'Some Conceptual Issues and Empirical Trends in the Study of Successful Mediation in International Relations'. *Journal of Peace Research*, 28(1), 7-17. Debiel, Tobias, 'Kriege', in *SEF: Globale Trends 1993/94*, FrankfurtM.: Fischer, 1993, pp. 177-97.

9 Transforming Conflict in Democratizing States: A New Agenda for Conflict Resolution

JANIE LEATHERMAN

The collapse of communism and the end of the Cold War opened the way to rapid and unprecedented gains for democracy. At its crest in the early 1990s, the third wave of democratization swept eighty-five percent of all countries into the pool of electoral democracies. By the mid-1990s, the had figure dropped to sixty-five percent, reflecting the hollowing out and break down of many transitions.[1] In spite of the fact that regimes in transition are prone to international conflict, as well as civil strife and even genocide (cf. Bosnia and Rwanda), the field of conflict management and resolution have lagged behind the challenges. The problem concerns the time frame, focus, scope and methods of much of the literature, including its implicit set of values and cultural assumptions.

But the high cost of managing failed states has helped to shift the attention of policy makers and scholars alike from intervening at the crisis stage to the early warning and prevention of conflict. If these approaches are to contribute to democratic consolidation, then more attention has to be given to the multifaceted nature of internal conflict, and its transformation than has been the case in the conflict management literature. Early warning and preventive action have the potential to be transformative, to the extent these methods help people in distressed societies (re)gain the key social functions of effective democracy: security and rule of law; effective representative political organizations at all levels; participation in civil and political society; and opportunities to build decent lives and hopes of the future. Such an agenda assumes preventive action is more than a stop-gap measure (i.e. a conflict management approach for buying time and space for solutions to be forced on, or agreed among the top political leaders). Instead, it has to be a tool for long-term capacity building and empowerment at all levels of society.

Shortcomings of Conflict Management

Traditionally, there have been two models for mitigating and ending violence: conflict settlement and conflict resolution. Conflict settlement has concerned itself with finding solutions to the issues of power politics (e.g. territorial sovereignty, power sharing arrangements, economic control). It relies on both coercive and positive inducements to get the parties to an agreement.[2] The conflict resolution model developed as an alternative focused on satisfying underlying human needs (e.g. security, identity, justice).[3] Though the deprivation of basic human needs typically stems from structural sources of violence,[4] much of the conflict resolution literature has been concerned with manipulating factors endogenous to the negotiation and mediation process.[5] Influenced by behavioralism, conflict resolution scholars have drawn extensively from bureaucratic, communicative,[6] bargaining,[7] and psychological theories.[8]

One of the leading approaches to emerge from the conflict resolution school is problem solving. This approach holds that 'authentic and effective face-to-face interaction among the parties themselves can lead to the de-escalation and resolution of destructive, intractable conflicts'.[9] It promotes interaction among the conflicting parties in a workshop setting that is presumed to offer 'an informal, low-risk, non-committal, and neutral forum in which unofficial representatives of the parties may engage in exploratory analysis and creative problem solving, free from the usual constraints of official policy and public scrutiny'.[10] Problem solving has traditionally engaged well placed individuals with access to policymakers who can influence decision making. But there has been little inquiry into how the interaction will lead to greater social and political justice and equality. Feminists have also contended that the micro-management of conflict that this approach implies, risks disempowering marginalized and oppressed communities.

Conflict settlement and conflict resolution both have their limitations as tools for strengthening democracy. Drawing on methods of power politics, the conflict settlement approach would impose or postpone democracy rather than promote it, if necessary. Internalization of democratic expectations and practices are not the first order of business, but rather order and international security. The conflict resolution school, on the other hand, has more often assumed than worked to achieve the attitudes, institutions and practices necessary for dealing constructively with conflicts in democratic societies.

The limitations of the conflict resolution school can be illustrated by examining six key assumptions of the problem solving method. First, the problem solving school assumes it is possible to separate the people from the problem.[11] Druckman and Mitchell[12] also argue that keeping positions separate from broad ideologies is key to negotiating flexibility, and hence a good problem solving approach. But how negotiators can do this is the critical question. In internal conflicts, people are usually perceived as the problem–a perception which ethnic and nationalist or religious ideologies play a fundamental role in shaping. Second, whereas getting the parties to the table is where much of the challenge lies,[13] (and I include the challenges of dealing with the affective dimensions of conflict here), the literature mostly tells us what to do after they are seated and now presumably able to proceed civilly (e.g. rationally). Third, the emphasis problem solving gives to openly discussing underlying interests and concerns presupposes the democratic awareness, tolerance and self restraint that people in democratizing states first need to learn about and internalize. Fourth, problem solving also presumes participants at the table are on an equal footing, rather than problematizing asymmetries of power, and how such differences affect who is included in conflict resolution, what advantages or disadvantages this implies, and what kinds of outcomes may eventually be legitimized.[14]

Fifth, although advocates of problem solving call for principled negotiations, the reality often is that principles have to be worked out first before substantive differences can be resolved. Finding agreement on basic principles is one of the first bridges the conflicting parties have to cross; the failure to do so often means negotiations will will never get going. Such problems arise, for example, when governments refuse to negotiate with opposition forces, because to do so implies a level of recognition or legitimacy they do not want to convey or accept from the outset. Another dilemma lies in finding the right principles for a peace settlement that will redress the injustices that define the status quo at war's end. For example, one of the challenges the international community faces in the aftermath of the Bosnian war is to ensure – partly through the work of the war crimes tribunal – that the territorial gains achieved through ethnic cleansing, are not, in effect, legitimized by the terms of the Dayton Peace Accords. As Donald Horowitz has noted, 'mediators have a process bias that keeps them from focusing on good institutional arrangements, in favor of "getting to yes" any yes'.[15] Part of the problem is that the idea of negotiation as a search for justice is relatively understudied.[16] But in democratizing states, unlike mature democracies, the rules of the game and parameters within which conflicts are to be resolved are all at stake.[17] Because principles are at the crux of the matter, they are more likely to be the stumbling block than the key to 'getting to yes'. As Zartman notes, 'individual notions of justice act as a substantive veto on agreement, and must be coordinated and accepted as the first stage of negotiation. This notion of justice constitutes a formula on the basis of which the parties then proceed to the disposition of details.[18]

Sixth, the lack of, or under-institutionalization of the political process in democratizing and conflict ridden states also means that the implementation of agreements is another important area for study. The study of success or failure begins, not ends, with the assumption that signed agreements will stick. Recent studies underscore this point, noting the importance of the continued intervention of a variety of third parties in the post-conflict phase of peacebuilding and reconstruction.[19] There is also a growing awareness that peacebuilding depends in many ways on how the international community continues to handle peace spoilers.[20]

These criticisms suggest that contextual variables (e.g. political system, structural and cultural factors, escalation dynamics, relationships, types of parties) in which internal conflicts unfold are highly salient for determining outcomes, but they have not been the principle focus of the literature nor its methods. This is often the case with training programs in conflict resolution, which 'approach peacebuilding merely as a matter of technique', rather than as a question of developing a more dynamic understanding that requires holistic thinking and careful grounding in the specific context of the intervention.[21] The lack of attention to these factors has instead helped to legitimize negotiation and mediation as technical and bureaucratic enterprises. Consequently, the conflict resolution literature has promoted the engagement of expert practitioners, who are typically outsiders, rather than the study of ways to transform conflict and empower people directly affected by its outcome.

However, the literature on conflict transformation has emphasized the structural causes of violence and injustice, as well as the importance of contingency thinking for matching appropriate intervention strategies to the stage of conflict,[22] and developing methods that engage all levels of society, and not just the elite, in the resolution process.[23] Its focus has also been more long-term, concerned not just with success as indicated by signed agreements, but as a function of the development of viable political institutions, securing of human rights and other democratic practices, and reconciliation. John Burton has made a similar point with his concept of 'provention'. He has called for conflict resolution as an area of study and practice not merely to be concerned with preventing or removing sources of conflict, but also to focus on promoting conditions that lead to cooperative relationships within states and internationally. It is in this sense that he treats conflict resolution as a political system and philosophy.[24]

Challenges of Democratization

By problematizing socioeconomic, cultural and political boundaries, the literature on conflict transformation calls us to question the applicability of the traditional tools of conflict management, and to develop a broader range of tools for conflict resolution. Dealing effectively with democratizing states poses a special challenge. In the rush to promote democratization, much of the focus has been on electoral democracy. This is democracy narrowly defined. It is like promoting an Olympics without rules of participating, competing and officiating, leaving the nascent political society vulnerable to partisan struggle and conflict. In states with deeply divided societies, elections often become a census on ethnic stakes, encouraging a winner-take-all approach to governing. What results is adversarial democracy. The exercise of political power comes to rest on aggressive nationalism, rather than on other sources of legitimacy.[25] In the worst cases, conflicts erupt into inter-ethnic war, or internal problems are displaced through reckless policies directed at neighboring states, as the disintegration of the former Yugoslavia illustrates.[26] In a recent study, Mansfield and Snyder found that the probability for war for democratizing states was 60% greater than states not undergoing regime change (or those moving toward autocracy).[27]

The prevention of conflict in democratizing states involves a range of challenges, depending on the extent of the political transition. In unconsolidated transitions, there are challenges stemming from the vulnerability of the state itself. For example, when the Republic of Macedonia declared its independence in 1991, it faced difficulties gaining international recognition, while Serbia also continued to treat their common border as an administrative, not international, border. In addition, Macedonia faced deep internal divisions, as evidenced, for example, by the refusal of the ethnic Albanian parties to vote for the new constitution drafted and approved by the parliament, in part because of their objections to the Preamble that set forth Macedonians as the new state's constituent people.

In contrast, a completed transition means that the authority and domain of the *polis* is clear; and that the identities and loyalties are not too conflicting. The initial democratization phase has been completed to the extent that free and fair elections are held regularly, and the government can exercise authority, including over the military. Linz and Stepan also include three other sets of indicators of a consolidated democracy.[28] These encompass behavioral, attitudinal, and constitutional factors. In behavioral terms, they mean the government is no longer plagued by opposition efforts to breakdown the democratic process. Attitudinally, the government and the great majority of the citizenry are prepared to adhere to democratic approaches to governing, even in the face of severe economic and political crises. Democracy is accepted as the new game in town. Finally, all groups of society are habituated to the idea of working out problems and conflicts according to established norms and procedures; there is an understanding that their violation will lead to costly and ineffective outcomes.

The key to conflict prevention in deeply divided, transitional states is the promotion of consensual, rather than adversarial democracy. While adversarial democracy is based on the assumption that over time losers in the previous round of elections will have an opportunity to compete and gain control of government in subsequent elections, in ethnically divided societies, the tyranny of the majority may result instead. As Ross notes, 'democracy's promise of access to all and a fair chance to win political contests is blatantly contradicted by experience'. In cases such as Northern Ireland, the real question concerns how the votes will be split within each religious group, not between them.[29]

In contrast, consensual democracy approaches the political process as one of joint problem solving. It endeavors 'to produce decisions that include and reflect the key concerns of all of a society's significant stakeholders, not just those of the ethnic majority'.[30] Consensual practices include joint problem solving approaches that seek to build common interests, inclusive political decision making processes (such as the Presidential Round Table in Estonia), power sharing arrangements that include minority parties in governing coalitions, and the adoption of policies that lower, rather than increase the salience of group identities. The importance of consensual democratic development cannot be overstated for former communist countries, where dissent was formerly the equivalent of treason. As Shonholtz notes, 'by creating a set of norms that disavowed the value, utility, and healing power of conflict, the former communist regimes failed to create cultural, institutional, or psychological foundations for constructive engagement in conflict'.[31]

It is also important to understand the background conditions, and the escalation dynamics that make ethnic divisions in society most salient during the democratization process. Among the key background factors are interest, identity, and the role of the state, all of which are closely related.[32] Interest based theories explain conflict in terms of competition for scarce resources. Such accounts draw attention to the structural injustices in society, especially the patterns of social organization, and the norms governing allocation of resources and rewards. As Leatherman et al. observe,[33] the key consideration is how various groups, their interests, and resources are related to each other. Such analysis considers how entitlements are distributed, including their linkage to property rights, material resources, economic and educational opportunities, and social welfare. Territory is also an important indicator, especially as a spatial arrangement for the disposition of power and resources. It can also convey a sense of identity, and thus potentially act not only as a structural, but also cultural source of conflict. Structural sources of conflict become salient to the extent they give rise to grievances and help to fuel the mobilization of opposition movements, and hence define competing interests and stakes in the democratization process.

There are at least three basic approaches for alleviating interest based conflicts. One strategy focuses on the administration of resource allocation to ensure that:

1. organizational practices and the attitudes and work ethic of personnel are consistent with the national legislation and its rules for implementation; and
2. the implementation itself does not undermine inter-ethnic relations. These were problems, for example, in Estonia and Latvia, especially concerning policies on naturalization that effected the Russian speaking minority who became essentially stateless when the Soviet Union collapsed.

A second approach ensures a more equitable distribution of resources to meet the minority community concerns, or to provide international assistance to alleviate the hardships endured by the marginalized group. A third approach is to promote cross-cutting ties in society, so that interests are shared more widely, and there is less likelihood of the mobilization of an ethnic community based on perceived group grievances. Measures focused on reallocation may, however, lead to more adversarial than consensual democratic processes. Majoritarian governments may well lack political incentives to undertake affirmative action policies. On the other hand, weak governing coalitions may lack the political capital with which to carry out such policies. While important for promoting equity and social justice, efforts focused on reallocation risk engendering a backlash.

The promotion of cross-cutting ties, while a time-consuming process that must encompass the grassroots of society, may help to build more consensual practices by enhancing communication, shared understandings, and perceived common stakes between majority and minority communities. Consensual approaches would also be enhanced through programs that retrain civil servants (especially those in key sectors, such as offices of naturalization), and through international assistance (such as the funding Estonia and Latvia have received from the international community to facilitate the acquisition of Estonian and Latvian language competency by Russian speakers, a hurdle that must be crossed to qualify for citizenship in these countries).

Identity based theories account for intercommunal conflict in terms of group attachments, and recognition needs, and assume conflicts are most severe when substantive issues are transformed into perceived threats to existence.[34] These theories emphasize the subjective nature of conflict, and thus the role that suspicions, myths, propaganda and conspiracy theories play in intensifying conflict. Indeed, they often become a self-fulfilling prophesy. Identity theories also draw our attention to the heavy emotional investment the parties make in inter-communal conflicts, so that threats to any particular group member are quickly and intensely perceived as threats to the group and its legitimacy and existence.

There are at least two main approaches for addressing the identity aspects of inter-ethnic conflict. One approach is to focus on the substantive issues that are identity-laden. These concern demands for cultural autonomy or recognition of specific kinds of minority rights, for example, language and education rights, and other entitlements. On the other hand, initiatives can target the relationship aspect of the inter-communal tensions, and work to reduce and transform the negative stereotypes, prejudices, suspicions, fears, miscommunication, and hatred that divide their society.

Attention focused on the substantive issues behind identity claims could, however, encourage adversarial politics, particularly to the extent the conflict is characterized by dichotomous reasoning (any recognition of the other ethnic community leads to one's own community's extinction). For example, 'all-or-nothing thinking' tends to prevail on issues concerning inter-ethnic tensions in the Republic of Macedonia: the majority Macedonian community feels if it concedes cultural and regional autonomy rights to the ethnic Albanians, this will lead to the establishment of parallel institutions and the secession of the mostly Albanian populated western region of Macedonia. The dismemberment of the country would then be completed as other neighboring states (Serbia, Bulgaria, and Greece) would act on their historical claims.

Third party measures that deal with the relational aspects of inter-communal conflict require time-consuming, long-term commitments on the part of third parties. But, by promoting empathy, understanding, trust, the identification of joint interests, mutual recognition and legitimacy, such measures could be expected to help mitigate many of the negative dynamics that fuel identity conflicts. Thus, the focus on relationship factors should facilitate consensual democratic practices.

There is a close relationship between interest and identity aspects of inter-ethnic conflict. Minority communities see the government response or refusal to respond to their demands for greater representation in civil administration, or more language schools for their children as a matter of recognizing the legitimacy of their community. As Ross notes, 'specific entitlement demands involving high-level political positions or public display of flags or street signs are often "tests" to gauge how a political system views a group'.[35] Such a test threatened to destabilize Macedonia in 1997, when the ethnic Albanian mayor of the predominantly Albanian community of Gostivar in western Macedonian opted to display the Albanian flag. The incident led to a clash with police, the death of three Albanians, the mayor's imprisonment, and a prolonged political impasse at the national level.

As the previous example illustrates, interest and identity conflicts in democratizing states can lead to a crisis of state legitimacy and authority itself. The challenge to the state arises when opposition groups contest the knowledge, status and authority claims of the responsible officials. A variety of factors are key to determining the seriousness of the situation, including the strength and unity of the opposition and the degree of mobilization. Repression is generally a sign of state weakness, not strength, and the 'more scarce the legitimate institutional means to redress grievances, the more likely it is that conflict management will become destructive. In fact the destruction of public institutions is a sure sign of troubles to come as it makes possible the further polarization of the society, along with use of ties, propaganda, and hate-inciting media'.[36] When such developments are accompanied by the rise of competing armed factions, civil war may well be on the horizon. Among the factors that led to Yugoslavia's collapse, Janjic notes how 'inadequate experience with democratic institutions and procedures for the management of conflicts, which was conducive to the use of violence. In effect, the absence of procedures for the management of conflicts created a "might makes right" situation'.[37]

Measures that address both interest and identity conflict in democratizing societies can help alleviate the erosion of state authority and the legitimacy of its institutions and policies. Yet strategies are also needed to engender support both within the state and the international community for moderate leadership. To these ends, the school of conflict settlement has traditionally focused on promoting various power sharing arrangements. Sisk defines these broadly as 'political systems that foster governing coalitions inclusive of most, if not all major mobilized ethnic groups in society'.[38] Problems of representation are addressed in divided societies by including legitimate representatives, and by promoting consensus decision making, rather than majoritarian forms of democracy.

Consociational forms rely on groups being represented as such in the political system, but emphasize elite accommodation, especially through veto prerogatives for the minority. While consociational approaches have their strength in promoting cultural and political autonomy, they risk reifying the structures of conflict, and promoting inefficient decision making. In addition, critics like Horowitz contend that post-election multi-ethnic coalitions are coalitions of convenience, not commitment, as would result from preelection coalitions or multiethnic parties.[39] The latter are classic integrationist strategies. This approach also relies on forces of economic and social integration to create cross-cutting ties, thereby helping groups transcend differences by virtue of shared stakes. Integrative strategies aim to disperse power, and help to reduce disparities between groups by managing the distribution of resources. However, this approach favors individual over group rights. This has numerous implications, including, for example, the adoption of a lingua franca.[40] Eliminating ethnic traits of national identity to promote civic conceptions generally means that one ethnic group's identity will be favored over others, outcomes minority groups are likely to see as fundamental threats to their identity.

How support for power sharing policies are conveyed by third parties to the leadership of divided societies is especially critical. The timing of the intervention is also important, as are the kinds of tools used to encourage the desired behaviors or decisions. For example, policies based on economic sanctions that result in widespread humanitarian costs, risk engendering a rally around the flag effect that may exacerbate adversarial politics, rather than help encourage consensual practices. Achieving success may also be more difficult when the international community faces multiple domestic parties as was the case in negotiating and then implementing the Dayton Peace Accords,[41] or when dealing with non-state actors as US officials' attempts to mediate a political settlement to the war in Kosovo in 1998 attests. These kinds of complexities are typical of internal conflicts, and thus need to be better understood.[42]

Conflict Early Warning and Prevention: Problems and Possibilities for Democracy Building

The high cost of managing complex humanitarian emergencies, coupled with deep reductions in foreign aid, defense and intelligence budgets in many countries have converged to thrust the early warning and prevention of conflicts onto the international agenda. To date, there exists, however, no systematic means for the international community to engage in such activity. Neither is such a global system likely to emerge. The present trend is for conflict early warning and prevention to be coordinated mostly on an ad hoc basis among governments and international organizations, but relying increasingly on non-governmental organizations (NGOs) both for vital information on global hot spots, and for helping to implement responses.

Despite these limitations, throughout the 1990s the international community has begun to develop a greater variety of tools of intervention that can be used for conflict prevention and democracy building. These encompass military, political, economic, and socio-cultural resources, which may be used in conjunction with punitive or proactive strategies. Punitive strategies, what Nicolaïdis calls a 'hands off' approach, extend threats and promises to shape the incentives of the parties concerned.[43] The approach can be ad hoc or systemic. Ad hoc approaches, such as those associated with coercive diplomacy, aim at mitigating escalatory dynamics over the immediate term. In contrast, systemic approaches (such as offers to democratizing states of membership in international organizations), are long-term strategies. They are broader in scope, and aimed at the institutionalization of peacebuilding norms and practices.

Alternatively, preventive action can take a 'hands on' approach, by which Nicolaïdis means capacity building. These methods involve outside intervention that is unconditional. The outside intervener seeks to change the preferences in society that led to conflict by enhancing the capacity of society to thwart violence. These approaches can also be ad hoc, concerned with assisting the conflicting parties at developing means to address root causes of conflict over the short term, or also of a more systemic nature. In the latter case, the transformation of the structural, cultural and institutional sources of conflict are sought over the long term by working for change from within the society at risk – not by manipulating events from the outside through a mix of carrots and sticks. Thus, a hands on approach is more likely to lead to lasting changes than a hands off approach.[44]

Coercive diplomacy usually involves the threat of, or use of force, or sanctions. Military coercion is probably of limited utility in the promotion of democratization and democratic consolidation. While threats or the selective use of military action can be employed to avert the escalation of conflict to violence, to prevent its spread or intensification, or to bring about de-escalation and a cease fire, they may be difficult to use successfully against recalcitrant leaders.[45] In order for military threats to work, the target of the policy must be convinced the threat is credible, and the costs of the threatened action too great to withstand. If the action is multilateral, then success depends heavily on the political skill of the targeting state(s) in organizing a collective response and sustaining consensus for its implementation. In addition, 'coercive diplomacy is most likely to work at the late prevention stage simply because threats are more credible as a response to an encroachment already taken'. Moreover, too early use of coercive threats may harden the parties resolve, not increase their flexibility for making compromises.[46]

Because enforcement action risks escalating conflict, there is good cause for resorting to less coercive means, such as the preventive deployment of military forces or the establishment of demilitarized zones and safe havens. In some instances, preventive action may also be taken to protect democratizing states which face threats to their security. For example, NATO strikes against the Bosnian Serbs during the war in Bosnia, as well as its threats of air strikes against Serbia again in 1998 in response to the escalation of violence in Kosovo, have had the objective not only to promote de-escalation in those specific conflicts, but also to thwart the spillover of conflict into the Republic of Macedonia. Together with the deployment of peacekeeping troops along Macedonia's border with Serbia and Albania,[47] and an international force in Albania since 1997 under the auspices of the Organization for Security and Cooperation in Europe (OSCE), the international community has lent support to a weak, democratizing state that lacked sufficient military defense capabilities of its own.

The UN preventive peacekeeping forces in Macedonia have diffused crises on the Macedonia-Serbian border, including a potentially dangerous build-up of forces in July 1994, and helped create an atmosphere of stability within the country. The general public considered the UN presence an indication of general political support, at a time when the country lacked recognition as an independent state. The peacekeeping mission helped to stabilize the situation also by paving the way for other international organizations to begin work in Macedonia, and to coordinate their efforts (e.g., assisting in needs assessments and delivery of humanitarian supplies). In addition to its military operations, the peacekeeping mission's civilian command also has monitored tensions, and worked with other international mediators to encourage inter-ethnic dialogue and moderation. The failure of the international community to find solutions to the regional conflicts in which Macedonia's inter-ethnic relations are inserted, has threatened, however, to undermine all the preventive initiatives to date. The 750 member peacekeeping mission in Macedonia, nearly half its earlier size, is at best a symbolic line of defense against the war in Kosovo. The October 1988 accord that US envoy Richard Holbrooke negotiated with Slobodan Milosevic, is to lead, however, to the establishment of a NATO rapid reaction force in Macedonia. This may give the international community's commitment to Macedonia's security more teeth, though its stated purpose is to provide a means for the emergency evacuation of some 2,000 verifiers of the OSCE, who are to monitor the implementation of the accord.

Sanctions have sometimes been used as a prelude to, or in combination with military force to support democratic processes and promote democratic regime change. But as Weiss, et. al. note, sanctions have typically been imposed under ad hoc arrangements, and managed 'by improvisation, with little consistency from one setting to the next'. However, Haiti, South Africa, and Serbia offer a study in contrasts.[48] For the elites in Haiti the sanctions were, at worst, an inconvenience, and at best, an opportunity for enrichment through the black market. In contrast, poor Haitians, whose own economic conditions and quality of life deteriorated, supported sanctions because they saw them as a symbol of international concern for their plight, and because this was practically the only option available to them. But after three years of suffering under the sanctions regime, the Haitians saw democracy and freedom restored more as a result of the third party mediation of former President Jimmy Carter backed by the impending threat of a military attack by the US, than the sanctions regime itself.[49]

Similar skepticism may also be in order in the case of sanctions on the former Yugoslavia. The record suggests Slobodan Milosevic may have been more compelled to negotiate a settlement to the conflict in Bosnia as a result of the strengthening Croatian and Bosnian Federation military capabilities, and NATO air strikes than by the sanctions themselves–though the significant economic dislocations and high humanitarian costs also contributed to a sense of war weariness and may have given Milosevic a face saving argument for the internal political forces in the former Yugoslavia. But by embargoing educational, scientific, and cultural exchanges, sanctions also cut off people from the outside world and denied international support to those figures who represented the possibility of a democratic alternative. Devin and Dashti-Gisbon conclude sanctions hurt the antiwar movement and civil society by isolating not only these groups, but also the independent media from international support and resources.[50]

The South African case illustrates the moral hazards of a policy of 'constructive engagement' as a means to work for democratic reform, while also pointing to the possibility of promoting fundamental political and social change through a sanctions regime that hurts its target. Crawford's study concludes that 'corporate executives were primarily concerned with profitability and economic efficiency, and many saw the restrictions of apartheid and the international isolation of South Africa as obstacles to business growth. Over time, the concerns of business executives served as a moderating influence on elements of the National Party and generated pressure for reform and the eventual abandonment of apartheid.'[51]

Economic and political inducements, while running the risk of moral appeasement, do provide important policy alternatives that may be more appropriate in some cases for promoting democratization.[52] The international community can use inducements to enhance regional security, and generate domestic political support for moderate policies, consensual democracy, and minority rights in the recipient state. For example, when Russia balked at withdrawing its troops from Estonia and Latvia in protest of the mistreatment of Russian speaking peoples in these two successor states of the Soviet Union, the West offered a variety of financial incentives to Russia to facilitate the withdrawal.[53] In addition, the West effectively used the promise of association in international political organizations (Council of Europe, as a first step on the road to NATO and European Union membership) to pressure Estonia and Latvia for more moderate citizenship laws concerning the Russian speaking minority. As a result, Russia refrained from its earlier attempts to condemn Estonia and Latvia and lower their status in international organizations.

Incentives policies also have their limitations. In the Baltic states, they did nothing to fundamentally alter tensions between the majority and minority communities; the Russian speaking population still faces discrimination, and Latvia and Estonian relations with Russia have remained tense over minority rights.[54] The international community's limited success in this case is also a function of the consensus reached on the need for action; agreement on the key goals; and the coordination of international efforts and commitment of resources.

There is a considerable spectrum of political instruments which may be used to deal with conflicts threatening to undo democratic transitions. Third party interventions can range from unilateral initiatives undertaken by specific states to mediation sponsored by inter-governmental and non-governmant organizations. However, there are many barriers to achieving effective, timely responses.[55] Policymakers prefer to error on the side of doing nothing, hoping for positive outcomes, rather than take the more highly visible route of risking action that could turn negative and cost them politically. This is all the more problematic, in that most of the large-scale humanitarian disasters take place in parts of the world where the West has few strategic interests, and the general public gets little systematic press coverage. All this translates into problems of developing a consensus and building coalitions among domestic and international partners for action to deal with impending crises. Generally, it is not the lack of information, but the reluctance to act quickly along with the impediments to organizing collective action that explain why the international community fails to keep new democracies from breaking down, or wars and famines breaking out.

To date, there is more emphasis on the monitoring and early warning of conflict than on developing remedial actions and means of implementing them. Scholars have played a role in this, promoting essentially two different kinds of approaches to early warning. The first is centered on remote, computer based models for forecasting violent conflicts, and the second on qualitative and field-based case studies. Computerized models provide prospective analysis and empirical mapping of indicators of incipient and escalating violence (and now also indicators of decelerators). They help narrow the focus of policy makers on the set of cases most crisis prone. But an almost exclusive reliance on news feeds (typically Reuters) has its own limitations, while real time analysis is no panacea when considerable lead time is needed to mobilize a response.

The second school of monitoring focuses on qualitative analysis and the case study method. Its strength is that it relies on field assessments and requires an engagement in, and deep knowledge of local conditions. While both computer models and case studies can provide the analysis of background conditions fueling conflict in society, qualitative analyses are better suited to assess the pattern of accumulating tensions and breaking points in a particular society. This often involves making politically and culturally sensitive judgments, e.g. the threshold above which conflict will spiral out of control – judgments generally outside the scope of remote methods. Such nuanced information is important for developing recommendations on targeting preventive actions.

But getting from the point of knowing about a conflict to doing something about it is the real challenge. What is then critical for the promotion of democracy is how the policy options are framed. The choice of frames may determine whether the policy response calls for conflict management approaches to maintain international security, or the investment of resources in the political, economic and social capital of a society for the purposes of democracy building.

The timing of the response is also critical. Early conflict prevention affords opportunities to strengthen existing institutional capacities in society to manage internal conflict, and help political leaders, as well as leaders from civil society search for solutions to specific problems. It also provides an opportunity to invest in the development of conditions that sustain democracy, e.g. a viable state, working bureaucracy, autonomous political and economic society, effective rule of law, and self-organized civil society. Many governments are regularly committing foreign assistance for such a deepening of democracy, while there are numerous NGOs specialized in developing local capacities in each of these sectors. An excellent example of this is Catholic Relief Services (CRS) program in Macedonia to develop a national Parent Teacher Association, which CRS launched by bringing together multiethnic groups of community leaders to help repair schools.[56] Larry Diamond, in a 1995 report to the Carnegie Commission on the Prevention of Deadly Violence, has made a strong appeal for the United States government not to reduce this kind of foreign aid.

Missions of long duration (of six months or longer) deployed by international organizations such as the OSCE to countries like Estonia and Latvia and Macedonia, along with the first UN deployment of preventive peacekeepers in the latter, have helped to shore up the viability of the state in a threatening regional context and during a period of instability, while enhancing domestic security and the local capacity to resolve conflicts. Their contributions are reinforced by the efforts of many other international mediators, focusing on different aspects of internal and regional conflict.

More typically, the international community responds only when the situation has already reached the crisis stage. Then the main challenge is to contain and reverse the escalation of violence, and create the space for political solutions to emerge. While finding the right mix of power sharing approaches is often critical to getting a peace settlement, and for ensuring a viable democratic system, there is little systematic analysis of what works on the ground and why. Cyprus illustrates how failure can devolve into protracted communal disputes. Rwanda and Angola remind us how failure can prove even more costly in terms of lives and destruction than the civil strife that initially precipitated the crisis. The key here is to know as much as possible about the incentives the various parties have for any given agreement, and how to deal with the spoilers.

All these problems still need to be kept in focus in the post-conflict period, along with the rebuilding of society itself. Nevertheless, some scholars contend this may be the most applicable phase for prevention. First, this phase does not require early warning per se, but rather an assessment of conflict resolution patterns and progress. The benchmark against which this is measured is the recent outbreak of conflict. Thus, there may be fewer problems with early warning judgments about what constitutes a critical threshold, than exist in earlier phases. This means there are likely to be fewer problems with under warning (i.e. failure to warn), or over warning (the cry wolf syndrome). Moreover, the success of preventive action in this phase is likely to be more credible. Whereas successful prevention in the early phase erases the evidence of its concern, in the post-conflict phase, the danger of inaction (of failed action like Rwanda) will loom large, and be more costly politically in the donor nations.

Second, there may be fewer problems of operationalizing a response to prevent conflict in the post-conflict phase, since many actors are already on the ground and have programs running throughout the crisis. Resources already deployed may only need to be retooled, or redirected to reconstruction and peacebuilding objectives. Finally, the population itself may be more tolerant of the international community's involvement at this stage, since memories of recent suffering may make them more ready to push for international assistance.

However, a major problem is that the international community typically has little stick-to-it-ness to sustain commitments on the scope and time frame needed to make a lasting difference. In those cases where there is a concerted effort, there is often too much coordination among the international community and too little effort to engage the local people in the process. This can undermine the quality of the political intelligence, and thus, judgments about what kinds of programs are most needed. On the other hand, efforts at coordination may breakdown over competing agendas and priorities of the donor communities. Both of these problems have been documented in the response of the international community to the 1994 Rwandan genocide.

Conclusions

The emerging culture of conflict early warning and prevention has shifted the time frame, focus, scope and methods of much of the conflict management literature. It has brought renewed attention to the context of the conflict, and opened up opportunities for remedial actions by the international community before violence has erupted. It also expands the focus of the field by calling attention to the need for long-term commitments to support democratization and peacebuilding. Yet to date there has been little discussion of the implicit values informing early warning and conflict prevention. There is concern among some practitioners that increasingly a security discourse is contaminating the humanitarian discourse, e.g. we respond to starvation not because of the suffering itself, but because of the threat of refugees. This amounts to a policy of distanciation from human suffering, not, in fact, a greater concern for it.

A transformative agenda would ask for much more. It also means that not only national leaders, but also community leaders are partners in the process of making judgments about the kinds of assistance needed, and its implementation. A transformative agenda requires mechanisms for conflict resolution not only involving the elites (top-top), but at the grass roots level (bottom-bottom up), and in-between, to ensure the latter a voice in the democratic process, and the former, accountability. What kind of mechanisms, what problems they address, and how they are used should all be part of the discussion, so that as many people as possible become apprentices and stakeholders in the democratic and peacebuilding processes. Ultimately, international involvement of the transformative type would serve to build up and enhance local capacity, not substitute for it. Finally, the objectives are not to target problems over the short term, but to transform the society with a long-term commitment to rooting out the causes or production of violence in society. Altogether this means comprehensive approaches that cover the multidimensional and multileveled nature of internal conflicts.

Notes

1 Diamond, Larry (1997), *Consolidating the Third Wave Democracies: Themes and Perspectives.* Baltimore, Maryland: Johns Hopkins University Press.
2 George, Alexander, et. al. (1971), *Limits of Coercive Diplomacy: Laos-Cuba-Vietnam.* Boston: Little Brown and Company; Baldwin, David A. (1985), *Economic Statecraft.* Princeton, New Jersey: Princeton University Press.
3 Burton, John W. (ed.) (1990), *Conflict: Human Needs Theory*, New York: St.

Martin's Press.
4 Galtung, Johan (1969), 'Peace, Violence and Peace Research', *Journal of Peace Research* 6, pp. 167-191; Azar, Edward (1990), *The Management of Protracted Social Conflict*, Hampshire, UK: Dartmouth.
5 Druckman, Daniel (1993), 'An Analytical Research Agenda for Conflict and Conflict Resolution', in Dennis J.D. Sandole and Hugo van der Merwe (eds), *Conflict Resolution Theory and Practice*, New York: Manchester University Press; Druckman, Daniel and Christopher Mitchell (eds) (1995), 'Flexibility and International Negotiation and Mediation', *The Annals of the American Academy of Political and Social Science* 542.
6 Burton, John W. (1969), *Conflict and Communication. The Use of Controlled Communication in International Relations*, London: MacMillan; Burton, John W. (1990), *Conflict: Conflict Resolution and Provention*, New York: St. Martin's Press; Kelman, Herbert C. and Stephen P. Cohen (1976), 'The Problem Solving Workshop: A Social-Psychological Contribution to the Resolution of International Conflict', *Journal of Peace Research* 13, pp. 79-90; Kelman, Herbert C. (1986), 'Interactive Problem Solving: A Social-Psychological Approach to Conflict Resolution', in William Klassen (ed.), *Dialogue toward Interfaith Understanding*, Jerusalem: Ecumenical Institute for Theological Research; Mitchell, Christopher R. (1973), 'Conflict Resolution and Controlled Communication: Some Further Comments', *Journal of Peace Research* 10, pp.123-132.
7 Hopmann, P. Terrence (1996), *The Negotiation Process and the Resolution of International Conflicts*, Columbia, South Carolina: University of South Carolina Press; Pruitt, Dean G. and Steven A. Lewis (1977), 'The Psychology of Integrative Bargaining', in Daniel Druckman (ed.), *Negotiations: Social-Psycholgocial Perspectives*, Beverly Hills: Sage.
8 Rubin, Jeffrey Z., Dean G. Pruitt and Sung Hee Kim (1994), *Social Conflict: Escalation, Stalemate and Settlement*, New York: McGraw-Hill, 2nd edition; Pruitt, Dean G. and Peter Carnevale (1993), *Negotiation in Social Conflict*, Pacific Grove, California: Brooks/Cole Publishing.
9 Fisher, Ronald J. (1997), 'Interactive Conflict Resolution', in I. William Zartman and J. Lewis Rasmussen (eds), *Peacemaking in International Conflict: Methods and Techniques*, Washington, DC: United States Institute of Peace Press, p. 241.
10 Ibid.
11 Fisher, Roger and William Ury (1991), *Getting to Yes. Negotiating Agreement Without Giving In*, New York: Penguin Press, 2nd edition.
12 Druckman and Mitchell (1995), *op.cit.* note 5, p. 18.
13 Cf. Gross Stein, Janice (1989), *Getting to the Table: the Processes of International Prenegotiation*, Baltimore: The Johns Hopkins University Press.
14 Cf. Zartman, I. William and Jeffrey Rubin (1996), *The Structural Dilemma:*

Negotiating in Asymmetry, Laxenburg: International Institute of Applied Systems Analysis.

15 Sisk, Timothy (1996), *Power Sharing and International Mediation in Ethnic Conflicts*, Washington, DC: United States Institute of Peace, p. 94, citing personal correspondence

16 Zartman, I. William (1997a), 'Conflict and Order: Justice in Negotiation', *International Political Science Review* 18(2), pp. 121-138.

17 Linz, Juan and Alfred Stepan (1996), 'Toward Consolidated Democracies', *Journal of Democracy* 7(2), pp. 14-33.

18 Zartman (1997a), *op.cit.* note 16, p. 123.

19 Hampson, Fen Osler (1996), *Nuturing Peace: Why Peace Settlements Succeed or Fail*, Washington, DC: United States Institute of Peace Press.

20 Stedman, Stephen (1997), 'Spoiler Problems in Peace Processes', *International Security* 22, pp. 5-53.

21 Lederach, John Paul (1997), *Building Peace: Sustainable Reconciliation in Divided Societies*. United States Institute of Peace Press, p. 118.

22 Fisher, Ronald J. (1995), 'Pacific, Impartial Third Party Intervention in International Conflict: A Review and an Analysis', in John A. Vasquez et al. (eds), *Beyond Confrontation: Learning Conflict Resolution in the Post-Cold War Era*. Ann Arbor, Michigan: Michigan University Press; Fisher, Ronald J. and Laura Keashly (1991), 'The Potential Complementarity of Mediation and Consultation within a Contingency Model of Third Party Intervention', *Journal of Peace Research* 28(1), pp. 29-42.

23 Lederach, John Paul (1997), *Building Peace: Sustainable Reconciliation in Divided Societies*, United States Institute of Peace Press; Lederach, John Paul (1995), *Preparing for Peace: Conflict Transformation across Cultures*, Syracuse: Syracuse University Press.

24 Burton, John W. (1993), 'Conflict Resolution as a Political Philosophy', in Dennis J.D. Sandole and Hugo van der Merwe (eds), *Conflict Resolution Theory and Practice*, New York: Manchester University Press, pp. 60-63.

25 Werlin, Herbert (1994), 'A Primary/Secondary Democracy Distinction', *PS: Political Science and Politics* 3(27), pp. 530-34.

26 Cohen, Leonard J. (1995), Broken Bonds. Yugoslavia's Disintegration and Balkan Politics in Transition, Boulder, Colorado: Westview.

27 Mansfield, Edward and Jack Snyder (1995), 'Democratization and the Danger of War', *International Security* 20(1), pp. 5-38.

28 Linz, Juan and Alfred Stepan (1996), 'Toward Consolidated Democracies', *Journal of Democracy* 7(2), pp. 14-33 (pp. 15-16).

29 Ross, Marc Howard (1998), Culture of Conflict: Interpretations and Interests in Comparative Perspective. New Haven: Yale University Press, p. 11.

30 Ibid., p. 12.

31 Shonholtz, Raymond (1997), 'Conflict Management Training: A

Transformative Vehicle for Transitional Democracies', *International Negotiation* 2, pp. 437-450 (p. 438).

32 Ross, Marc Howard (1998), *op. cit.* note 29, p. 2; Ross, Marc Howard (1999), forthcoming, *Democracy as Joint Problem Solving: Addressing Interests and Identities in Divided Societies*. Nationalism and Ethnic Politics.

33 Leatherman, Janie, William Demars, Patrick Gaffney and Raimo Väyrynen, forthcoming, *Breaking Cycles of Violence: Conflict Prevention in Intrastate Crises*. West Harford, Connecticut: Kumarian Press, p. 79.

34 Ross, Marc Howard (1998), *op. cit.* note 29, p. 6.

35 Ibid., p. 9.

36 Leatherman et. al. (1999), *op. cit.* note 33, p. 105.

37 Janjic, Dusan (1995), 'Resurgence of Ethnic Conflict in Yugoslavia: The Demise of Communism and the Rise of the "New Elites" of Nationalism', in Payam Akhavan (ed.), *Yugoslavia: the Former and the Future*. Washington, DC: The Brookings Institution, p. 33.

38 Sisk, Timothy (1996), *op. cit.* note 15.

39 Ibid., pp. 45, 60.

40 Ibid., p. 75.

41 Väyrynen, Raimo (1997), 'Economic Incentives and the Bosnian Peace Process', in David Cortright (ed.), *The Price of Peace: Incentives and International Conflict Prevention*. Lanham, Maryland: Rowman and Littlefield.

42 Zartman, I. Willilam (1997b), 'Intervening to Prevent State Collapse', *World Affairs*, 4/2, pp. 13-23.

43 Nicolaïdis, Kalypso (1996), 'International Preventive Action: Developing A Strategic Framework', in Robert I. Rotberg (ed.), *Vigilance and Vengeance: NGOs Preventing Ethnic Conflict in Divided Societies*, Washington, DC: Brookings Institution Press.

44 Ibid., pp. 39-40.

45 Leatherman, Janie et al. (1999), *op. cit.* note 33, p. 167.

46 Nicolaïdis (1996), *op. cit.* note 43, p. 44.

47 Archer, Clive (1994), 'Conflict Prevention in Europe: the Case of the Nordic States in Macedonia', *Cooperation and Conflict* 29(4), pp. 367-86.

48 Weiss, Thomas G., David Cortright, George Lopez, and Larry Minear (eds) (1997), *Political Gain and Civilian Pain: Humanitarian Impacts of Economic Sanctions*, Lanham, Maryland: Rowman and Littlefield, p. 218.

49 Zaidi, Sarah (1997), 'Humanitarian Effects of the Coup and Sanctions in Haiti', in Thomas G. Weiss, David Cortright, George Lopez, and Larry Minear (eds), *Political Gain and Civilian Pain: Humanitarian Impacts of Economic Sanctions*, Lanham, Maryland: Rowman and Littlefield, p. 210.

50 Devin, Julia and Jaleh Dashti-Gibson (1997), 'Sanctions in the Former Yugoslavia: Convoluted Goals and Complicated Consequences', in Thomas G. Weiss, David Cortright, George Lopez, and Larry Minear (eds), *Political Gain*

and Civilian Pain: Humanitaridn Impacts of Economic Sanctions, Lanham, Maryland: Rowman and Littlefield, pp. 180-181.

51 Crawford, Neta (1997), 'The Humanitarian Consequences of Sanctioning South Africa: A Preliminary Assessment', in Thomas G. Weiss, David Cortright, George Lopez, and Larry Minear (eds), *Political Gain and Civilian Pain: Humanitarian Impacts of Economic Sanctions*, Lanham, Maryland: Rowman and Littlefield, p. 75.

52 Cortright, David (ed.) (1997), *The Price of Peace: Incentives and International Conflict Prevention*, Lanham, Maryland: Rowman and Littlefield.

53 Hurlburt, Heather (1997), 'Gaining Leverage for International Organizations: Incentives and Baltic -Russian Relations, 1992-94', in Cortright, David (ed.), *The Price of Peace: Incentives and International Conflict Prevention*. Lanham, Maryland: Rowman and Littlefield, p. 233.

54 Ibid., p. 239.

55 The following discussion draws in part from discussions by scholars, policymakers, and practitioners summarized in the author's 'Report on the Synergy in Early Warning Conference', March 15–18 1997, Westin Harbour Castle, Toronto, Canada.

56 Leatherman, Janie (1999), forthcoming, 'Catholic Relief Services' Peacebuilding Role in the Republic of Macedonia: Using Humanitarian Assistance to Promote Democratic Awareness and Civic Participation', in Marc Howard Ross and Jay Rothman (eds), *Theory and Practice in Conflict Management: Conceptualizing Success and Failure*, London: MacMillan.

10 Forms of Third Party Intervention: Typology, Theoretical Approaches, Empirical Results

Marta Martinelli

In everyday language, the term 'conflict' tends to be vaguely or not at all defined.[1] In one sense of the term, a conflict between two or more parties is there to the extent that it is not possible in the given situation, for all of them to achieve their goals at the same time. In extreme cases, the situation is structured in a way that entails that one party loses what the other wins ('zero-sum game'). The more normal case is one where the parties have interests that collide and some that coincide ('mixed-motive game') which often means that all parties can get better off by a suitable combination of strategies – if, e.g., co-ordination or credibly binding agreements are possible in the situation.

In another sense the term refers to behaviour: there exists a conflict when the parties try to deprive each other of something valuable, be it life and health, liberty, material goods, social reputation or self-esteem – in other words when they engage in violence in the most extended sense of that term.

In either sense conflict will always be with us – which does not mean that any single conflict is inescapable, insoluble or necessarily has effects that the parties, on balance, see as evil. How parties act in situationally defined conflicts is an empirical question, as are the effects of actions on the eventual resolution of a conflict and on who comes out of it how well. Whether common or colliding interests will predominate the actors' choices of strategies is often hard to predict, and it can be difficult for a party to foresee whether its actions will bring the conflict closer to a solution that is favourable for it or for all – or, on the contrary, make the conflict more difficult and costly. Hostile behaviour may be self defeating; co-operative behaviour may facilitate a mutually beneficial solution – or have catastrophic effects for the actor if exploited by other actors.

Throughout the course of history all kind of societal and international actors (from individuals to states) have striven to find a way to deal with their conflicts in order to effectively manage them and, whilst maximising their gains, to contain their costs.

Third party intervention as a response to conflict has been used everywhere and in a variety of contexts as well as with regard to a variety of issues. In particular, effective mediation by a third party can help minimise the risks involved in establishing communication between opposing parties to a conflict.

Mediators interpose between the conflicting parties with the expressed intent of helping them in their conflict management efforts [2] (whether this constitutes their primary agenda or hides other ends, varies from case to case and from actor to actor). This 'interposition effort' can occur when a) a conflict is long, drawn out and complex, b) the parties have reached a deadlock with their own conflict management efforts,[3] c) continuation of the conflict is seen as an exacerbating factor by all concerned, (sometimes referred to as conflict fatigue) and d) there exists some premise for communication or co-operation between the parties.[4]

Among the initiatives that mediators try to perform is to act as an instrument to establish or re-establish sufficiently good communications between conflicting parties, so that they can talk sensibly to each other by reducing exaggerated reciprocal perceptions and contributing to make them more realistic. This does not necessarily resolve the conflict. Mediation must be followed up by skilled negotiation,[5] usually directly between two protagonists.

Because mediators are expected to facilitate dialogue between conflicting parties, they should help the parties by providing reliable means of communication, by helping them to re-formulate their ideas into clearer patterns and more precise terms (sometimes summarising statements and asking direct or indirect questions), or by suggesting a non-threatening or neutral language. Most of all they help the parties to listen to each other in order to unlock the issues at stake.[6]

In traditional international negotiation, both sides to a dispute tend to think that their opponent is pursuing an interest. Traditional diplomatic methods adopted in response to this kind of perception are typical of a legal adjustment. These methods are a) *good offices*: it is usually practised by carrying out specific requests by the parties, for instance presenting one side's message to the other; it is not rare that the third party acts merely as observer or point of reference for the parties;[7] b) *facilitation*: implies a more continued role in organising and sustaining a dialogue; c) *mediation*: is the (ideally impartial) management of the dialogue through the power to influence the agenda and format for the talks and to formulate proposals for discussion as well as designing alternatives. This power is better attained when the mediators have access to some form of leverage including punishments and rewards that can be applied to the parties when they favour or hinder the mediation process; d) *arbitration*: involves the parties' consensual delegation of power to a third party, which will design the dispute settlement. It is reasonable to expect that in this case negotiations between the parties will precede (contrary to the cases named above), rather than follow, the third party's intervention. In this case the decision power is removed from the parties and transferred to an external authority. Nevertheless the parties themselves can be said to have had an active stand in that it is still *their* decision, taken in the ad hoc situation, to hand over their decisional power that has to be taken into account by the third party whom will have a mandate to respect; e) *adjudication*: is, contrary to all the other methods, removed from the ad hoc dispute arising between the parties in that the latter agree to authorise a third party (who can also be authorised by others or by itself) to decide on the solution of a conflict between them *in advance*, that is prior to the insurgence of the conflict itself, and even to enforce the chosen solution. Similar to the case of arbitration, it is reasonable to assume that direct negotiations between the parties will take place before the intervention by a third party.

Third party involvement can theoretically start at any point of the mediation activities named above. Empirically, one can notice that they tend to move 'upward' in the range, starting out as good offices. In some processes the mediator's intervention will not develop into different forms, but will just be carrying messages, or waiting outside the meeting room doors available at any request. In others the third parties change their roles from mediators to arbitrators thus 'escalating' the degree of their involvement in the dispute considered. Yet in others, good offices might not be needed at all and the process can start at the level of negotiations.

A common feature to all kinds of third party intervention (not aimed at a direct involvement in the conflict in a belligerent capacity) is that 'it must be seen as an extension of the negotiation process whereby an acceptable third party intervenes to change the course of action or outcome of a particular conflict'.[8] What is relevant in the relationship that will grow among the parties is that, both the conflicting and the intervening parties, will try to affect each other's behaviour, perception and alternatives of action in order to attain a defined outcome. Following this, it is very important to remove the misperception that intermediaries of any kind act only for altruistic reasons and do not have any personal aim. Because by the very fact of intervening third parties become parts to the conflict process, they bring with them careful consideration of the costs, interests and potential rewards to their involvement. This might be less true of states interposing in a dispute, when one thinks of the pressure imposed upon them by the media and the urgency for action that their leaderships might experience as a consequence. What is relevant here is that attempts by a third party to 'unmake' a problem can at times complicate it by adding 'third goals' which clash with the parties and therefore form a different issue.

As Christopher Mitchell explains 'The process of mediation is customarily carried out by individuals... at the level of the individual the nature of motivations involved can run from a genuinely altruistic desire to bring an end to some conflict regarded as tragic or misguided, to a wish for an increase in personal status and reputation, or for a desire for "a place in history" rewards may be given by a sense of gratification... by a career advancement... or by a sense of being in a position to affect important events'.[9] Mitchell claims that at the individual level, underlying motivations can be conscious or unconscious. They can range from highly altruistic to those involving any form of personal advancement. Following this and moving to the organisational level, individuals representing or acting on behalf of organisations (be they voluntary, charitable or state-led ones) bring with them also the need to respond and foster the aims of the organisation they represent thus following a more or less rigid definition of their mandate, and pursuing an interest of political and economic influence.

While acknowledging that these may exist, it is noteworthy that both Adam Curle (Quaker mediator) and Don Matteo Zuppi (mediator belonging to the Italian NGO Community of Sant'Egidio) stress the necessity that the mediator be not *perceived* as favouring one outcome instead of another for his/her personal ends. To be viewed as impartial he/she must not take sides but act as striving *with* the parties for them to find their own solutions to their shared problem represented by the conflicting situation. If any, a mediator's interest has to be one of aiming at a win-win solution and at maintaining the facilitation process he/she has established. This is the ideal image of the mediator, in reality things can be slightly different. It has been suggested that there might be two basic forms of bias in mediation: a) one is called *bias of content*, which refers to the mediator's behaviour in favouring one side over the other in a settlement proposal; and b) the other is the so called *bias of source characteristic*, which pertains to the expectations that stem from the mediator's closer personal, political, or economic ties with one party.[10] Furthermore, as suggested above in the case of intervention by states, a factor leading to biased proposals is once again represented by the media. Whilst reporting and commenting on events, in fact, they can alter the relative weight of reality images, thus leading to erroneous assessments of the same.

Whilst the first kind of bias makes it difficult to mediate effectively with the non-favoured side it is sometimes possible to ignore the second kind of bias as convincingly illustrated by Paul Lederach in his study of the Esquipulas Agreement.[11] At times a perception of 'fair decisions fairly arrived at' appears to be more important in the approval of the mediator than the attachment to a theoretical notion of bias and impartiality.

The same cannot be said with regard to the third kind of bias, where effective tools are still to be devised to correct media 'mis-representations'.

Character of the Third Party

Mediation can be a low cost and highly flexible approach to conflicts and may be adopted by private citizens, international organisations, and any actor whose behaviour can affect the dynamics of the conflicting parties' relations. In an environment lacking a centralised authority, the range of possible mediators is quite varied, but they can be categorised as: a) Individuals; b) States; and c) Institutions and/or Organisations.[12]

Individuals: although the individual mediator who engages in activities aimed at conflict settlement is usually an official representing his/her government in formal interactions with representatives of the disputing parties, less formal mediation efforts can be carried out by an altogether different type of 'individual'. This is exemplified by the image of unofficial, informal means made available to members of adversary groups or nations by the deeds of private citizens (church leaders and representatives, professors, members of parliaments, journalists, and businessmen)[13] that are willing to offer their expertise, personal contacts, and sensitivity in order to help them to resolve their conflict. Such individuals approach a dispute as private citizens only and in virtue of this can offer to the parties a very flexible arena in which to try out alternative solutions to a dispute. Nevertheless this kind of individuals typically intervene without any formal invitation by the disputants so that as a result the mediator's legitimate power is likely to be relatively modest[14] as long as its acceptance is not formally sanctioned by the parties. Its acceptability in spite of the mentioned shortcoming, depends on the fact that in this case he/she can be disowned easily without loss of face, he/she may be available at any time, and may allow the parties to be more in control with their own conflict management efforts. This kind of mediation seems to be particularly sought when all else has failed and communications have severely deteriorated.

Despite the increase in number and relevance of this kind of activities in both intra- and inter-state conflicts, it is clear that private citizens alone do not have all the means, the status or the resources to warrant and guard an eventual peace-agreement, thus, making official diplomacy's entry on the stage necessary anyway.

States: it is undeniable that, although one cannot disregard the increasing number of non-state actors in the international arena, states are still widely regarded as the most significant actors in international policy and the world structure of relative power gives some governments a more or less appropriate status to provide mediation activities. The diplomatic system as it has developed nowadays, has been devised to deal with this kind of actors and the great majority of the rules shaping the international system are addressed to states. Even if it is true that the options available to states' representatives in a mediation context can be more limited than those available to informal mediators, the assertion that officials can affect political outcomes more directly is undeniable. Representatives of all states interact formally in various international forums. The strength and the weaknesses of their stance and their bargaining position often depends on the power and economic resources available to the state they represent. In the same way, the relative political, economic and military weight of a state in the international arena can determine the strategy it chooses to mediate a dispute. In fact depending on the amount of its resources, a state can not only assist and suggest options for the resolution of a conflict, but also dictate and enforce the solution which is most functional to its own interests. The notion of the resources is relevant in that it makes credible any 'stick-and-carrot' policy a mediator-state might choose, thus letting the disputants realise that the mediator has the actual capacity (and the political will, one may add) to either reward or sanction them eventually even with military means. In doing so a state can shift its mediating role from a less to a more intrusive one (i.e. from an 'offer of good offices' to actual arbitration exemplified by punishing and rewarding actions) thus altering also the parties' perception of its impartiality. For the sake of the conflict situation if a third party such as a state has got enough power as to apply sufficient leverage then it may subdue or suppress the conflicting behaviour of the original parties, thus ending the violence. This way the problem would be settled rather than resolved and in the long run this kind of accommodation can prove both unable to secure stability and undesirable for those involved.[15]

Institutions and Organisations: What has been said with regard to the states, can largely be understood also with regard to international and regional institutions and organisations, the difference being only that because their representatives act in representation of (ideally) concerted policies of the member states, their status is relatively higher than that of representatives of a single state, whilst they also enjoy a reputation of more impartiality.

In reality, international organisations can be led by the strongest amongst their members (thus becoming a 'directorium' of 'elite states') as it has often been suggested in the case of the UN, or they can be paralysed by inertia due to the need to come to an agreement with all their members. It is my opinion that due to the great amount of resources nominally available, international organisations can be tempted to assume a more directive role than individuals or states, thus becoming more intrusive. In reality, the mobilisation of such resources can prove extremely difficult due to the need to make all members consistent with and accountable to the agreement international organisations enter upon. Nevertheless, it is my conviction that their entry onto the stage is most recommendable in the final stage of a conflict-resolution process and in the aftermath of it, in order to support its implementation economically and to better monitor the consistency of the implementation process with the agreement itself.

The question of effectiveness

The effectiveness of mediation actions is usually defined in terms of success or failure. The definition of success though, remains difficult and can range from minimalist to maximalist. In the first case success is seen as a situation in which both parties to the conflict formally or informally accept a mediator and a mediative attempt within five days after the first attempt.[16] On the other hand a maximalist view maintains that successful outcomes can be said to be the production of a cease-fire, a partial settlement or a full settlement.[17] Others focus on the equation between mediation success and effectiveness, taking the mediator's (or the parties') objectives as their starting point.

The success of an attempt at mediation depends also on the proper timing of mediation initiatives.[18] According to one view, which supports late entry, mediation is most fruitful when failure to reach an agreement is precipitating an emergency. On the contrary some think that mediation needs to be initiated at an early stage, i.e. well before the adversaries cross a threshold of violence and begin to inflict heavy losses on each other, which makes them more and more inflexible.

Other analysts focus on the logic of the events in order to make an assessment of the right timing entry of the mediators. In this case what matters is the parties' perception of each other. Thus a conflict would be ripe for resolution when: a) a mutually hurting stalemate exists; b) unilateral solutions proposed by the parties have failed and bilateral solutions can begin to be considered as one can observe the insurgence of convergent expectations by the parties; c) there is an ongoing shifting of power so that the party that had the upper hand at the beginning is now slipping and the underdog starts rising[19] and the parties come to some similar perception of the options available.[20]

It seems that some conflicts are inherently easier to resolve peacefully because the degree of the conflict of interest is less or the threats to the goals and values of the parties are minimal. Thus another characteristic thought to be important to the outcomes of mediation concerns the issues at stake. These can be listed as follows: a) sovereignty issues involving adversaries with incompatible claims to a specific piece of a territory; b) ideology issues, in which the parties disagree on the nature of a political system or/and on basic values and beliefs; c) security issues concerning the stability of the system designed to embody and actuate the issues named in b); d) issues of self-determination and national selfhood.[21] It is possible to argue that some issues, such as those arising from deep rooted values or ideologies, are basically zero-sum, leaving no room for assisted negotiation, while more interest-related ones would be more easily manageable in an attempt to mediate, so that one strategy for seeking peaceful resolution should be to reformulate a conflict apparently over power or justice in terms of interests.[22] However, some authors think that it is possible to split the problem into different, more negotiable sub-units. Fisher states that where no permanent agreement is possible, perhaps a provisional one is. Once the disputed issues are clarified the parties could try a partial agreement, involving fewer parties, covering only selected subject matters, applying it only to some geographical areas, or testing it within a limited amount of time. This way the mediators can challenge them to devise new solutions and to explore those sub-issues where a co-operative behaviour is possible.[23] Indeed, the very fact of the parties choosing agreed procedures to deal with their conflicts (irrespective of the substance of the disagreement) signals the creation of momentum for settlement.

It is important to notice that in characterising a particular outcome as either a success or a failure, the general background conditions to the conflict are of the utmost importance. In fact, it is possible that whilst the process of mediation in itself may have been excellent, the background circumstances might have prevented the conflict transformation towards a mutual accommodation; on the other hand it is also possible that what is scholarly considered a clumsy mediation process turns out to be very successful in terms of conflict settlement because the time for resolution was 'so ripe' that the conflict would have moved towards resolution anyway.[24]

This could lead to the conclusion that it is not the mediators' efforts that can bring about a settlement, but only and exclusively the parties' will and commitment and the set of circumstances characterising the emergence as well as the transformation of the conflict in terms of fighting actors, escalation and variation of issues at stake and destructiveness. In reality the success of a mediation initiative depends heavily on the capability of the mediator to understand those conditions and to construct a set of activities that well respond to them, identifying possibilities for changes in roles and functions that have results appropriate for them.

Following this, a mediator's effective entry on the stage should also consider (together with what was stated above): 1) the international context,

2) the support of the various constituencies for either escalation or de-escalation of the conflict, and 3) the relationship between the adversaries.[25]

In particular the last aspect involves a careful consideration of the character of the conflicting parties: it does make a difference if the parties are a) states vs. states, b) non-state actors vs. non-state actors, or c) states vs. non-state actors.

States vs. states: It is my opinion that in the first case power considerations[26] will be important in the definition of the dispute settlement which will most likely 'reward' the most powerful state thus creating dissatisfaction with the opponent and bringing about an accommodation which could fall apart in the long run. On the other hand if both actors in the conflict are states, the very difficult issue of the status of the parties and of the mutual recognition will not be a major concern of the mediator who will be engaged with either dissensual (when the parties differ on their values and thus may find it difficult to understand 'what they disagree about') or consensual (where the parties value the same resources and agree on the issues at stake) matters.[27]

The status of the mediator will most likely not be less than that of the representatives of the states involved. Mediators are thus likely to be representatives of a third state with high status or envoys of international organisations, which may act at a formal or informal level, even if there are examples of non-governmental mediators involved in state disputes. The level of intrusion by the mediators will depend on their status and power in relation to those of the parties and on the level of disruption that the dispute may cause to the power and alliance structures of the international system. I would also assume that in the case of state-representatives acting as mediators the balance of impartiality and the level of the interests involved may create confrontational issues that are exogenous to the conflict.

Non-state actors vs. non-state actors: In the case of non-state actors involved in disputes against non-state actors most of the considerations on status and mutual recognition in the case of states vs. states apply whilst the issue of power disparity is more difficult to measure than it is with regard to nations. In this case the mediator can be a government that is not regarded as a party to the conflict or a representative of an international organisation. Nevertheless the parties might feel 'threatened' by the status and the resources of the intervener which could be perceived as more likely to have the capacity for imposing rather than facilitating a solution, thus performing a more intrusive role. Non-governmental actors may be especially apt in dealing with disputes that involve the same kind of actors because they belong to the same category, they would more easily understand each other, and most of all the conflicting parties might feel that there are no exogenous interests brought into the conflict arena. Moreover, non-governmental mediators are sometimes able to remain engaged for a longer period of time than governments subject to electoral change, and giving time to the parties to come to an agreed solution, they manage to reach more stable agreements.[28] A major feature of this sort of mediation is its long duration, often running on for several years, at times marking the substantive difference between regulating and terminating a conflict and reaching a real settlement of the *underlying* issues.[29] The case of disputes between intra-state groups can be particularly difficult to solve and to classify, as the issues at stake can be identity, territory, equal status with other groups or the right to have equal access to decision making. Polarisation can be very strong especially where there is the identification of the government with one ethnic group (like in the case of Sudan) or a struggle between ethnic groups for the control over a government.

States vs. non-state actors: Finally, in disputes involving governmental actors vs. non-governmental ones, both the issues of power and status can be more exacerbating to the conflict than in the cases analysed above. This is due to the fact that the conflict seems to be between a legally recognised and legitimate authority on one hand and on the other hand, a movement that may be ill defined and possibly made illegal by that authority. Parity of power is often assumed as a prerequisite for a mutually satisfactory accommodation but in this case it would be misleading to measure it purely in terms of material means as the motivation behind a non-governmental actor can be such as to compensate for the lack of resources and can keep a state seriously engaged for years (as in the case of Mozambique vs. Renamo). With regard to this third typology of conflict, a lot of the mediator's attention and efforts will be focused on the question of mutual recognition by the parties, factions or movements that may not be easily identified. In fact, when adversaries do not recognise each other as legitimate, a negotiated end to any conflict between them is most difficult. The denial of legitimacy involved in this case means that not only do the parties disagree on the issues at stake, but they also deny the very existence of the counterpart as a political actor worth negotiating with. Like in the above mentioned case, this kind of disputes is more likely to be over values and relationship, thus more difficult to solve peacefully and more prone to an escalation of violence, than disputes involving only state actors.

Conclusion

The increasing popularity of third party intervention between conflicting parties at all levels demands that our understanding and skills be substantially increased. Making distinctions within the categories of mediation activities, actors and stages of conflict de-escalation is useful, as it offers a basis for understanding which kinds of action contribute to mutual accommodation and which kinds do not. In particular, reference to past initiatives and to successful as well as unsuccessful experiences can suggest new or alternative ways to provide mediation services.

In the debate about the effectiveness of conflict resolution techniques, there are those who think that some types of conflict can never be resolved peacefully and therefore armed conflict is inevitable. There are others who believe that all kinds of conflicts can be resolved given sufficient goodwill and skills. Various study cases have proved that: a) conflicts involving issues of territory, resources, independence, post independence, jurisdiction and ethnicity all include peacefully resolved cases; b) conflicts involving ideological and minority issues include cases which were partially or peacefully resolved; c) conflicts involving violent secession, religious confrontations and struggles for control of government included no peacefully resolved cases.

The fact that conflicts over interests have proved easier to resolve than those over ideological issues seems to prove that the international dispute settlement system is better with coping with conflicts over interests between states, rather than with conflicts over values and relationships involving non state actors. This is due to two reasons: first, governments and their representatives are accustomed to negotiating and bargaining over tangible assets and are less ready to deal with issues where fundamental clashes of values arise: if power and material benefits can be shared, conflicting senses of identity seem more irreconcilable; furthermore, the international system seems to be ready to deal with inter-state conflicts but was not designed, with the UN and the regional organisations at its core, to deal with intra-state ones: the problem is that civil or intra-state conflicts are now the great majority. In particular the UN has not seriously addressed the question of what are the proper feasible roles for it to play at all levels (thus including the mediation one) in intra-state conflicts.[30]

The theory of conflict resolution as it has evolved until now, seems to privilege the assumption that the outcomes of the conflict should be of a 'win-win' type. This view assumes the fact that decision-makers indeed want to reach a peaceful settlement. The reality is that often they do not want to and they might see a winning solution as their priority.

In the study led by Hugh Miall in his 'The Peacemakers', it is suggested that a number of procedures, though not certain to produce a peaceful settlement, have been important in some of the peaceful settlements of the past. I will shortly list below those that appear more relevant for my considerations:

1. Mediation can help to separate issues and reach agreement on the less contentious, as a way to move towards the agreement on more complex issues.
2. A declaration of willingness to settle peacefully can trigger a process that ends in a peaceful resolution of the conflict, even if at the beginning both sides seemed unwilling to shift their positions.
3. Agreement on the procedures for settling the dispute (such as a joint study group to examine the issues at stake) is often conducive to peaceful settlement even if at the beginning the parties are divided on substantive points.
4. It may be conducive to a settlement to allow a conflict to proceed to the point where the parties are aware of the costs each is imposing on the other, because then a shared interest is created in resolving the conflict to avoid these costs.
5. On the other hand, removing the factors which impose costs can create momentum for reciprocal co-operation.
6. Parties sometimes cannot explore the possibility of a mutually acceptable outcome without adequate channels of communication and the creation and maintenance of these channels is itself conducive to peaceful settlement although it is not a sufficient condition of a settlement.
7. In the absence of regular two-way communications between the parties mediation is an important alternative.

8. Early third party intervention is associated with peaceful resolution of conflicts.
9. Conflicts are more likely to be peacefully resolved if the parties respond to the situation they are in as a whole and take account of others' interests as well as their own.[31]

Without disregarding what stated above and with regard to the intervening parties rather than the dynamics of the conflict, it is also possible to suggest that:

1. It is important that the mediator be perceived as not favouring one side over the other, as bias of content in the proposals will be most likely despised by the less favoured side, thus preventing it from reaching an agreement. Consequently, the more impartial the mediator, the more easily he/she will be accepted.
2. A biased behaviour on the mediator's part can only be accepted by the parties if the mediator's reward and leverage power is such as to make his/her acceptance inevitable. In this case the mediator's high status will make possible a high degree of intrusiveness.
3. This kind of strong intrusiveness can only be practised by actors with ample access to economic and power resources which will make their 'stick and carrot' policy credible. It is most likely that these actors will be state or international organisations representatives intervening in inter-state conflict.
4. When this kind of strong mediation is practised in intra-state conflicts such as the one in Yugoslavia, it is most likely that it will leave one side discontented with the agreement attained and that conflict will surface again in the long run.
5. In formal mediation the explicit consent by the conflicting parties to any change in the scale on intrusiveness is usually not always given on a step by step basis, once the initial involvement by a state or an international organisation has been agreed. This was illustrated by the approach to the Yugoslav conflict of the UN and the EU.
6. Conversely, in informal mediation the mediator's intrusiveness is strictly monitored throughout his/her involvement and furthermore any escalation or reduction in that intrusiveness is dependent upon an express consent by the conflicting parties. This was illustrated in the case of the Norwegian state representatives acting in an informal

capacity during the Oslo negotiations, whose role was not allowed to go any further than the initial facilitation; and in the case of the Mozambican peace process where the non-governmental informal mediation had the explicit consent of both parties to move from a lesser to a more intrusive role.

7. With respect to both formal and informal mediative intervention the voluntary acceptance of the conflicting parties of any assistance is essential to any successful third party intervention and the concurrent peaceful settlement of the dispute.

Despite the great amount of propositions available like those listed above, devising a list of successful mediation outcomes is a complicated matter. In fact, there is still little agreement on what constitutes the outcome of a mediation process and how to identify the terminal point of a process that is dynamic and ever changing. Furthermore, every scholar of conflict resolution theory as well as observers of empirical studies will have to admit that mediation outcomes and the level of satisfaction with them may be perceived and defined very differently, depending on who is called to give a definition: an observer, the parties involved, the international community, or the mediators themselves. Whilst there has been a lot of study on the conditions, the chosen dynamics and the characteristics of the parties and the mediators in order to identify which is more conductive to a peaceful resolution, little has been done to seriously identify what is a success if one does not believe that a mediation can be considered successful when it is offered only.[32] If one thinks of it in terms of a 'mutually satisfying resolution of the underlying issues', the successful cases that one can observe are very meagre; on the other hand, if one is happy with the 'attainment of a cease fire' as the result of a successful mediative attempt, then the statistics show more relevant numbers.

It seems to me that the conflict resolution theory has in practice failed to account for those conflicts that *seem* in fact *intractable* i.e., *by means of mediation*. The choice of the verb *seem* is a conscious one as it wants to stress the fact that we might not have the right categories to define *intractable* conflicts objectively. The theory of conflict resolution has gained credibility by stressing the necessity that each conflict be treated on a case by case basis and by referring to past attempts at mediation in order to identify mediation patterns and processes that could ideally be used 'to resolve' future conflicts. This is ·testified by the great amount of case studies available.

However, what is still missing is the acceptance that 'mediation' as an answer to conflict does not always work towards its resolution, because at times it stops short at its settlement, with unforeseeable consequences for the long term. In reality, mediation is not even needed to come to a settlement as it can be enforced by both internal and external parties whose coercive power is strong enough as not to require its services.

For example in the former Yugoslavia the accepted mediators were state representatives and UN and EU officials. It appears clear to observers that they have obtained an agreement which did not resolve the underlying sources of conflict because it moved from relationship issues to more interest related ones such as territorial issues. This was possible because of their status and of their access to resources of power which allowed them a coercive behaviour and a very intrusive role, that moved from one of *facilitation* to one of *arbitration* and even one of *adjudication*.

It seems to me that there are such conflicts where such behaviour by the external parties is possible (and most likely will occur) because what is really missing is a willingness by the conflicting parties to come to a shared level of communication. Regardless of the long term underlying issues this approach by external parties can bring, in the short term, the end of the violence in the field (and for this reason is in itself a success) but it usually conceals the defence of the intervener's interests.

What conflict resolution theory seems unable to explain and consequently face, is the fact that not all political leaders want to come to a peaceful resolution of their disputes. Thus the international community, if threatened in its stability by them, will answer to these situations with the only means that it knows, that is coercion and negotiation over interests, which in turn will create new causes of conflict.

What is needed in my opinion, is a study of deep-rooted *intractable* conflicts and how to appeal to their perpetrators for them to accept the services of mediation. The strategy for this is twofold: firstly to extend conflict resolution theory to accept the above problematique and identify its approach to such *intractable* conflicts. And secondly for the international community to acknowledge and adapt its procedures to the reality of these increasingly occurring 'unmanageable' conflict scenarios. This would enable it to face the responsibility of dealing with such underlying factors, which it has thus far relegated to the realm of conflict resolution theory.

Notes

1 For a better definition of the contradictions inherent to the term 'conflict', see: Johan Galtung, *Peace by Peaceful Means, Peace and Conflict, Development and Civilisation*, London, SAGE Publications, chapter II, pp. 70-88.
2 A more precise definition of the term will be provided later on in the chapter.
3 In this case the disputants may want to choose a face-saving way out of the conflict. In such situations negotiation through an intermediary may help protect a party's prestige. Because the desire for a settlement implies the need to make concessions, the parties could feel that conceding by means of a third party is less harmful to their reputation and their future bargaining positions than conceding to the adversary in direct negotiations. S. Touval and I.W. Zartman (eds), *International Mediation in Theory and Practice*, Colorado, Westview Press, 1985, p. 255. Conversely, the parties may use the third party's proposal as a way to justify, in the eyes of their constituencies, their refusal of concessions to their opponent. This can happen when the parties feel the need to present an actual refusal, as a concession done to their constituencies.
4 Jacob Bercovitch, *Social Conflicts and Third Parties. Strategies of Conflict Resolution*, Colorado Westview Press, 1984, p.13.
5 But at times the two initiatives can go hand in hand, and in some cases, which we will deal with later on, negotiation can actually precede mediation.
6 C. Hume, *Ending Mozambique's War. The Role of Mediation and Good Offices*, Washington, US Institute of Peace, p. 73.
7 This behaviour has been observed in the case of the Oslo Channel, where the Norwegians were never present at the meetings between the parties but kept 'handy' in order to grant any kind of needed assistance.
8 J. Bercovitch and A. Houston, 'The Study of International Mediation: Theoretical Issues and Empirical Evidence', in J. Bercovitch (ed.), *Resolving International Conflicts. The Theory and Practice of Mediation*, London, Lynne Rienner, 1996, p. 12.
9 C. R. Mitchell, 'The Motives for Mediation', in C. R. Mitchell and K. Webb (eds), *New Approaches to International Mediation*, London, Greenwood Press, 1988, p. 31.
10 P .J. Carnevale and S. Arad, 'Bias and Impartiality in International Mediation', in J. Bercovitch, *Resolving International Conflicts*, op. cit., p. 45.
11 This is the analysis of a regional process of conflict resolution as it has evolved in Nicaragua within the Esquipulas II Agreement of 1987 where Lederach has developed his concept of the 'insider partial' as opposed to the 'outsider neutral'. He suggests that a an intervention from a mediator whose acceptability is based in connectedness and trusted relationship with the conflicting parties rather than in his/her distance from them, might prove significantly effective.
12 J. Bercovitch, 'The Structure and Diversity of Mediation in International

Relations', in Jacob Bercovitch and Jeffrey Z. Rubin (eds), *Mediation in International Relations, Multiple Approaches to Conflict Management*, London, Macmillan, 1992, p. 10.

13 A good example of a businessman entering in a process of conflict resolution is given by Tiny Rowland. A man with enormous economic interests threatened by the war in Mozambique, he decided to help the peace process providing flights and accommodation for many RENAMO representatives. Conversely, his presence seems to be exacerbating the ongoing conflict in Sudan.

14 J. Bercovitch and J.Z. Rubin (eds), op. cit., p. 257.

15 Christopher R. Mitchell, *Handbook of Conflict Resolution: Analytical Problem Solving Approach*, London, 1996, p. 3.

16 Marieke Kleiboer, 'Understanding Success and Failure of International mediation', *Journal of Conflict Resolution*, Vol. 40, No.2, Sage Publications, Inc., June 1996, p. 361.

17 Ibidem.

18 This factor has repeatedly been stressed by Cameron Hume in his description of the mediation performed by the Community of Sant'Egidio in the war in Mozambique. C. Hume, *Ending Mozambique's War, The Role of Mediation and Good Offices*, Washington, U.S. Institute of Peace, 1994.

19 Marieke Kleiboer, op. cit., p. 363.

20 The ongoing shifting of power *per se* does not necessarily lead to a more co-operative behaviour or contribute to convergent expectations: in fact if the underdog perception is one of a rising status and stronger bargaining power, it may as well come to more rigid stances. What a shift of power makes possible in reality is a change in the equation 'risks-costs-gains' considered by the parties for the choice of their course of action.

21 Ibidem, p. 364.

22 Hugh Miall, *The Peacemakers: Peaceful Settlement of Disputes since 1945*, Oxford, MacMillan, 1992, p. 110.

23 See: Roger Fisher and William Ury, *Getting to Yes. Negotiating Agreement Without Giving In*, London, Hutchinson Business, 1981, p. 72-73.

24 Louis Kriesberg, 'Varieties of Mediation Activities and Mediators in International Relations', in J. Bercovitch (ed.), *Resolving International Conflicts*, op. cit., p. 220.

25 Ibidem.

26 The definition of power here must be considered in connection with the goals for which it is being exercised and must comprehend military, geopolitical, economic, ideological, social and cultural resources. Ibidem, p. 222.

27 Ibidem.

28 In all cases conflicts involving a higher degree of violence have a proportionally higher mediation duration than those involving minor violence. H. Miall, op. cit., p. 125.

29 Oran R. Young, *The Intermediaries. Third Parties in International Crises*, Princeton, Princeton University Press, 1967, p. 35.
30 R. Cooper and M. Berdal, 'Outside Intervention in Ethnic Conflicts', in Michael E. Brown (ed.), *Ethnic Conflict in International Security*, Princeton, N.J., Princeton University Press, 1993, pp. 199-201.
31 H. Miall, op. cit., p. 188-189.
32 J. Bercovitch, *Resolving International Conflicts*, op. cit., p. 20.

PART IV

CASE STUDIES

11 Identity Conflicts and Their Resolution: The Oslo Agreement and Palestinian National Identities

HELENA LINDHOLM SCHULZ

Introduction[1]

Five years after the buoyant hand-shake between the two arch-enemies, Israel's Prime Minister Yitzhak Rabin and PLO Chairman Yasir Arafat, an end to the conflict between Israel and the Palestinians appears on the surface as far-fetched as ever. Israel's 50-year anniversary celebrations in 1998 symbolized in a concrete way how identities and stereotypes remain on both sides. Israel demonstrated its control over land and air with military parades and air shows, while Palestinian protest[2] took on the semblance of the struggle of the deprived. The celebrations and their counteractions were also instrumental in portraying identities; in marking the Jewish Israeli identity as manifested in and through the state, and the Palestinian identity as created out of the disasters befalling them. Any analysis of that conflict as well as the attempts to resolve it needs to take as its starting point the issue of identity. The conflict is ultimately a clash between two nationalist movements colliding on the same territory. One, Zionism, has been able to create a strong state on part of that territory and the other, Palestinianism is struggling to do so, implying a grossly unequal relationship and struggle. However, despite all the shortcomings of the Oslo process[3] as well as recent backlashes, the process set in motion by the Declaration of Principles between Israel and the PLO (signed in September 1993) have cast both Israelis and Palestinians upon an uncertain road implying deep-reaching questioning of long-lasting identity-concepts and enemy-images.

The aim of this chapter is to analyse how identity has been approached in the Oslo process, in order to contribute to the literature on ethnic conflict and the discussion in conflict resolution through the case of the Palestinian-Israeli conflict. Although the discussion will use the experiences of both

229

Palestinian and Israeli identity formations, emphasis will be placed on Palestinian identities within the context of the overall conflict. The case will be used so as to underline the problematique of national(ist) identities in conflict resolution approaches.[4]

Ethnicity, identity and conflict theory

In a world increasingly defined by internal conflicts,[5] ethnicity has thrown itself upon conflict research and international relations. Rather than taking account of the works establishing ethnicity as a form of social organization[6] ('Ethnicity is an aspect of social relationship between agents who consider themselves as culturally distinctive from members of other groups with whom they have a minimum of regular interaction'),[7] there is still a tendency in conflict research to view ethnicity in static and absolute categories.

> *Ethnic groups* are large groups of people who share ancestral, language, cultural, or religious ties and a common *identity* (individuals identify with the group). Although conflicts between ethnic groups often have material aspects notably over territory and government control ethnic conflict itself stems from a dislike or hatred that members of one ethnic group systematically feel toward another ethnic group.[8]

This mode of definition stand in contrast to identity studies, which portray identity socially as constructed in discursive systems, as fragmented, de-centered and in constant motion, never completely fulfilled:[9]

> [N]ot only are there no 'natural' or 'original' identities, since every identity is the result of a continuing process, but this process itself must be seen as one of permanent hybridization and nomadization. Identity is, in effect, the result of a multitude of interactions that take place inside a space whose outlines are not clearly defined.[10]

A primordialist perspective may be detrimental to our understanding of conflicts of identity and serve counter-productive aims when it comes to resolution attempts. Identity, nationalist and ethnicist discourses about selfhood and sameness, should be viewed in its constant relation to an outside, something which it is not;[11] identity is constructed in polarization, exclusion and power hierarchizations.[12] It is only in relation to an 'Other' that it becomes meaningful to identify a 'Self'. Often, a negative stereotyping is emphasized, but 'Others' must not mean 'strangers', 'aliens', but could involve co-residents in encompassing social systems and lead (in fact) more often to questions of how 'we' are distinct from 'them', rather than to a hegemonic and unilateral view of 'the other'.[13] A 'them' must not refer to a specific group of people, it must not be well-defined or delimited, but rather relate to a general 'them', a non-us, 'out there'.[14] Roosens's clarification is important in the sense that through emphasizing boundaries between 'Us' and 'Them', there is a risk of overemphasizing difference and negative interaction, or conflict. Stereotypes carry information which help individuals structure and order a chaotic 'reality'.[15] There are, however, 'Others' of different kinds: 'Others' could be friendly or indifferent. Furthermore, ethnic or national identities are, like other identities, formed not only in relation to an 'outside', to something which is different, but involve attempts at being *similar* to others. To recognize oneself as an individual in the behaviour of a larger collectivity, the in-group, is also to sense security. To conform with a norm is a way to enhance security. 'Self' and 'Other' thus represent similarity and difference. Differences or boundaries between 'Self' and 'Other' do not preclude peace and coexistence.[16] Groups defining themselves in different cultural identity categories must not end up in conflict.

The tendency in conflict theory to treat ethnicity as a static variable, as an explanatory factor, risks augmenting nationalist discourses and legitimise politics of difference. It is never ethnicity or difference in itself which leads to conflict. A constructivist approach would rather emphasize ideologies of difference and homogeneity as conflict-bound. This goes back to modernist theories on nationalism,[17] emphasizing nationalism as the main instrument for the state in creating homogeneity out of 'multi-cultural', 'multi-ethnic' populations. As both Gellner (1983) and Hobsbawm (1990) note, it is *nationalism* that creates the *nation* and not the other way around.

Another tendency in international relations theory about ethnic conflict portrays an instrumentalist image of ethnic conflicts.[18] However, although not natural, given or fixed, neither are ethnicities and nationalisms to be reduced to strategies and politics only. There *are* existential sides to ethnicity. What needs to be done within international relations and conflict theory is to scrutinize links between nationalism much more explicitly as the core instrument in creating perceptions of cultural differences and conflicts as well as to analyse group perceptions of 'Self' and 'Other'.

Nationalism

The main elements of nationalism are 'territory, place and environment (i.e. spatial entities), in relation to people and their collective memories (i.e. temporal entities).' Nationalism focuses on the 'distribution of land among nations'.[19] Space, i.e. the territory embraced by state-borders, is important both in the sense of providing modes of production and in the sense of emotional attachments. A territory, a 'homeland', is crucial in determining the nation's location.

Nationalism is an ideology of *boundedness* and a believed or claimed congruity between people, territory and state, or population, geography and politics. The general belief of nationalism is that the world is organized and divided into 'nations' who *possess* territories.[20] 'Each nation is thus a unity of people, territory and state',[21] although I would stress a *perceived* or *claimed* unit.

Nationalism is thus about homogenization, about attempts to make similar, to create a common identity out of whatever building-stones within a certain space and about claims on territory. Official nationalism is not only based on assumptions on who 'we' are and who 'they' are, on mechanisms of exclusion and inclusion, but on conscious attempts of homogenization; it thrives on myths of homogeneity so as to legitimate administrative functions of statehood. Institutional and administrative aspects of statehood are used in the process of homogenization.

Through the process of homogenization, difference becomes visible. Those who fail to have this 'something', however defined, in common become marginalized,[22] in what Hettne has called the 'nation-state' project,[23] and Connor[24] has called 'nation-destroying' rather than 'nation-building'. Stavenhagen[25] elaborates the notion of 'ethnocide' to describe the process of homogenization wherein cultural systems are marginalized. Hettne, Connor and Stavenhagen all view this process with a bias towards sympathy for 'ethnic groups' and 'nations' out there, without problematizing on the idea of ethnicities as fundamental. Nevertheless, they all strongly point out the role of the *state in creating ethnic tensions or reactions* in abortive attempts of homogenization. The failure lies in the paradox that it is precisely the *process or project of creating homogeneity which renders difference more important.* Nationalism and national/ethnic identity are created in and through a relationship, but also by the works of state and/or other élites. This is not to say that a nationalist élite is always capable of manipulation, but there is an aspect of active craft-work. However, this must find a chord among populations, why society perceptions are equally important. Moreover, national/ethnic identity-perceptions are not equally distributed within a population: there is a myriad of variations and differences,[26] as ethnic/national identity criss-crosses with class, gender, regional and other identification processes, as well as institutional power, political economy and large-scale structures.

The Palestinian-Israeli conflict

The Palestinian-Israeli conflict has become almost an 'archetype' of modern national/nationalist conflict. It has plagued the peoples of both sides for almost a century. The conflict is precisely a conflict between two nationalist movements: 'Zionism and Palestinianism were the very origins, the very generative forces which have brought into existence both the Israeli and Palestinian societies as well as the conflicts between them'.[27] In fact, Israeli and Palestinian societies 'enfold each other to the extent that neither is definable today independent of the other'.[28] Israeli and Palestinian societies and identities are mirror images of each other, and part of each other, although it needs to be pointed out that Zionism was initially formed as a European phenomenon, i.e. as a reaction against nationalism in Europe, anti-semitism and pogroms, persecution and annihilation. There is today no Israeli society which 'exists' completely independent of the Palestinian and vice versa. It is as though both societies carry with them the other, as a perceived burden but also a potential asset.

'Selfs' between traumas and assertion

The Palestinian-Israeli conflict is for both sides an *existential* conflict as much as anything else. This is true for many ethnic/national conflicts, certainly including aspects of material resources in the form of land, territory, economic development, economic opportunities, political influence and power. The distribution of land is of course important in nationalist conflicts. However, an *experienced* (whether 'objectively' relevant or not) feeling of a humiliated, threatened or denied identity is equally fundamental. This is also held by for example Burton, in the problem-solving approach. In attempts at conflict resolution, such immaterial values must be given increased emphasis. Both Palestinians and Israelis represent troubled and traumatized identities. For Israeli Jews, the Holocaust still serves as a prime principle in framing experiences of a 'Self' endangered by annihilation.[29] Further, the sense of an exposed and threatened identity in the midst of an 'Arab sea' threatening to drive out the Jews from the Middle East feeds directly into Israeli discourse about vulnerability and unsafety. Although from a Palestinian viewpoint, Israeli Jews represent a rationally calculating superagent, always on top of the Palestinians, it remains that Israeli-Jewish identity is vulnerable and questioned. This is a 'fact' which must be taken into account in attempts at conflict resolution. The 'Arab threat' is felt as real. However, most academic undertakings about Israeli identity are still moving in the spheres of Judaism/Jewishness, the holocaust, intra-state ethnic relations and diaspora-state relations and do not take into sufficient acccount the extent to which Israeli-Jewish identity is formed in relation to its Palestinian Arab other.[30]

> On the one hand, the Jewish-Israeli polity is driven by a code of self-perceived weakness, permanent wretchedness, and existential threat. A sense of permanent siege and potential annihiliation in a hostile Gentile world of antisemites be they Christians, Muslims, Buddhists or agnostics is perceived as the state of nature, or the cosmic order. [...] On the other hand, Jewish Israelis are well aware of their country's status as a regional military power with one of the best-equipped and trained armed forces. [...] The 'new Israeli', in counter-distinction to the 'Jew-of-exile', shaped and disdained by Zionist ideology and mythology is first and foremost a warrior. [...] The weakness and power-oriented components of this culture complement each other, yet they are also a source of internal strain within the Jewish-Israeli collective identity.[31]

The Holocaust serves as the root structure of Israeli-Jewish identity as represented through immense collective suffering. Conceptions of a victimized 'Self' have been strengthened by the wars between Israel and the Arab states, as well as the violent conflict between Israel and the Palestinians. Threats feed into a discourse of fear and anxiety. As a counterpole to this side of Israeli-Jewish identity as a passive victim, the 'new state' Israeli is crafted through his or her attempts at securing identity. That is, strength, power and action (defined in male terms) are the other side of Israeli-Jewish identity, centring around those dual poles. The 'new state Israeli Jew' was to overcome the traumas and the suffering; and was to eliminate the weakness. However, the victimized Israeli Jew has not waned but has continued to exist as a necessary motivating aspect of the warring Israeli Jew.

Palestinian national identity is equally troubled. A Palestinian national(ist) identity is in fact quite recent, although embryonic national identity crystallized around its clash with Zionism as well as large-scale sociological processes in relation to the First World War and related events.[32] The changing fortunes of the Arab-Israeli, Palestinian-Israeli conflict have provided the contextual framework for the ups and downs of Palestinian identity. Homelessness and insecurity constitute the main representations of Palestinian identity, and it seems reasonable to claim that politicized identities, in general terms, arise out of peril and anxiety. Dispossession and uprootedness amplify feelings of being deserted and at the mercy of stronger forces.

> The quintessential Palestinian experience, which illustrates some of the most basic issues raised by Palestinian identity, takes place at a border, an airport, a checkpoint: in short, at any one of those modern barriers where identities are checked and verified. What happens to Palestinians at those crossing points brings home to them how much they share in common as a people. For it is at these borders and barriers that the six million Palestinians are singled out for 'special treatment', and are forcefully reminded of their identity: of who they are, and why they are different than others. [...] As a result, at each of these barriers which most others take for granted, every Palestinian is exposed to the possibility of harassment, exclusion and sometimes worse simply because of his or her identity.[33]

Through commemorating disasters representing the suffering of the Palestinians as well as battles representing pride and resistance, a Palestinian history is produced centred around the notions of 'suffer' and 'struggle'. Catastrophes have become crucial in structuring Palestinian narratives of identity. 1948, the creation of Israel and the Palestinian exodus is referred to as 'the catastrophe', the *nakba*. The notion of the struggling Palestinian dates back to the Great Revolt (1936–39), and has experienced transformation through the revolution of the 1960s and 1970s, the resistance and the intifada of the late 1980s. 'Struggle' has persisted as the main means of overcoming processes of victimization and to transcend the current state of dispossession, denial and statelessness. Armed struggle has been a basic foundation of Palestinian nation-building.[34]

236 Helena Lindholm Schulz

The driving force in the philosophy and ideological outlook of Fateh, to the extent that they existed, was profoundly existential. It derived overwhelmingly from the physical circumstances and deep alienation of the majority of uprooted and exiled refugees, rather than the minority of Palestinians who still resided in their original homes after the end of the 1948 war. The same existential drive imbued Fateh's notion of 'revolution'. 'With revolution we announce our will [hence existence], and with revolution we put an end to this better surrender, this terrifying reality that the children of the Catastrophe [of 1948] experience everywhere.[35]

In the same way that the warring Israeli soldier was to transcend images of 'Self' as on the brink of extinction, the Palestinian *feday*[36] (the guerilla-fighter), the new 'PLO-Palestinian' and the resisting 'intifada-Palestinian' were to eclipse the catastrophe, the *nakba*.[37]

While I am struggling against the occupation I am a Palestinian.[38]

It is in the *action*, in participation in resisting the occupation, that one becomes Palestinian. Palestinians perceived themselves as having an inherent right in their resistance. Perhaps the most substantial representation of Palestinian national identity is to 'struggle', which serves as the action, the strategy through which to transcend the denial, the conditions of the present and reach the future, the state. 'A pervasive quality or ethos of contemporary Palestinian culture is militancy (*nidal*)'.[39] Embedded in Palestinian identity is also the endeavour for elevation to statehood, to become like others, to have what others have, 'to have a passport', to be able to have your identity firmly *written* into a document which can then not be questioned.

I have suffered a lot and sacrificed a lot for Palestine. I have lost my brother, my cousin, four of my uncles, all because of Palestine.[40]

I am proud to be a Palestinian, even though it is very difficult to be a Palestinian in this stage. In this century, or in this time. Because being a Palestinian means to suffer, to be refused all over the world.[41]

Loss of family members is *because* of Palestine, and like Israeli-Jewish identity representations, Palestinian identities are epitomized in the duality of suffering and struggle.

Israeli-Jewish and Palestinian identities thus in fact constitute twin concepts and mirror images in a very concrete sense. Both are centred around the poles of victim-warrior/struggler. Their suffering gives them no option but to struggle to -aintain their identities in the eyes of the world and to maintain the rights which belong to peoples. Perhaps this is one of the most crucial aspects of the Palestinian-Israeli conflict as such, i.e. the way that identities are manifested through the duality of insecurities and strain.

The 'Other' discourse

A pattern of interaction characterized by conflict obviously creates an emphasis on difference and otherness. Stereotypes or fixed perceptions of the 'Other' provide norms and patterns for behaviour and action. In line with Simmel,[42] 'Self' and 'Other', friend and foe, are the basic forms of sociation. They help to bring order in chaos; 'inside' is purity, order, truth, beauty, good and right. 'Outside' of the boundary is pollution, chaos, falsity, ugliness, bad and wrong;[43] although as has previously seen underlined, the 'outside' might also be characterized by indifference.

> The repugnant and frightening 'out there' of the enemies is, as Derrida would say, a supplement: both the addition to, and displacement of the cosy and comforting 'in here' of the friends.[44]

Israeli 'Other'-discourse is based on stereotypes of Israel as a Western incarnation of modernization, rationality and science in a dark environment of tradition, superstition and backwardness. In Israeli-Jewish Zionism, Arabs and Palestinians have come to represent everything which is backward, 'traditional', 'unprogressive', and is in those terms very much a part of Orientalist discourse.[45] 'Self' and 'Other' clearly entails notions of superior and inferior.[46] One of the Israeli discourses about Palestinians circles around the space of the West Bank and Gaza, depicted as the 'territories', feeding into the 'frontier' idea,[47] about an empty place to be settled by the pioneer society, but also and on the other hand an unknown field inhabited by backward, but dangerous 'others'.

Palestinian 'Other'-perceptions are the 'Other' side of how Israelis perceive Palestinians.[48] In Palestinianist discourse there are no associations with a superior Palestinian-ness. Instead, the Israelis are portrayed as smart and cunning, and as able to run the course of events in the direction they prefer, which is, needless to say, perceived as to the disadvantage of the Palestinians. The Israelis represent the superior to whom the Palestinians incessantly compare themselves. If Israelis are smart, then the Palestinians are not equally smart. A woman activist said: 'We have to be as foxy as them', i.e. the Israelis are perceived as wily and in order to gain a better influence over the negotiations, the Palestinians should *learn* from the Israelis and become sly themselves. These perceptions stem from the history of the Palestinian-Israeli conflict as it is experienced and felt by the Palestinians and the structural asymmetry between them. There is on the one hand a sense of almost total subordination vis-à-vis Israeli as the super-agent.

> The Israelis are very smart, very intelligent. They could manage to have somebody, like Yasir Arafat to sign, as if the whole Palestinian problem is solved, as if the Palestinian-Israeli conflict is solved, and as if the Arab-Israeli conflict has been solved. And as a matter of fact, the agreement does not oblige Israel to do much.[49]

However, this Palestinian weakness and inferiority complex is compensated by their 'right' to the land and their unrelentless 'struggle' for the land. Palestinian rightfulness make them morally superior. There is a Palestinian asset in the struggle for 'what is right'. Israeli superiority is in fact based on false premises, since it is 'better' to be 'right' than to be 'smart'.

We have previously asserted that one important aspect of national identity is the relation to the 'Other'. The 'Other' is in fact part of 'Self', which is evident not least in the Palestinian case where 'self-image' is linked to the Israelis in a very direct and entangled way. This leads to a highly suspicious attitude towards Israelis. Although the Oslo process provided for a softening of 'enemy-images', such distrust has again increased after the coming to power of Benyamin Netanyahu in Israel and the reverse trend of the peace process. Palestinians increasingly suspect that there will be no more Israeli withdrawals, but that the end-solution will entail the fragmented, Bantustan-like, self-rule which exists today. Likewise, the terror attacks by Palestinian Islamist movements resulting in a skyrocketing of Israelis killed have served to reinforce Israeli perceptions of Palestinians as terrorists and have fed into the anxiety discourse. Security becomes the logical outcome, both in terms of sealing Israel from contact with Palestinians from the West Bank and Gaza and in terms of Israeli requirements on the Palestinian Authority to combat terrorism.

The Declaration of Principles and the mutual recognition

Although the Declaration of Principle[50] is not and was not a peace agreement, it remains the most successful attempt to bring the actors closer to a negotiated solution. 'This was not peace, but a mutual expression of peaceful intentions.'[51] Rather, the DOP was an agreement that the parties aspired for a peaceful solution and a time-schedule and a plan for how to do so. It also contained an acknowledgement that this would be a painstaking effort and that it could only be realized through a gradual process in which trust and confidence were to be gradually erected.

The main achievement of the Oslo process is usually described as the mutual recognition expressed in letters by Israel's Prime Minister Yitzhak Rabin and PLO Chairman Yasir Arafat respectively and exchanged a few days prior to the signing of the actual DOP. Mutual recognition implied a willingness on behalf of the parties to break down ideological foundations on which both sides had built their 'Other'-perceptions.[52] To the Palestinians, the most important gain was that Palestinian identity was recognized, that in the eyes of the world the Palestinians had become a *somebody*.

> The essence in the agreement and the mutual recognition between the PLO and Israel, it was that the Israelis [were] saying, they exist, they have rights, they have national rights, and this openly stood [in the agreement], [it was as though] someone said: 'We lied for the past 70 years, we can no longer lie. They are there.'[53]

Highlighted in these remarks is the fact that the revolutionary PLO had now been elevated to the finest salons of international politics. A denied nationality was no longer denied. The Palestinians fearfully remember Golda Meir's statement in the late 1960s, implying that 'there are no Palestinians',[54] and Israel is still chilled by the Palestinian National Charter of 1964 (amended in 1968), denying the existence of a Jewish nation. With Israel's recognition, the USA also followed, and the PLO received full international recognition. International recognition is also a way to place oneself as a collective identity in the international structure of sovereign nation-states. Recognition was an achievement in itself. Its significance was that the Palestinians now constituted a 'somebody' in the eyes of others, i.e. an immaterial value had been partly fulfilled. On behalf of Israel, recognition of the PLO accounted for a revolutionary change in nationalist discourse(s).[55] Although the result of gradual change within the Labour Party, the PLO had up to that point been depicted as the ultimate symbol of terrorism and the man who since 1969 had reincarnated the Palestinian struggle was delineated as global evil.

> [Arafat] was perceived and presented by most of the Jewish Israeli media in caricature; shaped as an appalling but ridiculous terrorist, a cunning conspirator with a limited performance record, a loser survivalist, a non-trustworthy consistent pragmatist, and, above all, as the personification of ultimate evil.[56]

The PLO recognition of Israel and its right to exist within secure borders was also the outcome of a gradual process of acknowledgement beginning in 1974 and formalized through the PLO recognition of UN resolutions 242 and 338 in 1988. The formalization of this recognition was accompanied with the writings in the letter by Chairman Arafat to Prime Minister Rabin affirming that 'those articles of the Palestinian Covenant which deny Israel's right to exist and the provisions of the Covenant which are inconsistent with the commitments of this letter are now inoperative and no longer valid'.[57] The PNC was not called upon to take this crucial discussion of the Covenant until April 1996. At this meeting, the PLO specified the paragraphs in the Charter which were now nullified. However, the Charter has still not been redrafted making this issue a perpetual thorn in Palestinian-Isareli relations. Israel's Prime Minister Netanyahu has constantly made a redraft a requirement for further progress in the peace process. However, the PLO standpoint needs to be understood in relation to struggle as the main embodiment of Palestinian national identity. Although the PLO might not have a problem to do away with the struggle as a strategy, it is far more complicated to negotiate away struggle as discourse. To do so would be to deny the content of Palestinian identity as it has been formed during the last decades.[58]

For both Palestinians and Israelis such fundamental changes in nationalist identity discourses were sudden and not prepared.

> In fact, for both Palestinians and Israeli Jews, the agreement hurt longstanding cognitive maps of who the 'enemy' is, of the 'intentions' of the 'other', and of the imperatives of collective memories and amnesia – without any proper preparation.[59]

One of the main effects of the peace process was thus the beginning of a deconstruction of enemy images. Enemy images and constructions of 'Self' and 'Other' had until then provided an unquestioned, secure sphere in which to place oneself and to find categories for acting. When all of a sudden cooperation was the favoured action, this created confusion on popular levels on both sides. Israel was now to assist in Palestinian institution-building and to create an economic bases for the agreements, and the Palestinians were to defend Israelis from violence and terror. The peace process also gave way to new images of Israelis as the Palestinian 'neighbour', implying a softening of the boundaries.[60] When the stereotype changes in character, it might actually provide problems since it is no longer as clear how to act and behave vis-à-vis the 'Other'. Turbulence replaces the previous sense of order and harmony. However, it might also be argued that the Oslo process has served as to further fragment identities on both sides. For the Palestinian diaspora left aside by the agreements, there is an augmented sense of despair and desertedness, together with a potential sharpening the boundary between 'Us' and 'Them'. On both sides, political hard-liners using politico-religious discourse, tend to see the agreements as betrayal of identity, of what is 'right', and a cheap 'sell-cut' of territory to the unrightful 'other'.

The Oslo process and identity

It could be argued that the particular mode of mediation and third-party intervention provided by the Norwegians[61] provided for a setting where old identity concepts were questioned and new ones in the form of boundary transcending friendships materialized. The Oslo formula was based on non-interference and flexibility on behalf of the Norwegian facilitators, secrecy, problem-solving and smallness in size (i.e. the negotiating teams had to be small in size) and a working personal chemistry.[62] In the secret Oslo channel, personal chemistry was to a large extent the key to constructive communication between the parties:

> It is obvious that this personal chemistry was completely crucial. That is one of the secrets behind the success. There were such exceptional personalities on all sides. It was very much that which was Terje's strength in this; his way of dealing with the persons. At least towards the end, the relationship between Uri Savir[63] and Abu Ala[64] became very special.[65]

This creation of an unusual friendship allowed for the parties to become constructive in understanding the other's point of view. There was a mutual interest between the interlocutors who were sometimes posed at odds with their superiors.[66] Enemy images were explicitly addressed by the Norwegian mediators. One of the motivating forces for Terje Rød Larsen to get involved in the process was his conviction that Other descriptions and enemy images on both sides were 'completely wrong'.[67] To build trust between the negotiators, the Norwegians placed a great deal of effort in finding the right spatial context for the discussions as well as to create the 'right' atmosphere. Negotiations were accompanied by walks in the woods, dinners and nightly talks. Also, in the capacity of carrying messages, the Norwegians were able to explain standpoints and assure each side about the sincerity of the other side.

Although this personal mode of partial boundary transcending was the main factor behind the relative success of Oslo, it also proved the most vulnerable. It made the agreements, the understanding of the agreements as well as all subsequent modalities a too personalized affair to transform properly into a process where a Likud-led Israeli government could take as active part as a Labour-government. Neither could the process be easily picked up by populations on each side.

Official Palestinian nationalism, was during the first years of the peace process in effect *allied* with Israel's government in the peace process as well as in protecting Israeli security, representing drastic change of the enemy image. The ones who were previously fought were now to be protected. For the first time in the history of Palestinian nationalism, Israeli security was interpreted as a Palestinian *national* interest.[68] Although potentially crafting new forms of togetherness, such partially boundary transcending steps may be hard to swallow for populations, and serve as to augment internal polarizations.

Thus, this relationship worked primarily on the level of the negotiating teams and an elite level. In extension, a working relationship was able to unfold also on leadership level, and although not characterized by absolute warmth, there was a kind of chemistry especially by Simon Peres and Yasir Arafat; Rabin obviously feeling more difficulties in overcoming the image of Arafat as the arch-terrorist of global politics.

It could be argued that the reconstruction of the 'Other' becomes even more important in the post-agreement phase, when agreement is to be implemented.[69] 'The persistence of old enemy images is a major reason why we see breakdowns of peace agreements in the implementation phase, since new interpretations of the post-war phase may be bitterly contested among the parties.'[70]

Concluding comments

Decline of external conflict implies a change of the setting and creates turbulence and disorder in the sense that inside and outside of the boundary are becoming blurred. This decline leads to a deconstruction of images of 'Self' and 'Other'. New forms of togetherness or empathy must be created, not necessarily in order to replace old ones, but to complement them. Any conflict resolution attempt with aspirations of a long-term settlement must realize that the main factor is troubled national identities and that any package must allow for the recognition of identities as well as mechanisms to overcome negative stereotypes. The boundary between Us and Them has to become softer.

The lesson from the Oslo-channel seems thus to be to provide for peoples and leaders to engage in problem-solving affairs dealing not necessarily with the ultimate and fundamental issues in the first round, but more small-scale issues, where cooperation could realistically be envisaged from the beginning. If confidence can be established in such fields, one can then move on to larger issues. The main rationale behind this is for identities framed as exclusive categories to meet concretely, not only in abstract construction, and get to know the diabolic 'Other'. The main way to do this ought to be to find things to *do together*, such as, in this case, all the negotiation teams working on various issues, the joint security patrols, economic cooperation etc. However, such processes must be popularized and social arenas must be found where people from various experiences and backgrounds meet to build confidence.

A pattern of interaction characterized by conflict obviously creates an emphasis on difference and otherness. Interaction in a context of common problem-solving can rather serve to emphasize similarities and provide for the creation of new identities, not replacing old ones, but offering complementary political constructs which do have an impact upon ideologies of boundedness. This may provide new mechanisms of exclusion and inclusion which might reduce or change conflict patterns. In addition, 'people's categories are for action',[71] that is identities are formed in the crossing-point between what groups of people experience are happening to them and how they act to deal with such historical traumas. Identities are crafted through the action, not by primordial givens, and not out of raw interest. 'Hence "identity", though ostensibly a noun, behaves like a verb'.[72] It is in a constant process of action that self and other are being incessantly reconstituted and never fulfilled. The lesson of the Oslo agreement and the process behind it is to recognize the problematique of identity and the deep meanings associated with 'Self' and 'Other'. It is to make symbolic recognition and acceptance of the 'Other' an aim in itself. It is also, however, to rapidly find a way to popularize such processes and not let boundary-transcending become an opportunity for élites only.

Notes

1 Many thanks to Elisabeth Abiri, Maria Eriksson Baaz, Peter Johansson, Henrik Norberg, Camilla Orjuela and Michel Schulz at the Department for Peace and Development Research, Göteborg University for substantial and valuable comments.
2 Palestinian protest demonstrations on 15 May 1998 turned violent and left a number of Palestinian protesters dead as Israeli Defence Forces opened fire.
3 The process set in motion by secret negotiations in Norway in 1993, leading to the Declaration of Principles (1993), the Gaza-Jericho Agreement (1994), and the Interim Agreement on the West Bank and the Gaza Strip (1995).
4 This is due to the fact that my own research has primarily dealt with Palestinian nationalism and national identity. This chapter is to a large extent based on my dissertation: *Reconstruction of Palestinian Nationalisms: Between Revolution and Statehood* to be published by Manchester University Press in 1999.
5 Heldt, Birger (ed.) (1992) *States in Armed Conflict 1990–91*, Report No. 35, Department of Peace and Conflict Research Uppsala University; Wallensteen, Peter and Karin Axell (1993) 'Armed Conflicts at the End of the Cold War, 1989–92', in Karin Axell (ed.), *States in Armed Conflict 1992*, Report No. 36, Department of Peace and Conflict Research, Uppsala University; SIPRI Yearbook, 1993, 1994, 1995, 1996, *World Armamants and Disarmaments*. Oxford and New York: Oxford University Press.
6 Barth, Fredrik (1969) *Ethnic Groups and Boundaries, The Social Organization of Culture Difference*. Bergen, Oslo: Universitetsforlaget and London: George Allen and Unwin; Eriksen, Thomas Hylland (1993) *Ethnicity and Nationalism, Anthropological Perspectives*. London, Boulder, Colorado: Pluto Press.
7 Eriksen (1993), *op. cit.*, p. 12.
8 Goldstein, Joshua, S. (1996) *International Relations*, 2nd edn, American University, Washington D.C., Harper Collins College Publishers, p. 198. Cf. also Gurr, Ted and Barbara Harff, 1994, *Ethnic Conflict in World Politics,* Boulder Westview Press
9 For example, Hall, Stuart (1992) 'The Question of Cultural Identity', in Stuart Hall, David Held and Tony McGrew (eds), *Modernity and its Futures*. Polity Press in Association with the Open University; Hall, Stuart (1996) 'Introduction: Who Needs Identity?', in Stuart Hall and Paul du Gay (eds), *Questions of Cultural Identity*, Sage Publications London: Baumann, Zygmunt

(1990) 'Modernity and Ambivalence', in Mike Featherstone (ed.), *Global Culture: Nationalism, Globalization and Modernity*. Sage Publications, pp. 143-169; Laclau, E. (1990) *New Reflections on the Revolution of Our Time*. London: Verso; Derrida, J. (1981) *Positions*. Chicago: University of Chicago Press.

10 Mouffe, Chantal (1994) 'For a Politics of Nomadic Identity', in George Robertson *et al.*, (eds), *Travelers' Tales: Narratives of Home and Displacement*, p. 109 ff. (139-74).

11 Hall (1996), *op. cit.*

12 Said, Edward (1978) *Orientalism*. Penguin Books; Derrida (1981), *op. cit.*; Laclau (1990) *op. cit.*

13 Barth, Fredrik (1994) 'Enduring and Emerging Issues in the Analysis of Ethnicity', in Hans Vermuelen and Cora Govers (eds), *The Anthropology of Ethnicity: Beyond Ethnic Groups and Boundaries*. Amsterdam: Het Spinhius, p. 13 (11-32).

14 Roosens, Eugeen (1994) 'The Primordial Nature of Origins in Migrant Ethnicity', in Vermuelen and Govers (1994), *op. cit.*, pp. 81-104.

15 Cf. Eriksen (1993), *op. cit.*

16 Brown, Michael E. *et al.* (eds) (1996–97) *Nationalism and Ethnic Conflict*. Cambridge, MA and London: The MIT Press, p. 3 ff.

17 Gellner, Ernest (1983) *Nations and Nationalism*. Oxford: Basil Blackwell Ltd; Anderson, Benedict (1991) *Imagined Communities*, London: Verso; Hobsbawm, Eric (1990) *Nations and Nationalism since 1780: Programme, Myth, Reality*. Cambridge: Cambridge University Press.

18 Brown *et al.* (1996–97), *op. cit.*

19 Portugali, Yuvali (1993) *Implicate Relations: Society and Space in the Israeli-Palestinian Conflict*. Dordrecht: Kluwer Academic Publishers, p. 37.

20 Cf. Smith, Anthony (1991) *National Identity*. London: Penguin Books, p. 40.

21 Portugali (1993), *op. cit.*, p. 44.

22 Verdery, Katherine (1994), 'Ethnicity, Nationalism and State-making: Ethnic Groups and Boundaries: Past and Future', in Vermuelen and Govers (1994), *op. cit.*, pp. 33-58.

23 Hettne, Björn, 1992, *Etniska Konflikter och internationella relationer*. Lund: Studentlitteratur (in Swedish).

24 Connor, Walker (1972) 'Nation-building or Nation Destroying', *World Politics* 24(3), April, pp. 319-355.

25 Stavenhagen, Rodolfo (1991) *The Ethnic Question: Conflicts, Development, and Human Rights*. United Nations University Press.

26 For example, Hobsbawm (1990) *op. cit.*

27 Portugali (1993), *op. cit.*, p. 36

28 Ibid., p. 39

29 For example, Baumel, Judith (1995) 'In Everlasting Memory': Individual and

Communal Holocaust Commemoration in Israel', in Robert Wistrich and David Ohana (eds), *The Shaping of Israeli Identity: Myth, Memory and Trauma.* Frank Cass, London, pp. 146-70, Handelman, Don and Lea Shamgar Handelman (1997) *ThePresence of Absence: The Memoralism of National Death in Israel,* in Eyal Ben-Ari and Yoram Bilu (eds.),1997, *Grasping Land: Space and place in Contemporary Israeli Discourse and Experience,* State University of New York Press.

30 The main exception to this trend may well be Kimmerling, Baruch (1983) *Zionism and Territory: The Socio-Territorial Dimensions of Zionist Politics.* University of California, Berkely, Institute of International Studies;

31 Kimmerling, Baruch (1997) 'The Power-Oriented Settlement: PLO – Israel: The Road to the Oslo Agreement and Back?', in Avraham Sela and Moshe Ma'oz (eds), *The PLO and Israel: From Armed Conflict to Political Solution, 1964–1994.* New York, St Martin's Press, p. 229 (223-252).

32 Khalidi, Rashid (1997) *Palestinian Identity: The Construction of Modern National Consciousness.* New York: Columbia University Press; Muslih, Muhammad (1988) *The Origins of Palestinian Nationalism.* New York: Columbia University Press; Lesch, Ann Mosley (1973) 'The Palestine Arab Nationalist Movement Under the Mandat', in William Quandt, Fuad Jabber and Ann Mosley Lesch, *The Politics of Palestinian Nationalismi.*Berkeley, Los Angeles, London: University of California Press, pp. 5-42; Ann Mosley Lesch (1979) *Arab Politics in Palestine 1917–1939: The Frustration of a Nationalist Movementi.* Ithaca and London: Cornell University Press.

33 Khalidi (1997), *op. cit.,* p. 1 ff.

34 Sayigh, Yezid (1997) *Armed Struggle and the Search for State: The Palestinian National Movement, 1949–1993.* Oxford: Clarendon Press.

35 Ibid., p. 88.

36 *Feday* means one who sacrifices.

37 See Lindholm Schulz, Helena (1999) *Reconstruction of Palestinian Nationalisms. Between Revolution and Statehood,* forthcoming Manchester University Press.

38 Interview with Fateh-leader, 29 October 1994.

39 Peteet, Julie M. (1993) 'Authenticity and Gender: The Presentation of Culture', in Judith E. Tucker (ed.), *Arab Women.* Indiana University Press, p. 56 (49-62).

40 Interview with Fateh-activist, 26 August 1994.

41 Interview with Fateh-activist, 22 April 1995.

42 Simmel, Georg (1971) 'The Stranger' in *On Individuality and Social Forms* (original edition, 1908). Chicago: Chicago University Press.

43 Baumann, Zygmunt (1990) 'Modernity and Ambivalence', in Mike Featherstone (ed.), *Global Culture: Nationalism, Globalization and Modernity.* London: Sage Publications, pp. 143-170.

44 Baumann (1990), *op. cit.,* p. 143.

45 See Said (1978), *op. cit.;* Said, Edward (1993) *Culture and Imperialism,*

Vintage.

46 Cf. Kimmerling (1997), *op. cit.*, p. 229.

47 See Kimmerling (1983), *op. cit.*

48 Lindholm Schulz (1999), *op. cit.*

49 Interview with DFLP-sympathizer, 21 and 28 September 1994

50 For a critique of the DOP and the Oslo-process as such, see Butenschøn, Nils (1998) 'The Oslo Agreement: From the White House to Jabal Abu Ghneim', in George Giacaman and Dag Jørund Lønning (eds), *After Oslo: New Realities, Old Problems*. London and Chicago: Pluto Press, pp. 16-44.

51 Butenschøn (1998), *op. cit.*, p. 17.

52 Aggestam, Karin and Christer Jönsson (1997) '(Un)Ending Conflict: Challenges in Post-War Bargaining, *Millennium: Journal of International Studies* 26(3), p. 785 (771-793).

53 Interview with PA-Minister, Fateh, 3 February 1995

54 Golda Meir, quoted in London *Sunday Times*, 15 June 1969.

55 Raz-Krakotzkin, Amon (1998) 'A Peace without Arabs: The Discourse of Peace and the Limits of Israeli Consciousness', in Giacaman and Lønning (1998), *op. cit.*, p. 59 (59-77).

56 Kimmerling (1997), *op. cit.*, p. 231.

57 PLO Chairman Yasir Arafat to Israeli Prime Minister Yitzhak Rabin, PLO and Israeli Letters of Mutual Recognition, Tunis and Jerusalem, 9 September 1993, in *Journal of Palestine Studies* 23(1), Autumn 1993, pp. 114-115,

58 Cf. Lindholm Schulz (1999), *op. cit.*; Sayigh (1997), *op. cit.*

59 Kimmerling (1997), *op. cit.*, p. 241.

60 Interviews with leading Palestinian political personalities, see Lindholm Schulz (1996), *op. cit.*

61 See Corbin, Jane (1995) *Gaza First: The Secret Norway Channel to Peace Between Israel and the PLO*. London: Bloomsbury.

62 Interview Terje Rød Larsen, 8 June 1995, the Norwegian academic who became chief negotiatior in the Norwegian channel.

63 Then director general at the Israeli foreign department and towards the latter part of the negotiations, head of the Israeli team.

64 Leading PLO official and head of the Palestinian negotation team.

65 Inteview with Mona Juul, 7 June 1995. Mona Juul is a career diplomat with the Middle East as her specialty and is married to Terje Rød Larsen.

66 Ibid.

67 Interview, Terje Rød Larsen, 8 June 1995.

68 Lindholm Schulz (1999), *op. cit.*

69 Cf. Aggestam and Jönsson (1997), *op. cit.*, p. 783.

70 Ibid., p. 784

71 Barth (1969), *op. cit.*

72 Bauman (1990), *op. cit.*, p. 19.

12 Cultural Roots of Russian Nationalism: Dilemmas of Existential Conflict

ANTON IVANOV

Introduction

This chapter presents an attempt to map out ways to understand present-day Russian nationalism as a culture-specific system of values and underlying beliefs, represented both at the grassroots and élite levels, as well as the conflict-free alternatives to it. Nationalism in Russia appears to play an increasingly important role as a powerful mobilization doctrine, defining political preconceptions and affecting the conflict and peace dynamics in the Russian Federation and neighbouring states. Cultural roots of the contemporary Russian nationalism are seen as a variety of key ideas and concepts that continue to provide a constant input to national interests and policy formulation and implementation in the course of decades and are firmly established either in a philosophical or political discourse. In terms of academic genre, this chapter is meant to provide a philosophical framework based upon cultural-historical data. Still, I regard it as a policy-oriented work, in the broadest sense of the term.

I should also like to position this chapter in terms of the dominant conceptual frameworks, somewhere between the analysis of civic (or state) nationalism and the examination of ideas that belong to the realm of ethnic nationalism, because I tend to share the opinion that in societal reality these two types overlap. This distinction is very fruitful as an analytical instrument that is applied for theorizing, but it may seem inept for a cultural context. Furthermore, the elements of political culture and phraseology that draw on nationalism as a mobilizing force and a catalyst for political action are almost identical in both civic and state 'mantras', at least in the case of Russian nationalism, that used to be official in history. Both have a tendency to search for a philosophical and moral firmament, or to invent one, if the search proves unsuccessful.

There is a great difference, however, between the initial universalist precepts of V. S. Solovyov's imperative[1] ('love other peoples as your own'), for example, and ideas, shared by the ideologues of racism and fascism. The distinction along these lines is independent from the dichotomy of civic and ethnic nationalisms. Unfortunately, it has lately become fashionable to construct certain types of nationalism that are inherently prone to aggressive xenophobia, and to advance other kinds as conducive to state-building, in order to adjust one's discourse to the perceived notions of political correctness. These constructs do not produce an impression of being intellectually valid and seem to do more harm than cure, so far as handling flesh-and-blood nationalisms is concerned.

Finally, it should be mentioned that nationalism as a manner of speaking and, generally, of communication, appears to have a super-segmental level, to put it in linguistic terms. In other words, the meaning is conveyed by means of context and 'social intonation', just as much as by the utterances and texts. Derogatory statements and self-praise may be expressed in a very subtle way, which mainly depends on the agenda and peculiarities of style of the proponents of nationalist ideas. Being an emotional discourse by nature, a nationalist sentiment can also easily increase or decrease the level of collective egoism and aggression, depending on the subject and situation. All this makes it particularly difficult to address super-segmental components of nationalism, since any critique of such kind lends itself to accusations of witch-hunting, subjectivity, and excessive rhetorical fervour. Nevertheless, it is necessary to tackle the deeply rooted ideas that exercise their power precisely on the super-segmental level, because they play a critical role in shaping the very genesis of nationalist sentiment. The goal of this chapter is to trace the conflict-generating implications and peace-building potential of the two main versions of Russian nationalism: inclusive and exclusive.

'Inclusive' nationalism as a group's self-cognition (ideology of Eurasianism)

A perception of certain ethnic and historical affinities between the peoples inhabiting the Central and North Eurasia has been characteristic of many ideological movements. Eurasianism tackles not just historical and geographical components of this unity, but also economic, political and ideological aspects that transcend purely ethnic, linguistic and cultural boundaries. The movement of Eurasianism began to form in the 1920s in the intellectual circles of the 'first wave' of Russian emigrants. It was originally a reaction to the insurmountable challenges posed by the Revolution of 1917 that brought about a regime lasting much longer than was expected by the majority of the upper-class intelligentsia. The new movement was represented by a number of outstanding scholars such as geographer P. N. Savitsky, historian G. V. Vernadsky, linguist, anthropologist and philosopher Prince N. S. Trubetskoy[2] and others. L. P. Karsavin, a prominent religious philosopher, who associated himself with Eurasianism, even returned to Stalinist Russia and eventually perished in the Gulag camp in Abez.

Contemporary historian and geographer L. N. Gumlilev considered himself to be the last Eurasianist, but post-Soviet history has evidenced the appearance of new and rather eccentric proponents of the old doctrine, who probably would not even agree that they were taking part in such a thoroughly forgotten philosophic paradigm. For example, some of the speeches by Kazakhstani president Nursultan Nazarbaev and the Krasnoyarsk governor with presidential ambitions, General Alexander Lebed, seem to rely upon key ideas rooted in Eurasianism. N. Nazarbaev has invested much energy in the development of the political programme for a 'Eurasian Union' – a form of closer economic and political integration between the post-Soviet states with a supra-national government of member-nations, headed by a Council of Presidents.[3]

A. Lebed, in his usual laconic manner, has referred to close affinities of cultures that can be observed between peoples of Slavic and non-Slavic descent within the Russian Federation, when running for his position of governor. While Lebed's texts allow little room for interpretative analysis, many of the other statements, programmes and academic publications that appear in Russian intellectual journals,[4] demonstrate that the ideas and concepts characteristic to Eurasianism continue to play an important role at present.

In his article 'On True and False Nationalism', N. S. Trubetskoy states

> a human being with a marked ego-centric psychology, unconsciously considers oneself to be the centre of universe. [...] That is why any natural group to which such humans belong, is regarded *a priori* as the most perfect. One's family, tribe, class and race seem to be better than others. People of Romano-Germanic stock, partaking in this psychology, base their assessment of other cultures on that assumption.[5]

This statement is very characteristic of Eurasianism, which tended to accuse the West of cultural expansion and a sort of cosmopolitan chauvinism. At the same time, it regarded the Eurasian super-ethnos as an entity with a mission to counter-balance the Western influence and combine Eastern and Western perspectives in the unique economic, political and ideological environment of Russia. Any possibility of a global culture was categorically denied by N. S. Trubetskoy and most of the other Eurasianists.

True nationalism, according to Trubetskoy and L. N. Gumilev, has nothing to do with imposing one's lifestyle and culture upon others. It is based on the idea of an individual and collective self-cognition and a simple behavioural rule – be yourself. False nationalism, according to Trubetskoy, is a misleading association of national and ethnic peculiarities with culturally extinct historical phenomena. He stresses that it is equally misleading to assert one's uniqueness and dignity at the expense of others. Generally, any assumptions and inventions that are not based on impartial self-cognition as well as little intellectual dishonesties make nationalism false and transform it into chauvinism. The Eurasianists failed to acknowledge the universalism of European culture and did not see its tolerance and inclusiveness in relation to other cultures. Their philosophical constructs were mainly determined by the active search for an answer to the severe geopolitical challenges of the 1920s–30s, as far as the role of Russia is concerned.

Modern Eurasianists maintain that the creation of Eurasian Union, or any such formation that would re-unite the culturally similar nations of the post-Soviet space, will bring no more harm than the creation of the European Union and will answer the aspirations of the majority of the populations on the ground. They share the opinion that the self-determination of ethnic groups should not necessarily proceed along the path of statehood, which brings about rivalries of élites, dividing lines and a variety of conflict-generating factors. But the nationalist precepts, quite paradoxically, transform this very reasonable assumption into the assertion of the leading role the Russian people should play in the process of building the Russian state, that eventually leads to precisely the same cultural expansion of which the West is being accused.

The significance of Eurasianism for the conflict and peace dynamics in the territories of the former Soviet Union lies with the fact that this ideology continuously presents itself as neither left nor right for the regional and sub-regional policy actors, offering a comparatively peaceful and constructive channel for the manifestation of nationalist sentiments. Although, it may pose new challenges to the West in terms of managing geopolitical equilibrium, especially if the CIS frameworks develop towards further integration in economic, political and military sphere, this ideology may well offer a constructive context for intra-state conflict prevention. Indeed, if nationalism cannot be escaped, it can be transformed into a less conflicting form. In this setting, nationalism understood as self-cognition, if consistently pursued, brings us to the end of nationalism, provided that a more general and preferably universal ethical framework is adhered to. In the case of Kazakhstan, the example of President Nazarbaev demonstrates an evolution of ideology that, somehow, went beyond nationalism, being essentially nationalistic.

'Exclusive' nationalism as messianism (Slavophiles and the 'Third Rome')

Orthodox religious messianism was a child born from philosophy and misunderstood patriotism, rather than religion itself. A. S. Khomyakov and other so-called 'old' Slavophiles believed, according to V. V. Zenkovsky,[6] that the Russian Orthodox world-view contained a qualitatively different approach to Christianity, which was based upon the preservation of the religious tradition, whereas in the West the very notion of Christianity was such that it was bound to evolve into secularism. Slavophiles appeared to look for a newer form for the old content, and the spiritual expectation of the new epoch made them struggle against the old one. In a way, they have been struggling against the tradition and foundations of their own faith, that called for tolerance and forgiveness.

The historical views of the Slavophiles were influenced by the ancient idea of Moscow's being a 'Third Rome', or the last spiritual leader of the Christian world after Rome and Byzantium. This idea relates to the time of Ivan the Terrible, when it acquired specific significance for a consolidating state power, lacking spiritual backup. Nevertheless, the concept of the third Roman Empire always belonged to realm of the unspoken and unwritten mystical perceptions. Even in the sixteenth to seventeenth centuries, when it first emerged as a cultural phenomenon, it always existed in the background, never reaching the surface of political life. The fact that stress was always laid on the notion of the third Roman Empire as the *last* one appears to be of particular importance. If one accepts that spiritual leaders of humanity shift as in a relay race, the inevitable question, in the case of the third and possibly the fourth Roman Empire, would be what kind of cultural content is being transferred from one leader to another when shifts occur and why the third Roman Empire should necessarily be the last one. This question, abstract as it is, seems to contain the key to understanding the mechanism of how agreeable patriotism turns into somewhat unpleasant nationalism.

Zenkovsky, being a Russian Orthodox priest himself, was one of the first scholars (after N. A. Berdyaev) [7] to point out a very interesting feature of the Slavophiles' group that formed around A .S. Khomyakov and I. V. Kireevsky in the 1840s. It usually passed unnoticed that the very term 'Slavophiles' was not quite appropriate, because the main emphasis within this movement was always upon the Russian culture only. It would have been much more exact to apply the term 'Russophiles'. Unlike Eurasianism, this movement never really managed to transcend the boundaries of the Russian cultural circle. Its brilliant insights about *sobornost* (spiritual collectivism) of the Russian ethnos and holistic realism of spiritual cognition lacked spiritual universalism and inclusiveness. Starting from the theological dispute, Slavophiles ended up struggling against the Western culture as such. It was the tragedy of misplaced benevolence, when a little flaw and seemingly unimportant assumption developed into an impregnable dividing line between Orthodox 'us' and Western 'them'.

The noteworthy linkage between a system of religious beliefs and ethnicity became a catalyst for a nationalist sentiment in the context of conflict of world-views, based not so much on the lack of communication between the cultures, but the lack of desire to communicate. As far as Slavophile religious messianism is concerned, nationalism seems to have begun at the point when group self-perception shifted from the flexible and temporary *'primus inter pares'* to the static and finite *'primus inter pares sub specie aeternitatis'*[8] yet another instance of the delusion of intrinsic superiority.

This transformation seems to be of critical importance. The subtlety of this *shift of meaning,* that lies at the very heart of a nationalist-messianic mythology is one of the resources that makes it a very powerful mobilization tool. Even those messianic ideas that lie very far from the 'mainstream spirituality' of Russians and are strongly associated with neo-paganism bear a certain degree of validity for the nationalist leaders due to the quick and tangible effects on the followers. Neo-pagan beliefs and ideas tend to be utilized by the most radical part of the nationalist ideologies, that address the marginalized stratum of society. Some of these ideas and 'great historical discoveries' are shocking, or even absurd (like the 'ethnogenetic' constructs by V. Kandyba and P. Zolin, who seem to believe that prehistoric people were 'transmuted into proto-Russians as a result of the arrival of an intelligent beam of light from the constellation of Orion 18 million years ago').[9]

The notions of being Russian and being Orthodox were practically interchangeable in the vision of Russian culture (and Russian nationalism, one may add), created by F. M. Dostoevsky. The messianic pathos was especially intense in his idea of the Russian people as '*narod-bogonosets*' (people that accepted and embodied God). According to V. V. Rosanov,[10] Dostoevsky started with all-embracing love, but ended up suspecting Catholicism of being anti-Christian and considering anything non-Russian to be at least ridiculous.[11] It was that little shift of meaning (from patriotic *primus inter pares* to nationalist *primus inter pares sub specie aeternitatis* that made it possible to refer to both names in one text: the great author of *Crime and Punishment* and V. Kandyba, with his 'Oriono-centric' theory and reference to Christianity as 'the ideology of hatred'.[12]

Inclusive paradigms in political discourses (*Derzhavnost* doctrine)

According to the contemporary Russian anthropologist V. A. Tishkov,[13] civil nationalism cannot be neutral in the cultural sense. In Russia, this is exemplified by the dominance of the Russian language and culture. Ethnonationalism cannot avoid claiming cultural authority and the necessity of state support. This is evidenced by the fact that practically all post-Soviet culturally distinct ethnic communities would like to have their 'own' statehood. Those who do make a distinction between civil and state nationalism regard the former as a liberal ideology and a practice of nation-building, i.e. the creation of nation-states. It exists in many forms: from patriotism and isolationism, to chauvinism and messianism. Ethnic nationalism (ethnonationalism) is usually interpreted as a collectivist-authoritarian one. It is defined as a form of particularism and exclusivity and, furthermore, as a means for a certain group to gain political power and control over resources and create ethnically homogenous states which are alien to pluralistic democracy and a civil society.

It is precisely within the framework of this approach that V. A. Tishkov identifies two main types of 'nationalism' with regard to the USSR and Russia. The first type is a 'hegemonist' nationalism, usually referring to the ruling ethnic group or state. The second one is a 'peripheral' or 'protective' ethnonationalism which more often refers to ethnic minorities and the domestic structures controlled by them. The latter manifests itself in different forms, ranging from cultural nationalism to armed separatism.

The constructivist interpretation of nationalism, embodied in the well-known phrase by Benedict Anderson, 'Imagined Communities', with which Tishkov tends to side, regards the notion of 'nation' as a social construct and an imagined group, the members of which do not know each other personally and do not interact, but who nevertheless consider themselves to be a single community with a common character, hopes and fate. This imagined community becomes a reality as the masses begin to believe in the idea of a community and its components. In this case, nationalism is a sort of mechanism for the reconceptualization of a political community which could have been categorized as an empire, colonial administration or tribal formation prior to that. According to Benedict Anderson, it is significant to note that this phenomenon had arisen in the Latin-American colonial governorships and spread, either simultaneously or afterwards, throughout Europe and then the rest of the world.

In the case of Russia, this approach helps to explain how the idea of a nation has been translated in the public consciousness into the notion of '*derzhava*' (a notion that unites the perception of the state as the great power and a certain identification with the native land as the motherland). The modern *derzhava* nationalists do not seem to be exclusively Russian nationalists at all. They are much closer to the Eurasian paradigm with a very strong geopolitical element to it. The obvious involvement of politics in the reconceptualization of the *derzhavnost* doctrine is explained mainly by the new geopolitical competition in the world in the aftermath of the Cold War and the emergence of the intra-state conflicting ethnicity as a new challenge to stability and development. At the same time, dominance and even hegemonism are characteristic of *derzhavnost* doctrine vis-à-vis local separatism.

According to S. Kortunov,[14] Russia as heir to the Ancient Rus, Moscow state, Russian empire and the USSR, occupies a unique place in Eurasia, between the Eastern and Western civilizations. This allowed Russia to play an important stabilizing role in the global equilibrium of forces and interests. Kortunov believes that Russia has evolved into a complex ethnic community – or a *supra-nation* consolidated by the historical destiny of the Russian people, that interacts with other ethnic groups within Russia on the basis of equality and freedom. Russian empire, according to Kortunov, is a kind of a natural function of the supra-nation. It has nothing to do with Russian ethnic imperialism. It was and is an imperialism of the supra-national state, whose interests have consistently been ranking higher than the interests of society.

The fact that the Russian people had no privileges in the 'Russian empire' has been underlined by many authors, including J. B. Dunlop, Alain Besançon, Milovan Djilas and others. According to Dunlop,[15] if the Tsarist empire cannot, except for in its closing years (i.e. the russification policy under Alexander III and Nicholas II), be termed a Russian empire, much less can the Soviet empire be so considered. As Carl Linden[16] pointed out in 1983, 'the [Soviet] party-state in its strict conception acts not in the name of those it rules but as a proxy of the future 'communised' humanity freed of political rule and no longer separated into nation-states'. Similarly, and quite paradoxically, the *derzhava* nationalism acts as a proxy of the more or less utopian future well-being and greatness of the supra-nation.

Imperial mentality of the supra-national state, as it is conceived by Kortunov, can be defined as a system of values aimed at the search for a certain 'common path' towards a political union of multiethnic populations of Russia in which the Russian people is supposed to play a catalysing and consolidating role. The responsibility for the creation of this union lies with the supra-national state, or the so-called 'imperium', which Kortunov defines as a 'spirit-centred, supra-national state uniting peoples by the strong idea'.

The very essence of the *derzhavnost* doctrine, Kortunov's concept being one of its re-incarnations, is precisely in this idea of the powerful state the interests of which override the interests of the society it is supposed to represent. Despite numerous disclaimers along these lines, voiced by the proponents of *derzhavnost*, they indeed seem to be enchanted by an almost physical sensation of supreme power that creates and crushes what it deems necessary. This sensation is very similar to the one expressed by Rosanov in the nineteenth century, when this exceptionally talented intellectual felt an almost mystical womanly love for the regiment of heavy cavalry passing him by.

Unlike Slavophiles, who thought that Russians did not have a firmly established notion of statehood (on the level of ethnic stereotypes), the ideologists of *derzhava* nationalism appear to be absolutely convinced of the opposite. In fact, the strong notion of statehood and the necessity to sacrifice societal interests to the state is one of the foundations of *derzhavnost* doctrine. *Derzhavnost* is preoccupied with power and the designs of re-engineering political, economic, social and even historical space. Due to its serious mobilizing potential, the ideology of *derzhavnost* is utilized both by the Yeltsin's administration and the most influential opposition figures.

In his book *Derzhava*, the leader of the Communist Party of the Russian Federation, Gennady Zyuganov, defines Russia's vital interests as gathering together under the protection of the unified and powerful state all Russian people, all who consider Russia as their Motherland, and all those peoples who agree to share with Russia their historical fate.[17] This type of rhetoric offers Zyuganov a convenient compromise between the political efficiency of nationalism and the doctrinal internationalism of communist ideology. The organization founded by a group of Russian nationalist leaders, including Zyuganov, in 1992 – 'Russkii Natsionalny Sobor' (Russian National Assembly) attempts to build a coalition of patriotic groups, operating in Belarus, Ukraine and the Baltic states, as well as Moldova and Georgia. The RNS's manifesto refers to the unity of Russia's citizens on the basis of traditional moral and religious values. The importance of the *derzhavnost* doctrine as a 'winning strategy' in the semantic games of the present-day Russian politics cannot be overestimated. Suffice it to say, that Zyuganov appears to have the best chances for presidency at the coming elections, according to numerous public opinion surveys.

Ethical patriotism vs. existential dualism of 'us' and 'them' (overcoming nationalism)

The reason for examining the realities of the Russian collective psyche is not simply to measure the extent to which the nationalist portrayal of it is a distortion but to try to understand why it is portrayed in such a fashion and how the distortion occurs. It is obviously not sufficient to establish that the

Russian culture is socially and culturally different from the Western cultures. Differences between nations are commonplace. It is necessary to tackle the affinities and common roots, as the only socially constructive foundation that may serve to overcome nationalist sentiment by means of transforming it into a more inclusive form. It is not possible to resolve or prevent conflict of any kind using the pressure of degrading terms.

The reality of nationalism for nationalists themselves is neither more nor less than a reality of a dominant paradigm that arranges and organizes a highly emotional content. This paradigm and the manner of thinking about its constituent values is *not the only possible reality* for the people who tend to share it and this basic fact should be kept in mind.

Fortunately, the authority of a dominant paradigm is never absolute. Where it does not reflect the actual experiences as well as aspirations of people and appears to misrepresent them and, therefore, to mislead them, then it tends (sooner or later) to become displaced and people look for alternative explanations. In so far as people in Russia realize that their spiritual, economic and political position is precarious and even threatening, they will continue to generate responses to improve the situation. Whether or not they will do it at the expense of their neighbours or in cooperation with them, whether they will turn nationalist or patriotic in an inclusive and co-operative way is not exclusively their own choice. It is the common responsibility in the world that seems to be turning into a global neighbourhood. The reproduction of divisions and suspicions is definitely not conducive to the positive scenario and, therefore, the management of the emerging interdependence based on respect and compromise is of critical importance.

The displacement of inappropriate ideas is continually underway but it is a long and extremely painful process that unfolds unevenly and erratically. Among Russians, who experienced tremendous pressure during the period of totalitarianism and the demoralizing effect of the ideological vacuum and various degrees of massive societal disappointment, patriotism is often perceived as the only hope and the last resort. Any attempt to construct a causal link between the patriotic feeling and aggressive nationalism in political and academic rhetoric is utterly destructive and harmful. Furthermore, it is dangerous as it consolidates and radicalizes the nationalist sentiments and agendas. An example of the lengths to which this construction process can go is the notorious statement by one of the Russian nationalist leaders: 'If nationalism is fascism, then I am a fascist'.

Ethical patriotism has deeper roots in the grassroots Russian culture than any kind of aggressive nationalism, especially fascism, to which Russia has had a very strong immunity since the Second World War. In the history of Russian philosophic thought ethical patriotism was characteristic of such figures as V. S. Solovyov, N. N. Strakhov and N. A. Berdyaev, for example. Academician D. S. Likhachev can be regarded as a contemporary representative of this modest movement, which should at last be recognized.

At the end of the nineteenth century, Solovyov wrote:

> cosmopolitanism that requires an unconditional application of moral law without the slightest concern with ethnic diversity is more ethically appropriate than nationalism. However, it is precisely the moral principle itself, if consistently adhered to, that does not allow us to be satisfied with the negative freedom of cosmopolitanism in relation to multiple ethnicities.[18]

The viewpoint of the ethical patriotism is centred around the perception of ethnicity as a continuation and widening of individual's personality as a whole. Ethnic identity is accepted by the act of personal self-consciousness, self-cognition and will and becomes interiorized as a part of individuality – something that constitutes value for a human being. How can the relationships between humans be morally acceptable if this important value is not recognized and respected? Ethical principle does not allow one to view a living human being as some kind of an abstract subject, arbitrarily selecting some qualities and distinctive features as acceptable and condemning other features and components of an integral personality as alien or even unacceptable. In other words, if we respect human beings we must respect their ethnicity. It is equally wrong to ignore it or to pretend that it does not exist. Therefore, the positive moral principle of patriotism is a direct derivative from the ethical imperative of at least *respecting* others as oneself. The complete definition of patriotism, according to Solovyov is 'love other peoples as you love your own people'.

There is a good logic to the argument that hatred or indifference to one's own ethnicity and people is something unnatural and dangerous, because it leads to the same feelings in relation to other ethnicities and peoples. It is a logic of a spiritual discipline rather than pure rationalism. The question of whether or not we can justifiably view ethnicity and ethnic diversity as values in their own right depends upon the dominant definition of ethnicity and the dominant paradigm in general. For nationalist consciousness ethnicity is first and foremost a dividing line in a fragmented world of 'us' and 'them'. For ethically correct patriotism it is a set of positive peculiarities that may be respected and appreciated. The imperative requirement of respecting other ethnicities and nations as one's own does not imply a psychologically identical feeling. It refers only to the ethically identical act of will.

In political discourse it is far more appropriate to advance the focus from the 'political correctness' that is essentially instrumentalist and can justify virtually anything, depending on the political ends, to *'ethical correctness'* as an act of will directed to inclusiveness, universality and freedom. The values of individuality (or personality), universality (or openness) and freedom, including the freedom from bias and prejudice achieved through communication and well-informed decision-making, constitute a complex of indispensable prerequisites of the ethically correct inter-ethnic policy. It appears that any distortion of this framework results in the re-emergence of hostile ethnic division and paradigmatic rivalries. Formulation of national interests should also follow this threefold ethical correctness as much as it is possible at all.

Notes

1 Solovyov, V. S. (1988) 'Opravdanie dobra' (Justification of Good), in *Collection of Works in Two Volumes*, Vol. 1. Mysl, Moscow, pp. 378-379.
2 Trubetskoy, N. S. (1927) *Ob istinnom I lozhnom natsionalisme* (On true and false nationalism), *Nasledie Tchingizkhana: vzgyad na russkuyu istoriu ne s zapada, a s vostoka* (Chingyzkhan's heritage: a perspective on Russian history that comes not from the West but from the East), *K probleme russkogo samopoznania* (On the problem of Russian self-cognition), Sofia; Gumilev, L. N. (1991) 'Zametki poslednego Evrasiitsa' (Notes by the laast Eurasianist), in *Nashe Nasledie* (Our Heritage) 3, pp. 19-26.
3 The complete proposal was printed in *Nezavisimaya Gazeta*, 8 June 1994; see also Olcott, Martha Brill (1997) 'Kazakhstan: Pushing for Eurasia', in Ian Bremmer and Ray Taras (eds), *New States, New Politics: Building the Post-Soviet Nations*. Cambridge University Press, Cambridge, pp. 548-549.
4 See e.g. journal called *Pro et Contra* referred to in this chapter, *Nezavisimaya Gazeta*, *Obshaya Gazeta* and other periodicals with large print-runs.
5 See note 2, *Ob istinnom I lozhnom natsionalisme*, quoted from Gumilev (1991), op. cit., p. 20.
6 Zenkovsky, V. V. (1948) *Istoria russkoy filosofii* (History of Russian

philosophy), Vol. I. YMCA-Press, Paris, pp. 5-38.

7 Berdyaev, N. A. (1990) *Sudba Rossii* (The fate of Russia). Sovetski Pisatel, Moscow, p. 131. (The article 'Slavyanofilstvo I slavyanskaya idea' (Slavophiles and the Slavic idea) was written in 1915.)

8 *Primus inter pares sub specie aeternitatis.* Unconscious identification of one's ethnic group as the 'best' or the most 'proper' cannot yet be regarded as nationalism. Nationalism as a form of exclusivity requires a philosophical pretext to justify superiority and association with eternity is probably the most widespread one. It is the starting point where nationalism begins.

9 Kandyba, V. and Zolin, P. (1997) *Istoria I ideologia russkogo naroda* (History and the ideology of the Russian people), Vol. 2. Lan, St. Petersburg, p. 324 (quoted from Izmozik, Vladlen (1998) 'Alexander Makedonsky: nash rossiisky geroi' (Alexander the Great: our Russian hero), *Obshaia Gazeta* 24, 18–24 June 1998, p. 254.

10 Rosanov, V. V. (1991) 'Razmolvka mezhdu Solovyovym I Dostoevskim' (Disagreement between Solovyov and Dostoevsky), reprinted in *Nashe Nasledie* (Our Heritage), 6, pp. 70-72.

11 See note 7. Rosanov's comment should not be understood literally so far as the development of views in time is concerned. It points to the fact that Dostoevsky did have a negative perception of Catholicism, although he professed the idea of universal love, no matter how contradictory it may seem. Generally, this comment may be misunderstood if taken out of context of the whole article by Rosanov, where he attempts to show the complexity and profundity of Dostoevsky's philosophical views, pointing to some nationalistic components.

12 See note 5. p. 219.

13 Quoted from the text of the lecture on the problems of nationalism (manuscript), May 1998.

14 Kortunov, S. (1997) 'Kakaya Rossia nuzhna miru' (What kind of Russia does the world need?), *Pro et Contra*, 2(1), Winter.

15 Dunlop, J. B. (1997) 'Russia: In Search of an Identity?', in Bremmer and Taras (1997), op. cit., pp. 30-31.

16 Linden, C. A. (1983) *The Soviet Party-State: the Politics of Ideocratic Despotism.* Praegner, New York, p. 95.

17 Zyuganov, G. (1994) *Derzhava*, 2nd edn. Informpechat, Moscow, p. 77.

18 See note 1, pp. 377-378.

13　Ethnic Conflict as Political Smokescreen: The Caucasus Region

TAMARA DRAGADZE

The aim of my paper is very direct: let us be aware of the way we use terminology. What may be appropriate for the seminar room is not always so for the decision making corridors of power in the UN after it leaves the seminar room. My example will be the use of the term 'ethnic conflict' and the area to which it is applied will be the Caucasus region.

Hegemonic discourse

First of all I must acknowledge my intellectual debt to the pioneering work of Neumann and Eriksen.[1] As they have stated in their characteristically succinct way, the age of the nation state today is concomitant with the age of the first world wide international system and it is an age marked by social organisation and information transmission on an unprecedented scale. No wonder a search is on for discursive consensus. Since political elites create collective identities of an emblematic kind, in order to communicate, their use of terms such as 'Islamic' or 'secular' or indeed of 'ethnic' are always goal orientated. Thus, in my view, you observe the following:

The three bases for variations on the intended use of the given terms are by necessity provided through: a) the identity of the person who utters goal orientated communications, b) the intended audience and c) the implicit agenda for the discourse.

Some of my work has been on the relationship, in this context, between official representatives of the Russian Federation, the institutions of the international community and the Federation's aim of retaining for itself the management of crises in the Caucasus.

Again, I agree with Eriksen and Neumann that in international relations there tends to be dominant, hegemonic discourse on the one hand and on

262

the other hand there develops a subordinate, mediated discourse particular to neophyte states. The Newly Independent States of the former Soviet Union tend to be perceived as neophyte states in contrast with the Russian Federation which was the self declared successor state to the Soviet Union with its seat on the UN Security Council, ownership of all the Soviet Embassies and main mass media agencies.

A useful analogy to this train of thought is Edwin Ardener's work on dominant and 'muted' discourse in relation to men and women's discourse in any given society.[2] This idea implies that subordinate discourse mirrors only partially the dominant one because it necessarily reflects an alternative experience. In my view the 'muted' or subordinate discourse would have to express contrived, conformist images as a measure of self-defence but the underlying sentiment – if one can talk of sentiment here – in no way parallels that of the source of the dominant lexicon. Using the term 'ethnic conflict' can convey different meanings in hegemonic and subordinate discourse on the international arena although neophyte states receive, on the whole, much less of a platform – or perhaps one could say 'microphone' – for expressing their views.

The power relations between dominant discourse and the alternative, contesting voices is noticeable not only in the efficiency of their creation but also in their distribution. We witness 'packages' of discourse which are formulated to dominate and which are validated and supported by strong emblems devised by the most powerful media channels. As regards the Caucasus, since most international media are based in Moscow it was only with the war in Chechnya, for example, that Western television reporting became less Moscow dominated. Sometimes there are episodes of deliberate mishandling when, for example, in 1988 the anti-Soviet demonstrations in Baku, the capital of Azerbaijan, were depicted as being of a 'fundamentalist Islamic' inspiration because the Islamic crescent had appeared on some of the flags being waved. It was not reported that the flags with the crescent in question represented the Azerbaijan flag when it was an independent state from 1918 to 1920 which the demonstrators were hoping to re-establish. Admittedly, there is a sharp contrast between the internal and external discourse of representatives of neophyte states who vary the expression of their opinions according to the audience before them. My main interest here, though, is to remark on the use of the term 'ethnic conflict' in the hegemonic discourse used in the international community and which some African intellectuals as well as Caucasians have often called 'The big get out clause'.

Ethnic conflict

There is within most seminar rooms a shared usage of the term 'ethnic group' which usually imples:

- putative common ancestors;
- shared language;
- shared territory (the main 'ethnic' problem, see below);
- shared culture (also known as 'shared ethno-psychology');
- shared self-labeling (ethnonym);
- self-awareness of distinctiveness from other designated groups; and
- a sense of shared destiny (my own addition here: 'we are a tragic people' and so on).

We must remember that all the above exercise is a social construction, fluid and redefined by constant shifts. Physical attributes are absent and I have to say this for the sake of some of my post-Soviet colleagues who insist on emphasising the existence of a 'shared genetic pool' for ethnic groups which, in turn, affect their collective behaviour – a most dubious assertion.

The flexibility itself of this social construction makes the idea amenable to both internal and external political manipulation:

- internally when, for example, political leaders describe the characteristics of their ethnic group as being 'organically' linked to a particular territory: 'we are the people of the hills' and 'We are the people of those hills over there, between this river and that one'. It is indeed this 'biologistic' aspect of some ethnic ideology which is devised to create a morality of violence to extend uncontested administrative power to a formally ethnically mixed territory.
- external manipulation, for example where there is a deliberate mystification of ethnicity created by interested parties, for example, when Russia in the UN successfully excluded close examination of the troubles in the Caucasus by claiming their own superior experience of

calming and managing 'centuries old ethnic conflicts between Armenians and Azerbaijanis or Abkhazians and Georgians' which defy rational understanding and therefore need expert intervention, namely theirs.

Concepts of 'ethnicity' come out of what I call a 'familiar repertoire' in both the Western and post-communist worlds which make political manipulation easier both in the international community such as the UN and in the mass media.

Ethnic conflict: In the strict sense this should mean violent acts committed between two or more ethnic groups whose motivation lies solely in the perceived differences between themselves, that is, for example, 'Because "they" over there do not share our ancestors, do not share our habits and so on...we will fight them'.

David Carlton and Simon Bekker rightly premise that ethnic conflict is different from all other forms of conflict, insofar as it embodies the assertion of difference.[3] Yet when the term 'ethnic conflict' is bandied about as a kind of 'buzz word' I find that it nearly always masks a different agenda to the one proclaimed. The fact is that 'ethnic conflict' in the strict sense of the term as I have just defined it is relatively rare. Many conflicts popularly labeled 'ethnic conflicts' by the mass media and by politicians who direct public opinion are often related more closely to:

- power struggles (between political factions);
- economic struggles (competition for scarce or coveted resources);
- colonial or post colonial exercises to rule more effectively (by dividing residentially adjacent communities among themselves);
- irredentism, to extend administrative control, as in Karabagh; and
- disputes over land ownership, and many other examples.

One may sum up the above by stating that differently to the imagery which the deliberately politicised use of the term 'ethnic conflict' is supposed to conjure up, these fights are what one may call 'rationally motivated struggles' with tangible goals that are not too difficult to recognise.

The subtext

In hegemonic discourse there is a subtext which implies a scale between rationality and extreme irrationality, on a continuum, for example:

- Sectarianism, a conflict within a religion, as in Northern Ireland which is perceived as intellectual even if 'a bit irrational' and therefore could in principle be defeated through verbal and written argument
- Communalism, a conflict within the same ethnicity, as in India between Muslims and Hindus, seen as less rational than the fine arguments of sectarian differentiation but communalism is perceived as capable of self regulation
- 'Ethnic conflict', irrational and always out of control, needing a strong, outside hand, but not just any hand, an experienced handler to contain the strange manifestations of aggression and fighting tactics, as in the Caucasus where Russia could present itself as the expert to handle the 'mad Caucasians'.

The underlying assumption of all these assertions is the implicit acceptance of ethnic stereotypes: the Irish and Celtic obsessiveness, the excessive religiosity in the Indian subcontinent and the wildness of the Caucasians (if not of all East Europeans).

General background of post-Soviet ethnicity

There have, of course, been changes in political arrangements at a global level, not least in the African sub-continent, but likewise in the former communist lands although these have been more elusive than when a public ceremony marking independence from a colonial power marks the change.

In the Soviet Union, after decades of centralised, totalitarian rule there was a beginning tendency towards devolution of power to localised power groups. This tendency, I would argue, began well before the formal demise of communist rule. I am therefore inclined to disagree with authors such as Michael Ignatieff who attribute a cathartic resonance to the so-called sudden disappearance of communism which left a gaping ideological hole which, such authors say, nationalism appealed to and came to fill instead.[4]

I would argue that in the last years of the Brezhnev era, in both East, Central and Soviet Europe, the growth of technology and the wearing down of the central economy led to a slow but steady erosion of power from the centre in Moscow. This in turn encouraged the growth of local ambitions for political and economic power and with it a search for a local identity which could reflect the growing assertiveness. I have written elsewhere [5] about the relationship between democracy and the search for authenticity, citing Marshall Berman, for example, who defines authenticity as a 'celebration of self'. In the closing years of the USSR, a sort of regionalism grew through the tendency to wish to 'do your own thing' locally. Out of the ashes of strong totalitarian rule 'Economic regionalism' began to grow [6] which asserted that authority and control over local natural resources and local labour should be transferred from the centre to a particular territory (their own) within their own defined territorial boundaries, an action-based orientation.

The basic problem, however, is how you define the boundaries of your territory and how to seek legitimacy for your definition of these boundaries. The Soviet legacy heightened the significance of the territorial factor to produce what I have termed 'ethnicised regionalism'.

When the political administrative structures of the Soviet Union and 'autonomous republics' were devised in the 1920s and 1930s, these were based either – grudgingly – on ultimate recognition, in the case of the South Caucasian republics, of their previous internationally recognised status as independent and sovereign states or, in the case of the so-called 'autonomous republics', a status gelled around the notion of titular nationality. The result was that no administrative units of the above kinds could exist without displaying ethnicity as the key to their legitimacy.

Ethnically defined provinces, or administrative units, in the Soviet experience engendered a two-way experience: the ethnicisation of political, cultural and economic discourse in the local context and the territorialisation of ethnicity. Thus, the Soviet system reenforced the local view that a given territory has emblematic significance for a people's understanding of self and their ethnicity.

The Caucasus region

This is an interesting region for comparative work, not only for its 'drama' in recent years but as an example where a) the importance of indigenous perceptions cannot be ignored despite their feeble voice in the international arena when recent confrontations began there, and b) the geo-political location produces a ripple effect in the international world order, being at the crossroads between Russia, Turkey, Iran and Central Asia on the one hand and, on the other, lying between the Black Sea and the oil rich Caspian Sea.

The South Caucasus consists of three independent republics: Armenia, Azerbaijan and Georgia (the term 'Transcaucasus' is viewed as 'colonial' since it expresses the view from the North, where the Russian colonisers were situated, and not from within the Caucasus). In the North Caucasus, all of which is within the Russian Federation, there are three subjects of the Russian Federation which are included formally within the North Caucasus region but which cannot boast a titular ethnic group and are given the lesser status of 'Region' – Rostov oblast – or 'District' – Stavropol and Krasnodar krayi. The autonomous republics are: Daghestan (multi-ethnic, with four dominant groups – Lesghin, Dargyn, Kumyk and Avar and several lesser groups), Chechenia, Ingushetia, Kabardo-Balkaria (two dominant ethnic groups), Karachai-Cherkessia (two dominant groups again), Adighei and North Ossetia.

The Caucasus region as a whole must necessarily embrace both North, at least in reference to the 'autonomous republics' and South over the international borders of the Russian Federation and the three independent, sovereign states.

The people of the region share common features

Culturally linked to the larger arenas of Persia, Turkey, Greece and Russia, historically all were subjected to the 19th century military conquest by Russia (Georgia annexed and held within the Tsarist empire from 1802).

All, with the exception of some Ossets, attempted to seize back independence when the 1917 revolution occurred in Russia, and all were taken back by armed force into the Russian orbit through Red Army activity.

All were subject to the same nationalities policy during the Soviet era which has already been described above, where ethnicity alone justified a separate administrative unit and no full recognition of ethnicity was given to those groups who could not claim a defined territorial administrative unit.

All, except Armenia, have significantly multi-ethnic populations finally, all the Caucasus region in cultural life and social customs have more in common with each other than their neighbours: dance, music, singing (polyphony frequent), marriage patterns (exogamy frequent), hospitality rules and so on.

Differing features

Religious differences insofar as Islam is the dominant religion in Azerbaijan and the republics of the North Caucasus whereas Christianity dominates in Georgia and Armenia. Yet there is also evidence that indigenous religious practice, such as worshipping holy sites, have most features of worship and ritual in common.

The most significant difference was that between the 'Union' republics and 'autonomous' republics, even during the Soviet period when centralisation and Moscow dominance were so strong, because it prepared for what was perceived locally, in the 'autonomous' republics within the Union republics as an unfair post-Soviet position, where the Union republics obtained UN recognised independence and no autonomous republic, whether within the South Caucasus or within the Russian Federation was able to emulate them.

The historic legacy is shared by the whole Caucasian region

Under Tsarist rule they shared:

- the 'carrot and stick' attitude of government where, for example, the Tsarist government was ruthless towards the Georgian church, having priceless mediaeval frescoes whitewashed inside the churches and cathedrals but integrating the nobility into the highest ranks of the army and at the same time creating a 'dikaja divizia' (wild division) for the Muslim combatants as a way of absorbing them into what were considered glorious military exploits.
- the Caucasus region was divided into 'gubernias' (provinces) which paid scant regard to indigenous administrative demarcations.
- the Caucasus region was used as dumping ground for political dissidents (such as the Decembrists) and persecuted religious minorities (such as the Dukhobors).
- the mass deportations of Muslim Caucasians to the Ottoman Empire and the settlement of Greeks in various parts of the Tsarist Empire

which included parts of the Caucasus had a significant impact on the region, to put it mildly.

* the main interest in the Caucasus region for the Tsarist government was military, with the exception of oil development when it began in Baku.
* partly because of the illustrious dissidents such as Lermontov who were exiled to the Caucasus there began to develop a romantic image among the literati of the region as a kind of 'Byron's Italy for the Russian poets'.

In the Soviet era the shared experience of the Caucasus region was obviously not that different from that of all the other minorities of the Soviet Union and of the Russian majority too. The All Union Communist Party was a vehicle for Moscow domination. You could not publish a single book or pass a single thesis, for example, without the permission of the appropriate Moscow organ's imprematur. Furthermore, with Moscow being a 'Category 1' city it enjoyed greater access to commodities than the others so, for instance, millions of Soviet citizens from the whole Soviet Union had to come to Moscow to purchase some goods. All benefited from the increases in education, health services and cultural programs under the Soviet system. They also were victims of purges and repression under Stalin and later. There were, however, some experiences particular to the peoples of the Caucasus region:

* some of the purges were exceptionally vicious under Stalin, for example, 1924 and 1937, were both terrible years in Georgia. In Azerbaijan the political leader Narimanov who had combined a deep national pride with an acceptance of Communism died in as yet unexplained circumstances.
* the Union republics of Armenia, Azerbaijan and Georgia had the requisites for Union status: a non-Russian titular nationality and a border with a foreign state outside the Soviet Union. Within the Soviet constitution they had the right of secession, even under Brezhnev's revised constitution.
* 'Disintegration' may be a good description of, for instance, the hypothetical break-up of India into 'separatist states' with no constitutional provisions for separation; but this was not the case in the Soviet Union. Thus the independence movements in Georgia and Azerbaijan were for upholding their Soviet constitutional rights.

- the legacy of the Soviet constitution is that there is no provision for the 'autonomous' republics to gain sovereign independence, a view accepted by the international community, and this is viewed as unacceptable by those 'autonomous republics' seeking full independence.

For the Newly Independent States the post-Soviet era has brought shared experiences in coping with the Russian Federation, because it was the self-declared successor state to the Soviet Union so it controlled the rouble (the sole available currency for the first years of independence), controlled the entire military arsenal of the Soviet Union (through the Tashkent Agreement) and had unique diplomatic and media access. The currency dependency on the rouble is now a thing of the past but the other problems continue, and these have affected in particular the conflicts in the Caucasus.

The Caucasian conflicts

There have been four main conflicts, and one less known, in the Caucasus region, all of them fought with Soviet Russian weapons.

The Karabagh conflict

It began with a demand by its ethnically Armenian population, supported by Armenians of Soviet Armenia, for a transfer of administration from Baku (capital of Azerbaijan which Karabagh was a part of) to Erevan, capital of Armenia. Over time and with greater contact with the international arena, the demand was formally turned into one for independence.

The true background to the outbreak of war will probably take a long time in coming to light and one can only suspect that it was not an entirely spontaneous movement, but even if it were, and there is still a lot of evidence that it was, the acquiescence of the Soviet government to the growing agitation could scarcely have been by accident. The Soviet Army was still able to crush unrest ruthlessly when it wanted to in the 1980's and the Soviet Intelligence services (the KGB) were centrally controlled and still relatively efficient. It has been claimed by Arif Yunusov (oral communication) that over 90% of KGB personnel in the relevant locations for Karabagh were changed by Moscow in the period leading up to the fighting. Finally, regiments of the Soviet Army and all their arsenal were present in all areas where battles were fought and there is no question of their complicity either in active participation or in surprising neglect. The Azerbaijani view, which also needs more data collection when the relevant archives are finally opened, is that its national liberation movement was well organised and supported by trade unions and the working classes in an obvious way and so posed the greatest threat to the stability of the Soviet Union. The classically imperial reaction, in their view, was that the Moscow authorities should revert to 'divide and rule' tactics against Azerbaijan.

Whatever the origins of the Karabagh war, which only informed guesses and speculation can uncover for the foreseeable future, until greater access is offered to the relevant government and military data, the interest here is in how the war was presented.

It is understandable that the large Armenian diaspora should have the upper hand in the propaganda war that ensued but the Armenian Soviet Republic and – after 1991 – the independent Armenian Republic were able to rely on Russian sympathy. Since, as has already been said, the Russian Federation has the dominant position, it has been an important factor for opinion forming. It is important to stress that I am discussing discourse and not passing judgement on the perpetrators of violence on one side or the other.

All the elements of the presentation of the Karabagh war as 'ethnic conflict' were temptingly there to mislead: allegations of 'centuries old' traditional enmity between Azeris and Armenians 'religious enmity' between Muslims and Christians 'Pan-Turkic illusions of grandeur' (according to this allegation the only obstacle to a mighty land mass of Turkic people from Anatolia to Chinese Sinjian was the presence of Armenians on Armenian territory which had to be eliminated) 'the massacre in 1915 of Armenians in Turkey and the Azerbaijani action in Karabagh are related in intent', yet again demonstrating the irrationality of historic tendencies even if both peoples had lived side by side and had even inter-married, this was the result of Communist repression of ethnic conflict and not because of genuine good neighbourly relations.

It is interesting to note that these were not arguments put forward by the Armenian leader of the Karabagh movement, Levon Ter Petrossian, who instead focussed on the democratic principle of the right to self determination. This argument, however, is not an integral part of discussions in the international community regarding the altering of borders of sovereign states. Neither would such a principle have served the aims of the Russian Federation which was to keep all negotiations on Karabagh within their own 'sphere of influence'.

It seemed more advantageous to present the Karabagh war as 'ethnic conflict' in which only the experience of the Russian government would be sufficient to find a solution. Russian envoys either went on parallel missions to the self appointed international ones (such as the 'Minsk group' initiative) or became co-chair of the same Minsk group. It was not peace camps, reconciliation exercises and other actions that were proposed to bring the two warring ethnicities together, whether over-idealistic or not. Their 'package approach' to negotiations, however, was unlikely to meet with success, where the practice of linking a peace agreement with other demands (such as the stationing of Russian troops and a controlling stake in oil contracts in this case), was de rigueur.

It is good to report that at the present time of writing negotiations have moved away from the fantasies of 'ethnic conflict' arguments, are more evenhanded in the extent of international participation. At present the guiding pinciple is to find an acceptable legal and administrative status for arabagh which will also accommodate the refugees who fled the fighting.

Abkhazia

From the outset, the then Minister of Defence, Pavel Grachev, stated that the ussian Federation had to support the Abkhazian side against the Georgian tate because Russia needed an extended Black Sea coast (which it had lost wen Georgia gained independence). In Soviet times some Abkhazians had emanded that their 'autonomous republic' should transfer its position from being part of Soviet Georgia to becoming part of the Russian Federation. This was subsequently modified into a demand for full independence and sovereignty for the Abkhazian Republic which, as could have been expected, was deemed unacceptable by the Georgian government. Once again, 'ethnic conflict' was presented as the most important reason for the war, despite evidence of good neighbourly relations and inter-marriage in the past, in order to present events as 'exotic' and therefore needing, yet again, the experienced hand of Russian peace mediators.

It is not my intention to trivialise the very serious and genuine problems of the Abkhazian population in organising their political and administrative affairs in the wake of the Georgian independence movement and the actual independence that followed.

Instead, it appears once again that it was unhelpful to portray the war as the 'ethnic conflict' of mad Caucasians who were incapable of understanding where their own interests lay in a rational way and to facilitate peace negotiations between the parties in a direct way. At one stage the mediation efforts were quite fanciful, where under the auspices of the United Nations, the Georgian negotiators spoke with the Russian facilitators, who spoke to the Abkhazian negotiators, who spoke again to the Russian facilitators, who in turn spoke with the UN representatives, with the result that none of the three elements in the negotiation spoke to anybody except the Russian facilitators. It is difficult to know at present whether the tremendous expenditure of effort by these Russian facilitators gained any reward in the actual peace talks. The Russian military forces that act as peace keepers in the region have at least a symbolic role in keeping the de facto cease fire. Formally a CIS force, it is controlled and financed by the Russian government. Since this is a considerable burden to the Russian Federation there is at present a recognised need to have realistic expenditure policies and an accountable democracy and foreign policy on the one hand, and at the same time fulfil Russian wishes to have a military base in Abkhazia and to extend and maintain its influence in the region. These considerations have to be included in an evaluation of both the war that took place, the continual skirmishes and the chances of a realistic peace agreement.

South Ossetia

Once again this enclave in Georgia, with the formal status of 'autonomous region' and an ethnically mixed population of Ossets and Georgians (and a minority of several others) was caught up in conflict, in the presence of Soviet troops, among peoples that had lived side by side and inter-married and where the titular nationality wanted a change of administration. Again the initial wish was for entry into the Russian Federation where North Ossetia, an 'autonomous republic', would be conveniently joined to the territory of South Ossetia. This position progressed to a general emphasis on extricating the region from its ties with Georgia. Displaced people suffered – as refugees always do, lives were lost and the rhetoric on both sides reached unacceptable levels of intolerance – as it always does. In the meantime, there were still more ethnic Ossetians living outside the enclave and in mainland Georgia than within the autonomous region of South Ossetia. Many left and many then returned, especially when it became evident that this conflict was a good candidate for the international peace industry, from the OSCE to small NGOs, to become involved. It rapidly became evident that the best way forward was to foster direct talks between the representatives of both governments. To date, the preparations to bring about a relatively long lasting compromise and satisfactory resolution to the conflict between South Ossetia and the Georgian government in Tbilisi have been the most successful in the Caucasus.

Chechnya

The tragic conflict in Chechnya, an 'autonomous republic' of the North Caucasus within the Russian Federation had most of the characteristics of an anti-colonial war and few of those which even the most imaginative presentations of 'ethnic conflict' could lay claim to. If a majority of the combatants in the Armed Forces of the Russian Federation and the troops of the Ministry of the Interior were ethnically Russian on the one hand and the independence fighters were mostly ethnically Chechen, this fact bore little relation to the nature of the war and could barely have more than the status of a 'numbers game'. Yet the Russian Federation representatives were initially successful in some cases in portraying the fighting in Chechnya as being an 'ethnic conflict' in which the Federal Armed Forces had to intervene to protect the Russians from the wild Caucasians, or as an internal affair consisting of a war against common criminals (the ethnic Chechen mafiosi) or better still, to protect the whole world from the growth of the influence of Islamic fanatics. As the brutality increased so did the fighting reveal its more political character: to maintain the territorial integrity of the Russian Federation when confronted with a demand for independence from a people who no longer recognised the moral authority of the Russian state as a whole over its own affairs, for both historical and contemporary reasons. Economic interests were thrown in for good measure, that the fighting was allegedly over the control of the oil pipeline routes where it was assumed that the Western market oriented international community would sympathise with a country trying to protect its interests against local insurgents. The action of the indigenous peace groups, led by Russians of profound convictions and commitment to moral fortitude soon demonstrated the lack of ethnic character in this war. The Soldiers Mothers Union and similar mothers' unions witnessed an unprecedented degree of collaboration between Chechen and Russian women. Much of the data they collected testified, moreover, to a puzzling lack of regard by the commanders of the Federal Armed forces for their own fellow ethnic young Russian soldiers who were often treated with the same contempt as the enemy, for example in making few efforts to collect and identify their corpses.

Most significant for our discussion is the fact that the long lasting solution to the problems in Chechnya is a political one, not one of inter-ethnic reconciliation, and that the 'smokescreen' of ethnic conflict to explain the Chechen war has evaporated.

Ingushetia-North Ossetia

This conflict in the North Caucasus took place, again with the participation, or some would say 'the presence', of Federal Russian troops, when Ingushetians living in a particular territory of North Ossetia asked for its return to Ingush jurisdiction as it had been before their deportation by Stalin in the wake of the Second World War. The Ingushetians were driven out of the area with much loss of life. One of the results is that the closed borders in the region of the conflict make travel through the North Caucasus so difficult that it seriously impedes any endeavours to create a more integrated and thus economically more viable region. This fact has not escaped the eye of conspiracy theorists, of course. It is the least visible of the recent Caucasian conflicts, kept relatively successfully within the confines of the 'internal affairs' of the Russian Federation, but one can only hope for both the North Ossetians and the Ingushetians that a lasting solution can be found which will in some way attenuate the suffering of the bewildered and bereaved populations of that part of the Caucasus.

Conclusion

In the Caucasus there have been serious armed conflicts, much loss of life and countless refugees all within less than one decade. For this reason, given its formal commitment to the alleviation of human suffering, the international community, such as it is, could not ignore the region. On the one hand the Russian Federation, as successor state to the Soviet Union, has been able to be chief advocate, expert and mediator for the affairs of this troubled region. On the other hand, the presence of Soviet forces followed by Russian Federation forces and the declared interest of the Russian Federation to maintain the Caucasus under its zone of influence prevent it from being a disinterested party. This is not the place to pass judgement in any way on this position. The aim has rather been rapidly to consider some examples of the disassociation between concepts conveyed through a particular use of terminology – 'ethnic conflict' in this case – and the actual Caucasian problems.

It should be remembered, however, that except in the Chechen case ethnic terminology has been used by some, but not all, of the political leaders of the warring parties to mobilise public opinion in their favour. It is also important to note that subsequently the degree of ethnic self awareness became more acute during the transition from Soviet status to independence, with all the accompanying anxieties for the ethnic minorities within the republics of Georgia and Azerbaijan. One should not fail to acknowledge the serious political and administrative difficulties, often couched in ethnic symbolism, which accompany such profound changes as those experienced in the closing years of the Soviet Union and those that followed independence. It is important also to draw upon the examples of other parts of the world when colonial rule was threatened and then ended to see that this process is often accompanied by severe internal dissent and rivalry which offer golden opportunities for external intervention for ulterior purposes. In many instances, ethnic identity acquires rapidly changing significance in the struggle for power and the control of wealth. There is, however, a significant difference between ethnic self awareness and ethnic assertion on the one hand, and on the other hand when aggression, through the obtaining of the necessary arsenal from external interested sources, becomes 'weaponised ethnicity', as I have called it. There is a different quality to ethnic aggression, if one can name it that, when it is expressed through the use of sophisticated weaponry such as surface to air missiles, fighter bombers and all the arsenal put at the disposal of both fighting sides in Abkhazia and Karabagh, for example.

Finally, why should we be concerned by intellectual endeavours to sharpen our usage of terms such as 'ethnic conflict', in the Caucasus for example?

The Russian Federation cannot become a politically stable world power, with a strong democracy and a thriving economy, playing a positive role on the world stage, one it rightly deserves, while the international community shows itself much too willing to accept Russia's present explanations and insistence to dominate the outcomes of past conflicts in the Caucasus. I see our analysis of terminology as an 'unmasking' activity.

'Ethnic conflict' is a term used to camouflage violations of human rights, for example when attention is deliberately diverted away from the way young Russian soldiers themselves are abused in the Armed Forces in order to focus on the allegedly exotic behaviour of belligerent Caucasians.

'Ethnic conflict' is a term often used to promote general resolutions to take no intervening action at all to stop violence. If we take as a starting point that 'ethnic conflict ' itself is highly unlikely, in the strictest sense in a given situation and that we look behind the presentations by interested parties, we are more likely to get intervention of a sensible kind from the international community to assist in stopping violence 'tout court'.

By taking the stance that 'ethnic conflict' is unlikely to be the underlying cause of tensions and war, the quicker it will be to get direct talks going between the conflicting parties.

The undue cost and futility of imposing 'influence' where political players' desire for hegemony is very much an emotional factor should be a subject of open discussion by all parties to the above mentioned conflicts in the Caucasus. On the other hand, when 'interests' lead to economic activity, investment and trade then ethnic difference is easier to come to terms with, as it always has been in the Caucasus, and good neighbourly relations can be promoted, good transport and communications can be restored as well.

In conclusion, therefore, there are good, sound reasons why the Caucasus region, the Russian Federation, the Commonwealth of Independent States, the Baltic and European states and international relations as a whole could benefit if we could be a little more mindful of how we use conceptual terms such as 'ethnic conflict' but, above all, of where we use them.

Notes

1 Eriksen, Thomas Hylland and Iver B. Neumann, (1993), 'International Relations as a Cultural System: an Agenda for Research', in *Cooperation and Conflict*, Vol. 28(3), London, Newbury Park and New Delhi, Sage, pp. 233-264.

2 Ardener, Edwin (1972), 'Belief and the Problem of Women', in J. La Fontaine (ed.), *The Interpretation of Ritual*, London: Tavistock.
3 Bekker, Simon and David Carlton (eds) (1996), *Racism, Xenophoobia and Ethnic Conflict*, Durban: Indicator Press.
4 Ignatieff, Michael (1993), *Blood and Belonging*, New York: Farrar, Straus and Giroux.
5 Dragadze, Tamara (1993), 'Soviet Economics and Nationalism in the Gorbachev Years. Regionalism, Ethnicised Regionalism and Constitutional Regionalism', in Marco Buttino,(ed.) *In a Collapsing empire: Underdevelopment, Ethnic Conflicts and Nationalisms in the Soviet Union*, Milano, Fondazione Giangiacomo Feltrinelli.
6 Ibid.

14 Ethnicity and Intra-State Conflict: Types, Causes and Peace Strategies – a Survey of sub-Saharan Africa

FÉLIX NKUNDABAGENZI

Introduction

Since the end of the Cold War, numerous peripheral zones have gone through conflict situations, which have required the curative or preventive intervention of the international community. Africa, and in particular sub-Saharan Africa, is one of the most destabilized regions in this new geopolitical context. The international community has developed instruments and accomplished actions that have so far not been successful in coping with these situations.

Our main purpose is to investigate those paradigms that can help us deal with specific African conflictual situations. One has to take into account the fact that obviously the classical instruments of diplomacy have not yet proven their adequacy with crisis situations in sub-Saharan Africa. Our contribution will deal with three questions:

- the nature of African conflicts;
- the African State; and
- the instruments of conflict prevention, management and resolution in Africa and the role of NGOs in that context.

The nature of conflicts in sub-Saharan Africa

Two types of conflicts could be recorded in sub-Saharan Africa: border problems or intra-state wars.

Border conflicts[1]

The Berlin West African Conference of 15 November 1884 through 26 February 1885 gave birth to African States by designing the boundaries *in the frame of which modern nationhood were to be forged*. In 1964, the Cairo summit of the OAU adopted the *Uti possidetis* position that 'solemnly declares that all Member States pledge themselves to respect the borders existing on their achievement of national independence'.

This position has not however done away with border problems. At the 37th Session of the OAU Council of Ministers in Nairobi in 1981, Nigeria pushed for a OAU Boundary Commission that would tackle those relevant conflicts.[2] The same topic arose at the Abuja Summit in 1991.

Table 14.1   (Non-exhaustive) list of sub-African border problems

Actors	Dates	Main issue
Rwanda/Burundi	1962; 1972; 1988; 1993; 1994; 1997...	Destabilizing refugees; rebel movements
Burundi/Tanzania	1972–73; 1993; 1997...	Destabilizing refugees; rebel movements
Rwanda/Uganda	1990	Destabilizing refugees; rebel movements
Chad/Libya	1973–89	Border resources; destabilization
Chad/Sudan	1968; 1987–90	Destabilizing rebel-groups
Cameroon/Nigeria	1974; 1981, 1991	Border resources
Gabon/Eq. Guinea	1974	Border resources
Rwanda/Zaire-DRC	1994; 1997–98	Destabilizing refugees; liberation war in Zaire
DRC/Congo-Brazzaville	1997–98	Congo civil war spill-over; destabilizing refugees
Namibia/Botswana	1998	Border resources
Uganda/Sudan	1987–98	Sudan civil war spill-over
Eritrea/Ethiopia	1998	Border dispute

The manifestation of border wars ranges from simple disputes to war. Taking into consideration the West African situation one can distinguish the following causes for border conflicts:[3]

- *Economically motivated border conflicts.* The issues in these types of conflicts concern transborder natural resources (Nigeria-Chad in 1983; Nigeria-Cameroon in 1982; Mali-Burkina Faso in 1982; or today the dispute involving Namibia-Botswana regarding the Singobeka island) such as underground water in arid and semi-arid regions or offshore mineral oil and even fisheries in territorial waters.

- *Strategically motivated border conflicts.* The situations covered are those involving certain means used to destabilize a neighbouring country. Such situations were encountered these last years in the Great Lakes region when former Field-Marshal Mobutu used the Rwandan and Burundian hutu refugees in order to enhance his own role as a regional mediator and at the same time was instrumentalizing them in order to destabilize the Tutsi-led governments of Rwanda and Burundi.

- *Socio-politically motivated conflicts.* This refers to internal social or cultural conflicts with spillover effects. The late liberation war of Zaire was partially trigged by the Banyamulenges' nationality struggle. These populations being Tutsis found a logical support from the Tutsi-led government of Rwanda and from its ally Uganda.

Intra-state wars

However, an inventory of African conflicts would have to place intra-state war as the main form of conflict in sub-Saharan Africa. The 1994 UNDP Development report mentions that during the 1989–92 period only three out of 82 conflicts in the world were inter-state conflicts: 90% of the victims were civilian causalities. For example, since the independences, sub-Saharan Africa has been through more or less 190 *coup d'états* (with only 70 of them succeeding).[4] Among those intra-state conflicts one could also distinguish between succession and secessionist wars.[5]

The secessionist conflict's stake is to control a part of the former national territory in order to transform it into a sovereign entity. The conflict of succession considers the competition between social groups who either seek simply to replace the ruling élite or want to change the whole political system.

If one discriminates between these two forms of internal conflicts, the succession type of conflict appears to be the most common one in sub-Saharan Africa.

Table 14.2 Conflicts in Africa, 1989–92

Dates/conflict	1989	1990	1991	1992
Succession	7	8	9	7
Secession	3	3	3	1

Table 14.3 Number of victims resulting from conflicts in Africa since 1980[6]

Country	Population (1995)	Duration of war	Estimated number of victims
Sudan	28 million	1983	500,000/1 million
Ethiopia	54 million	1970–91	450,000/1 million
Mozambique	15 million	1979–92	450,000/1 million
Angola	10 million	1975–91	300,000/500,000
		1992–94	500,000
Uganda	20 million	1980–87	100,000/500,000
Somalia	9 million	1982	400,000/500,000
Rwanda	7 million	1994	500,000/1 million
Burundi	6 million	1972	100,000/300,000
		1988	250,000
Liberia	3 million	1989	200,000
Sierra Leone	3 million	1991	50,000

Consequences of intra-state conflicts

Humanitarian consequences Conflicts in Africa have had disastrous humanitarian consequences for the populations. During the last 25 years, the ten major conflicts in sub-Saharan Africa have claimed the lives of an estimated 3.8 to 6.8 million people; 90% of casualties were civilian. Everyone has of course in mind the figures of the civil wars in Rwanda and Mozambique, in which about 1 million and over half a million people died respectively.

The refugee crisis in sub-Saharan Africa is another consequence of ongoing conflicts in that region of the world. In 1993, the United Nations estimated that there were over 18.2 million refugees and 24 million displaced persons in the world. In 1995, in sub-Saharan Africa alone, the number of refugees and displaced persons reached about 8 million, as shown in Table 14.4. However, by 1996 that figure dropped to 6.5 million.[7] Furthermore, in the aftermath of the downfall of Field Marshal Mobutu's regime, 2 million Rwandan refugees returned back home. This should bring the total figure of refugees and displaced persons in Africa down to approximately 4.7 million in 1988.

Table 14.4 Estimated number of refugees and displaced people in sub-Saharan Africa, 1995–96

Region	Refugees and displaced persons in 1995	Refugees and displaced persons in 1996
Western Africa (Benin, Burkina Faso, Ivory Cost, Cameroon, CAR, Chad, Gabon, Gambia, Ghana, Guinea, Guinea-Bissau, Liberia, Nigeria, Senegal, Sierra Leone, Togo)	1,916,004	2,115,297
Central Africa (Burundi, Congo, DRC, Kenya, Rwanda, Uganda, Tanzania)	3,252,035	3,476,024
Horn of Africa (Djibouti, Eritrea, Ethiopia, Mali, Niger, Somalia, Sudan)	873,766	802,777
Southern Africa (Angola, Botswana, Malawi, Mozambique, Namibia, South Africa, Swaziland, Zambia, Zimbabwe)	1,979,442	227,137
Total	8,021,247	6,621,235

Table 14.4 also shows that there are two major depression areas in sub-Saharan Africa: western Africa and central Africa. In western Africa, the Liberian and Sierra Leone civil wars were undoubtedly at the origin of the humanitarian crisis in the sub-region. The recent unrest that broke out in Guinea in the beginning of 1988 has aggravated the already difficult humanitarian situation in the sub-region.

The aftermath of the Rwandan genocide and the ongoing civil wars in Burundi and the Democratic Republic of Congo (DRC) mean that the numbers of refugees and displaced persons in Central Africa remains extremely high by any account. The only good news, in 1996, was that the stabilization of the political situation in Mozambique allowed 1.8 million Mozambican refugees to return to their homes.

Political consequences The main consequence of these internal disputes and wars is that the State can no longer play its role as 'the federative factor' in those societies. This results in a 'breakdown of the State'. Social and individual loyalty turns to ethnic, clan or regional leaders who are in defiance of the central authority, incarnated by the political forces controlling the State apparatus. Civil disobedience soon changes into armed opposition, leaving little or no room for political and peaceful dialogue between belligerents. Moreover the governing élites in sub-Saharan Africa, unaccustomed to political contradiction, do not always find it necessary to deal with issues such as democracy, human rights or accountability.

The impossibility of political dialogue and the loss of the monopoly over armed force lead to the progressive disappearance of the State, both as a political actor and as a framework for political changes. When the conflict reaches high levels of antagonism, anomy is *de facto* the best word to describe the political stage on which the belligerents are evolving. Thus, bringing back peace means restoring the State as the centre of gravity of the political process. This therefore implies that the State can no longer be the monopoly of a specific political group.

Economic consequences The major economic consequence of war is the destruction of economic and social infrastructures, which often represents decades of efforts in development. Rwanda is probably one of the most dramatic illustrations of war-induced destruction. Until 1990, Rwanda was considered to have one of the best-managed economies in central Africa. As a result of war, Rwanda's exports dropped 33%, from 102.6 million

US\$ in 1990 to 68.5 million US\$ in 1992. During the same period, imports rose 5% (from 227 to 240 million US\$).[8] Of course, the Defence Department was the main beneficiary of the new government priorities, as the Rwandan Army grew from 5000 to about 40,000 men in less than two years.

Today, because of the ongoing military unrest in the northern and western parts of the country, the defence budget still represents more than 50% of public expenditure. One can easily understand how difficult it can be for any government to undertake serious steps towards economic and social development when most of its resources are devoted to security.

This brings us to the analysis of the African State in itself. It should help us narrow down the systemic elements that explain the nature of conflict in Africa and eventually the type of prophylactic measures to be taken in order to deal with African instability.

The African State

The study of the political mechanism of political transition in the African State is necessary in order to determine the nature of intra-State conflict. There is a link between the two phenomena.

In his chapter regarding hegemonic power (total political power) in sub-Saharan Africa, Jean-François Bayart[9] notes that competing social groups will use, for instance, the ethnic element as a political resource in order to fulfil three goals:

- to determine a territory on which the group can use its hegemony;
- the territory is the land on which primary accumulation of wealth is made possible; and
- the State machinery is the best instrument to accomplish the above objectives at a national level.

Inequality between competing groups was a reality before Independence but it has deepened afterwards thanks to the fact that the dominant groups, by controlling the State machinery, had extremely efficient coercive mechanisms.[10] Thus many African States have harboured various competing social groups with predatory behaviours and what has been seen as stability in the post-independence period would be better understood as an equilibrium reached in the struggle for power.

The end of the cold war saw a shift in the Western countries' priorities.[11] The economic internal crisis, the redeployment in eastern and central Europe has put sub-Saharan Africa at the end of that priority list. The international financial institutions (IMF and WB) pushed for economic reforms that implied political ones as well.

The financial size of the African State had to shrink to a status compatible with its real economic performances. This had an immediate effect: the social contract between the élite in those countries and their 'clientele' was broken. Scarce resources forced these governments to concentrate their generosity upon the 'family', the clan or the ethnic group. The general social equilibrium was thus broken as well. A new internal redistribution of wealth and economic power took place in those countries. Whether this redistribution would take place in a violent or a non-violent mode was the main political issue in most sub-Saharan states in the 1990s. Would this redistribution happen through reformism or revolutionary means?

Most African States adopted, under international pressure, the reformism path. Democratization should be the way to achieve a new redistribution of forces. Almost ten years after the first signs that such a redistribution process was taking place, one can evaluate the global situation in sub-Saharan Africa. The first observation would be to admit that African States have never been this instable since the colonization period. State structures have collapsed, governmental legitimacy is difficult to achieve and ongoing civil unrest is still the reality.[12]

Rephrasing Francis Fukuyuma[13] one can consider that democracy is seen by the third-world populations as a mean to attain equality at the socio-economic level. It is a tool for self-improvement for certain marginalized individuals or social groups. Therefore African populations, just as the Europeans a century ago and Latin Americans a decade ago, strive for democracy not because of the beauty of its substance but because it is merely a mechanism that can permit the numerous poor to be heard at executive level. If democracy or political reforms do not work then violence becomes the only other viable option.[14]

The instruments of conflict prevention in sub-Saharan Africa[15]

Three levels of intervention on conflict prevention can be distinguished. First, the regional level which studies the OAU action; secondly, the sub-regional level which brings us to analyse organizations such as ECOWAS or SADC; and thirdly, civil society's contribution (NGOs etc).

OAU's instruments

Although 'asleep' during the Cold War period, the Organisation of African Unity has tried to live up to its mission and purposes ever since the Berlin Wall went down. In terms of conflict prevention nevertheless one has to acknowledge the fact that the OAU's stand on borders has certainly provided, even before 1989, a basis on which certain frontier conflicts were avoided.

Before the adoption of the OAU Mechanism for Conflict Prevention, Management and Resolution in June 1993, the OAU used its Commission of Mediation, Conciliation and Arbitration in order to deal with conflict situations. As for any other intergovernmental organization, it goes without saying that the OAU could not get involved in internal disputes. On the other hand, when the conflicting parties brought in the OAU, it could manage those conflicts thanks to *ad hoc* committees that operated as mediation fora more than arbitration institutions. The Algerian-Morrocan conflict saw the end of the adhocism approach. The OAU then turned over the role of mediators to the Head of States. However, none of these methods produced the expected results, hence forcing the OAU Head of States and Governments to adopt yet another mechanism in June 1993: the Mechanism for Conflict Prevention.

The Mechanism has a political element called the Central Organ, which comprises the Member States of the OAU Bureau, the Conference of Head of States and the past and present President of the organization. The Organ's decisions are executed by the Secretary General. The financial wing of the Mechanism is the OAU Peace Fund whose aim is to collect the means for peace operations sponsored by the Mechanism. In 1997, the Fund had collected more or less 15 million US dollars in contributions. For example, the United States' contribution helped build the OAU Conflict Prevention Centre (4,150,000 US$). The Fund financed Observation mission in Burundi (716,000 US$), in Rwanda (572,000 US$), Mozambique (251,000 US$) or Liberia (200,000 US$).

Table 14.5 Contributions to the OAU Peace Fund[16]

Foreign countries	US$ (thousands)	African countries	US$ (thousands)
USA	4150	OAU	4204
Canada	2500	South-Africa	716
Belgium	902	Namibia	250
Denmark	300	Maurice	52
Germany	248	Lesotho	15
UK.	157	Algeria	10
Spain	150	Ethiopia	10
Sweden	137		
China	100	Individual	
Norway	17	contributions	35
Indonesia	15		
Subtotal	9209		5392
Total	14,601		

A striking element is the contradiction between the letter of the Mechanism's mandate and the empirical application. Being a product of an intergovernmental institution, the mechanism can not formally deal with internal situations. However, the Secretary General, taking into consideration the fact that the vast majority of African crisis are intra-State conflicts, considered that the OAU had to take part in the management and resolution of those type of conflicts as well.

Bearing in mind its financial limits, the OAU has decided to concentrate its efforts on organizing a continental Early Warning System (EWS). A series of seminars will be held by the organization in order to draw up the architecture of this African EWS.[17] Among the interesting elements of this EWS is the idea of the network of focal points: this network will comprise political institutions, academic centres (universities and study centres), NGOs, civilian associations who will have to send any useful data, information and analysis to the EWS to prevent a crisis that might trigger a conflict. The OAU will then orchestrate the traditional diplomatic instruments necessary to cope with such a situation at the earliest stage possible. This could lead to the intervention of either the UN or the competent sub-regional organization.

Sub-regional organizations

African countries have created numerous sub-regional organizations. The utility of many of them is questionable. The reasons behind the creation or adhesion to one or the other of these organizations range from economic interest to cultural ties. Most of these institutions have, first and foremost, an economic purpose that extends, today, to security considerations. This shift in institutional goals reflects the current evolution in development studies, where stability and security are increasingly considered as prerequisites for a sound and durable development.[18] We will examine two sub-regions: Western Africa and Southern Africa.

Western Africa In Western Africa the most significant sub-regional organization involved in conflict prevention has been the Economic Community of Western African States[19] (ECOWAS). The member States of ECOWAS have created a mechanism of mutual assistance. This mechanism has enforced solidarity among member States in defence matters, allowing any member State to intervene in the internal affairs of other member States when the sub-regional security is at risk (risk of a spillover of the internal dispute). This is the only limit to national sovereignty of the member States. It was on these grounds that ECOWAS was able to send peace restoring and peacekeeping troops to Liberia and Sierra Leone.[20]

Taking into consideration the experience in those two countries, ECOWAS head of States and Government decided, on 17 December 1997,[21] to create a sub-regional mechanism for prevention, management and resolution of conflicts in western Africa. This instrument could also be used for peacekeeping matters. Furthermore, an observatory of political and social unrest will be monitoring the different member States, providing ECOWAS with an early warning capability. Finally, a permanent Western African peacekeeping rapid reaction force should, eventually, be created in the short to medium term.

Southern Africa Southern Africa has gone through dramatic changes since apartheid was abolished. In 1996, SADC,[22] originally an economic organization, created a political structure, the Organ, to deal with security aspects as well. The Organ co-ordinates foreign and security matters of the member States. There are interesting elements to be observed here. The Organ releases updates on the political and socio-economic situation of member States. Therefore the Organ functions as an actor of the continental EWS. Furthermore in very specific fields, such as arms trafficking control, the southern African co-operation has enforcing instruments such as the Southern African Regional Police Chiefs Cupertino Organisation (SARPCCO) which helps governments to tackle regional organized crime that could potentially destabilize member States.

Civil society and conflict prevention

In this part of the study we shall focus on civil societies' role in the frame of political transition and in relation to conflict prevention, management and resolution.

Identification of civil society The Ghanaian sociologist Claude Akpokavie[23] considers that the appearance of African civil society as an actor is one of the most remarkable political experience of the last years. Achille Mbembe,[24] on the other hand, offers us the vision of a civil society that has always existed and 'rebelled' against the political power: organizing its own economic network (informal economy), obeying informal authorities (traditional or religious leaders outside the formal political institutions etc.). In Mbembe's view civil society would only combine with the formal order when its interests commanded it to do so but not otherwise.

In Mali, when dealing with the Touareg war, civil society involved in the compromise procedure defined itself as 'anonymous citizens associated around a common interest that is not the access to political power'.[25] Government officials, civil servants, the army and political parties are thus not part of this civil society. Therefore non-governmental associations such as NGOs, trade unions, merchant associations, churches, youth or women's associations etc. are then part of the so-called 'civil society'. Such a broad definition can hardly be applied as such to every single national political system, and rather requires a case by case analysis. For instance, here a trade union can really be a member of the civil society but there it can merely be an extension of a political force.

Civil society and political transition The political reforms in Africa called for a redistribution of power that could leave the civil society out of the game, at least for one simple reason: the members of civil society were often among the numerous casualties of war.

If we bear in mind Fukuyama's paradigm about democratic revolutions, civil society can also be seen as a force for social change. It can be another channel through which a social category can enhance its egalitarian claim or maintain its privileges.

In the 1990s, civil society was primarily made of new-born actors demanding political reforms in order to promote the social categories they represented. Many national conferences integrated it as such, giving these new actors direct political participation in the process of constitutional changes (ex-Zaire). In other instances, former civil society associations, such as trade unions, transformed themselves into political forces that competed for political power (Zambia). The third situation would be the political posture held mainly by the churches, coming in between antagonist political forces and presiding over the transition to multiparty democracy (Benin, Zaire, Congo-Brazzaville).

Civil society and conflict management When acting as mediators, NGOs take into consideration several systemic elements that allow them to deal with conflictual situations:

a) *Governance in African politics.* Since independence a growing gap has appeared between the idea of politics and technocratic democracy on the one hand and the sense of community or welfare on the other hand. This has been pointed out by some NGOs. In a majority of traditional political systems, governance was based on transparency and accountability whereas modern administration only seemed to function in the secretive mode. Adopting the IMF or World Bank's view on accountability thus implies that some of these sub-Saharan African élites would need to return to the kind of 'normality' that their own traditional heritage had in common with a proper contemporary exercise of political power.

b) *Peace and reconciliation.* In dealing with the search for peace and reconciliation between the parties, NGOs realize that peace can be obtained if the needs (causes of conflicts) of the belligerents are taken into consideration and if the reconciliation process leads to the establishment of new social relations.

One pragmatic question occurs when dealing with the transition to a new political regime. Should reconciliation precede elections or not? This is not a rhetoric question considering the fact that sub-Saharan countries are confronted today with this methodological and political question. One can observe that national conferences (Zaire, Congo, Benin and South Africa) have served simultaneously as peace, reconciliation and political transition fora.

c) *The mediation process.* NGOs might be accepted as mediator as long as they can be considered as being capable of having the following qualities and means:[26]

- impartiality regarding the issues in the dispute;
- independence from all parties to the conflict;
- the respect and acceptability to all protagonists;
- the knowledge and skill to deal with the issues;
- international support for the mediator; and
- leverage, i.e. the possibility for the mediator to put pressure on one or both parties to accept a proposed settlement.

d) *The goal.* The goal is either peace, safe and stable political transition, reconciliation or all of them at once. The interesting element that can be drawn from NGOs' experience is that one has to bear in mind social justice (intérêt général) when dealing with peacemaking operations. In other words, it is only when social justice lies next to economic performance at the core of the élites' political action that sustainable peace and development can be met.

e) *The evaluation of NGOs' contribution to conflict prevention.*[27] NGOs' intervention in internal conflicts comes as a back-up to the official talks that often concentrate on the causes of the conflicts and therefore on the fundamental claims of the belligerents. The NGOs have so far been extremely useful in getting the parties to be on speaking terms. Initiating and creating a forum for political dialogue when there was a stalemate have been a considerable input for these organizations.

The Sant Egidio Community in Italy has for instance been extremely useful in bringing the belligerents to the negotiating table in the

Mozambique and in the Burundi conflicts. One has also to acknowledge the role of certain media in creating a climate propitious to negotiation. NGOs such as Search for Common Ground have been active in Burundi in helping Hutu and Tutsi radio professionals in putting up a radio station that dealt in a constructive way with the political crisis in that country.

There should nevertheless be questions about NGOs' own ethics when dealing with such sensitive matters. Certain NGOs have been put negatively in the spotlight when dealing with sensitive situations. International Alert in Sierra Leone or MSF and Caritas International in former Eastern-Zaire have been seen as an obstacle or a partisan organization. Therefore, there is a call for a code of conduct of NGOs dealing with matters related to political questions. This code of conduct would therefore insist on impartiality, neutrality, independence and accountability of NGOs.

Another ambiguous aspect of NGOs' intervention in conflict prevention is the one regarding relations between Western organizations and local ones. Western NGOs by definition have more financial and technical means that African ones. Furthermore, due to this inequality in means and to cultural patterns, there could be a tendency to ignore the work done by local African NGOs in dealing with conflict situations. A sometimes unconscious paternalistic approach can lead western NGOs to bypass the endogenous expertise and knowledge. In the Horn of Africa, the Life and Peace Institute has had a fruitful experience combining local and international cooperation between NGOs to deal with the situation in that part of Africa.

The European Union's cooperation policy towards sub-Saharan Africa

Since the genocide in Rwanda, and the mid-term revision of the Lomé Convention in 1994, the European Union has taken seriously the question of conflict prevention and political cooperation with sub-Saharan African States. This has led to the adoption of numerous political positions [28] that have in common the promotion of human rights, good governance and conflict prevention by insuring structural stability in African States.

Conditionality in the European Union's development policy

Conceptual framework The European Union has voted a series of legal instruments that define its vision of relations with third-party countries. The Council resolution of 28 November 1991 indicates that the promotion of human rights, democracy and the rule of law should be the goal and the framework of its cooperation policy. When considering development cooperation with sub-Saharan Africa, the EU will translate the above framework into article 5 of the Lomé Convention which specifically imposes democracy, respect of human rights and the rule of law as conditions for a full and total cooperation with the EU.

However the latest developments regarding political transition have forced the EU to consider the political instability of African States as a major source of non-development. This instability can go from social unrest (caused by hunger, riots etc.) to open civil war. The EU thus had to adopt another political instrument that could allow the Commission to help its African counterparts in dealing with crisis and conflicts: the Common Position of the Council of 2 June 1997 regarding conflict prevention and resolution in sub-Saharan Africa. It goes without saying that in these situations, cooperation would have to focus on rehabilitating the State in its basic functions in order to avoid total chaos. And thus, human rights, democracy and rule of law would come second on the agenda after ensuring structural stability.[29]

First evaluations of the European cooperation policy regarding both conditionality and conflict prevention are controversial. Methodologically, one has to determine, first and foremost, if a country is stable or not. If a country is stable, political conditionality will be directly imposed; otherwise, structural stability would become the first goal of cooperation.

The NGOs role in the EU's approach

This European approach deals not only with bilateral EU-State cooperation but has also decided to enhance and support decentralized cooperation through which NGOs are called upon to play an active role in this field. The Dutch and the British presidencies of the Union, and the Luxembourg and Belgian foreign ministries have, during the last two years, put the questions of peace and stability in sub-Saharan Africa at the top of their political agenda. In the European institutional approach NGOs are an essential actor of the double-track diplomacy in dealing with conflict prevention or management.

In the light of this recognition, European NGOs and their African counterparts are trying to establish working methods that can allow them to benefit from European subsidies in order to cope with the local stakes. In that framework, NGOs have still to establish efficient networks of information-exchange that can circulate information on methodology in conflict mediation and/or serve as early warning devices, thanks to the rapid exchange and analysis of sensible informations.

Conclusions

Conflicts have had disastrous consequences in sub-Saharan Africa. More than 90% of all casualties are civilians, about 5 millions people were forced into exile or displaced and the economic and social development efforts have been destroyed. In other words, African States are either facing latent instability or open anomie.

Sub-Saharan Africa is slowly organising itself to meet this political challenge. On a regional level, the OAU adopted in June 1993 a Mechanism for conflict prevention, management and resolution that aims to deal mainly with intra-States conflict. Whereas that regional Mechanism is in its earliest stage, some sub-regional organizations, such as ECOWAS, have developed efficient tools to deal with conflict situations. The experience accumulated by these organizations can be considered as milestones for the future.

Civil society and NGOs have also been involved in conflict prevention and resolution. One has to acknowledge their contributions in conflict management, mainly in the mediation processes.

As for international cooperation, the EU is undoubtedly the most involved partner in the prevention and resolution of conflicts in Africa. The EU and sub-Saharan Africa are linked by a structured cooperation framework, whose aim is to lead unstable African States to structural stability. Within this framework, the EU is convinced that NGOs and civil society can largely participate in the curative process resulting from conflicts in sub-Saharan Africa.

Notes

1 Anthony, Asiwaju (1993), 'Workshop on the Role of Border Problems: West Africa', in *Disarmament: African Peace and Security*. UN.

2 OAU: Document CM/119-CXXXVII/Add.I.

3 Anthony (1993), op. cit, pp. 82-88.

4 Bigo, D. (1987) 'Les coups d'Etat en Afrique 1945–1985', *Etudes Polémologiques* 41, 1er trimestre.

5 Ayissi, A. (1994) 'Le défi de la sécurité collective régionale en Afrique après la guerre froide: vers la diplomatie préventive et la sécurité collective', *UNIDIR Travaux de recherches* 27, Genève, pp. 44-53.

6 Adam, Bernard (1997) 'Arms Transfers to African Countries: The Control', in *Conflicts in Africa, An Analysis of Crisis and Crisis Prevention Measures*, GRIP, p. 108.

7 'L'Afrique subsaharienne: les perspectives en matière de sécurité', *Centre d'études et de défense*, colloque du 2/3 décembre 1986, p. 176.

8 Nkundabagenzi, Fabien (1996) 'Un partenariat politique pour un développement politique',in *Rwanda: Les enjeux de la reconstruction nationale*, Edifie LLN, p.186.

9 Bayart, Jean-François (1989) *L'Etat en Afrique*, Seuil, pp. 14-67.

10 'Autant dire que les luttes factionnelles n'ont pas seulement pour objet la ventilation du statut et du pouvoir. Elles ont aussi trait à celles des richesses ou, plus exactement, à celle des possibilités de réaliser une véritable accumulation primitive, au sens précis du concept, par la confiscation des moyens de production et d'échange. Combats sans merci car ils se déroulent dans un double contexte de rareté matérielle et de précarité politique', ibid., p.287.

11 Cf. the discussions about the Lomé Convention, for instance.

12 Mbembe, Achille (1992) 'Le véritable enjeu des débats sur la démocratie', *Le Monde Diplomatique*, January.

13 Fukuyuma, Francis (1993) 'Capitalism and Democracy: The Missing Link', *Dialogue* 100(2), pp.2-7.

14 The Zaïrean political reform illustrates perfectly this assumption: it started out with a 'Conférence nationale souveraine' and ended with the *liberation* war led by Laurent Kabila.

15 Nkundabagenzi, Félix (1997) *La prévention des conflits en Afrique. L'Europe et la sécurité internationale*, GRIP, pp. 98-110.

16 *Jeune Afrique*, 24 June 1993.

17 Ibok, S.Bassey and Nhara, W. (1996) *OUA Early Warning System on Conflict Situations in Africa*, Addis Ababa.

18 Collins, N. (1993) 'Confidence Building Measures in Africa: From Economic Cooperation to Confidence Building Measures in the Security Fields', *Disarmament*, Tropical Papers 17, United Nations, New York, p. 73.

19 ECOWAS is composed of Benin, Burkina Faso, Cape Verde, Ivory Coast, Gambia, Ghana, Guinea-Bissau, Liberia, Mali, Mauritania, Niger, Nigeria, Senegal, Sierra-Leone and Togo.
20 ECOWAS ceasefire monitoring group.
21 Communiqué final, *Togo Presse*, 18 December 1997 and 'Réunion des ministres affaires étrangères de la CEDAO: communiqué final', *Fraternité Matin*, Abidjan, 15 March 1998.
22 The member States are Angola, Botswana, Lesotho, Malawi, Mozambique, Namibia, South Africa, Swaziland, Tanzania, Zambia, Zimbabwe, Mauritius and the Democratic Republic of Congo.
23 Akpokavie, Claude (1993) *Démocratie multiforme et transitions multiples: une contribution à la réfelxion sur la démocratie et le développement*, 10–11 May.
24 Mbembe, Achille (1988) *Afrique indociles*, Karthala.
25 Poulton, Robin E. (1996) 'Vers la réintégration des Touaregs au Mali', *Le Monde Diplomatique*, November.
26 Assefa, H. and Wachira, G. (1996) *Peacemaking and Democratization in Africa*, East African Educational Publishers, p. 90.
27 Tongeren, Paul van (1998) 'Le rôle des ONG: la valorisation des capacités locales pour la paix', *Le Courrier* 168, March–April, pp. 70-72.
28 Résolution du conseil et des Etats membres du 28/11/1997 portant sur les droits de l'homme, la démocratie et les droits de l'homme; article 5 de la convention de Lomé; Communication de la Commission au conseil du 6/03/97; Position commune du conseil du 2/06/1997 concernant la prévention et la résolution des conflits en Afrique (subsaharienne).
29 Commission communication to the Council of 6 March 1996 regarding conflict prevention and resolution in subsaharan Africa.

Bibliography

Adam, Bernard (1997), 'Arms Transfers to African Countries: The Control', in *Conflicts in Africa, An Analysis of Crisis and Crisis Prevention Measures*, GRIP.

Aggestam, Karin and Christer Jönsson (1997), '(Un)Ending Conflict: Challenges in Post-War Bargaining, *Millennium: Journal of International Studies*, 26(3), pp. 771-793.

Aho, James (1994), *This Thing of Darkness: A Sociology of Enemy*, Seattle and London: University of Washington Press.

Akpokavie, Claude (1993), *Démocratie multiforme et transitions multiples: une contribution à la réfelxion sur la démocratie et le développement*, 10–11 May.

Anderson, Benedict (1983), *Imagined Communities: Reflections on the Origins and Spread of Nationalism*, London: Verso.

Angoustures, Aline and Pascal, Valérie (1996), 'Diasporas et finanncement des conflits', in Francois Jean and Jean Christophe Rufin (eds), *Economie des guerres civiles*, Paris: Hachette, pp. 495-542.

Anthony, Asiwaju (1993), 'Workshop on the Role of Border Problems: West Africa', in *Disarmament: African Peace and Security*. UN.

Aoki, D. S. (1995), 'Using and Abusing of French Discourse Theory: Misreading Lacan and the Symbolic Order', *Theory, Culture and Society* 12(4), pp. 47-70.

Appadurai, Arjun (1990), 'Disjuncture and Difference in the Global Cultural Economy', *Theory, Culture and Society*, 7(2-3), pp. 295-310.

Archer, Clive (1994), 'Conflict Prevention in Europe: the Case of the Nordic States in Macedonia', *Cooperation and Conflict*, 29(4), pp. 367-86.

Ardener, Edwin (1972), 'Belief and the Problem of Women', in J. La Fontaine (ed.), *The Interpretation of Ritual*, London: Tavistock.

Arendt, Hannah (1958), *The Human Condition*, New York: Doubleday & Company.

Arendt, Hannah (1970), *On Violence*, San Diego, New York and London: Harcourt Brace & Company.

Ashley, Richard (1989), 'Living on Border Lines: Man, Poststructuralism, and War', in James Der Derian and Michael Shapiro (eds), *International/Intertextual Relations*, Lexington: Lexington Books, pp. 259-322.

Assefa, H. and Wachira, G. (1996), *Peacemaking and Democratization in Africa*, East African Educational Publishers.

Auvinen, Juha Y. (1995), 'Socio-Political and Economic Indicators for Conflict Early Warning'. Paper prepared for the 36th Annual ISA Convention, 21–25 February 1995, Chicago, IL.

Ayissi, A. (1994), 'Le défi de la sécurité collective régionale en Afrique après la guerre froide: vers la diplomatie préventive et la sécurité collective', *UNIDIR Travaux de recherches*, 27, Genève.

Ayto, John (1990), *Dictionary of Word Origins*, London: Bloomsbury.

Azar, Edward (1990), *The Management of Protracted Social Conflict, Theory and Cases*, Aldershot: Dartmouth.

Bächler, Günther, Volker Böge, Stefan Klötzli, Stephan Libiszewski and Kurt R. Spillmann (1996), *Kriegsursache Umweltzerstörung: Ökologische Konflikte in Der Dritten Welt und Wege ihrer friedlichen Bearbeitung*, Zürich: Verlag Rüegger.

Bakhtin, M. M. (1986), *Speech Genres and Other Essays*, Austin: University of Texas Press.

Baldwin, David A. (1985), *Economic Statecraft*. Princeton, New Jersey: Princeton University Press.

Barth, Fredrik (ed.) (1969), *Ethnic Groups and Boundaries, The Social Organization of Culture Difference*, Boston: Little, Brown and Company.

Barth, Fredrik (1994), 'Enduring and Emerging Issues in the Analysis of Ethnicity', in Hans Vermuelen and Cora Govers (eds), *The Anthropology of Ethnicity: Beyond Ethnic Groups and Boundaries*, Amsterdam: Het Spinhius, pp.11-32.

Baudrillard, Jean (1995), *The Gulf War Did Not Take Place*, Bloomington: Indiana University Press.

Bauman, Zygmunt (1990), 'Modernity and Ambivalence', in Mike Featherstone (ed.), *Global Culture: Nationalism, Globalization and Modernity*, London: Sage Publications, pp. 143-170.

Bauman, Zygmunt (1991), *Modernity and Ambivalence*, Ithaca, New York: Cornell University Press.

Bauman, Zygmunt (1992), 'Soil, Blood and Identity', *The Sociological Review*, 40(4), pp. 675-701.

Baumel, Judith (1995), 'In Everlasting Memory': Individual and Communal Holocaust Commemoration in Israel', in Robert Wistrich and David Ohana (eds), *The Shaping of Israeli Identity: Myth, Memory and Trauma*, Frank Cass, London, pp. 146-70.

Bayart, Jean-François (1989), *L'Etat en Afrique*, Paris: Seuil.

Beaumont, Roger (1996), 'Small Wars: Definitions and Dimensions', in W.M.J. Olson (ed.), 'Small Wars', *Annals of the American Academy of Political and Social Science*, vol. 541, London: Sage Publications, pp. 20-35.

Bekker, Simon and David Carlton (eds) (1996), *Racism, Xenophoobia and Ethnic Conflict*, Durban: Indicator Press.

Bellamy, Christopher (1996), *Knights in White Armour. The New Art of War and Peace*, London: Hutchinson.

Benhabib, Seyla (1992), *Situating the Self*, Cambridge: Polity Press.

Bercovitch, Jacob (1984), *Social Conflicts and Third Parties. Strategies of Conflict Resolution*, Colorado: Westview Press.

Bercovitch, Jacob *et al.* (1991), 'Some Conceptual Issues and Empirical Trends in the Study of Successful Mediation in International Relations', *Journal of Peace Research*, 28(1), pp. 7-17.

Bercovitch, Jacob (1992), 'The Structure and Diversity of Mediation in International Relations', in Jacob Bercovitch and Jeffrey Z. Rubin (eds), *Mediation in International Relations, Multiple Approaches to Conflict Management*, London: Macmillan.

Bercovitch, Jacob and A. Houston (1996), 'The Study of International Mediation: Theoretical Issues and Empirical Evidence', in Jacob Bercovitch (ed.), *Resolving International Conflicts. The Theory and Practice of Mediation*, London: Lynne Rienner.

Berdyaev, N. A. (1990), *Sudba Rossii* (The fate of Russia), Sovetski Pisatel, Moscow.

Berkowitz, Leonard (1990), 'Biological Roots: Are Humans Inherently Violent?, in Betty Glad (ed.), *Psychological Dimensions of War*, London: Sage Publications, pp. 24-40.

Bigo, D. (1987), 'Les coups d'Etat en Afrique 1945–1985', *Etudes Polémologiques*, 41, 1er trimestre.

Boucaud, André and Boucaud, Louis (1996), 'Burma: Verließ mit goldenem Boden', *Der Überblick*, 3, pp. 35-38.

Boutwell, Jeffrey, Michael T. Klare and Laura W. Reed (eds) (1995), *Lethal Commerce: The Global Trade in Small Arms and Light Weapons*, Cambridge, MA: American Academy of Arts and Sciences.

Brass, Paul (1991), *Ethnicity and Nationalism: Theory and Comparison*, New Delhi: Sage Publications.

Brock, Lothar (1997), 'The Environment and Security: Conceptual and Theoretical Issues', in Nils Petter Gleditsch (ed.), *Conflict and the Environment*, Dordrecht, Boston and London: Kluwer Academic Publishers. Published in cooperation with NATO Scientific Affairs Division, pp. 17-35.

Broome, Benjamin (1993), 'Managing Differences in Conflict Resolution: The Role of Relational Empathy', in Dennis J. D. Sandole and Hugo van der Merwe (eds), *Conflict Resolution Theory and Practice, Integration and Application*, Manchester and New York: Manchester University Press, pp. 97-111.

Brown, Michael E. (ed.) (1993), *Ethnic Conflict and International Security*, Princeton, NJ: Princeton University Press.

Brown, Michael E. (ed.) (1996), *The International Dimensions of Internal Conflict*, Cambridge, MA: MIT Press.

Brown, Michael E., Sean Lynn-Jones and Steven E. Miller (eds) (1996), *Debating the Democratic Peace*, Cambridge, MA: The MIT Press.

Brown, Michael E. *et al.* (eds) (1997), *Nationalism and Ethnic Conflict*, Cambridge, MA and London: The MIT Press.

Brown, Neville (1989), 'Climate, ecology and international security', *Survival* 31(6), November–December, pp. 519-532.

Brundtland, Gro et al. (1987), *Our Common Future. World Commission on Environment and Development*, Oxford: Oxford University Press.

Buchanan, Allen (1997), 'Theories of Secession', *Philosophy and Public Affairs*, 26(1), pp 31-61.

Buchanan, Allen (1998), 'Self-Determination, Secession, and the Rule of Law', in Robert McKim and Jeff McMahan (eds), *The Morality of Nationalism*, New York: Oxford University Press.

Burton, John W. (1969), *Conflict and Communication. The Use of Controlled Communication in International Relations*, London: MacMillan.

Burton, John W. (1990), *Conflict: Conflict Resolution and Provention*, New York: St. Martin's Press.

Burton, John W. (ed.) (1990), *Conflict: Human Needs Theory*, New York: St. Martin's Press.

Burton, John W. (1993), 'Conflict Resolution as a Political Philosophy', in Dennis J.D. Sandole and Hugo van der Merwe (eds), *Conflict Resolution Theory and Practice*, New York: Manchester University Press.

Burton, John W. (1997), *Violence Explained*, Manchester: Manchester University Press.

Butenschøn, Nils (1998), 'The Oslo Agreement: From the White House to Jabal Abu Ghneim', in George Giacaman and Dag Jørund Lønning (eds), *After Oslo: New Realities, Old Problems*, London and Chicago: Pluto Press, pp. 16-44.

Buzan, Barry (1991), *People, States and Fear.* 2nd Ed. Boulder, CO: Lynne Reinner.

Byman, Daniel and Stephen Van Evera (1998), 'Hypotheses on the Causes of Contemporary Deadly Conflict', *Security Studies*, 7(3), pp. 1-50.

Camilleri, J.A. and Jim Falk (1992), *The End of Sovereignty? The Politics of a Shrinking and Fragmenting World*, London: Edward Elgar.

Campbell, David and Michael Dillon (eds), *The Political Subject of Violence*, Manchester and New York: Manchester University Press.

Campbell, David (1993), *Writing Security*, Minneapolis: University of Minnesota Press.

Campbell, David (1994), *Politics Without Principle. Sovereignty, Ethics, and the Narratives of the Gulf War*, Boulder, CO: Lynne Rienner.

Carnevale, P.J. and S. Arad (1996), 'Bias and Impartiality in International Mediation', in Jacob Bercovitch (ed.), *Resolving International Conflicts. The Theory and Practice of Mediation*, London: Lynne Rienner.

Clausewitz, Carl von (1980), *Vom Kriege. Ungekürzter Text nach der Erstauflage (1832-1834)*, Frankfurt a.M.: Ullstein Materialien.

Coakley, John (1994), 'Approaches to the Resolution of Ethnic Conflict: The Strategy of Non-territorial Autonomy', *International Political Science Review*, 15(3), pp. 297-314.

Cobb, Sara (1994), 'A Narrative Perspective on Mediation: Toward the Materialization of the "Storytelling" Metaphor', in Joseph Folger and Tricia Jones (eds), *New Directions in Mediation*, Thousand Oaks, London, New Delhi: Sage Publications.

Cock, Jacklyn (1997), 'The Cultural and Social Challenge of Demilitarization', in Gavin Cawthra and Bjørn Møller (eds), *Defensive Restructuring of the Armed Forces in Southern Africa*, Aldershot: Dartmouth, pp. 117-144.

Cohen, Leonard J. (1995), *Broken Bonds. Yugoslavia's Disintegration and Balkan Politics in Transition*, Boulder, Colorado: Westview.

Coker, Christopher (1994), *War and the 20th Century. The Impact of War on the Modern Consciousness*, London: Brassey's, UK.

Collins, N. (1993), 'Confidence Building Measures in Africa: From Economic Cooperation to Confidence Building Measures in the Security Fields', *Disarmament*, Tropical Papers 17, New York: United Nations.

Connolly, William (1991), *Identity/Difference: Democratic Negotiations of Political Paradox*, Ithaca, NY: Cornell University Press.

Connolly, William (1995), *The Ethos of Pluralization*, Minneapolis: The University of Minnesota Press.

Connor, Walker (1972), 'Nation-Building or Nation-Destroying?', *World Politics*, 24(3), April, pp. 319-355.

Cooper, R. and M. Berdal (1993), 'Outside Intervention in Ethnic Conflicts', in Michael E. Brown (ed.), *Ethnic Conflict in International Security*, Princeton, NJ: Princeton University Press.

Corbin, Jane (1995), *Gaza First: The Secret Norway Channel to Peace Between Israel and the PLO*, London: Bloomsbury.

Cortright, David (ed.) (1997), *The Price of Peace: Incentives and International Conflict Prevention*, Lanham, Maryland: Rowman and Littlefield.

Crawford, Neta (1997), 'The Humanitarian Consequences of Sanctioning South Africa: A Preliminary Assessment', in Thomas G. Weiss, David Cortright, George Lopez, and Larry Minear (eds), *Political Gain and Civilian Pain: Humanitarian Impacts of Economic Sanctions*, Lanham, Maryland: Rowman and Littlefield.

Creveld, Martin Van (1989), *Technology and War from 2000 B.C. to the Present*, New York: Free Press.

Däniker, Gustav (1995), 'The Guardian Soldier: On the Nature and Use of Future Armed Forces', *Research Paper* 36, New York and Geneva: UNIDIR, UNIDIR/95/28.

Debiel, Tobias (1993), 'Kriege', in *SEF: Globale Trends 1993/94*, Frankfurt/M.: Fischer, pp. 177-97.

Deleuze, Gilles and Felix Guattari (1988), *A Thousand Plateaus*, London: The Athlone Press.

Derian, James Der (1991), 'The Terrorist Discourse: Signs, States, and Systems of Global Political Violence', in Michael Klare and Daniel C. Thomas (eds.), *World Security. Trends and Challenges at Century's End*, New York: St. Martin's Press, pp. 237-65.

Derian, James Der (1992), *Antidiplomacy. Spies, Terror, Speed and War*, Oxford: Polity Press, pp. 173-202.

Derrida, Jacques (1981), *Positions*, Chicago: University of Chicago Press.

Deudney, Daniel (1991), 'Environment and Security: Muddled Thinking', *Bulletin of the Atomic Scientists*, 47(3), pp. 22-28.

Devin, Julia and Jaleh Dashti-Gibson (1997), 'Sanctions in the Former Yugoslavia: Convoluted Goals and Complicated Consequences', in Thomas G. Weiss, David Cortright, George Lopez, and Larry Minear (eds), *Political Gain and Civilian Pain: Humanitarian Impacts of Economic Sanctions*, Lanham, Maryland: Rowman and Littlefield.

Diamond, Larry (1995), *Promoting Democracy in the 1990s: Actors and Instruments, Issues and Imperatives*, A Report to the Carnegie Commission on Deadly Violence, Washington, DC.

Diamond, Larry and Marc F. Plattner (eds) (1996), *Civil-Military Relations and Democracy*, Baltimore: Johns Hopkins University Press.

Diamond, Larry (1997), *Consolidating the Third Wave Democracies: Themes and Perspectives*, Baltimore: Johns Hopkins University Press.

Dillon, Michael (1996), *Politics of Security*, London and New York: Routledge.

Doob, Leonard (ed.) (1970), *Resolving Conflict in Africa: The Fermeda Workshop*, New Haven, London: Yale University Press.

Dragadze, Tamara (1993), 'Soviet Economics and Nationalism in the Gorbachev Years. Regionalism, Ethnicised Regionalism and Constitutional Regionalism', in Marco Buttino (ed.), *In a Collapsing empire: Underdevelopment, Ethnic Conflicts and Nationalisms in the Soviet Union*, Milano, Fondazione Giangiacomo Feltrinelli.

Druckman, Daniel (1993), 'An Analytical Research Agenda for Conflict and Conflict Resolution', in Dennis J.D. Sandole and Hugo van der Merwe (eds), *Conflict Resolution Theory and Practice*, New York: Manchester University Press.

Druckman, Daniel and Christopher Mitchell (eds) (1995), 'Flexibility and International Negotiation and Mediation', *The Annals of the American Academy of Political and Social Science*, 542.

Duffield, Mark (1994), 'The Political Economy of Internal War: Asset Transfer, Complex Emergencies and International Aid', in Macrae, Joanna and Anthony

Zwi (eds) (1994), *War and Hunger: Rethinking International Responses to Complex Emergencies*. London: Zed, pp. 50–69.

Dunér, Bertil (1985), *Military Intervention in Civil Wars: The 1970s*, Aldershot: Gower.

Dunlop, J.B. (1997), 'Russia: In Search of an Identity?', in Ian Bremmer and Ray Taras (eds), *New States, New Politics: Building the Post-Soviet Nations*, Cambridge: Cambridge University Press.

Dupuy, Trevor N. (1980), *The Evolution of Weapons and Warfare*, London: Jane's.

Eastwood, Lawrence (1993), 'Secession: State Practice and International Law after the Dissolution of the Soviet Union and Yugoslavia', *Duke Journal of Comparative and International Law*, 3(2), pp. 299-349.

Eckstein, Harry and Ted Robert Gurr (1975). *Patterns of Authority: A Structural Basis for Political Inquiry*, New York: Wiley.

Ehrenreich, Barbara (1997), *Blood Rites. Origins and History of the Passions of War*, London: Virago Press.

Elias, Norbert (1989), *Über den Prozeß der Zivilisation, Bd. 2, Wandlungen der Gesellschaft, Entwurf zu einer Theorie der Zivilisation*, Frankfurt a.M.: Suhrkamp.

Elshtain, Jean Bethke (ed.) (1992), *Just War Theory*, Oxford: Blackwell.

Endres, Jürgen and Dietrich Jung (1998), 'Was legitimiert den Griff zur Gewalt? Unterschiede im Konfliktverhalten islamistischer Organisationen in Ägypten', *Politische Vierteljahresschrift*, 39(1), pp. 91-108.

Eriksen, Thomas Hylland and Iver B. Neumann (1993), 'International Relations as a Cultural System: an Agenda for Research', in *Cooperation and Conflict* 28(3), London, Newbury Park and New Delhi, Sage Publications, pp. 233-264.

Eriksen, Thomas Hylland (1993), *Ethnicity and Nationalism. Anthropological Perspectives*, London and Boulder, CO: Pluto Press.

Eriksen, Thomas Hylland (1995), 'We and Us: Two Modes of Group Identification', *Journal of Peace Research*, 32(4), 427-436.

Etzioni, Amitai (1993), 'The Evils of Self-Determination', *Foreign Policy*, 89, pp. 21-35.

Fairley, Lawrence (1986), *Plebiscites and Sovereignty. The Crisis of Political Illegitimacy*, Boulder: Westview Press.

Fearon, James D. (1995), 'Rationalist Explanations of War', *International Organization*, 49(3), pp. 379-414.

Feierabend, Ivo K., Rosalind L Feierabend and Betty Nesvold (1972), 'Social Change and Political Violence: Cross-National Patterns', in Ivo K. Feierabend, Rosalind L. Feierabend and Ted Robert Gurr (eds), *Anger, Violence and Politics*, Englewood Cliffs, NJ: Prentice Hall, pp. 107-125.

Feldman, Allen (1991), *Formations of Violence, The Narrative of the Body and Political Terror in Northern Ireland*, Chicago and London: The University of Chicago Press.

Fisher, Eric (1949), 'On Boundaries', *World Politics*, 1(2), pp. 196-222.
Fisher, Roger and William Ury (1981), *Getting to Yes. Negotiating Agreement Without Giving In*, London: Hutchinson Business.
Fisher, Roger and William Ury (1991), *Getting to Yes. Negotiating Agreement Without Giving In*, 2nd edition, New York: Penguin Press.
Fisher, Ronald J. and Laura Keashly (1991), 'The Potential Complementarity of Mediation and Consultation within a Contingency Model of Third Party Intervention', *Journal of Peace Research*, 28(1), pp. 29-42.
Fisher, Ronald J. (1995), 'Pacific, Impartial Third Party Intervention in International Conflict: A Review and an Analysis', in John A. Vasquez *et al.* (eds), *Beyond Confrontation: Learning Conflict Resolution in the Post-Cold War Era*, Ann Arbor, Michigan: Michigan University Press.
Fisher, Ronald J. (1997), 'Interactive Conflict Resolution', in I. William Zartman and J. Lewis Rasmussen (eds), *Peacemaking in International Conflict: Methods and Techniques*, Washington, DC: United States Institute of Peace Press.
Forsberg, Tuomas (1996), 'Beyond Sovereignty, Within Territoriality. Mapping the Space of Late-Modern (Geo)Politics', *Cooperation and Conflict*, 31(4), pp. 355-386.
Forsberg, Tuomas (1996), 'Explaining Territorial Disputes: From Power Politics to Normative Reasons', *Journal of Peace Research*, 33(4), pp. 433-450.
Fukuyuma, Francis (1993), 'Capitalism and Democracy: The Missing Link', *Dialogue*, 100(2), pp. 2-7.
Gadamer, Hans-Georg (1991), *Plato's Dialectical Ethics*, New Haven and London: Yale University Press.
Galtung, Johan (1969), 'Peace, Violence and Peace Research', *Journal of Peace Research*, 6, pp. 167-191.
Galtung, Johan (1982), *Environment, Development and Military Activity. Towards Alternative Security Doctrines*, Oslo: Norwegian University Press.
Galtung, Johan (1990), 'Neue Weltordnung: "Dialektik zwischen Orient und Okzident". Ein Gespräch mit Johan Galtung. Groningen. July 1990', *ECOR Papers Series*, 3.
Galtung, Johan (1994), 'Conflict Interventions', in J. Calließ and Ch. Merkel (eds), *Peaceful Settlement of Conflict*, Evangelische Akademie Loccum: Protokolle 24 (1 & 2), Loccum.
Galtung, Johan (1996), *Pace by Peaceful Means: Peace and Conflict, Development and Civilization*, London, Thousand Oaks and New Delhi: Sage Publications.
Galtung, Johan (1997), *Conflict Experience 1952–97*. www.transcend.org/
Galtung, Johan (1997), *Peace by Peaceful Means: Peace and Conflict, Development and Civilization*, London: Sage Publications.
Galtung, Johan (1998), *After Violence: 3R, Reconstruction, Reconciliation, Resolution. Coping With Visible and Invisible Effects of War and Violence*. www.transcend.org/

Gantzel, Klaus Jürgen and Schwinghammer, Thorsten (1995), *Die Kriege nach dem Zweiten Weltkrieg 1945–1992. Daten und Tendenzen*, Münster und Hamburg: LIT.

Gantzel, Klaus Jürgen (1997), 'Kriegsursachen – Tendenzen und Perspektiven', *Ethik & Sozialwissenschaft*, 8(3), pp. 257-266.

Gantzel, Klaus Jürgen (1997), 'War in the Post-World War II World: Some Empirical Trends and a Theoretical Approach', in David Turon (ed.), *War and Ethnicity. Global connections and Local Violence*, San Marino: University of Rochester Press.

Gat, Azar (1989), *The Origins of Military Thought. From the Enlightenment to Clausewitz*, Oxford: Clarendon Press.

Gellner, Ernest (1983), *Nations and Nationalism*, Oxford: Basil Blackwell Ltd.

Gellner, Ernest (1992), *Postmodermism, Reason and Religion*, London: Routledge.

Gelven, Michael (1994), *War and Existence. A Philosophical Inquiry*, University Park, Pennsylvania: Penn State Press.

George, Alexander *et al.* (1971), *Limits of Coercive Diplomacy: Laos-Cuba-Vietnam*, Boston: Little Brown and Company.

George, Jim (1994), *Discourses of Global Politics: A Critical (Re)Introduction to International Relations*, Boulder: Lynne Rienner.

Gibson, James William (1988), *The Perfect War. The War We Couldn't Lose and How We Did*, New York: Vintage.

Giddens, Anthony (1995), *The Nation-State and Violence*, Oxford: Polity Press.

Gilbert, Paul (1994), *Terrorism, Security and Nationality. An Introductory Study in Applied Philosophy*, London: Routledge.

Gleditsch, Nils Petter (1996), 'Det nye sikkerhetsbildet: Mot en demokratisk og fredelig verden?', *Internasjonal Politikk, 3.*

Gleditsch, Nils Petter and Håvard Hegre (1997), 'Peace and Democracy: Three Levels of Analysis', *Journal of Conflict Resolution*, 41 (2), April, pp. 283-310.

Gleditsch, Nils Petter (1998), 'Armed Conflict and the Environment: A Critique of the Literature', *Journal of Peace Research*, 35(3), May, pp. 381-401.

Gleick, Peter H. (1993), *Water in Crisis. A Guide to the World's Fresh Water Resources*, New York, Oxford: Oxford University Press, for Pacific Institute for Studies in Development, Environment and Security & Stockholm Environment Institute.

Goldstein, Joshua S. (1996), *International Relations*, 2nd edn, American University, Washington D.C.: Harper Collins College Publishers.

Gottlieb, Gidon (1994), *Nation Against State. New Approaches to Ethnic Conflicts and the Decline of Sovereignty*, New York: Council of Foreign Relations Press.

Gray, Chris Hables (1997), *Postmodern War. The New Politics of Conflict*, London: Routledge.

Gray, Colin S. (1996), 'The Continued Primacy of Geography', *Orbis*, 40(2), pp. 247-259.

Green, Philip (1966), *Deadly Logic. The Theory of Nuclear Deterrence*, Columbus, Ohio: Ohio State University Press.

Greenwood, Christopher (1992), 'In Defence of the Laws of War', in Robert A. Hinde (ed.), *The Institution of War*, New York: St. Martin's Press, pp. 133-147.

Grimes, Barbara F. (chief ed.), R. S. Pittman and J. E. Grimes (eds) (1996), *Ethnologue. Languages of the World*, 13ᵗʰ Edition. Dallas: Summer Institute of Linguistics.

Grosby, Steven (1995), 'Territoriality: The Transcendental, Primordial Feature of Modern Societies', *Nations and Nationalism*, 1(2), pp. 143-162.

Gross Stein, Janice (1989), *Getting to the Table: the Processes of International Prenegotiation*, Baltimore: The Johns Hopkins University Press.

Gumilev, L.N. (1991), 'Zametki poslednego Evrasiitsa' (Notes by the last Eurasianist), in *Nashe Nasledie* (Our Heritage) 3, pp. 19-26.

Gurr, Ted Robert (1993), *Minorities at Risk. A Global View of Ethnopolitcal Conflict*, Washington, D.C.: US Institute of Peace.

Gurr, Ted Robert and Barbara Harff (1994), *Ethnic Conflict in World Politics*, Boulder: Westview Press

Gurr, Ted Robert (1994), 'Peoples against States: Ethnopolitical Conflict and the Changing World System', *International Studies Quarterly*, 38 (3), pp. 348–77.

Hall, Stuart (1992), 'The Question of Cultural Identity', in Stuart Hall, David Held and Tony McGrew (eds), *Modernity and its Futures*, Polity Press in Association with the Open University.

Hall, Stuart (1996), 'Introduction: Who Needs Identity?', in Stuart Hall and Paul du Gay (eds), *Questions of Cultural Identity*, London: Sage Publications.

Halperin, Morton and David Scheffee with Patricia Small (1992), *Self-Determination in the New World Order*, Washington, D.C.: Carnegie Endowment for Peace.

Hampson, Fen Osler (1996), *Nuturing Peace: Why Peace Settlements Succeed or Fail*, Washington, D.C.: United States Institute of Peace Press.

Handelman, Don and Lea Shamgar Handelman (1997), *ThePresence of Absence: The Memoralism of National Death in Israel*, in Eyal Ben-Ari and Yoram Bilu (eds), *Grasping Land: Space and place in Contemporary Israeli Discourse and Experience*, New York: State University of New York Press.

Hannum, Horst (1990), *Autonomy, Sovereignty, and Self-Determination*, Philadelphia: University of Pennsylvania Press.

Hart, Basil Liddell (1974), *Strategy. The Indirect Approach*, 2nd edition (1967) reprint, New York: Signet Books.

Harvey, Neil (1994), *Rebellion in Chiapas: Rural Reforms, Campesino Radicalism and the Limits to Salinismo*, San Diego: Center for U.S.-Mexican Studies.

Hauge, Wenche and Håvard Hegre (1977), 'Economic Development and Civil War', Paper presented to the 38th Annual Conference of the International Studies Association, Toronto, 18–22 March 1977.

Hauge, Wenche and Tanja Ellingsen (1998), 'Beyond Environmental Scarcity: Causal Pathways to Conflict', *Journal of Peace Research*, 35(3), May, pp. 299-319.

Hechter, Michael (1975), *Internal Colonialism: The Celtic in British National Development 1536–1966*, London: Routledge & Kegan Paul.

Heisler, Martin (1990), 'Ethnicity and Ethnic Relations in the Modern West', in Joseph Montville (ed.), *Conflict and Peacemaking in Multiethnic Societies*, Lexington, MA: Lexington Books.

Heldt, Birger (ed.) (1992), *States in Armed Conflict 1990–91*, Report No. 35, Department of Peace and Conflict Research, Uppsala University.

Hensel, Paul (1996), 'Charting a Course to Conflict: Territorial Issues and Interstate Conflict, 1816–1992', *Conflict Management and Peace Science*, (1), pp. 43-73.

Heraclides, Alexis (1993), 'Secessionist Conflagration. What Is to Be Done?', *Security Dialogue*, (3), pp. 283-293.

Hettne, Björn (1992), *Etniska Konflikter och internationella relationer*, Lund: Studentlitteratur.

Hettne, Björn (1995), *Development Theory and the Three Worlds*, Essex: Longman Scientific & Technical.

Hibbs, Douglas A. (1973). *Mass Political Violence: A Cross-National Causal Analysis*, New York: John Wiley & Sons.

Hobsbawm, Eric (1990), *Nations and Nationalism since 1780: Programme, Myth, Reality*, Cambridge: Cambridge University Press.

Holsti, Kalevi J. (1991), *Change in the International System. Essays on the Theory and Practice of International Relations*, Aldershot, Brookfield: Ashgate.

Holsti, Kalevi J. (1991), *Peace and War: Armed Conflict and International Order 1648–1989*, Cambridge: Cambridge University Press.

Holsti, Kalevi J. (1992), 'International Theory and War in the Third World', in Job, Brian L. (ed.), *The Insecurity Dilemma. National Security of Third World States*, Boulder, Co.: Westview Press.

Homer-Dixon, Thomas F. (1991), 'On the Threshold. Environmental Changes as Causes of Acute Conflict', *International Security*, 16(2), pp. 76-116.

Homer-Dixon, Thomas F., Jeffrey H. Boutwell and George W. Rathjens (1993), 'Environmental Change and Violent Conflict', *Scientific American*, 268(2), pp. 38-45.

Homer-Dixon, Thomas F. (1994), 'Environmental Scarcities and Violent Conflict: Evidence from Cases', *International Security*, 19(1), pp. 5-40.

Hopmann, P. Terrence (1996), *The Negotiation Process and the Resolution of International Conflicts*, Columbia, South Carolina: University of South Carolina Press.

Horowitz, Donald (1985), *Ethnic Groups in Conflict*, Berkeley, Los Angeles, London: University of California Press.

Howard, Michael (1976), *War in European History*, Oxford: Oxford University Press.

Hume, C. (1994), *Ending Mozambique's War. The Role of Mediation and Good Offices*, Washington, D.C.: US Institute of Peace.

Huntington, Samuel P. (1991). *The Third Wave: Democratization in the Late Twentieth Century*, Norman, OK and London: University of Oklahoma Press.

Hurlburt, Heather (1997), 'Gaining Leverage for International Organizations: Incentives and Baltic-Russian Relations, 1992–94', in David Cortright (ed.), *The Price of Peace: Incentives and International Conflict Prevention*, Lanham, Maryland: Rowman and Littlefield.

Huth, Paul K. (1996), *Standing Your Ground. Territorial Disputes and International Conflict*, Ann Arbor, MI: The University of Michigan Press.

Ibok, S. Bassey and W. Nhara (1996), *OUA Early Warning System on Conflict Situations in Africa*, Addis Ababa.

Ignatieff, Michael (1993), *Blood and Belonging*, New York: Farrar, Straus and Giroux.

Izmozik, Vladlen (1998), 'Alexander Makedonsky: nash rossiisky geroi' (Alexander the Great: our Russian hero), *Obshaia Gazeta* 24, 18–24 June 1998.

Jacobson, David (1997), 'New Frontiers: Territory, Social Spaces, and the State', *Sociological Forum*, 12(1), pp.121-133.

Janjic, Dusan (1995), 'Resurgence of Ethnic Conflict in Yugoslavia: The Demise of Communism and the Rise of the "New Elites" of Nationalism', in Payam Akhavan (ed.), *Yugoslavia: the Former and the Future*, Washington, DC: The Brookings Institution.

Jean, Francois (1996), 'Aide humanitaire et économie de guerre', in Francois Jean and Jean Christophe Rufin (eds), *Economie des guerres civiles*, Paris: Hachette, pp. 543-589.

Jomini, Antoine-Henri de (1811), *Traite des grandes operations militaires*, 2nd edition, vol. 4, Paris: Magimel. Librairie pour l'art militaire, pp. 275-286.

Jones, Archer (1988), *The Art of War in the Western World*, London: Harrap.

Jowitt, Ken (1991), 'The New World Disorder', *Journal of Democracy*, 2(4), December, pp. 11-20.

Jung, Dietrich (1995), *Tradition – Moderne – Krieg. Grundlegung einer Methode zur Erforschung kriegsursächlicher Prozesse im Kontext globaler Vergesellschaftung*, Münster und Hamburg: LIT.

Kandyba, V. and P. Zolin (1997), *Istoria I ideologia russkogo naroda* (History and the ideology of the Russian people), vol. 2, St. Petersburg: Lan.

Kaufman, Chaim (1996), 'Possible and Impossible Solutions to Ethnic Civil Wars', *International Security*, 20(4), pp. 136-175.

Keaney, Thomas A. and Eliot A. Cohen (1995), *Revolution in Warfare? Air Power in the Persian Gulf*, Annapolis, Maryland: Naval Institute Press.

Kellett, Anthony (1990), 'The Soldier in Battle: Motivational and Behavioral Aspects of the Combat Experience', in Betty Glad (ed.), *Psychological Dimensions of War*, London: Sage Publications, pp. 215-235.

Kelman, Herbert C. and Cohen, Stephen P. (1976), 'The Problem Solving Workshop: A Social-Psychological Contribution to the Resolution of International Conflict', *Journal of Peace Research*, 13, pp. 79-90.

Kelman, Herbert C. (1986), 'Interactive Problem Solving: A Social-Psychological Approach to Conflict Resolution', in William Klassen (ed.), *Dialogue toward Interfaith Understanding*, Jerusalem: Ecumenical Institute for Theological Research.

Kelman, Herbert C. (1991), 'Informal Mediation by the Scholar/Practitioner', in Jacob Bercovitch and Jeffrey Rubin (eds), *Mediation in International Relations, Multiple Approaches to Conflict Management*, Basingstoke, London: Macmillan Press, pp. 64-96.

Khalidi, Rashid (1997), *Palestinian Identity: The Construction of Modern National Consciousness*, New York: Columbia University Press.

Kiernan, Ben (1996), *The Pol Pot Regime: Race, Power, and Genocide in Cambodia under the Khmer Rouge, 1975–79*, New Haven, London: Yale University Press.

Kimmerling, Baruch (1983), *Zionism and Territory: The Socio-Territorial Dimensions of Zionist Politics*, Berkeley: University of California, Institute of International Studies.

Kimmerling, Baruch (1997), 'The Power-Oriented Settlement: PLO – Israel: The Road to the Oslo Agreement and Back?', in Avraham Sela and Moshe Ma'oz (eds), *The PLO and Israel: From Armed Conflict to Political Solution, 1964–1994*, New York: St. Martin's Press, pp. 223-252.

Kimura, Masato and David Welch (1998), 'Specifying "Interests": Japan's Claim to the Northern Territories and Its Implications for International Relations Theory', *International Studies Quarterly*, 42(2), pp. 213-244.

Kleiboer, Marieke (1996), 'Understanding Success and Failure of International mediation', *Journal of Conflict Resolution*, 40(2), Sage Publications.

Klein, Bradley S. (1994), *Strategic Studies and World Order. The Global Politics of Deterrence*, Cambridge: Cambridge University Press.

Knight, David (1988), 'Self-Determination for Indigeneous Peoples: The Context for Change', in R. J. Johnston, David Knight and Eleonore Kofman (eds), *Nationalism, Self-Determination and Political Geography*, London: Croom Helm.

Kocs, Stephen A. (1995), 'Territorial Disputes and Interstate War 1945–1987', *The Journal of Politics*, 57(1), pp. 159-175.

Kortunov, S. (1997), 'Kakaya Rossia nuzhna miru' (What kind of Russia does the world need?), *Pro et Contra*, 2(1), Winter.

Kratochwil, Friedrich, Paul Rohrlich and Harpreet Mahajan (1985), *Peace and Disputed Sovereignty. Reflections on Conflict over Territory*, Lanham, Maryland: University Press of America.

Kriesberg, Louis (1996), Varieties of Mediation Activities and Mediators in International Relations, in Jacob Bercovitch (ed.), *Resolving International Conflicts. The Theory and Practice of Mediation*, London: Lynne Rienner.

Krippendorff, Ekkehardt (1984), *Staat und Krieg. Die historische Logik politischer Unvernunft*, Frankfurt: Suhrkamp Verlag.

Kull, Stephen (1990), 'War and the Attraction to Destruction', in Betty Glad (ed.): *Psychological Dimensions of War*, London: Sage Publications, pp. 41-55.

Laclau, Ernesto (1990), *New Reflections on the Revolution of Our Time*. London, New York: Verso.

Laclau, Ernesto (1994), 'Introduction', in Ernesto Laclau (ed.), *The Making of Political Identities*, London, New York: Verso.

Laclau, Ernesto and Lilian Zac (1994), 'Minding the Gap: The Subject of Politics', in Ernesto Laclau (ed.), *The Making of Political Identities*, London, New York: Verso, pp. 11-39.

Laclau, Ernesto (1996), 'Universalism, Particularism, and the Question of Identity', in Edwin Wilmsen and Patric McAllister (eds), *The Politics of Difference*, Chicago, London: University Chicago Press pp. 45-58.

'L'Afrique subsaharienne: les perspectives en matière de sécurité', *Centre d'études et de défense,* colloque du 2–3 décembre 1986.

Lapid, Yosef and Friedrich Kratochwill (1995), 'Revisiting the "National": Toward an Identity Agenda in Neorealism', in Yosef Lapid and Friedrich Kratochwill (eds), *The Return of Culture and Identity in IR Theory*, Boulder: Lynne Rienner, pp. 105-126.

Lapidoth, Ruth (1996), *Autonomy. Flexible Solutions to Intrastate Conflicts*, Washington, D.C.: United States Institute of Peace Press.

Laqueur, Walter (1996), 'Postmodern Terrorism', *Foreign Affairs*, 75(5), September-October, pp. 24-36.

Lawrence, Thomas Edward (1935), *The Seven Pillars of Wisdom. A Triumph*, London: Jonathan Cape, pp. 192-193.

Leatherman, Janie, William Demars, Patrick Gaffney and Raimo Väyrynen, forthcoming, *Breaking Cycles of Violence: Conflict Prevention in Intrastate Crises*. West Harford, Connecticut: Kumarian Press.

Leatherman, Janie, forthcoming, 'Catholic Relief Services' Peacebuilding Role in the Republic of Macedonia: Using Humanitarian Assistance to Promote Democratic Awareness and Civic Participation', in Marc Howard Ross and Jay Rothman (eds), *Theory and Practice in Conflict Management: Conceptualizing Success and Failure*, London: MacMillan.

Lechervy, Christian (1996), 'L`économie des guerres cambodgiennes: accumulation et dispersion', in Francois Jean and Jean Christophe Rufin (eds), *Economie des guerres civiles*, Paris: Hachette, pp. 189-232.

Lederach, John Paul (1995), *Preparing for Peace: Conflict Transformation across Cultures*, Syracuse, NY: Syracuse University Press.

Lederach, John Paul (1997), *Building Peace: Sustainable Reconciliation in Divided Societies*, Washington D.C.: United States Institute of Peace Press.

Leitenberg, Milton (1977), *A Survey of Studies of Post WW II Wars, Conflicts and Military Coups*, Ithaca, New York: Cornell University Press.

Lesch, Ann Mosley (1973), 'The Palestine Arab Nationalist Movement Under the Mandat', in William Quandt, Fuad Jabber and Ann Mosley Lesch, *The Politics of Palestinian Nationalismi*, Berkeley, Los Angeles, London: University of California Press, pp. 5-42.

Lesch, Ann Mosley (1979), *Arab Politics in Palestine 1917–1939: The Frustration of a Nationalist Movement*, Ithaca and London: Cornell University Press.

LeShan, Lawrence (1992), *The Psychology of War. Comprehending its Mystique and its Madness*, Chicago: Noble Press.

Levy, Marc A. (1995), 'Is the Environment a National Security Issue', *International Security*, 20(2), pp. 35-62.

Lewer, Nick and Steven Schofield (1997), *Non-Lethal Weapons: A Fatal Attraction?*, London: Zed Books.

Lichbach, Mark Irving (1989), 'An Evaluation of Does Economic Inequality Breed Political Conflict', *World Politics* XLI, (4), pp. 431-70.

Linden, C.A. (1983), *The Soviet Party-State: the Politics of Ideocratic Despotism*, New York: Praegner.

Lindholm Schulz, Helena, forthcoming, *Reconstruction of Palestinian Nationalisms. Between Revolution and Statehood*, Manchester University Press.

Linklater, Andrew (1990), *Men and Citizens in the Theory of International Relations*, London: Macmillan.

Linklater, Andrew (1994), 'Dialogue, Dialectic and Emancipation in International Relations at the End of the Post-War Age', *Millennium: Journal of International Studies*, 23(1), pp. 119-131.

Linz, Juan and Alfred Stepan (1996), 'Toward Consolidated Democracies', *Journal of Democracy*, 7(2), pp. 14-33.

Lipschutz, Ronnie D. (1997), 'Environmental Conflict and Environmental Determinism: The Relative Importance of Social and Natural Factors', in Nils Petter Gleditsch (ed.), *Conflict and the Environment*. Dordrecht, Boston and London: Kluwer Academic Publishers. Published in cooperation with NATO Scientific Affairs Division, pp. 35-51.

Lodgaard, Sverre (1992), 'Environmental Security, World Order and Environmental Conflict Resolution', in Nils Petter Gleditsch (ed.), *Conversion and the Environment. Proceedings of a Seminar in Perm, Russia, 24–27 November 1991*, PRIO Report, No. 2, pp. 115-136.

Luke, Timothy W. (1989), 'On Post-War: The Significance of Symbolic Action in War and Deterrence', *Alternatives*, 14(3) (July 1989), pp. 343-362.

Luttwak, Edward N. (1987), *Strategy. The Logic of War and Peace*, Cambridge, MA: Harvard University Press.

Luttwak, Edward N. (1996), 'A Post-Heroic Military Policy', *Foreign Affairs*, 75(4), July-August 1996, pp. 33-44.

Malmberg, Torsten (1980), *Human Territoriality: Survey of Behavioural Territories in Man with Preliminary Analysis and Discussion of Meaning*, The Hague, Paris and New York: Mouton.

Mansfield, Edward D. (1994), *Power, Trade and War*, Princeton, NJ: Princeton University Press.

Mansfield, Edward D. and Jack Snyder (1995), 'Democratization and the Danger of War', *International Security*, 20(1), pp. 5-38.

Mathews, Jessica Tuchman (1989), 'Redefining Security', *Foreign Affairs*, 68 (Spring), pp. 162-177.

Mbembe, Achille (1988), *Afrique indociles*, Karthala.

Mbembe, Achille (1992), 'Le véritable enjeu des débats sur la démocratie', *Le Monde Diplomatique*, January.

McGarry, John and O'Leary, Brendan (1993), 'Introduction. The Macro-political Regulation of Ethnic Conflict', in John McGarry and Brendan O'Leary (eds), *The Politics of Ethnic Conflict Regulation*, London, New York: Routledge, pp. 1-39.

McKitrick, Jeffrey *et al.* (1995), 'The Revolution in Military Affairs', in Barry R. Schneider and Lawrence E. Grinter (eds), *Battlefield of the Future. 21st Century Warfare Issues*, Maxwell Air Force Base, Alabama: Air University, pp. 65-97.

McNeill, William H. (1983), *The Pursuit of Power. Technology, Armed Force, and Society since A.D. 1000*, Oxford: Basil Blackwell.

Melvern, Linda (1997), 'Genocide behind the Thin Blue Line', *Security Dialogue*, 28(3) (September 1997), pp. 333-346.

Mendler, Martin and Wolfgang Schwegler-Rohmeis (1988), 'Weder Drachhentöter noch Sicherheitsingenieur – Bilanz und kritische Analyse der sozialwissenschaftlichen Kriegsursachenforschung', Frankfurt a.M.: HSFK Forschungsbericht.

Miall, Hugh (1992), *The Peacemakers: Peaceful Settlement of Disputes since 1945*, Oxford: MacMillan.

Middleton, Hugh (1992), 'Some Psychological Bases of the Institution of War', in Robert A. Hinde (ed.), *The Institution of War*, New York: St. Martin's Press, pp. 30-46.

Midlarsky, Manus I. (ed.) (1992), *The Internationalization of Communal Strife*, London: Routledge.

Millwood, David (chief ed.) (1996), *The International Response to Conflict and Genocide: Lessons from the Rwanda Experience*, 5 vols, Copenhagen (JEEAR) 3/1996.

Mitchell, Christopher R. (1973), 'Conflict Resolution and Controlled Communication: Some Further Comments', *Journal of Peace Research*, 10, pp.123-132.

Mitchell, Christopher R. (1988), 'The Motives for Mediation', in Christopher R. Mitchell and K. Webb (eds), *New Approaches to International Mediation*, London: Greenwood Press.

Mitchell, Christopher R. and Michael Banks (1996), *Handbook of Conflict Resolution: The Analytical Problem-Solving Approach*, New York, London: Pinter.

Montville, Joseph (ed.) (1990), *Conflict and Peacemaking in Multiethnic Societies*, Lexington, MA: Lexington Books.

Morehouse, David A. (1996), *Nonlethal Weapons. War Without Death*, Westport, CT: Praeger.

Moskos, Charles C. and James Burk (1994), 'The Postmodern Military', in James Burk (ed.), *The Military in New Times. Adapting Armed Forces to a Turbulent World*, Boulder: Westview, pp. 141-162.

Mouffe, Chantal (1994), 'For a Politics of Nomadic Identity', in George Robertson *et al.* (eds), *Travelers' Tales: Narratives of Home and Displacement*, pp. 139-74

Mueller, John (1989), *Retreat from Doomsday: The Obsolescence of Major War*, New York: Basic Books.

Murswiek, Dietrich (1993), 'The Issue of a Right of Secession – Reconsidered', in Christian Tomuschat (ed.), *Modern Law of Self-Determination*, Dordrecht: Martinus Nijhoff.

Muslih, Muhammad (1988), *The Origins of Palestinian Nationalism*, New York: Columbia University Press.

Myers, Norman (1993), *Ultimate Security: The Environmental Basis of Political Stability*, New York: W.W. Norton & Co.

Nardin, Terry (ed.) (1996), *The Ethics of War and Peace. Religious and Secular Perspectives*, Princeton, NJ: Princeton University Press.

Nicolaïdis, Kalypso (1996), 'International Preventive Action: Developing A Strategic Framework', in Robert I. Rotberg (ed.), *Vigilance and Vengeance: NGOs Preventing Ethnic Conflict in Divided Societies*, Washington, D.C.: Brookings Institution Press.

Nietschmann, Bernard (1987), 'Militarization and indigenous peoples', *Cultural Survival Quarterly*, 11(3), Cambridge, MA, Cultural Survival, Inc., pp.1-16.

Nkundabagenzi, Fabien (1996), 'Un partenariat politique pour un développement politique', in *Rwanda: Les enjeux de la reconstruction nationale*, Edifie LLN.

Nkundabagenzi, Félix (1997), *La prévention des conflits en Afrique. L'Europe et la sécurité internationale*, GRIP, pp. 98-110.

Norris, Christopher (1992), *Uncritical Theory. Postmodernism, Intellectuals, and the Gulf War*, Amherst, MA: University of Massachusetts Press.

O'Brien, William V. (1996), 'The Rule of Law in Small Wars', in W.M.J. Olson (ed.), 'Small Wars', *Annals of the American Academy of Political and Social Science*, vol. 541, London: Sage Publications, pp. 36-46.

Olcott, Martha Brill (1997), 'Kazakhstan: Pushing for Eurasia', in Ian Bremmer and Ray Taras (eds), *New States, New Politics: Building the Post-Soviet Nations*, Cambridge: Cambridge University Press.

Omaar, Rakiya and Alex de Waal (1995), *Rwanda: Death, Despair and Defiance*, London (African Rights) 9/1994 (revised edition 8/95).

Orentlicher, Diana (1998), 'Separation Anxiety: International Responses to Ethno-Separatist Claims', *Yale Journal of International Law*, 23(1), pp. 1-78.

Østerrud, Øyvind (1996), 'Antinomies of Postmodernism in International Studies', *Journal of Peace Research*, 33(4), November, pp. 385-90.

Percival, Val and Thomas Homer-Dixon (1998), 'Environmental Scarcity and Violent Conflict: The Case of South Africa', *Journal of Peace Research*, 35(3), May, pp. 279-299.

Peteet, Julie M. (1993), 'Authenticity and Gender: The Presentation of Culture', in Judith E. Tucker (ed.), *Arab Women: Old Boundaries, New Frontiers*, Bloomington, Indiana: Indiana University Press, pp. 49-62.

Pettman, Jan Jindy (1996), 'Border Crossing/Shifting Identities: Minorities, Gender, and the State in International Perspective', in Michael Shapiro and Hayward Alker (eds), *Challenging Boundaries: Global Flows, Territorial Identities*, Minneapolis, London: University of Minnesota Press.

Philpott, Daniel (1995), 'In Defense of Self-Determination', *Ethics*, 105, pp. 352-385.

Pieterse, Jan (1996), 'Varieties of Ethnic Politics and Ethnicity Discourse', in Edwin Wilmsen and Patric McAllister (eds), *The Politics of Difference, Ethnic Premises in a World of Power*, Chicago and London: The University of Chicago Press, pp. 25-44.

Pirages, Dennis (1991), 'Social Evolution and Ecological Security', *Bulletin of Peace Proposals*, 22(3), pp. 329-334.

Polanyi, Karl (1957), *The Great Transformation. The Political and Economic Origins of Our Time*, Boston: Beacon.

Porter, Bruce (1994), *War and the Rise of the State*, New York: The Free Press.

Portugali, Yuvali (1993), *Implicate Relations: Society and Space in the Israeli-Palestinian Conflict*, Dordrecht: Kluwer Academic Publishers.

Posen, Barry R. (1993), 'Nationalism, the Mass Army, and Military Power', *International Security*, 18(2) (Fall 1993), pp. 80-124.

Poulton, Robin E. (1996), 'Vers la réintégration des Touaregs au Mali', *Le Monde Diplomatique*, November.

Pruitt, Dean G. and Steven A. Lewis (1977), 'The Psychology of Integrative Bargaining', in Daniel Druckman (ed.), *Negotiations: Social-Psycholgocial Perspectives*, Beverly Hills: Sage Publications.

Pruitt, Dean G. and Peter Carnevale (1993), *Negotiation in Social Conflict*, Pacific Grove, California: Brooks/Cole Publishing.

Rabehl, Thomas and Trines, Stefan (eds) (1997), 'Das Kriegsgeschehen 1996. Register der Kriege und bewaffneten Konflikte', Arbeitspapier 6/1997, Research Unit of Wars, Armament and Development, University of Hamburg.

Rapkin, David P. and William P. Avery (1986), 'World Markets and Political Instability within Less Developed Countries', *Cooperation and Conflict* XXI, pp. 99-117.

Rapoport, Anatol (1970), 'Critique of Strategic Thinking', in Naomi Rosenbaum (ed.), *Readings on the International Political System*, Englewoood Cliffs, NJ: Prentice-Hall, pp. 201-227.

Ratner, Steven (1996), 'Drawing a Better Line: Uti Possidetis and the Borders of New States', *American Journal of International Law*, 10(4), pp. 590-624.

Raz-Krakotzkin, Amon (1998), 'A Peace without Arabs: The Discourse of Peace and the Limits of Israeli Consciousness', in George Giacaman and Dag Jørund Lønning (eds), *After Oslo: New Realities, Old Problems*, London and Chicago: Pluto Press, pp. 59-77.

Renner, Michael, Mario Pianta and Cinzia Franchi (1991), 'International Conflict and Environmental Degradation', in Raimo Väyrynen (ed.), *New Directions in Conflict Theory. Conflict Resolution and Conflict Transformation*. London: Sage Publications, in association with the International Social Science Council, pp. 108-128.

Reuck, Anthony de (1990), 'A Theory of Conflict Resolution by Problem-Solving', in John Burton and Frank Dukes (eds), *Conflict: Readings in Management and Resolution*, London: Macmillan, pp. 183-198.

Richardson, Lewis Fry (1960), *Statistics of Deadly Quarrels*, Chicago: Boxwood & Quadrangle.

Riggs, (1994), 'Ethno-National Rebellions and Viable Constitutionalism', Paper presented at the XVI Congress of Political Science, Berlin, 21–25 August 1994.

Roosens, Eugeen (1989), *Creating Ethnicity: The Process of Ethnogenesis*, London: Sage Publications.

Roosens, Eugeen (1994), 'The Primordial Nature of Origins in Migrant Ethnicity', in Hans Vermuelen and Cora Govers (eds), *The Anthropology of Ethnicity: Beyond Ethnic Groups and Boundaries*, Amsterdam: Het Spinhius, pp. 81-104.

Ropers, Norbert (1997), 'The Role of NGOs in Conflict Situations', Paper, Moscow: IFPR-RAS.

Rosanov, V. V. (1991), 'Razmolvka mezhdu Solovyovym I Dostoevskim' (Disagreement between Solovyov and Dostoevsky), reprinted in *Nashe Nasledie* (Our Heritage), 6, pp. 70-72.

Rosenau, James N. (1994), 'Neue Perspektiven in der Weltpolitik: Anmerkungen zur Antiquiertheit zwischenstaatlicher Kriege', in Krell, Gert and Müller, Harald (eds), *Frieden und Konflikt in den internationalen Beziehungen. Festschrift für Ernst-Otto Czempiel*, Frankfurt a.M., New York: Campus, pp. 116-132.

Ross, Marc Howard (1998), *Culture of Conflict: Interpretations and Interests in Comparative Perspective*, New Haven: Yale University Press.

Ross, Marc Howard, forthcoming, *Democracy as Joint Problem Solving: Addressing Interests and Identities in Divided Societies*, Nationalism and Ethnic Politics.

Ross, Marc Howard and Jay Rothman (eds), forthcoming, *Theory and Practice in Conflict Management: Conceptualizing Success and Failure*, London: MacMillan.

Rotberg, Robert I. and Thomas G. Weiss (eds) (1996), *From Massacres to Genocide. The Media, Public Policy, and Humanitarian Crises*, Washington, D.C.: The Brookings Institution and The World Peace Foundation.

Rubin, Jeffrey Z., Dean G. Pruitt and Sung Hee Kim (1994), *Social Conflict: Escalation, Stalemate and Settlement*, 2nd edition, New York: McGraw-Hill.

Ruggie, John (1993), 'Territoriality and beyond: Problematizing Modernity in International Relations', *International Organization*, 47(1), Winter 1993, pp. 139-174.

Rummel, Rudolph J. (1994), 'Power, genocide and mass murder', *Journal of Peace Research*, 31(1).

Rummel, Rudolph J. (1995), 'Democracies ARE more Peaceful', *European Journal of International Relations*, vol. 1, no. 4, December, pp. 457-479.

Rupesinghe, Kumar (1992), 'The Disappearing Boundaries between Internal and External Conflicts, in Kumar Rupesinghe (ed.), *International Conflict and Governance*, New York: St. Martin's, pp. 1-26.

Ryan, Stephen (1990), *Ethnic Conflict and International Relations*, Aldershot: Dartmouth.

Ryan, Stephen (1996), 'The Voice of Sanity Getting Hoarse?: Destructive Processes in Violent Ethnic Conflict', in Edwin Wilmsen and Patric McAllister (eds), *The Politics of Difference*, Chicago and London: The University of Chicago Press, pp. 144-161.

Sack, Robert (1986), *Human Territoriality*, Cambridge: Cambridge University Press.

Said, Edward (1978), *Orientalism*, Harmondsworth: Penguin Books.

Said, Edward (1993), *Culture and Imperialism*, London: Vintage.

Santoni, Ronald E. (1992), 'Nurturing the Institution of War: "Just War" Theory's "Justifications" and Accomodations', in Robert A. Hinde (ed.), *The Institution of War*, New York: St. Martin's Press, pp. 99-120.

Sayigh, Yezid (1997), *Armed Struggle and the Search for State: The Palestinian National Movement, 1949–1993*, Oxford: Clarendon Press.

Scherrer, Christian P. (1996), 'Ethno-Nationalismus im Weltsystem: Prävention, Konfliktbearbeitung und die Rolle der internationalen Gemeinschaft', in *Handbuch zu Ethnizität und Staat*, I, Münster: Agenda.

Scherrer, Christian P. (1996, 1997, 1998/99, forthcoming), *Ethno-Nationalismus*. Vols 1-3. Münster: Agenda.

Scherrer; Christian P. (1997), *Ethnicization and Genocide in Central Africa*. Frankfurt a.M., New York: Campus.

Scherrer, Christian P. (1997), *Ethnisierung und Völkermord in Zentralafrika: Genozid in Rwanda, Bürgerkrieg in Burundi und die Rolle der Weltgemeinschaft*. Frankfurt a.M.: Campus.

Scherrer, Christian P. (1997), 'Ethno-Nationalismus im Zeitalter der Globalisierung: Ursachen, Strukturmerkmale und Dynamik ethnisch-nationaler Gewaltkonflikte', in *Handbuch zu Ethnizität und Staat*, II, Münster: Agenda.

Scherrer, Christian P. (1998), 'Fundamental Human Rights must be Protected', Working Paper, Copenhagen: COPRI.

Schlichte, Klaus (1996), *Krieg und Vergesellschaftung in Afrika. Ein Beitrag zur Theorie des Krieges*, Münster und Hamburg: LIT.

Schlichte, Klaus (1997), 'Das Chaos der Gewalt und die Regeln des Marktes: Zur Behinderung von Friedensprozessen durch Kriegsökonomien', in *Jahrbuch Frieden*, München: C.H. Beck, pp. 140-148.

Schneider, Barry R. (1995), 'Principle of War for the Battlefield of the Future', in Barry R. Schneider and Lawrence E. Grinter (eds), *Battlefield of the Future. 21st Century Warfare Issues*, Maxwell Air Force Base, Alabama: Air University, pp. 1-42.

Schöneberg, Regina (1996), 'Environmental Conflicts in the Amazon Region of Brazil', in Günther Bächler and Kurt R. Spillmann (eds), *Kriegsursache Umweltzerstörung (Environmental Degradation as a Cause of War: Country Studies of External Experts)*, vol. 111, Zürich: Verlag Rüegger.

Schonholtz, Raymond (1997), 'Conflict Management Training: A Transformative Vehicle for Transitional Democracies', *International Negotiation*, 2, pp. 437-450.

Schulte-Sasse, Jochen and Linda Schulte-Sasse (1991), 'War, Otherness, and Illusionary Identification with the State', *Cultural Critique*, 9, pp. 67-95.

Schutz, Alfred (1964), *Collected Papers I*, The Hague: Martinus Nijhoff.

Schutz, Alfred and Thomas Luckmann (1974), *The Structures of the Life-World*, Vol. 1, London: Heinemann.

Schwarzer, Gudrun (1994), 'Friedliche Konfliktregulierung: Saarland – Österreich – Berlin', *Zeitschirft für internationale Beziehungen*, 1(2), pp. 243-277.

SEF (Stiftung Entwicklung und Frieden / Development and Peace Foundation) (1993), *Globale Trends 1993/94. Daten zur Weltentwicklung*, Frankfurt: Fischer.

SEF (Stiftung Entwicklung und Frieden / Development and Peace Foundation) (1997), *Global Trends 1998*, Frankfurt: Fischer.

Senghaas, Dieter (1994), *Wohin driftet die Welt? Über die Zukunft friedlicher Koexistenz*, Frankfurt a.M.: Suhrkamp.
Shapiro, Michael (1997), *Violent Cartographies*, Minneapolis, London: University of Minnesota Press.
Siegelberg, Jens (1994), *Kapitalismus und Krieg. Eine Theorie des Krieges in der Weltgesellschaft*, Münster und Hamburg: LIT.
Simmel, Georg (1971), 'The Stranger', in Donald N. Levine (ed.), *On Individuality and Social Forms* (original edition, 1908), Chicago: Chicago University Press.
Singer, Max and Aaron Wildawsky (1993), *The Real World Order. Zones of Peace / Zones of Turmoil*, Chatham, NJ: Chatham House Publishers.
SIPRI Yearbook, 1993, 1994, 1995, 1996, *World Armamants and Disarmaments*, Oxford and New York: Oxford University Press.
Sisk, Timothy (1996), *Power Sharing and International Mediation in Ethnic Conflicts*, Washington, DC: United States Institute of Peace.
Small, Melvin and David J. Singer (1982), *Resort to Arms International and Civil Wars 1816–1980*, Beverly Hills, London, New Dehli: Sage Publications.
Smith, Anthony D. (1981), 'States and Homelands: the Social and Geopolitical Implications of National Territory', *Millennium*, 10(3), pp. 187-201.
Smith, Anthony D. (1986), *The Ethnic Origin of Nations*, Oxford: Basil Blackwell.
Smith, Anthony D. (1991), *National Identity*, London: Penguin Books.
Smith, Dan (1997), *The State of War and Peace Atlas*, London: Penguin.
Smith, Steve, Ken Booth and Marysia Zalewski (eds) (1996), *International Theory: Positivism and Beyond*, Cambridge: Cambridge University Press.
Smith, Steve (1997), 'Epistemology, Postmodernism and International Relations Theory', *Journal of Peace Research*, 34(1), pp. 330-336.
Snow Donald M. (1996), *UnCivil Wars: International Security and the New Pattern of Internal War*, Boulder: Lynne Rienner.
Snow, Donald M (1997), *Distant Thunder. Patterns of Conflict in the Developing World*, 2nd edn, Armonk, NY: M.E. Sharpe.
Sollenberg, Margareta and Peter Wallensteen (1997), 'Major Armed Conflicts', in *SIPRI Yearbook 1997: Armaments, Disarmament and International Security*, Oxford: Oxford University Press, pp. 16-30.
Solovyov, V.S. (1988), 'Opravdanie dobra' (Justification of Good), in *Collection of Works in Two Volumes*, vol. 1, Moscow: Mysl.
Sorokin, Pitirim A.(1937), *Social and Cultural Dynamics*, vol. 3, New York: American Book Co.
Sponsel, Leslie E. and Thomas A Gregor (eds) (1994), *The Anthropology of Peace and Violence*, Boulder: Lynne Rienner.
Spruyt, Hendrik (1994), *The Sovereign State and Its Competitors*, Princeton, NJ: Princeton University Press.
Stavenhagen, Rodolfo (1991), *The Ethnic Question: Conflicts, Development, and Human Rights*, Tokyo: United Nations University Press.

Stedman, Stephen (1997), 'Spoiler Problems in Peace Processes', *International Security*, 22, pp. 5-53.

Stein, George (1995), 'Information War – Cyberwar – Netwar', in Barry R. Schneider and Lawrence E. Grinter (eds), *Battlefield of the Future. 21st Century Warfare Issues*, Maxwell Air Force Base, Alabama: Air University, pp. 153-179.

Steiner, Hillel (1996), 'Territorial Justice', in Simon Caney, David George and Peter Jones (eds), *National Rights, International Obligations*, Boulder: Westview Press.

Tamir, Yael (1993), *Liberal Nationalism*, Princeton, NJ: Princeton University Press.

Taw, Jennifer Morrison and Bruce Hoffman (1994), 'Operations Other Than War', in Paul K. Davis (ed.), *New Challenges for Defense Planning. Rethinking How Much is Enough*, Santa Monica: RAND, pp. 223-250.

Tétreault, Mary Ann (1997), 'Justice for All: Wartime Rape and Women's Rights', *Global Governance*, 3(2), May-August, pp. 197-212.

Thompson, William R. (1994), 'The Future of Transitional Warfare', in James Burk (ed.), *The Military in New Times. Adapting Armed Forces to a Turbulent World*, Boulder: Westview, pp. 63-92.

Thornberry, Patrick (1989), 'Self-Determination, Minorities, Human Rights: A Review of International Instruments', *International and Comparative Law Quarterly*, 38(4), pp. 867-889.

Tillema, Herbert, K. (1995), '690 foreign overt military interventions, 1945–1991', in Isabelle Duyvesteyn, *Wars and Military Interventions since 1945*, Working Paper 88/95, Hamburg: AKUF.

Tilly, Charles (1985), 'War Making and State Making as Organized Crime', in Peter Evans, Dietrich Rueschemeyer and Theda Skocpol (eds) (1985), *Bringing the State Back In*, Cambridge: Cambridge University Press.

Tilly, Charles (1990), *Coercion, Capital and European States, AD 900–1900*, Cambridge, MA: Basil Blackwell.

Toffler, Alvin and Heidi Toffler (1993), *War and Antiwar: Survival at the Dawn of the 21st Century*, Boston: Little, Brown & Co.

Tongeren, Paul van (1998), 'Le rôle des ONG: la valorisation des capacités locales pour la paix', *Le Courrier* 168, March–April.

Touval, S. and I.W. Zartman (eds) (1985), *International Mediation in Theory and Practice*, Colorado: Westview Press.

Tromp, Hylke: 'On the Nature of War and the Nature of Militarism', in Robert A. Hinde and Helen E. Watson (eds) (1995), *War: A Cruel Necessity? The Bases of Institutionalized Violence*, London: I.B. Tauris, pp. 118-131.

Trubetskoy, N. S. (1927), *Ob istinnom I lozhnom natsionalisme* (On true and false nationalism), *Nasledie Tchingizkhana: vzgyad na russkuyu istoriu ne s zapada, a s vostoka* (Chingyzkhan's heritage: a perspective on Russian history that comes not from the West but from the East), *K probleme russkogo samopoznania* (On the problem of Russian self-cognition), Sofia.

Tuan, Yi-Fu (1977), *Space and Place. The Perspective of Experience*, Minneapolis: The University of Minnesota Press.

Ullman, Richard H. (1983), 'Redefining Security', *International Security*, 8 (Summer), pp. 129-153.

United Nations Conference on Trade and Development, Annual, *UNCTAD Handbook on International Trade and Development Statistics*, Geneva: United Nations Publication.

Van Creveld, Martin (1991), *The Transformation of War*, New York: The Free Press, pp. 57-62.

Vasquez, John A. (1976), 'Statistical Findings in International Politics: A Data-Based Assessment', *International Studies Quarterly*, vol. 20, no. 2, June, pp. 171-218.

Vasquez, John A. (1988), 'The Steps to War: Toward a Scientific Explanation of Correlates of War Findings', *World Politics*, 40(1), pp. 108-145.

Vasquez, John A. (1993), *The War Puzzle*, Cambridge: Cambridge University Press.

Vasquez, John A. (1995), 'The Post-Positivist Debate: Reconstructing Scientific Enquiry and International Relations Theory After Enlightenment's Fall', in Ken Booth and Steve Smith (eds), *International Relations Theory Today*, Cambridge: Polity Press, pp. 217-240.

Väyrynen, Raimo (1997), 'Economic Incentives and the Bosnian Peace Process', in David Cortright (ed.), *The Price of Peace: Incentives and International Conflict Prevention.* Lanham, Maryland: Rowman and Littlefield.

Väyrynen, Tarja (1995), 'Going Beyond Similarity: The Role of Facilitator in Problem-Solving Workshop Conflict Resolution', *Paradigms*, 9(2), pp. 71-85.

Väyrynen, Tarja (1998), 'Ethnic Communality and Conflict Resolution', *Cooperation and Conflict*, 33(1), pp. 59-80.

Verdery, Katherine (1994), 'Ethnicity, Nationalism and State-making: Ethnic Groups and Boundaries: Past and Future', in Hans Vermuelen and Cora Govers (eds), *The Anthropology of Ethnicity: Beyond Ethnic Groups and Boundaries*, Amsterdam: Het Spinhius, pp. 33-58.

Volkan, Vamik and Itzkowtz, Norman (1994), *Turks and Greeks, Neighbours in Conflict*, Huntington: The Eothen Press.

Waldmann, Peter (1997), 'Bürgerkrieg – Annäherungen an einen schwer faßbaren Begriff', *Leviathan*, 25(4), pp. 480-500.

Walker, R.B.J. (1993), *Inside/Outside: International Relations as Political Theory*, Cambridge: Cambridge University Press.

Wallensteen, Peter and Karin Axell (1993), 'Armed Conflicts at the End of the Cold War, 1989–92', in Karin Axell (ed.), *States in Armed Conflict 1992*, Report No. 36, Department of Peace and Conflict Research, Uppsala University.

Wallensteen, Peter and Margareta Sollenberg (1995), 'After the Cold War: Emerging Patterns of Armed Conflict 1989–1994', *Journal of Peace Research*, 32(3), pp. 345-360.

Wallensteen, Peter and Margareta Sollenberg (1996), 'The End of International War? Armed Conflict 1989-95', *Journal of Peace Research*, 33(3), August, pp. 353-370.

Wallensteen, Peter and Margareta Sollenberg (1997), 'Armed conflicts, conflict termination and peace agreements, 1989-96', Journal of Peace Research, 34(3), pp. 339-358.

Walton, John and David Seddon (1994), *Free Markets and Food Riots The Politics of Global Adjustment*, London: Basil Blackwell.

Waltz, Kenneth N. (1988), 'The Origins of War in Neorealist Theory', *Journal of Interdisciplinary History*, XVIII/4, pp. 615-628.

Wayman, Frank Whelon, David Singer and Meredith Sarkees (1996), 'Inter-State, Intra-State, and Extra-Systemic Wars 1816–1995', Paper presented at the annual meeting of the International Studies Association, San Diego, April 16–21, 1996.

Weiss, Thomas G., David Cortright, George Lopez, and Larry Minear (eds) (1997), *Political Gain and Civilian Pain: Humanitarian Impacts of Economic Sanctions*, Lanham, Maryland: Rowman and Littlefield.

Welch, David (1993), *Justice and the Genesis of War*, Cambridge: Cambridge University Press.

Wellman, Christopher (1995), 'A Defense of Secession and Political Self-Determination', *Philosophy and Public Affairs*, 24(2), pp. 357-372.

Werlin, Herbert (1994), 'A Primary/Secondary Democracy Distinction', *PS: Political Science and Politics*, 3(27), pp. 530-34.

Whelan, Frederick (1983), 'Prologue: Democratic Theory and the Boundary Problem', in J. Roland Pennock and John Chapman (eds), *Liberal Democracy* XXV, New York: New York University Press.

Wiberg, Håkan (1997), 'Kriegsursachenforschung: wie dürftig ist sie?', *Ethik & Sozialwissenschaft*, 8(3), pp. 308-12.

Williams, Colin and Anthony D. Smith (1983), 'The National Construction of Social Space', *Progress in Human Geography*, 7(4), pp. 502-517.

World Bank, The, *World Development Report*, Washington: Oxford University Press.

Wright, Quincy (1942), *A Study of War*, Chicago: Chicago University Press.

Wæver, Ole, Barry Buzan, Morten Kelstrup, Pierre Lemaitre *et al.* (1993), *Identity, Migration and the New Security Agenda in Europe*, London: Pinter.

Young, Oran R. (1967), *The Intermediaries. Third Parties in International Crises*, Princeton: Princeton University Press.

Zaidi, Sarah (1997), 'Humanitarian Effects of the Coup and Sanctions in Haiti', in Thomas G. Weiss, David Cortright, George Lopez, and Larry Minear (eds),

Political Gain and Civilian Pain: Humanitarian Impacts of Economic Sanctions, Lanham, Maryland: Rowman and Littlefield.

Zartman, I. William and Jeffrey Rubin (1996), *The Structural Dilemma: Negotiating in Asymmetry*, Laxenburg: International Institute of Applied Systems Analysis.

Zartman, I. William (1997a), 'Conflict and Order: Justice in Negotiation', *International Political Science Review*, 18(2), pp. 121-138.

Zartman, I. William (1997b), 'Intervening to Prevent State Collapse', *World Affairs*, 4(2), pp. 13-23.

Zenkovsky, V.V. (1948), *Istoria russkoy filosofii* (History of Russian philosophy), vol. 1, Paris: YMCA-Press, pp. 5-38.

Zinnes, Dina A. (1980), 'Why War? Evidence on the Outbreak of International Conflict', in Ted Robert Gurr (ed.), *Handbook of Political Conflict: Theory and Research*, New York: Free Press.

Zyuganov, G. (1994), *Derzhava*, 2nd edn., Moscow: Informpechat.

Name Index

For Product Safety Concerns and Information please contact our EU
representative GPSR@taylorandfrancis.com
Taylor & Francis Verlag GmbH, Kaufingerstraße 24, 80331 München, Germany

www.ingramcontent.com/pod-product-compliance
Lightning Source LLC
Chambersburg PA
CBHW070901270326
41926CB00057B/2295